Agile Data Warehouse Design

Collaborative Dimensional Modeling, from Whiteboard to Star Schema

Lawrence Corr
with Jim Stagnitto

decisionone.co.uk

Agile Data Warehouse Design

by Lawrence Corr with Jim Stagnitto

Published by DecisionOne Press, Burwood House, Leeds LS28 7UJ, UK.
Email: information@decisionone.co.uk, Tel: +44 7971 964824.

Proofing: Laurence Hesketh, Geoff Hurrell

Indexer: Jim Stagnitto

Illustrators: Gill Guile and Lawrence Corr

Cover Design: After Escher

Printing History:

       November 2011: First Edition.
       January 2012: Revision.
       October 2012: Revision.
       May 2013: Revision.
       February 2014: Revision.

ISBN: 978-0-9568172-0-4

[2014-02-03]

For Lucy Corr

1923-2009

Thank you for listening

ABOUT THE AUTHORS

Lawrence Corr is a data warehouse designer and educator. As Principal of DecisionOne Consulting, he helps organizations to improve their Business Intelligence systems through the use of visual data modeling techniques. He regularly teaches agile dimensional modeling courses worldwide and has taught DW/BI skills to thousands of IT professionals since 2000.

Lawrence has developed and reviewed data warehouses for healthcare, telecommunications, engineering, broadcasting, financial services and public service organizations. He held the position of data warehouse practice leader at Linc Systems Corporation, CT, USA and vice-president of data warehousing products at Teleran Technologies, NJ, USA. Lawrence was also a Ralph Kimball Associate and has taught data warehousing classes for Kimball University in Europe and South Africa and contributed to Kimball articles and design tips. He lives in Yorkshire, England with his wife Mary and daughter Aimee. Lawrence can be contacted at:

lcorr@decisionone.co.uk

Jim Stagnitto is a data warehouse and master data management architect specializing in the healthcare, financial services and information service industries. He is the founder of the data warehousing and data mining consulting firm Llumino.

Jim has been a guest contributor for Ralph Kimball's Intelligent Enterprise column, and a contributing author to Ralph Kimball & Joe Caserta's *The Data Warehouse ETL Toolkit*. He lives in Bucks County, PA, USA with his wife Lori, and their happy brood of pets. Jim can be contacted at:

jim.stagnitto@llumino.com

ACKNOWLEDGEMENTS

We would like to express our gratitude to everyone who made this book about BEAM✲ possible (using BEAM✲ notation):

ACKNOWLEDGMENTS [RE]

AUTHOR	**would like to thank** PERSON	at PLACE	for VERY GOOD REASON
[who] MV, C	[who] MV, ML, C	[where] MV, ML, C	[why] T
Lawrence and Jim	Ralph and Julie Kimball	The Kimball Group	Dimensional modeling inspiration and much more
Lawrence	Pat Harrell, Dave Taylor, and Richard Synoradzki	Linc Systems	Collaborative modeling inspiration
Lawrence	Bob Hefner	Linc Systems	Career oportunities and the chance to meet all of the above
Lawrence	Alan Simpson	Standard Life	Fact-specific calendar technique
Lawrence	John Telford and Ian Raven	Channel 4	Timelines and proactive design inspiration
Lawrence	Laurence Hesketh Geoff Hurrell	Northwards Fidelity	Eagle eyes
Lawrence	Mary and Aimee	Home	Peace, love and understanding
Lawrence	Ian Fleming John le Carré	In print, on screen	Entertainment, suspense
Jim	Joe Caserta	Caserta Concepts	Introduction to Lawrence, coaching
Jim	Lori	Home	Endless patience, love and support
Jim	Sadie the kitten	Home	Comic relief
Lawrence and Jim	Our clients	UK, USA, RSA	Numerous design challenges
Lawrence and Jim	Our business partners	UK, USA, RSA	Their hard work
Lawrence and Jim	Roger Thomas Bob Young	JCK Consulting Ideal Systems	Allowing us to adapt BEAM
Lawrence and Jim	Chris Adamson	Oakton Software	Author advice, dimensional modeling techniques
Lawrence and Jim	Rudyard Kipling	Any library, Project Gutenberg	Six honest serving-men, Baloo

CONTENTS

CHAPTER 3

CHAPTER 4

CHAPTER 7

CHAPTER 8

CHAPTER 9

WHY AND HOW: Design Patterns for Cause and Effect 261

INTRODUCTION

Dimensional modeling, since it was first popularized by Ralph Kimball in the mid-1990s, has become the accepted (data modeling) technique for designing the high performance data warehouses that underpin the success of today's business intelligence (BI) applications. Yet, with an ever increasing number of BI initiatives stumbling long before they reach the data modeling phase, it has become clear that Data Warehousing/Business Intelligence (DW/BI) needs new techniques that can revolutionize BI requirements analysis in the same way that dimensional modeling has revolutionized BI database design.

> Dimensional modeling is responsible for today's DW/BI successes, yet we still struggle to deliver enough BI

Agile, with its mantra of creating business value through the early and frequent delivery of working software and responding to change, has had just such a revolutionary effect on the world of application development. Can it take on the challenges of DW/BI? Agile's emphasis on collaboration and incremental development coupled with techniques such as Scrum and User Stories, will certainly improve *BI application development*—once a data warehouse is in place. But to truly have an impact on DW/BI, agile must also address *data warehouse design* itself. Unfortunately, the agile approaches that have emerged, so far, are vague and non-prescriptive in this one key area. For *agile BI* to be more than a marketing reboot of business-as-usual business intelligence, it must be *agile DW/BI* and we, DW/BI professionals, must do what every true agilist would recommend: adapt agile to meet our needs while still upholding its values and principles (see Appendix A: The Agile Manifesto). At the same time, agilists coming afresh to DW/BI, for their part, must learn our hard-won data lessons.

> Agile techniques can help, but they must address data warehouse design, not just BI application development

With that aim in mind, this book introduces BEAM✲ (*Business Event Analysis & Modeling*): a set of collaborative techniques for *modelstorming* BI data requirements and translating them into dimensional models on an agile timescale. We call the BEAM✲ approach "modelstorming" because it combines data modeling and brainstorming techniques for rapidly creating inclusive, understandable models that fully engage BI stakeholders.

> This book is about BEAM✲: an agile approach to dimensional modeling

BEAM✲ modelers achieve this by asking stakeholders to tell *data stories,* using the *7W* dimensional types—*who, what, when, where, how many, why,* and *how*—to describe the business events they need to measure. BEAM✲ models support modelstorming by differing radically from conventional entity-relationship (ER) based models. BEAM✲ uses tabular notation and example data stories to define business events in a format that is instantly recognizable to spreadsheet-literate BI stakeholders, yet easily translated into atomic-detailed star schemas. By doing so, BEAM✲ bridges the business-IT gap, creates consensus on data definitions and generates a sense of business ownership and pride in the resulting database design.

> BEAM✲ is used for *modelstorming* BI requirements directly with BI stakeholders

Who Is This Book For?

This book is for the whole agile DW/BI team, to help you not only gather requirements but also communicate design ideas

This book is intended for data modelers, business analysts, data architects, and developers working on data warehouses and business intelligence systems. All members of an agile DW/BI team—not just those directly responsible for gathering BI requirements or designing the data warehouse—will find the BEAM✲ notation a powerful addition to standard entity-relationship diagrams for communicating dimensional design ideas and estimating data tasks with their colleagues. To get the most from this book, readers should have a basic knowledge of database concepts such as *tables, columns, rows, keys,* and *joins.*

It is aimed at both new and experienced DW/BI practitioners. It's a quick-study guide to dimensional modeling and a source of new dimensional design patterns

For those new to data warehousing, this book provides a quick-study introduction to dimensional modeling techniques. For those of you who would like more background on the techniques covered, the later chapters and Appendix C provide references to case studies in other texts that will help you gain additional business insight. Experienced data warehousing professionals will find that this book offers a fresh perspective on familiar dimensional modeling patterns, covering many in more detail than previously available, and adding several new ones. For all readers, this book offers a radically new agile way of engaging with business users and kick-starting their next warehouse development project.

Meet The Modelstormers or How To Use This Book

Hello, I'm over here and I'm your fast track through this book

You may have already noticed the marginalia (non-contagious), on your left at the moment. This provides a "fast track" summary for readers in a hurry. This agile path through our text was inspired by David A. Taylor's object technology series of books. The margins of this book also contain a cast of anything but marginal characters. They are the *modelstormers* you need on your agile DW/BI team. We used them to highlight key features in the text such as *tips, warnings, references* and *example modeling dialogues.* They appear in the following order (in Chapters 1-9):

The bright modeler, not surprisingly, has some bright ideas. His tips, techniques and practical modeling advice, distilled from the current topic, will help you improve your design.

The experienced dimensional modeler has seen it all before. He's here to warn you when an activity or decision can steal your time, sanity or agility. Later in the book he follows the *pattern users* (see below) to tell you about the consequences or side effects of using their recommended design patterns. He would still recommend you use their patterns though—just with a little care.

The note takers are the members of the team who always read the full instructions before they use that new gadget or technique. They're always here to tell you to "make a note of that" when there is extra information on the current topic.

The agilists will let you know when we're being particularly agile. They wave their banner whenever a design technique supports a core value of the agile manifesto or principle of agile software development. These are listed in Appendix A.

The modelstormers appear en masse when we describe collaborative modeling and team planning, particularly when we offer practical advice and tips on using whiteboards and other inclusive tools for modelstorming.

The scribe appears whenever we introduce new BEAM✳ diagrams, notation conventions or short codes for rapidly documenting your designs. All the scribe's short codes are listed in Appendix B.

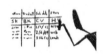

The agile modeler engages with stakeholders and facilitates modelstorming. She is here to ask example BEAM✳ questions, using the *7Ws*, to get stakeholders to tell their *data stories*.

The stakeholders are the subject matter experts, operational IT staff, BI users and BI consumers, who know the data sources, or know the data they want—anyone who can help define the data warehouse who is not a member of the DW/BI development team. They are here to provide example answers to the *agile modeler's* questions, tell data stories and pose their own tricky BI questions.

The bookworm points you to further reading on the current topic. All her reading recommendations are gathered in Appendix C.

The agile developer appears when we have some practical advice about using software tools or there is something useful you can download.

The head scratcher has interesting/vexing DW/BI problems or requirements that the data warehouse design is going to have to address.

The pattern users have a solution to *the head scratcher's* problems. They're going to use tried and tested dimensional modeling design patterns, some new in print.

How This Book Is Organized

This book has two parts. The first part covers agile dimensional modeling for BI data requirements gathering, while the second part covers dimensional design patterns for efficient and flexible star schema design.

Collaborative modeling with BI stakeholders

Part I: Modelstorming

Part I describes how to modelstorm BI stakeholders' data requirements, validate these requirements using agile data profiling, review and prioritize them with stakeholders, estimate their ETL tasks as a team, and convert them into star schemas. It illustrates how agile data modeling can be used to replace traditional BI requirements gathering with accelerated database design, followed by BI prototyping to capture the real reporting and analysis requirements. Chapter 1 provides an introduction to dimensional modeling. Chapters 2 to 4 provide a step-by-step guide for using BEAM✲ to model business events and dimensions. Chapter 5 describes how BEAM✲ models are validated and translated into physical dimensional models and development sprint plans.

Chapter 1: How to Model a Data Warehouse

Why we need new agile approaches for gathering BI requirements. Why they should be dimensional. What they should look like

Data warehouses and operational systems: Understanding the motivation for using dimensional modeling as the basis for agile database design.

Dimensional modeling fundamentals: Contrasting dimensional modeling with entity-relationship (ER) modeling, and learning the basic concepts and vocabulary of facts, dimensions, and star schemas that will be used throughout the book.

Agile data modeling for analysis *and* design: The BI requirement gathering problem. The challenges and opportunities of proactive DW/BI. The benefits of agile data warehousing. Why model with BI stakeholders? The case for modelstorming: using *agile* dimensional modeling to gather BI data requirements. **Introduction to BEAM✲**: Comparison of BEAM✲ and ER diagrams.

Chapter 2: Modeling Business Events

Step-by-step modeling of a business event using BEAM✲

Discovering business events: Using subjects, verbs, and objects to discover business events and tell *data stories*.

Documenting business events: Using whiteboards and spreadsheets and BEAM✲ tables to collaboratively model events.

Discovering event details: Using the *7Ws: who, what, when, where, how many, why,* and *how* to discover atomic-level event details. Using prepositions to connect details to events, and *data story themes* to define and document them. Using BEAM✲ *short codes* to document *event story types* (discrete, recurring, and evolving) and potential fact table granularity.

Chapter 3: Modeling Business Dimensions

Modeling *"detail about detail"*: Discovering dimensions and documenting their attributes with stakeholders. Telling *dimension stories* and overcoming weak narratives.

Discovering dimensional hierarchies: Using *hierarchy charts* to model hierarchical relationships and discover additional dimensional attributes.

Documenting historical value requirements: Using *change stories* and BEAM✲ short codes to define and document *slowly changing dimension* policies for supporting current (as is) and historically correct (as was) analysis views.

Step-by-step modeling of dimensions and hierarchies

Chapter 4: Modeling Business Processes

Modeling multiple business events: Modelstorming with an *event matrix* to storyboard a data warehouse design by identifying and documenting the relationships between events and dimensions. Using event stories to prioritize requirements and plan development sprints.

Modeling for agile data warehouse development: Defining and reusing *conformed* dimensions. Generalizing dimensions and documenting their roles. Supporting incremental development and creating a *data warehouse bus architecture.*

Step-by-step modeling multiple business events and conformed dimensions

Chapter 5: Modeling Star Schemas

Agile data profiling: Reviewing and adapting stakeholder models to data realities. Using BEAM✲ annotation to document data sources and physical data types, provide feedback to stakeholders on model viability and help estimate ETL tasks as a team.

Converting BEAM✲ tables to star schemas: defining and using surrogate keys to complete dimension tables, and convert event tables to fact tables. Using BEAM✲ technical codes to document the database design decisions and generate database schemas using the BEAM✲*Modelstormer* spreadsheet. Prototyping to define BI reporting requirements. Creating enhanced star schemas and physical dimensional matrices for a technical audience.

Validating stakeholder models and converting them into star schemas

Part II: Dimensional Design Patterns

Part II covers dimensional modeling techniques for designing high-performance star schemas. For this, we take a **design pattern approach** using a combination of BEAM✲ and star schema ER notation to capture significant DW/BI **requirements,** explain their associated issues/**problems,** and document pattern **solutions** and the **consequences** of implementing them. We have organized these design patterns around the *7W* dimensional types discovered in Part I. By using the *7Ws* to examine the complexities of modeling customers and employees (*who*), products and services (*what*), time (*when*), location (*where*), business measures (*how many*), cause (*why*), and effect (*how*), we document new and established dimensional techniques from a *dimensional perspective* for the first time.

Collaborative modeling within the DW/BI team. Using design patterns associated with each of the 7W dimensional types

Chapter 6: Who and What: People and Organizations, Products and Services

Design patterns for customer, employee and product dimensions

Modeling customers, employees, and organizations: Handling large, rapidly changing dimension populations. Tracking changes using *mini-dimensions*.

Mixed business models: Using *exclusive attributes* and *swappable dimensions* to model heterogeneous customers (businesses and consumer) and products (tangible goods and services).

Advanced slowly changing Patterns: Modeling micro and macro-level change. Supporting simultaneous current, historical, and previous value reporting requirements using *hybrid SCD views*.

Representing complex hierarchical relationships: Using *hierarchy maps* to handle recursive hierarchies, such as customer ownership, employee HR reporting structures, and product composition (component bill of materials and product bundles).

Supporting variation within business events: Using *multi-level dimensions* to describe events with variable granularity such as sales transactions assigned to individual employees or to teams, web advertisement impressions for single products or whole product categories.

Chapter 7: When and Where: Time and Location

Design patterns for time and location dimensions

Modeling time dimensionally: Using separate calendar and clock dimensions and defining date keys.

Year-to-date (YTD) analysis: Using *fact state* tables and *fact-specific calendars* to support correct YTD comparisons.

Time of day bracketing: Designing custom business clocks that vary by day of week or time of year.

Multinational calendars: Modeling multinational dimensions that cope with time *and* location. Supporting time zones and national language reporting.

Modeling movement: Overloading events with additional time and location dimensions to understand journeys and trajectories.

Chapter 8: How Many: Facts and Measures and KPIs

Design patterns for modeling efficient fact tables and flexible facts

Designing fact tables for performance and ease of use: Defining the three basic fact table patterns: *transactions*, *periodic snapshots*, and *accumulating snapshots*. Using event timelines to model accumulating snapshots as evolving events.

Providing the basis for flexible measures and KPIs: Defining atomic-level *additive facts*. Documenting *semi-additive* and *non-additive facts*, and understanding their limitations.

Fact table performance optimization: Using indexing, partitioning, and aggregation to improve fact table ETL and query performance.

Cross-process analysis: Combining the results from multiple fact tables using *drill-across* processing and *multi-pass* queries. Building *derived fact tables* and consolidated data marts to simplify query processing.

Chapter 9: Why and How: Cause and Effect

Modeling causal factors: Using promotions, weather, and other causal dimensions to explain *why* events occur and *why* facts vary. Using text dimensions to handle unstructured reasons and exception descriptions.

Modeling event descriptions: Using *how* dimensions to collect any additional descriptions of an event. Consolidating excessive degenerate dimensions as *how* dimensions, and combining small *why* and *how* dimensions.

Multi-valued dimensions: Using *bridge tables* and weighting factors to handle fact allocation ('splitting the atom') when dimensions have multiple values for each atomic-level fact. Using *optional bridge tables* and *multi-level* dimensions to efficiently handle *barely* multi-valued dimensions. Using *pivoted* dimensions to support complex multi-valued constraints.

Providing additional *how* dimensions: Using *step* dimensions for understanding sequential behavior, *audit* dimensions for tracking data quality/lineage, and r*ange band* dimensions for treating facts as dimensions.

Design patterns for modeling cause and effect

Appendix A: The Agile Manifesto

Appendix A lists the four values of, and the twelve principles behind, *the manifesto for agile software development*.

Appendix B: BEAM✳ Table Notation and Short Codes

Appendix B summarizes the BEAM✳ notation used throughout this book for modeling data requirements, recording data profiling results and representing physical dimensional modeling design decisions.

Appendix C: Resources for Agile Dimensional Modelers

Appendix C lists books, websites, and tools (hardware and software) that will help you adopt and adapt the ideas contained in the book.

Companion Website

Visit **modelstorming.com** to download the BEAM✳*Modelstormer* spreadsheet and other templates that accompany this book. On the site you will find example models and code listings together with links to articles, books, and the worldwide schedule of training courses and workshops on BEAM✳ and agile data warehouse design. Register your paperback copy online to receive a discounted eBook version.

PART I: MODELSTORMING

AGILE DIMENSIONAL MODELING, FROM WHITEBOARD TO STAR SCHEMA

Dimensional Modeling: it's too important to be left to data modelers alone
— *Anon.*

HOW TO MODEL A DATA WAREHOUSE

> Essentially, all models are wrong, but some are useful.
> — *George E. P. Box*

In this first chapter we set out the motivation for adopting an agile approach to data warehouse design. We start by summarizing the fundamental differences between data warehouses and online transaction processing (OLTP) databases to show why they need to be *designed* using very different data modeling techniques. We then contrast entity-relationship and dimensional modeling and explain why dimensional models are optimal for data warehousing/business intelligence (DW/BI). While doing so we also describe how dimensional modeling enables incremental design and delivery: key principles of agile software development.

Dimensional modeling supports data warehouse design

Readers who are familiar with the benefits of *traditional* dimensional modeling may wish to skip to **Data Warehouse Analysis and Design** on Page 11 where we begin the case for *agile* dimensional modeling. There, we take a step back in the DW/BI development lifecycle and examine the traditional approaches to data requirements *analysis*, and highlight their shortcomings in dealing with ever more complex data sources and aggressive BI delivery schedules. We then describe how *agile data modeling* can significantly improve matters by actively involving business stakeholders in the analysis *and* design process. We finish by introducing BEAM✲ (Business Event Analysis and Modeling): the set of agile techniques for *collaborative* dimensional modeling described throughout this book.

Collaborative dimensional modeling supports agile data warehouse analysis and design

- Differences between operational systems and data warehouses
- Entity-relationship (ER) modeling vs. dimensional modeling
- Data-driven analysis and reporting requirements analysis limitations
- Proactive data warehouse design challenges
- Introduction to BEAM✲: an agile dimensional modeling method

Chapter 1 Topics
At a Glance

3

OLTP vs. DW/BI: Two Different Worlds

OLTP and DW/BI have radically different DBMS requirements

Operational systems and data warehouses have fundamentally different purposes. Operational systems support the *execution* of business processes, while data warehouses support the *evaluation* of business processes. To execute efficiently, operational systems must be optimized for online transaction processing (OLTP). In contrast, data warehouses, must be optimized for query processing and ease of use. Table 1-1 highlights the very different usage patterns and database management system (DBMS) demands of the two types of system.

Table 1-1

Comparison between OLTP databases and Data Warehouses

CRITERIA	OLTP DATABASE	DATA WAREHOUSE
Purpose	Execute individual business processes ("turning the handles")	Evaluate multiple business processes ("watching the wheels turn")
Transaction type	Insert, select, update, delete	Select
Transaction style	Predefined: predictable, stable	Ad-hoc: unpredictable, volatile
Optimized for	Update efficiency and write consistency	Query performance and usability
Update frequency	Real-time: when business events occur	Periodic, (daily) via scheduled ETL (extract, transform, load). Moving to near real-time
Update concurrency	High	Low
Historical data access	Current and recent periods	Current + several years of history
Selection criteria	Precise, narrow	Fuzzy, broad
Comparisons	Infrequent	Frequent
Query complexity	Low	High
Tables/joins per transaction	Few (1–3)	Many (10+)
Rows per transaction	Tens	Millions
Transactions per day	Millions	Thousands
Data volumes	Gigabytes–Terabytes	Terabytes–Petabytes (many sources, history)
Data	Mainly raw detailed data	Detailed data, summarized data, derived data
Design technique	Entity-Relationship modeling (normalization)	Dimensional modeling
Data model diagram	ER diagram	Star schema

The Case Against Entity-Relationship Modeling

Entity-Relationship (ER) modeling is the standard approach to data modeling for OLTP database design. It classifies all data as one of three things: an entity, a relationship, or an attribute. Figure 1-1 shows an example entity-level ER diagram (ERD). Entities are shown as boxes and relationships as lines linking the boxes. The *cardinality* of each relationship—the number of possible matching values on either side of the relationship—is shown using *crow's feet* for many, | for one, and O for zero (also known as *optionality*).

ER modeling is used to design OLTP databases

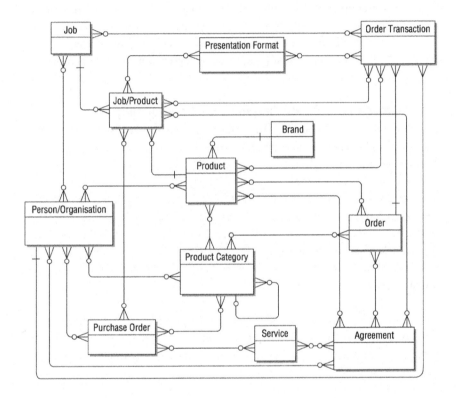

Figure 1-1
Entity-Relationship diagram (ERD)

Within a relational database, entities are implemented as tables and their attributes as columns. Relationships are implemented either as columns within existing tables or as additional tables depending on their cardinality. One-to-one (1:1) and many-to-one (M:1) relationships are implemented as columns, whereas many-to-many (M:M) relationships are implemented using additional tables, creating additional M:1 relationships.

Entities become tables, attributes become columns

ER modeling is associated with normalization in general, and *third normal form* (3NF) in particular. ER modeling and normalization have very specific technical goals: to reduce data redundancy and make explicit the 1:1 and M:1 relationships within the data that can be enforced by relational database management systems.

ER models are typically in third normal form (3NF)

Advantages of ER Modeling for OLTP

3NF is efficient for transaction processing

Normalized databases with few, if any, data redundancies have one huge advantage for OLTP: they make write transactions (inserts, updates, and deletes) very efficient. By removing data redundancies, transactions are kept as small and simple as possible. For example, the repeat usage of a service by a telecom's customer is recorded using tiny references to the customer and service: no unnecessary details are rerecorded each time. When a customer or service detail changes (typically) only a single row in a single table needs to be updated. This helps avoid update anomalies that would otherwise leave a database in an inconsistent state.

Higher forms of normalization are available, but most ER modelers are satisfied when their models are in 3NF. There is even a mnemonic to remind everyone that data in 3NF depends on "The key, the whole key, and nothing but the key, so help me Codd"—in memory of Edgar (Ted) Codd, inventor of the relational model.

Disadvantages of ER Modeling for Data Warehousing

3NF is inefficient for query processing

Even though 3NF makes it easier to get data in, it has a huge disadvantage for BI and data warehousing: it makes it harder to get the data out. Normalization proliferates tables and join paths making queries (SQL selects) less efficient and harder to code correctly. For example, looking at the Figure 1-1 ERD, could you estimate how many ways PRODUCT CATEGORY can be joined to ORDER TRANSACTION? A physical 3NF version of the model would contain at least 20 more tables to resolve the M:M relationships. Faced with such 3NF databases, even the simplest BI query requires multiple tables to be joined through multiple intermediate tables. These long joins paths are difficult to optimize and queries invariably run slowly.

3NF models are difficult to understand

More importantly, queries will only produce the right answers if users navigate the right join paths, i.e., ask the right questions in SQL terms. If the wrong joins are used, they unknowingly get answers to some other (potentially meaningless) questions. 3NF models are complex for both people and machines. Specialist hardware (data warehouse appliances) is improving query/join performance all the time, but the human problems are far more difficult to solve. Smart BI software can hide database schema complexity behind a semantic layer, but that merely moves the burden of understanding a 3NF model from BI users at query time to BI developers at configuration time. That's a good move but its not enough. 3NF models remain too complex for business stakeholders to review and quality assure (QA).

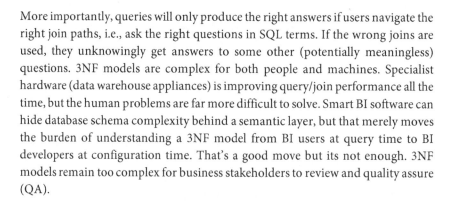

History further complicates 3NF

ER models are further complicated by data warehousing requirements to track history in full to support valid 'like-for-like' comparisons over time. Providing a true historical perspective of business events requires that many otherwise simple descriptive attributes become time relationships, i.e., existing M:1 relationships become M:M relationships that translate into even more physical tables and complex join paths. Such temporal database designs can defeat even the smartest BI tools and developers.

Laying out a readable ERD for any non-trivial data model isn't easy. The mnemonic "dead crows fly east" encourages modelers to keep crows' feet pointing up or to the left. Theoretically this should keep the high-volume volatile entities (transactions) top left and the low-volume stable entities (lookup tables) bottom right. However, this layout seldom survives as modelers attempt to increase readability by moving closely related or commonly used entities together. The task rapidly descends into an exercise in trying to reduce overlapping lines. Most ERDs are visually overwhelming for BI stakeholders and developers who need simpler, human-scale diagrams to aid their communication and understanding.

Large readable ER diagrams are difficult to draw: all those overlapping lines

The Case For Dimensional Modeling

Dimensional models define business processes and their individual events in terms of measurements (*facts*) and descriptions (*dimensions*), which can be used to filter, group, and aggregate the measurements. Data cubes are often used to visualize simple dimensional models, as in Figure 1-2, which shows the multidimensional analysis of a sales process with three dimensions: PRODUCT (*what*), TIME (*when*), and LOCATION (*where*). At the intersection of these dimensional values there are interesting facts such as the quantity sold, sales revenue, and sales costs. This perspective on the data appeals to many BI users because the three-dimensional cube can be thought of as a stack of two-dimensional spreadsheets. For example, one spreadsheet for each location contains rows for products, columns for time periods, and revenue figures in each cell.

Dimensional models appeal to spreadsheet-savvy BI users

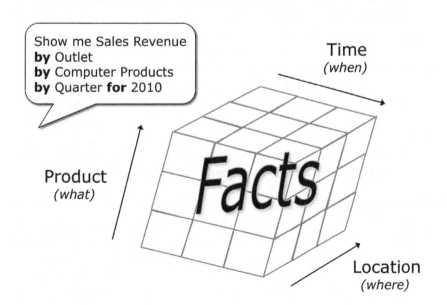

Figure 1-2
Multidimensional analysis

Star Schemas

Star schemas are used to visualize dimensional models

Real-world dimensional models are used to measure far more complex business processes (with more dimensions) in far greater detail than could be attempted using spreadsheets. While it is difficult to envision models with more than three dimensions as multi-dimensional cubes (they wouldn't actually be cubes), they can easily be represented using *star schema* diagrams. Figure 1-3 shows a classic star schema for retail sales containing a fourth (causal) dimension: PROMOTION, in addition to the dimensional attributes and facts from the previous cube example.

Figure 1-3

Sales star schema

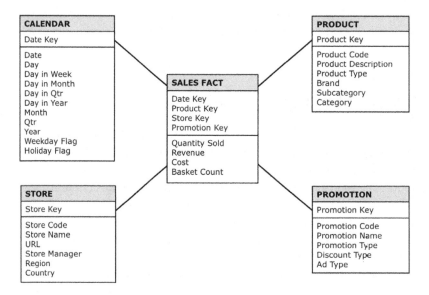

Star schema is also the term used to describe the physical implementation of a dimensional model as relational tables.

Star schema diagrams are non-normalized (N3NF) ER representations of dimensional models. When drawn in a database modeling tool they can be used to generate the SQL for creating fact and dimension tables in relational database management systems. Star schemas are also used to document and define the data cubes of multidimensional databases.

ER diagrams work best for viewing a small number of tables at one time. How many tables? About as many as in a dimensional model: a star schema.

Fact and Dimension Tables

Star schemas are comprised of fact and dimension tables

A star schema is comprised of a central fact table surrounded by a number of dimension tables. The fact table contains facts: the numeric (quantitative) measures of a business event. The dimension tables contain mainly textual (qualitative) descriptions of the event and provide the context for the measures. The fact table also contains dimensional foreign keys; to an ER modeler it represents a M:M relationship between the dimensions. A subset of the dimensional foreign keys form a composite primary key for the fact table and defines its *granularity*, or level of detail.

The term *dimension* in this book refers to a dimension table whereas *dimensional attribute* refers to a column in a dimension table.

Dimensions contain sets of descriptive (dimensional) attributes that are used to filter data and group facts for aggregation. Their role is to provide good report row headers and title/heading/footnote filter descriptions. Dimensional attributes often have a hierarchical relationship that allows BI tools to provide drill-down analysis. For example, drilling down from Quarter to Month, Country to Store, and Category to Product.

Dimensional hierarchies support drill-down analysis

Not all dimensional attributes are text. Dimensions can contain numbers and dates too, but these are generally used like the textual attributes to filter and group the facts rather than to calculate aggregate measures. Despite their width, dimensions are tiny relative to fact tables. Most dimensions contain considerably less than a million rows.

Dimensions are small, fact tables are large

The most useful facts are additive measures that can be aggregated using any combination of the available dimensions. The most useful dimensions provide rich sets of descriptive attributes that are familiar to BI users.

Advantages of Dimensional Modeling for Data Warehousing

The most obvious advantage of a dimensional model, noticeable in Figure 1-3, is its *simplicity*. The small number of tables and joins, coupled with the explicit facts in the center of the diagram, makes it easy to think about how sales can be measured and easy to construct the necessary queries. For example, if BI users want to explore product sales by store, only one short join path exists between PRODUCT and STORE: through the SALES FACT table. Limiting the number of tables involved and the length of the join paths in this way maximizes query performance by leveraging DBMS features such as star-join optimization (which processes multiple joins to a fact table in a single pass).

Dimensional models maximize query performance and usability

A deeper, less immediately obvious benefit of dimensional models is that they are *process-oriented*. They are not just the result of some aggressive physical data model optimization (that has denormalized a logical 3NF ER model into a smaller number of tables) to overcome the limitations of databases to cope with join intensive BI queries. Instead, the best dimensional models are the result of asking questions to discover which business processes need to be measured, how they should be described in business terms and how they should be measured. The resulting dimensions and fact tables are not arbitrary collections of denormalized data but *the 7Ws* that describe the full details of each individual business event worth measuring.

Dimensional models are process-oriented. They represent business processes described using the *7Ws* framework

The 7Ws
Framework

Who is involved?
What did they do? To *what* is it done?
When did it happen?
Where did it take place?
HoW *many* or much was recorded – *how* can it be measured?
Why did it happen?
HoW did it happen – in what manner?

The *7Ws* are interrogatives: question forming words

The *7Ws* are an extension of the 5 or 6Ws that are often cited as *the* checklist in essay writing and investigative journalism for getting the 'full' story. Each W is an *interrogative*: a word or phrase used to make questions. The *7Ws* are especially useful for data warehouse data modeling because they focus the design on BI activity: asking questions.

Fact tables represent *verbs* (they record business process *activity*). The facts they contain and the dimensions that surround them are *nouns*, each classifiable as one of the *7Ws*. 6Ws: *who, what, when, where, why*, and *how* represent dimension types. The 7th W: *how many*, represents facts. BEAM✲ *data stories* use the *7Ws* to discover these important verb and noun combinations.

Star schemas usually contain 8-20 dimensions

Detailed dimensional models usually contain more than 6 dimensions because any of the *6Ws* can appear multiple times. For example, an order fulfillment process could be modeled with 3 *who* dimensions: CUSTOMER, EMPLOYEE, and CARRIER, and 2 *when* dimensions: ORDER DATE and DELIVERY DATE. Having said that, most dimensional models do not have many more than 10 or 12 dimensions. Even the most complex business events rarely have 20 dimensions.

Star schemas support agile, incremental BI

The deep benefit of process-oriented dimensional modeling is that it naturally breaks data warehouse scope, design and development into manageable chunks consisting of just the individual business processes that need to be measured next. Modeling each business process as a separate star schema supports incremental design, development and usage. Agile dimensional modelers and BI stakeholders can concentrate on one business process at a time to fully understand how it should be measured. Agile development teams can build and incrementally deliver individual star schemas earlier than monolithic designs. Agile BI users can gain early value by analyzing these business processes initially in isolation and then grow into more valuable, sophisticated cross-process analysis. Why develop ten stars when one or two can be delivered far sooner with less investment 'at risk'?

Dimensional modeling provides a well-defined unit of delivery—the star schema —which supports the agile principles: *"Satisfy the customer through early and continuous delivery of valuable software."* and *"Deliver working software frequently, from a couple of weeks to a couple of months, with a preference to the shorter time scale."*

Data Warehouse Analysis and Design

Both 3NF ER modeling and dimensional modeling are primarily database *design* techniques (one arguably more suited to data warehouse design than the other). Prior to using either to design data structures for meeting BI information requirements, some form of *analysis* is required to discover these requirements. The two approaches commonly used to obtain data warehousing requirements are data-driven analysis (also known as supply driven) and reporting-driven analysis (also known as demand driven). While most modern data warehousing initiatives use some combination of the two, Figure 1-4 shows the analysis and design bias of early 3NF enterprise data warehouses compared to that of more recent dimensional data warehouses and data marts.

Analysis techniques are required to discover BI data requirements

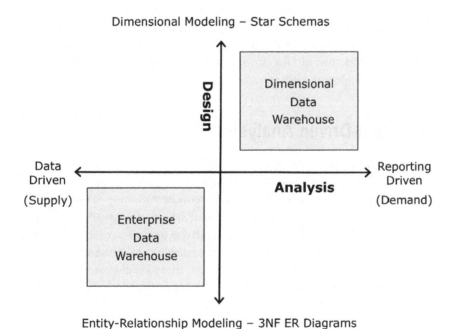

Figure 1-4
Data warehouse analysis and design biases

Data-Driven Analysis

Using a data-driven approach, data requirements are obtained by analyzing operational data sources. This form of analysis was adopted by many early IT-lead data warehousing initiatives to the exclusion of all others. User involvement was avoided as it was mistakenly felt that data warehouse design was simply a matter of re-modeling multiple data sources using ER techniques to produce a single 'perfect' 3NF model. Only after that was built, would it then be time to approach the users for their BI requirements.

Pure data-driven analysis avoided early user involvement

Leading to DW designs that did not met BI user needs !

Unfortunately, without user input to prioritize data requirements and set a manageable scope, these early data warehouse designs were time-consuming and expensive to build. Also, being heavily influenced by the OLTP perspective of the source data, they were difficult to query and rarely answered the most pressing business questions. Pure data-driven analysis and design became known as the "build it and they will come" or "field of dreams" approach, and eventually died out to be replaced by hybrid methods that included user requirements analysis, source data profiling, and dimensional modeling.

Packaged apps are especially challenging data sources to analyze

Data-driven analysis has benefited greatly from the use of modern data profiling tools and methods but despite their availability, data-driven analysis has become increasing problematic as operational data models have grown in complexity. This is especially true where the operational systems are packaged applications, such as Enterprise Resource Planning (ERP) systems built on highly generic data models.

IT staff are comfortable with data-driven analysis

In spite of its problems, data-driven analysis continues to be a major source of data requirements for many data warehousing projects because it falls well within the technical comfort zone of IT staff who would rather not get too involved with business stakeholders and BI users.

Reporting-Driven Analysis

Reporting requirements are gathered by interviewing potential BI users in small groups

Using a reporting-driven approach, data requirements are obtained by analyzing the BI users' reporting requirements. These requirements are gathered by interviewing stakeholders one at a time or in small groups. Following rounds of meetings, analyst's interview notes and detailed report definitions (typically spreadsheet or word processor mock-ups) are cross-referenced to produce a consolidated list of data requirements that are verified against available data sources. The results requirements documentation is then presented to the stakeholders for ratification. After they have signed off the requirements, the documentation is eventually used to drive the data modeling process and subsequent BI development.

User involvement helps to create more successful DWs

Reporting-driven analysis focuses the data warehouse design on efficiently prioritizing the stakeholder's most urgent reporting requirements and *can* lead to timely, successful deployments when the scope is managed carefully.

Accretive BI reporting requirements are impossible to capture in full, in advance

Unfortunately, reporting-driven analysis is not without its problems. It is time-consuming to interview enough people to gather '*all*' the reporting requirements needed to attain an enterprise or even a cross-departmental perspective. Getting stakeholders to think beyond 'the next set of reports' and describe longer term requirements in sufficient detail takes considerable interviewing skills. Even experienced business analysts with generous requirement gathering budgets struggle because detailed analytical requirements by their very nature are *accretive*: they gradually build up layer upon layer. BI users find it difficult to articulate future information needs beyond the 'next reports', because these needs are dependent upon the answers the 'next reports' will provide, and the unexpected new business initiatives those answers will trigger. The ensuing steps of collating requirements, feeding them back to business stakeholders, gaining consensus on data terms, and obtaining sign off can also be an extremely lengthy process.

Over-reliance on reporting requirements has lead to many initially successful data warehouse designs that fail to handle change in the longer-term. This typically occurs when inexperienced dimensional modelers produce designs that match the current report requests *too* closely, rather than treating these reports as clues to discovering the *underlying business processes* that should be modeled in greater detail to provide true BI flexibility. The problem is often exasperated by initial requirement analysis taking so long that there isn't the budget or willpower to swiftly iterate and discover the real BI requirements as they evolve. The resulting inflexible designs have led some industry pundits to unfairly brand dimensional modeling as too *report-centric*, suitable at the data mart level for satisfying the current reporting needs of individual departments, but unsuitable for enterprise data warehouse design. This is sadly misleading because dimensional modeling has no such limitation when used correctly to *iteratively* and *incrementally* model *atomic-level detailed* business processes rather than reverse engineer *summary* report requests.

Focusing too closely on current reports alone leads to inflexible dimensional models

Proactive DW/BI Analysis and Design

Historically, data warehousing has lagged behind OLTP development (in technology as well as chronology). Data warehouses were built often long after well established operational systems were found to be inadequate for reporting purposes, and significant BI backlogs had built up. This *reactive* approach is illustrated on the example timeline in Figure 1-5.

Early DWs were reactive to OLTP reporting problems

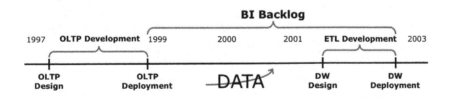

Figure 1-5
Reactive DW
timeline

Today, DW/BI has caught up and become *proactive*. The two different worlds of OLTP and DW/BI have become parallel worlds where many new data warehouses need to go live/be developed concurrently with their new operational source systems, as shown on the Figure 1-6 timeline.

The lag between OLTP and DW roll-out is disappearing

Figure 1-6
Proactive DW
timeline

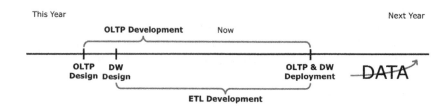

Proactive DW/BI
addresses
operational
demands, avoids
interim solutions
and preempts BI
performance
problems

DW/BI has steadily become proactive for a number of business-led reasons:

- DW/BI itself has become more operational. The (largely technical) distinction between operational and analytical reporting has blurred. Increasingly, sophisticated operational processes are leveraging the power of (near real-time) BI and stakeholders want a one-stop shop for all reporting needs: the data warehouse.

- Organizations (especially those that already have DW/BI success) now realize that, sooner rather than later, each major new operational system will need its own data mart or need to be integrated with an existing data warehouse.

- BI stakeholders simply don't want to support 'less than perfect' interim reporting solutions and suffer BI backlogs.

Benefits of Proactive Design for Data Warehousing

Proactive DW
design can
improve the data
available for BI

When data warehouse design preempts detailed operational data modeling it can help BI stakeholders set the data agenda, i.e., stipulate their ideal information requirements whilst the new OLTP system is still in development and enhancements can easily be incorporated. This is especially significant for the definition of mandatory data. Vital BI attributes that might have been viewed as optional or insignificant from a purely operational perspective can be specified as not null and captured from day one—before operational users develop bad habits that might have them (inadvertently) circumvent the same enhancements made later. Agile OLTP development teams should welcome these 'early arriving changes'.

Proactive DW
design can
streamline ETL
change data
capture

ETL processes are often thought of as difficult/impossible to develop without access to stable data sources. However, when a data source hasn't been defined or is still a moving target, it gives the agile ETL team the chance to define its 'perfect' data extraction interface specification based on the proactive data warehouse model, and pass that on to the OLTP development team. This is a great opportunity for ETL designers to ensure that adequate *change data capture* functionality (e.g. consistently maintained timestamps and update reason codes) are built into all data sources so that ETL processes can easily detect when data has changed *and* for what reason: whether genuine change has occurred to previously correct values (that must be tracked historically) or mistakes have been corrected (which need no history).

When source database schemas are not yet available, ETL development can still proceed if ETL and OLTP designers can agree on flat file data extracts. Once OLTP have committed to provide the specified extracts on a schedule to meet BI needs, ETL transformation and load routines can be developed to match this source to the proactive data warehouse design target.

Challenges of Proactive Analysis for Data Warehousing

While being proactive has great potential benefits for DW/BI, the late appearance of *data* on the Figure 1-6 timeline unfortunately heralds further analysis challenges for data warehouse designers: BI requirements gathering must take place before any real data is available. Under these circumstances proactive data modelers can rely even less upon traditional analysis techniques to provide BI data requirements to match their aggressive schedule.

Proactive analysis takes place before data exists

Proactive Reporting-Driven Analysis Challenges

Traditional interviewing techniques for gathering reporting requirements are problematic when stakeholders haven't seen the data or applications that will fuel their BI imagination. With no existing reports to work from, business analysts can't ask their preferred icebreaker question: "How can your favorite reports be improved?" and they have nothing to point at if and ask: "How do you use this data to make decisions?". Even more open questions such as "What decisions do you make and what information will help you to make them quicker/better?" can fall flat when a new operational systems will shortly enable an entirely new business process that stakeholders have no prior experience of measuring, or managing.

Reporting-driven analysis is difficult before data exists

Proactive Data-Driven Analysis Challenges

IT cannot fall back on data-driven analysis: data profiling tools and database remodeling skills are of little use when new source databases don't exist, are still under development, or contain little or no representative data (only test data). Even when new operational systems are implemented using package applications with stable, (well) documented database schemas they are often too complicated for untargeted data profiling: it would take too long and be of little value if only a small percentage of the database is currently used/populated and well understood by the available IT resources.

Data-driven analysis is impossible with no data to profile

Data then Requirements: a 'Chicken or the egg' Conundrum

Before there is data and users have lived with it for a time (with less than perfect BI access) both IT and business stakeholders cannot define genuine BI requirements in sufficient detail. Without these early detailed requirements proactive data warehouse designs routinely fail to provide the right information on time to avoid a BI backlog building up as soon as data is available. To solve this 'data then requirements'/'chicken or the egg' conundrum, proactive data warehousing needs a new approach to database analysis and design: not your father's data modeling, not even your father's dimensional modeling!

Proactive DW design requires a new approach to data analysis, modeling and design

Agile Data Warehouse Design

Traditional data warehousing follows a near-serial or *waterfall* approach to design and development

Traditional data warehousing projects follow some variant of *waterfall* development as summarized on the Figure 1-7 timeline. The shape of this timeline and the term 'waterfall' might suggest that its 'all downhill' after enough detailed requirements have been gathered to complete the 'Big Design Up Front' (BDUF). Unfortunately for DW/BI, this approach relies on a preternatural ability to exhaustively capture requirements upfront. It also postpones all data access and the hoped for BI value it brings until the (bitter) end of the waterfall (or rainbow!). For these reasons *pure* waterfall (analyze only once, design only once, develop only once, etc.) DW/BI development, whether by design or practice, is rare.

Figure 1-7
Waterfall DW development timeline

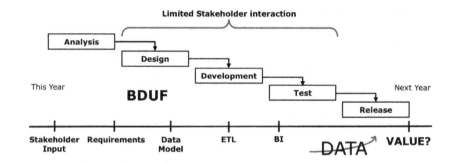

Dimensional modeling enables incremental development

Dimensional modeling can help reduce the risks of pure waterfall by allowing developers to release early incremental BI functionality one star schema at a time, get feedback and make adjustments. But even dimensional modeling, like most other forms of data modeling, takes a (near) serial approach to analysis and design (with 'Big Requirements Up Front' (BRUF) preceding BDUF data modeling) that is subject to the inherent limitations and initial delays described already.

Agile data warehousing is highly iterative and collaborative

Agile data warehousing seeks to further reduce the risks associated with upfront analysis and provide even more timely BI value by taking a highly iterative, incremental and collaborative approach to all aspects of DW design and development as shown on the Figure 1-8 timeline.

Figure 1-8
Agile DW development timeline

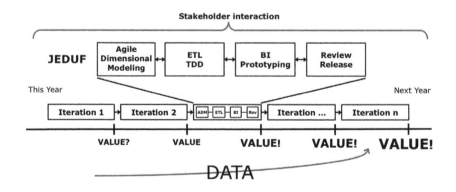

By avoiding the BDUF and instead doing 'Just Enough Design Upfront' (JEDUF) in the initial iterations and 'Just-In-Time' (JIT) detailed design within each iteration, agile development concentrates on the early and frequent delivery of working software that adds value, rather than the production of exhaustive requirements and design documentation that describes what will be done in the future to add value.

Agile focuses on the early and frequent delivery of working software that adds value

For agile DW/BI, the working software that adds value is a combination of queryable database schemas, ETL processes and BI reports/dashboards. The minimum set of valuable working software that can be delivered per iteration is a star schema, the ETL processes that populates it and a BI tool or application configured to access it. The minimum amount of design is a star.

For DW design, the minimum valuable working software is a star schema

To design any type of significant database schema to match the early and frequent delivery schedule of an agile timeline requires an equally agile alternative to the traditionally serial tasks of data requirements analysis and data modeling.

Agile database development needs agile data modeling

Agile Data Modeling

Scott Ambler, author of several books on agile modeling and agile database techniques (www.agiledata.org) defines *agile data modeling* as follows: *"Data modeling is the act of exploring data-oriented structures. Evolutionary data modeling is data modeling performed in an iterative and incremental manner. Agile data modeling is evolutionary data modeling done in a collaborative manner."*

Agile data modeling is collaborative and evolutionary

Iterative, incremental and *collaborative* all have very specific meanings in an agile development context that bring with them significant benefits:

- **Collaborative data modeling** obtains data requirements by modeling directly with stakeholders. It effectively combines analysis and design and 'cuts to the chase' of producing a data model (working software and documentation) rather than 'the establishing shot' of recording data requirements (only documentation).

Collaborative modeling combines analysis and design and actively involves stakeholders

- **Incremental data modeling** gives you more data requirements when they are better understood/needed by stakeholders, and when you are ready to implement them. Incremental modeling and development are scheduling strategies that support early and frequent software delivery.

Evolutionary modeling supports incremental development by capturing requirements when they grow and change

- **Iterative data modeling** helps you to understand existing data requirements better and improve existing database schemas through refactoring: correcting mistakes and adding missing attributes which have now become available or important. Iterative modeling and development are rework strategies that increase software value.

Agile Dimensional Modeling

DW/BI benefits from agile dimensional modeling

By taking advantage of dimensional modeling's unit of discovery—a business process worth measuring—agile data modeling has arguably greater benefits for DW/BI than any other type of database project:

Agile dimensional modeling focuses on business processes rather than reports

- Agile modeling avoids the 'analysis paralysis' caused by trying to discover the 'right' reports amongst the large (potentially infinite?) number of volatile, constantly re-prioritized requests in the BI backlog. Instead, agile dimensional modeling gets everyone to focus on the far smaller (finite) number of relatively stable business processes that stakeholders want to measure now or next.

Agile dimensional modeling creates flexible, report-neutral designs

- Agile dimensional modeling avoids the need to decode detailed business events from current summary report definitions. Modeling business processes without the blinkers of specific report requests produces more flexible, report-neutral, enterprise-wide data warehouse designs.

Agile modeling enables proactive DW/BI to influence operational system development

- Agile data modeling can break the "data then requirements" stalemate that exists for DW/BI just before a new operational system is implemented. Proactive agile dimensional modeling enables BI stakeholders to define new business processes from a measurement perspective and provide timely BI input to operational application development or package configuration.

Evolutionary modeling supports accretive BI requirements

- Agile modeling's evolutionary approach matches the accretive nature of genuine BI requirements. By following hands-on BI prototyping and/or real BI usage, iterative and incremental dimensional modeling allows stakeholders to (re)define their real data requirements.

Collaborative modeling teaches stakeholders to think dimensionally

- Many of the stakeholders involved in collaborative modeling will become direct users of the finished dimensional data models. Doing some form of dimensional modeling with these future BI users is an opportunity to teach them to think dimensionally about their data and define common, conformed dimensions and facts from the outset.

Collaborative modeling creates stakeholder pride in the data warehouse

- Collaborative modeling fully engages stakeholders in the design process, making them far more enthusiastic about the resultant data warehouse. It becomes *their* data warehouse, they feel invested in the data model and don't need to be trained to understand what it means. It contains their consensus on data terms because it is designed directly by them: groups of relevant business experts rather than the distillation of many individual report requests interpreted by the IT department.

Never underestimate the affection stakeholders will have for data models that they *themselves* (help) create.

Agile Dimensional Modeling and Traditional DW/BI Analysis

Agile dimensional modeling doesn't completely replace traditional DW/BI analysis tasks, but by preceding both data-driven and reporting-driven analysis it can make them agile too: significantly reducing the work involved while improving the quality and value of the results.

Agile dimensional modeling makes traditional analysis tasks agile

Agile Data-Driven Analysis

Agile data-driven analysis is streamlined by *targeted data profiling*. Only the data sources implicated by the agile data model need to be analyzed within each iteration. This targeted profiling supports the agile practice of *test-driven development* (TDD) by identifying the data sources that will be used to test the data warehouse design and ETL processes ahead of any detailed physical data modeling. If an ETL test can't be defined because a source isn't viable, agile data modelers don't waste time physically modeling what can't be tested, unless they are doing proactive data warehouse design. In this case the agile data warehouse model can assist the test-driven development of the new OLTP system.

Data-driven analysis becomes *targeted data profiling*

Agile Reporting-Driven Analysis

Agile reporting-driven analysis takes the form of BI prototyping. The early delivery of dimensional database schemas enables the early extraction, transformations and loading (ETL) of real sample data so that better report requirements can be prototyped using the BI user's actual BI toolset rather than mocked-up with spreadsheets or word processors. It is intrinsically fairer to ask users to define their requirements and developers to commit to them, once everyone has a sense of what their BI tools are capable of, given the available data.

Reporting-driven analysis becomes BI prototyping

Requirements for Agile Dimensional Modeling

Agile modeling requires both IT and business stakeholders to change their work practices and adopt new tools and techniques:

- Collaborative data modeling requires open-minded people. Data modelers must be prepared to meet regularly with stakeholders (take on a business analyst role) while business analysts and stakeholders must be willing to actively participate in some data modeling too. Everyone involved needs simple frameworks, checklists and guidelines that encourage *interaction* and prompt them through unfamiliar territory.

Collaborative modelers require techniques that encourage *interaction*

- Business stakeholders have little appetite for traditional data models, even conceptual models (see **Data Model Types**, shortly) that are supposedly targeted at them. They find the ER diagrams and notation favored by data modelers (and generated by database modeling tools) too complex or too abstract. To engage stakeholders, agile modelers need to create less abstract, more *inclusive* data models using simple tools that are easy to use, and easy to share. These inclusive models must easily translate into the more technically detailed,

Collaborative data modeling must use simple, *inclusive* notation and tools

logical and physical, star schemas used by database administrators (DBAs) and ETL/BI developers.

Data modeling sessions (*model-storms*) need to be *quick*: hours rather than days

- To encourage collaboration and support iteration, agile data modeling needs to be **quick**. If stakeholders are going to participate in multiple modeling sessions they don't want each one to take days or weeks. Agile modelers want speed too. They don't want to wear out their welcome with stakeholders. The best results are obtained by modeling with groups of stakeholders who have the experience and knowledge to define common business terms (*conformed dimensions*) and prioritize requirements. It is hard enough to schedule long meetings with these people individually let alone in groups. Agile data modeling techniques must support *modelstorming*: impromptu stand up modeling that is quicker, simpler, easier and more fun than traditional approaches.

Agile modelers must balance *JIT* and *JEDUF* modeling to reduce design rework

- Stakeholders don't want to feel that a design is constantly iterating (fixing what they have already paid for) when they want to be incrementing (adding functionality). They want to see obvious progress and visible results. Agile modelers need techniques that **support JIT** modeling of current data requirement in details **and JEDUF** modeling of 'the big picture' to help anticipate future iterations and reduce the amount of design rework.

Evolutionary DW development benefits from ETL/BI tools that support automated testing

- Developers need to **embrace database change**. They are used to working with (notionally) stable database designs, by-products of BDUF data modeling. It is support staff who are more familiar with coding around the database changes needed to match users' real requirements. To respond efficiently to evolutionary data warehouse design, agile ETL and BI developers need tools that support database impact analysis and automated testing.

DW designers must *embrace change* and allow their models to evolve

- Data warehouse designers also need to **embrace data model change**. They will naturally want to limit the amount of disruptive database refactoring required by evolutionary design, but they must avoid resorting to generic data model patterns which reduce understandability and query performance, and can alienate stakeholders. Agile data warehouse modelers need dimensional design patterns that they can trust to represent tomorrow's BI requirements *tomorrow*, while they concentrate on today's BI requirements *now*.

Agile dimensional modeling techniques exist for addressing these requirements

If agile dimensional modeling that is **interactive, inclusive, quick, supports JIT and JEDUF, and enables DW teams to embrace change** seems like a tall order don't worry; while there are no silver bullets that will make everyone or everything agile overnight, there are proven tools and techniques that can address the majority of these agile modeling prerequisites.

BEAM✲

BEAM✲ is an agile data modeling method for designing dimensional data warehouses and data marts. BEAM stands for Business Event Analysis & Modeling. As the name suggests it combines analysis techniques for gathering business event related data requirements and data modeling techniques for database design. The trailing ✲ (six point open centre asterisk) represents its dimensional deliverables: star schemas and the dimensional position of each of the *7Ws* it uses.

BEAM✲ consists of a set of repeatable, collaborative modeling techniques for rapidly *discovering* business event details and an inclusive modeling notation for *documenting* them in a tabular format that is easily understood by business stakeholders and readily translated into logical/physical dimensional models by IT developers.

Data Stories and the *7Ws* Framework

BEAM✲ gets BI stakeholders to think beyond their current reporting requirements by asking them to describe *data stories*: narratives that tease out the dimensional details of the business activity they need to measure. To do this BEAM✲ modelers ask questions using a simple framework based on the *7Ws*. By using the *7Ws* (*who, what, where, when, how many, why* and *how*) BEAM✲ conditions everyone involved to think dimensionally. The questions that BEAM✲ modelers ask stakeholders are the same types of questions that the stakeholders themselves will ask of the data warehouse when they become BI users. When they do, they will be thinking of *who, what, when, where, why* and *how* question combinations that measure their business.

Diagrams and Notation

Example data tables (or *BEAM✲ tables*) are the primary BEAM✲ modeling tool and diagram type. BEAM✲ tables are used to capture data stories in tabular form and describe data requirements using example data. By doing so they support collaborative *data modeling by example* rather than by abstraction. BEAM✲ tables are typically built up column by column on whiteboards from stakeholders' responses to the *7Ws* and are then documented permanently using spreadsheets. The resulting BEAM✲ models look more like tabular reports (see Figure 1-9) rather than traditional data models.

BEAM✲ (Example Data) Tables

BEAM✲ tables help engage stakeholders who would rather define reports that answer their specific business questions than do data modeling. While example data tables are not reports, they are similar enough for stakeholders to see them as

BEAM✲ is an agile dimensional modeling method

BEAM✲ is used to discover and document business event details

BEAM✲ modelers and BI stakeholders use the *7Ws* to tell *data stories*

BEAM✲ tables support *data modeling by example*

BEAM✲ tables look like simple tabular reports

visible signs of progress. Stakeholders can easily imagine sorting and filtering the low-level detail columns of a business event using the higher-level dimensional attributes that they subsequently model.

Figure 1-9
Customer Orders
BEAM✱ table

CUSTOMER ORDERS [DE]

CUSTOMER	orders PRODUCT	on ORDER DATE	QUANTITY	for REVENUE	with DISCOUNT	using ORDER ID
[who]	[what] MD, GD	[when] MD	[Retail Units]	[$, £, €]	[$, £, €, %]	[how] GD
Elvis Priestley	iPip Blue Suede	18-May-2011	1	$249	0	ORD1234
Vespa Lynd	POMBook Air	29-Jun-2011	1	£1,400	10%	ORD007
Elvis Priestley	iPip Blue Suede	18-May-2011	1	$249	0	ORD4321
Phillip Swallow	iPOM Pro	14-Oct-2011	1	£2,500	£150	ORD0001
Walmart	iPip G1	10 Years Ago	750	$200,000	$10,000	ORD0012
US Senate	iPOM + Printer	Yesterday	100	$150,000	$20,000	ORD5466
US Senate	iPip Touch	Yesterday	100	$25,000	$1,000	ORD5466

BEAM✱ Short Codes

BEAM✱ uses short codes to capture technical data properties

BEAM✱ tables are simple enough not to get in the way when modeling with stakeholders, but expressive enough to capture real-world data complexities and ultimately document the dimensional modeling design patterns used to address them. To do this BEAM✱ models use *short* (alphanumeric) *codes*: (mainly) 2 letter abbreviations of data properties that can be recorded in spreadsheet cells, rather than graphical notation that would require specialist modeling tools. By adding short codes, BEAM✱ tables can be used to:

- Document dimensional attribute properties including history rules
- Document fact properties including aggregation rules
- Record data-profiling results and map data sources to requirements
- Define physical dimensional models: fact and dimension tables
- Generate star schemas

BEAM✱ short codes act as dimensional modeling shorthand

BEAM✱ *short codes* act as dimensional modelers' shorthand for documenting generic data properties such as data type and nullability, and specific dimensional properties such as slowly changing dimensions and fact additivity. Short codes can be used to annotate any BEAM✱ diagram type for technical audiences but can easily be hidden or ignored when modeling with stakeholders who are disinterested in the more technical details. Short codes and other BEAM✱ notation conventions will be highlighted in the text in bold. Appendix B provides a reference list of short codes.

Comparing BEAM✱ and Entity-Relationship Diagrams

We will use Pomegranate Corp. examples to illustrate BEAM✱

Throughout this book we will be illustrating BEAM✱ in action with worked examples featuring the fictional Pomegranate Corporation (POM). We begin now by comparing an ER diagram representation of Pomegranate's order processing data model (Figure 1-10) with an equivalent BEAM✱ table for the Customer Orders event (Figure 1-9).

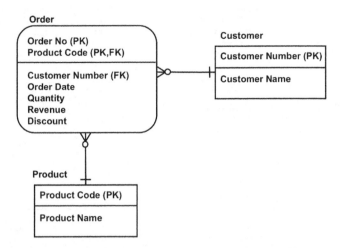

Figure 1-10
Order processing
ER Diagram

By looking at the ERD you can tell that customers may place orders for multiple products at a time. The BEAM✱ table records the same information, but the example data also reveals the following:

Example data models capture more business information than ER models

- Customers can be individuals, companies, and government bodies.
- Products were sold yesterday.
- Products have been sold for 10 years.
- Products vary considerably in price.
- Products can be bundles (made up of 2 products).
- Customers can order the same product again on the same day.
- Orders are processed in both dollars and pounds.
- Orders can be for a single product or bulk quantities.
- Discounts are recorded as percentages and money.

Additionally, by scanning the BEAM✱ table you may have already guessed the type of products that Pomegranate sells and come to some conclusions as to what sort of company it is. Example data speaks volumes—wait until you hear what it says about some of Pomegranate's (fictional) staff!

Example data speaks volumes!

Data Model Types

Agile dimensional modelers need to work with different types of models depending on the level of technical detail they are trying to capture or communicate and the technical bias of their collaborators and target audience. *Conceptual data models* (CDM) contain the least technical detail and are intended for exploring data requirements with non-technical stakeholders. *Logical data models* (LDM) allow modelers to record more technical details without going down to the database specific level, while *physical data models* (PDM) are used by DBAs to create database schemas for a specific DBMS. Table 1-2 shows the level of detail for each model type, its target audience on a DW/BI project, and the BEAM✱ diagram types that support that level of modeling.

Conceptual, logical and physical data models provide progressively more technical detail for more technical audiences

Table 1-2
Data Model Types

DETAIL	CONCEPTUAL DATA MODEL	LOGICAL DATA MODEL	PHYSICAL DATA MODEL
Entity Name	✓	✓	
Relationship	✓	✓	
Attribute	Optional	✓	
Cardinality	Optional	✓	✓
Primary Key		✓	✓
Foreign Key		✓	✓
Data Type		Optional	✓
Table Name			✓
Column Name			✓
DW/BI Audience	Data Modelers Business Analysts Business Experts Stakeholders BI Users	Data Modelers ETL Developers BI Developers	Data Modelers DBAs DBMS ETL Developers BI Developers Testers
BEAM✲ Diagram	Example Data Table Hierarchy Chart Timeline Event Matrix	Conceptual Diagrams with Short Codes Enhanced Star Schema	Enhanced Star Schema Event Matrix

BEAM✲ and ER notation are jointly used to create collaborative models for different audiences

Based on the detail levels described in Table 1-2 the order processing ERD in Figure 1-10 is a logical data model as it shows primary keys, foreign keys and cardinality, while the BEAM✲ event in Figure 1-9 is a conceptual model (we prefer "business model") as this information is missing. With additional columns and short codes it could be added to the BEAM✲ table but each diagram type suits its target audience as is. BEAM✲ tables are more suitable for collaborative modeling with stakeholders than traditional ERD based conceptual models. While other BEAM✲ diagram types and short codes compliment and enhance ERDs for collaborating with developers on logical/physical star schema design.

BEAM✲ Diagram Types

BEAM✲ also uses event matrices, timelines, hierarchy charts and enhanced star schemas

Example data tables are not the only BEAM✲ modeling tools. BEAM✲ modelers also uses event matrices, hierarchy charts, timelines and enhanced star schemas to collaborate on various aspects of the design at different levels of business and technical detail. Table 1-3 summarizes the usage of each of the BEAM✲ diagram types, and lists their model types, audience and the chapter where they are described in detail.

BEAM✲ supports the core agile values: *"Individuals and interactions over processes and tools."*, *"Working software over comprehensive documentation."* and *"Customer collaboration over contract negotiation."* BEAM✲ upholds these values and the agile principle of *"maximizing the amount of work not done"* by encouraging DW practitioners to work directly with stakeholders to produce compilable data models rather than requirements documents, and working BI prototypes of reports/dashboards rather than mockups.

Table 1-3 BEAM✳ Diagram Types

DIAGRAM	USAGE	DATA MODEL TYPE	AUDIENCE	PRINCIPAL CHAPTER
BEAM✳ (Example Data) Table CUSTOMER ORDERS [DE] orders / on / for CUSTOMER / PRODUCT / ORDER DATE / REVENUE [who] / [what] / [when] / [$, £, C] Elvis Priestley / iPip Blue Suede / 18-May-2011 / $249 Vespa Lynd / POMBook Air / 29-Jun-2011 / £1,400 Elvis Priestley / iPip Blue Suede / 18-May-2011 / $249 Phillip Swallow / iPOM Pro / 14-Oct-2011 / €2,500	Modeling business events and dimensions one at a time using example data to document their *7Ws* details. Example data tables are also used to describe physical dimension and fact tables and explain dimensional design patterns.	Business Logical Physical	Data Modelers Business Analysts Business Experts Stakeholders BI Users	2
Hierarchy Chart	Discovering hierarchical relationships within dimensions and prompting stakeholders for dimensional attributes. Hierarchy charts are also used to help define BI drill-down settings and aggregation levels for report and OLAP cube definition.	Business	Data Modelers Business Analysts Business Experts Stakeholders BI Users	3
Timeline	Exploring time relationships between business events. Timelines are used to discover *when* details, process sequences and duration facts for measuring process efficiency.	Business	Data Modelers Business Analysts Business Experts Stakeholders BI Users	8
Event Matrix	Documents the relationships between all the events and dimensions within a model. Event matrices record events in value-chain sequences and promote the definition and reuse of conformed dimensions across dimensional models. They are used instead of high-level ERDs to provide readable overviews of entire data warehouses or multi-star schema data marts.	Business Logical Physical	Data Modelers Business Analysts Business Experts Stakeholders BI Users Data Modelers ETL Developers BI Developers	4
Enhanced Star Schema	Visualizing individual dimensional models and generating physical database schemas. Enhanced star schemas are standard stars embellished with BEAM✳ short codes to record dimensional properties and design techniques that are not directly supported by generic data modeling tools.	Logical Physical	Data Modelers DBAs DBMS ETL Developers BI Developers Testers	5

Summary

- Data warehouses and operational systems are fundamentally different. They have radically different database requirements and should be modeled using very different techniques.

- Dimensional modeling is the appropriate technique for designing high-performance data warehouses because it produces simpler data models—star schemas—that are optimized for business process measurement, query performance and understandability.

- Star schemas record and describe the measureable events of business processes as fact tables and dimensions. These are not arbitrary denormalized data structures. Instead they represent the combination of the *7Ws* (*who, what, when, where, how many, why and how*) that fully describe the details of each business event. In doing so, fact tables represents verbs, while the facts (measures) they contain and the dimensions they reference represent nouns.

- Dimensional modeling's process-orientation supports agile development by creating database designs that can be delivered in star schema/business process increments.

- Even with the right database design techniques there are numerous analysis challenges in gathering detailed data warehousing requirements in a timely manner.

- Both data-driven and reporting-driven analysis are problematic, increasingly so, with DW/BI development becoming more proactive and taking place in parallel with agile operational application development.

- Iterative, incremental and collaborative data modeling techniques are agile alternatives to the traditional BI data requirements gathering.

- BEAM✲ is an agile data modeling method for engaging BI stakeholders in the design of their own dimensional data warehouses.

- BEAM✲ data stories use the *7Ws* framework to discover, describe and document business events dimensionally.

- BEAM✲ modelers encourage collaboration by using simple modeling tools such as whiteboards and spreadsheets to create inclusive data models.

- BEAM✲ models use example data tables and alphanumeric short codes rather than ER data abstractions and graphical notation to improve stakeholder communication. These models are readily translated into star schemas.

- BEAM✲ is an ideal tool for *modelstorming* a dimensional data warehouse design.

MODELING BUSINESS EVENTS

Think like a wise man but communicate in the language of the people.
— *William Butler Yeats (1865–1939)*

Business events are the individual actions performed by people or organizations during the execution of business processes. When customers buy products or use services, brokers trade stocks, and suppliers deliver components, they leave behind a trail of business events within the operational databases of the organizations involved. These business events contain the atomic-level measurable details of the business processes that DW/BI systems are built to evaluate.

BEAM✲ uses business events as incremental units of data discovery/data modeling. By prompting business stakeholders to tell their event *data stories,* BEAM✲ modelers rapidly gather the clear and concise BI data requirements they need to produce efficient dimensional designs.

In this chapter we begin to describe the BEAM✲ collaborative approach to dimensional modeling, and provide a step-by-step guide to discovering a business event and documenting its data stories in a BEAM✲ table: a simple tabular format that is easily translated into a star schema. By following each step you will learn how to use the *7Ws (who, what, when, where, how many, why, and how)* to get stakeholders thinking dimensionally about their business processes, and describing the information that will become the dimensions and facts of *their* data warehouse—one that they themselves helped to design!

- ▪ Data stories and story types: discrete, recurring and evolving
- ▪ Discovering business events: asking "Who does what?"
- ▪ Documenting events: using BEAM✲ Tables
- ▪ Describing event details: using the *7Ws* and stories themes
- ▪ Modelstorming with whiteboards: practical collaborative data modeling

Business events are the measureable atomic details of business processes

BEAM✲ modelers discover BI data requirements by telling *data stories*

This chapter is a step-by-step guide to using BEAM✲ tables and the *7Ws* to describe event details

Chapter 2 Topics
At a Glance

Data Stories

Data stories are to agile DW design as *user stories* are to agile software development

Data stories are comparable to *user stories*: agile software development's lean requirements gathering technique. Both are written or told by business stakeholders. While user stories concentrate on functional requirements and are written on index cards, data stories concentrate on data requirements and are written on whiteboards and spreadsheets.

Event stories use the narrative of a business event to discover BI data requirements

Business events, because they represent activity (verbs), have strong narratives. BEAM✳ uses these event narratives to discover their details (nouns) by telling *data stories*. BEAM✳ events are the archetypes for many similar data stories. "Employee drives company car on appointment date." is an event. "James Bond drives an Aston Martin DB5 on the 17th September 1964" is a data story. By following five *event story themes*, *event stories*, a specific type of data story, succinctly clarify the meaning of each event detail and help elicit additional details.

Story Types

Event stories are *discrete*, *evolving* or *recurring* depending on how they represent time

BEAM✳ classifies business events into three story types: *discrete*, *evolving*, and *recurring* based on how their stories play out with respect to time. Figure 2-1 shows example timelines for each type. Retail product purchases are examples of discrete events that happen at a point in time. They are (largely) unconnected with one another and occur unpredictably. Wholesale orders are evolving events that represent the irregular time spans it takes to fulfill orders. They too occur at unpredictable intervals. Interest charges are recurring events that represent the regular time spans over which interest is accrued. They occur in step with one another at predictable intervals.

Figure 2-1
Story type timelines

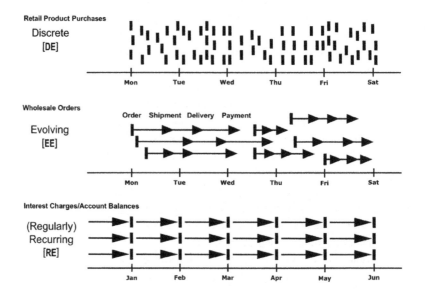

Discrete Events

Discrete events are "point-in-time" or short (duration) stories. They typically represent the atomic-level transactions recorded by operational systems. Example discrete events include:

- A customer buys a product in a retail store
- A visitor views a web page
- An employee makes a phone call

Discrete events are completed either at the moment they occur or shortly thereafter. By "shortly", we mean within the ETL refresh cycle of the data warehouse; i.e., they have "finished" or reached some end state by the time they are used for BI. Discrete event stories are generally associated with a single verb (e.g., "buys", "views", "calls") and a single timestamp. There are exceptions to the one verb, one timestamp rule, but for an event story to be discrete none of its details must change over time, otherwise it is evolving.

Evolving Events

Evolving events are longer-running stories (sagas) that can take several days, weeks, or months to complete. They are typically loaded into a data warehouse when their stories begin. Example evolving events include:

- A customer orders a product online and waits for it to be delivered
- A student applies for a place on a university course and is accepted
- An employee processes an insurance claim

Evolving events often represent a series of discrete events (chapters if you like) that BI stakeholders view as milestones of a complex/time-consuming business process. In Figure 2-1 the arrows that follow each evolving order event mark the shipment, delivery, and payment milestones that have been reached. Each of the verbs: "order", "ship", "deliver" and "pay" can be modeled as separate discrete events, but from the stakeholders' perspective the really important measures of the order fulfillment process only become visible when these events are combined to produce a *multi-verb* evolving event story.

Timelines (have you noticed how much we like them) are a great way to visualize evolving events stories and an invaluable tool for modeling milestones and interesting time intervals (duration measures). Modeling with timelines is covered in Chapter 8.

Recurring Events

Recurring events are periodic measurement stories that occur at predictable intervals, such as daily, weekly, and monthly (serials). In Figure 2-1 the arrowed line preceding each recurring event represents the period of time that the event measures. Example recurring events include:

Discrete events are "point-in-time" or short duration

Discrete event stories are "finished". They do not change

Evolving events represent irregular periods of times. Their stories may not have "finished"

Multi-verb evolving events combine the verbs of discrete events to support process performance measurement

Recurring events occur at predictable intervals

- Nightly inventory for a product at a retail location
- Monthly balance and interest charges/payments for a bank account
- Minute-by-minute viewing figures by audience for a TV channel

Recurring events summarize discrete events but can also represent the atomic detail for "automatic" measurements

Recurring events are typically used to sample and summarize discrete events, especially when cumulative measures, such as stock levels or account balances, are required that would be expensive to derive from the discrete events. For example, calculating an account balance at any point in time would require *all* the transactions against the account from all prior periods to be aggregated. Recurring events can also represent atomic-level measurement events that "automatically" occur on a periodic basis; for example, the hourly recording of rainfall at weather stations.

Events and Fact Tables

Events are business models for physical fact tables

The three BEAM✳ event story types are business models (conceptual models) for the three physical fact table types found in the star schemas of dimensional data warehouses. Table 2-1 shows how story types and fact table types are related.

Table 2-1
Story types and their matching star schemas

BEAM✳ STORY TYPE	STAR SCHEMA TYPE/PHYSICAL DIMENSIONAL MODEL
Discrete	Transaction fact table
Recurring	Periodic snapshot
Evolving	Accumulating snapshot

Discrete events are user models for *transaction fact tables*

Discrete events are implemented as *transaction fact tables*. All the detail that there is to know about discrete events is known before they are loaded into a data warehouse. This means that each discrete event story (fact record) is inserted once and never updated, greatly simplifying the ETL process.

Recurring events represent *periodic snapshots*

Recurring events are implemented as *periodic snapshot* fact tables. Many of their interesting measures are *semi-additive* balances that must be carefully reported over multiple time periods.

Evolving events represent *accumulating snapshots*

Evolving events are implemented as *accumulating snapshot* fact tables. They are loaded into a data warehouse shortly after the first event in a predictable sequence, and are updated each time a milestone event occurs until the overall event story is completed.

Chapter 5 describes the basic steps involved in translating events into star schemas. Chapter 8 provides more detailed coverage on designing transaction fact tables, periodic snapshots and accumulating snapshots.

The 7Ws

BEAM✱ uses the *7Ws: who, what, when, where, how many, why, and how* to discover and model data requirements as event details. Every event detail that stakeholders need falls into one of the 7 *W-types*. They are the nouns for people and organizations (*who*), things such as products and services (*what*), time (*when*), locations (*where*), reasons (*why*), event methods (*how*), and numeric measures (*how many*) that in combination form event stories.

Each of the *7Ws* is also an interrogative, a word or phrase that can be used to construct a question, and that is precisely what you do with them. By asking stakeholders a *who* question, you discover the people and organizations they want to analyze. By asking stakeholders a *what* question you discover the products and services they want to analyze. By asking these questions in the right combination and sequence you discover the business events they need to analyze.

As you capture event details you can record their dimension type in the type row of a BEAM✱ table. You will use this knowledge to help you model the details as dimensions and facts. Part 2 of this book has chapters dedicated to the *7Ws*, covering common BI issues and dimensional modeling design patterns associated with each type.

Thinking Dimensionally

The *7W* questions you ask to discover event details, mirror the questions that stakeholders will ask themselves when they define queries and reports. For example, a stakeholder will think about *where, when,* and *how many* to build a query that asks: "Which sales locations are performing better than last year?" and *who, when, what,* and *why* to ask: "Which customers are responding early to product promotions?" When stakeholders start using the *7Ws* they are thinking about their data dimensionally, because the *7Ws* represent how data is naturally modeled dimensionally. Table 2-2 shows the type of data that each of the *7Ws* represent together with examples of matching physical dimensions or facts.

Event stories are told using the *7Ws*

Each of the *7Ws* gives you a question to ask for story details

The *7Ws* help stakeholders think dimensionally about their data and BI queries

7WS	DATA	EXAMPLE DIMENSIONS (AND FACTS)
Who	People and organizations	Employee, Customer
What	Things	Product, Service
When	Time	Date/Calendar, Time of Day/Clock
Where	Locations	Store, Hospital, Delivery Address
Why	Reasons and causality	Promotion, Weather
How	Transaction IDs and status codes	Order ID (Degenerate Dimension), Call Status
How Many	Measures and Key Performance Indicators (KPIs)	Sales Revenue, Quantity (Facts)

Table 2-2
7Ws data, dimensions and facts

Using the *7Ws*: BEAM✳ Sequence

You ask *7W* questions in a specific, repeatable order to discover event details

The flowchart in Figure 2-2 shows the order (BEAM✳ sequence) for using the *7Ws*, along with the information that they give you at each stage. You start by using *who* and *what* to discover an event. From there you discover *when* the event happens and begin describing event stories using example data. After that, you ask as many *who*, *what*, *when*, and *where* questions as necessary to discover details for all of the people, organizations, products, services, timestamps, and locations related to the event. Then you ask *how many*, *why*, and *how* questions to discover the quantities, causes and other descriptive details needed to fully explain the event.

Figure 2-2
BEAM✳ sequence:
7Ws flowchart

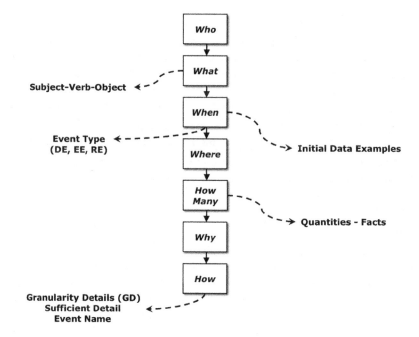

7W questions and event detail answers naturally flow from one to another

Once you become familiar with using the *7Ws* you will find they flow naturally from one to another; for example, quantity (*how many*) answers lead to *why* questions. If you discover a discount quantity this would naturally lead to the question: "*Why* do some orders have discounts?" Similarly, the *why* answer: "because of promotions" might lead to the *how* question: "*How* are promotions implemented?" and the answer: "with discount vouchers and codes."

Discovering event details out of sequence is okay

There is no need to be a slave to the BEAM✳ Sequence. If stakeholders call out relevant event details at random (hopefully not all at once) or remember details out of sequence, that's okay, but try to return to the flowchart as soon as possible to make sure all *7Ws* are covered.

Put a simple version of the *7Ws* flowchart up on the wall, so that *who, what, when, where, how many, why,* and *how* can start working on everyone's dimensional imagination and stakeholders know your next question type.

BEAM✳ in Action: Telling Stories

Modeling an event is an alliterative three-step process: *discover, document, describe*. Think of these as the *3Ds* to go along with the *7Ws*. Table 2-3 shows the steps and their matching techniques.

STEP	BEAM✳ TECHNIQUE
1. Discover an event	Ask "Who does what?"
2. Document the event	BEAM✳ table
3. Describe the event	The *7Ws* and event stories

Table 2-3
Event modeling
steps

The following sections describe each of the event modeling steps using an order processing example for Pomegranate Corp., our fictional multinational computer technology, consumer electronics, software, and consulting firm. In this initial worked example, order creation will be modeled in detail as a discrete event. In Chapter 4, shipments, deliveries and other related events will be modeled at a summary level. In Chapter 8, several of theses events are combined as a single evolving event that allows stakeholders to more easily measure the performance of the entire order fulfillment process.

Imagine you are modeling Pomegranate's order process

1. Discover an Event: Ask "Who Does What?"

BEAM✳ modelers discover business events by asking a deceptively simple question (using the first *2Ws*):

> **Who does what?**

The answer to this blunt opening question is an *event*. An event is an action. An action means that a *verb* is involved. When a verb is involved, there is *someone* or a *something* doing the action: the *subject*, and *someone* or a *something* having the action done to it: the *object*. So linguistically, the answer will be a *subject-verb-object* combination: the simplest story possible.

You are asking for a subject, a verb, and an object

"Who does what?" is really a mnemonic, a way of remembering to ask stakeholders to name the subject, verb, and object that identify an interesting event. It's a short way of saying: "Think of an activity. Who (or what) does it? What do they do? Who or what do they do it to?". Whatever form of the question you use, what you actually want to discover is an interesting *business* activity (verb) that is *in scope*, so it may need some qualification to work well. You might begin with your version of:

You do this to discover interesting business activity that needs to be measured

> **Who does what, that we want to report on within the scope of the next iteration/release?**

To which the stakeholders might reply:

> **Customer orders product?**

The answer to "Who does what?" is the *main clause* of an event

You now have what you need to begin modeling: a *subject*: customer, a *verb*: orders, and an *object*: product. This subject-verb-object combination is called the *main clause* of the event, and you will reuse it to ask most of the follow-up questions for discovering the "whole" story.

Focus on One Event at a Time

Stakeholders are typically interested in multiple events. Many share the same subject or object

Not surprisingly, you will find when asking a question as open as "Who does what?" that stakeholders can describe many subject-verb-object combinations that are interesting to them. In fact, they will typically bombard you with the subjects, verbs, and objects of several business events right off the top of their heads. Even reframing the question with a single chosen subject, for example, "Doctors do what?" or "Drivers do what?" can trigger a cascade of information. Stakeholders typically have several events that they need to measure for any given subject, each with a different verb. For instance, doctors *prescribe* medicines, but they also *diagnose* conditions, *perform* procedures, and *schedule* appointments. Drivers may *deliver* packages, but they also *depart* from depots, *accept* payments, and *collect* returns. Each subject-verb-object combination represents a different event which needs to be documented in its own BEAM✲ table.

Keep stakeholders focused on one event (verb) at a time

Getting an eager group of stakeholders to slow down and take things one event (verb) at a time can take some discipline. Try to reassure them (and yourself) that there will be plenty of time to capture all of this data, but you need to focus on one event at a time until it is complete—with all of its details. Don't worry about the stakeholders, they will not forget their other favorite events while you are documenting the current one.

Identifying the Responsible Subject

Responsible subjects (usually *whos*) help you discover *atomic-level* business events

Whenever possible, try to identify a *responsible subject* for the event's main clause. A responsible subject is a person or organization that actually performs the activity that the verb describes. This is important as it helps you discover the detailed *atomic-level* events of a business process rather than less flexible summary events that may only address the current report requirements. For example, if stakeholders are thinking too much about product reports they may respond "Product generates revenue" but you want to get them thinking about the underlying business process(es) by asking: "How does a product generate revenue? Who makes that happen?" To which the stakeholders might respond: "Customer buys product" or "Salesperson sells product". Both of these are better subject-verb-object combinations (main clauses) for an event that will help you identify the detailed transactions that should be modeled and loaded into the data warehouse.

Summary events can always be added afterwards for query efficiency, if necessary, so long as the details are there. You should make sure you initially model the most granular discrete events the stakeholders are interested in. You can then model recurring and evolving events from these (in subsequent iterations) to provide easier access to the performance measures that stakeholders need. Chapter 8 covers the event modeling and dimensional design techniques for doing this.

Asking: "Who does what?" does not always ensure that you will get actual *who* and *what* details. Objects especially can be any of the *7Ws*, including *how many*. For automated recurring events there may simply not be a responsible *who* subject that triggers them. For example, "Store stocks product" or "Weather station records temperature" are both perfectly valid events, but neither has *who* details. "Store" and "weather station" are *where*-type subjects, and "temperature" is an example of a *how many* object rather than a *what* object.

There is no need to fret over this, and try to coax stakeholders into supplying actual people (*who*) and things (*what*) in every case as this can get in the way of capturing their perspective on the event. The most important thing is that stakeholders supply a main clause containing a verb worth measuring. If their main clause doesn't contain a *who* or *what* you will soon discover any that belong to the event as you use each of the *7Ws* to discover more details.

> **Summary events can always be added later. You should initially concentrate on the atomic detail**
>
> **Subjects and objects are not always *who* and *what*. They can be any of the *7Ws***
>
> **As long as you have a verb you will find any *whos* or *whats* involved (if any) by asking more *W* questions shortly**

> ### Verbs
>
> Verbs are one of the most difficult parts of any language. Because of numerous tenses, cases, and persons, the possible ways of expressing a verb can be confusing. For instance, the verb "to buy" can be written as "buy", "bought", "buying" and "buys". To simplify events, use this last version "buys" which is the third-person singular present tense. This simply means it sounds right after "he", "she", or "it". In English, this version of the verb always end in "s". For example, "to call" becomes "calls", "reviewed" becomes "reviews", "auditing" becomes "audits", and "will sell" becomes "sells". This standard form is intuitive and avoids awkward verb variations.
>
> **For verbs, use the third-person singular present tense**

2. Document the Event: BEAM✳ Table

Now that the stakeholders have supplied an event, you need to document and display it on a whiteboard or screen where everyone can see it using a BEAM✳ example data table. Figure 2-3 shows the initial table for "Customer orders product." If this looks like it could be an "ordinary" spreadsheet table that's a good thing; Business stakeholders are the target audience for this model and they are usually very comfortable with spreadsheets.

> **An event is documented as a BEAM✳ table on a whiteboard or in a spreadsheet**

Figure 2-3
Initial event table

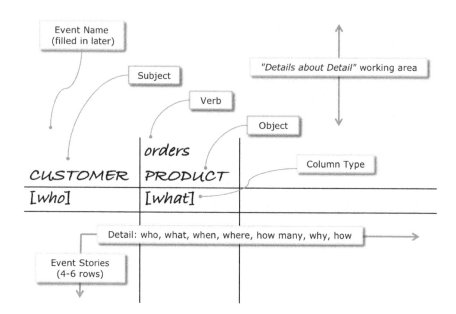

Several important BEAM✻ notation conventions are indicated in Figure 2-3. The subject (CUSTOMER) and object (PRODUCT) are capitalized, and have become column headers. The verb (orders) is in lowercase, and is placed in its own row above the object. This row will be used to hold other lowercase words shortly. The capitalized column headers are the event details that will eventually become facts or dimensions. The lowercase words will connect subsequent details to the event and clarify their relationships with the main clause. They make event stories readable, but are not components of the physical database design.

Draw data tables on whiteboards without borders between or below the example rows. Fewer lines make freehand drawing quicker and neater, while at the same time visually suggesting that the examples are open ended: that stakeholders can add to them at any point to illustrate ever more interesting stories that help to clarify exceptions.

Don't name the event until it is complete

The rest of the table is left blank, with several empty rows for example data and space above for an event name. Don't attempt to name the event just yet because this may prejudice the details that the stakeholders provide.

Leave some working space for *detail about detail*

The table is now ready to record event details and example data (event stories) to clarify the meaning of each detail. In Figure 2-3 there is also space reserved above the table as a scratchpad for recording *detail about detail*: important details that you may capture along the way that don't belong directly to the event (see **What?** later in this chapter) but will need to be modeled as dimensional attributes after the event is complete.

You can download a copy of the BEAM✳*Modelstormer* spreadsheet from **modelstorming.com.** It contains template BEAM✳ (example data) tables linked to formulas for generating customizable SQL DDL and simple table/entity graphics. You can use the DDL to define physical database tables or export your BEAM✳ model to other database modeling tools to produce star schemas.

3. Describe the Event: Using the *7Ws*

BEAM✳ obeys the maxim "show, don't tell" to describe and model an event using event stories rather than lengthy descriptive text. But before you can ask for useful example stories you need one more detail. You need to discover *when* the event occurs. You find out by asking your second simple "W" question: a *when* question.

Every event story needs a *when* detail

When?

Every event story has at least one defining point in time. No meaningful BI analysis takes place without a time element. Therefore, immediately following the discovery of an event, you should ask for its *when* detail. You do so by repeating the main clause of the event to the stakeholders as a question, with a "*when*" appended or prepended:

You discover *when* details by asking a *when* question

> **CUSTOMER orders PRODUCT *when?***
> or
> ***When do* CUSTOMERs order PRODUCTs?**

To which the stakeholders might respond (if you're lucky):

> **On order date.**

This is certainly what you are hoping for: a *prepositional phrase* containing a *preposition*: "on" followed by a *noun*: "order date." If they respond with actual dates/times, ask what these should be called. You are looking for a noun to name this detail; after you have it you can then use the date/time values for example stories to help you understand the time nature of the event. The general form of a *when* question is: "*Subject Verb Object **when?***" or "***When** does a Subject Verb Object*? What do you call that date/time?" The required response is in the form: "on/at/every *Time Stamp Name*"

You are looking for a preposition and a name for the *when* detail

The preposition *on* used with a *when* detail implies that the detail is recorded as a date, suggesting that the time of day is not available or is not important. An *at* preposition implies that time of day is recorded and is important. Whenever stakeholders give you example *when* values you should check that prepositions and examples match; so that event stories can be read correctly.

When prepositions contain clues to the level of time detail available/needed

Prepositions

Prepositions are the words that link nouns, pronouns and phrases in sentences and describe their relationships. These relationships include time (*when*), possession (*who/what*), proximity (*where*), quantity (*how many*), cause (*why*) and manner (*how*). Examples of typical prepositions include: with, in, on, at, by, to, from and for. BEAM✳ uses prepositions to:

- Link details to the main clause of an event.
- Construct event stories using natural language sentences made from main clause-preposition-detail combinations.
- Clarify the relationship between an event and its details.
- Discover event detail rules such as the time granularity of *when* details (on, at) and the direction implied by *where* details (from, to).

Add the *when* detail and preposition to the table

After you have confirmed the prepositional phrase you add it to the event table, as shown in Figure 2-4, with the *on* preposition above the new detail ORDER DATE. Now that you have the subject, object, and initial *when* details you can begin to fill out the table with event stories.

Figure 2-4
Adding the first
when detail

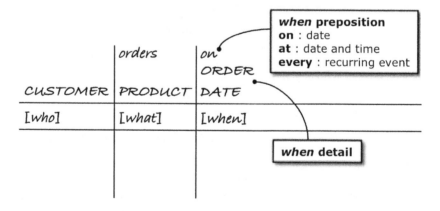

The preposition for a *when* detail is highly significant. "on order date," "at call time," and "every sales quarter" each contain an important clue to the level of time detail available (or necessary) for their respective events.

Collecting Event Stories

You ask the stakeholders to provide examples for every event detail you discover, for the following reasons:

- Asking for examples and getting useful answers is a clear indication that you are being agile, that you are modeling with the right people: stakeholders who know their own data.

- Example data clarifies the meaning of each event detail as you discover it with the minimum documentation.

- Examples avoid abstraction. Stakeholders can start to visualize how their data might appear on reports.

- Examples demonstrate how events behave over time by illustrating typical, exceptional, old, new, minimum, and maximum values amongst other event stories.

- Capturing examples quickly leads to an understanding of the story type, and eventually to a definition of the event *granularity* (the set of detail values that uniquely identify each event story).

Wait until you have at least one *when* detail before collecting example data. Having a *when* detail helps you get more interesting examples that tell a story.

Event Story Themes

To model events rapidly you want to describe each detail as fully as possible using the minimum number of example stories. You can discover and document most of what you need to know in five or six example rows by asking for stories that illustrate the following five *themes*:

Useful event stories follow five *themes*

- Typical
- Different
- Repeat
- Missing
- Group

Figure 2-5 shows how the themes vary slightly across the *7Ws*. The italic descriptions suggest the range of values that you want to illustrate for each "W" (by using the *typical* and *different* themes). Armed with this information you are now ready to start "modeling by example": asking the stakeholders to tell you event stories for each theme.

Themes help you discover data ranges for each of the *7Ws*

SUBJECT	**verb** OBJECT	on/at /every DATE/TIME	at/from/to LOCATION	with/for QUANTITY	for REASON	in/using MANNER
[who]	[what]	[when]	[where]	[how many]	[why]	[how]
Typical	Typical/Popular	Typical	Typical	Typical/Average	Typical/Normal	Typical/Normal
Different	Different	Different	Different	Different	Different	Exceptional
Repeat	Repeat	Repeat	Repeat	Repeat	Repeat	Repeat
Missing	Missing	Missing	Missing	Missing	Missing	Missing
Group	Multiple/Bundle		Multi-level		Multiple values	Multiple values
Range						
Old, Low value	*Old, Low value*	*Oldest needed* *Most recent*	*Near*	*Min, Negative* *0*	*Normal*	*Normal*
New, High value	*New, High value*	*Future*	*Far*	*Max, Precision*	*Exceptional*	*Exceptional*

Figure 2-5
Story theme
template

Typical Stories

You start by asking for a *typical* event story

Each event table should start with a *typical* event story that contains common/normal/representative values for each detail. For *who* data this could be a frequent CUSTOMER. For *what* details this might be a popular PRODUCT. Similarly, for *how many* details you are looking for average values that match the other typical values. To fill out this example story you simply ask the stakeholders for typical values for each detail.

Different Stories

Ask for *different* stories to explore value *ranges*

Following the typical example event you ask the stakeholders for another example with *different* values for each detail. If you ask for two *different* examples you can use them to discover the *range* of values that the data warehouse will have to represent. This is particularly important for *when* details because they indicate how much history will be required and how urgently the data must be loaded into the data warehouse.

Use *relative time descriptions* to document ETL urgency and DW history requirements

For *when* details, use *relative time descriptions* such as **Today, Yesterday, This Month,** and **5 Years Ago** to capture the most recent and earliest values so that the event stories remain relevant long after the model is completed. If the latest *when* is **Yesterday**, then you know that the data warehouse will demand a daily refresh for this particular business process. In Figure 2-6, the fourth and fifth example events show that the data warehouse will need to support 10 years of history for this event, and that a daily refresh policy is required.

If the latest *when* event story is **Today**, the data warehouse will need to be refreshed more urgently than daily—perhaps in near real-time. Because this will significantly complicate the ETL processing and increase development costs, you should confirm that this is a vital requirement with budgetary approval. If it is, you need to find out if **Today** means "an hour ago" or "10 minutes ago".

Look for old and new values as well as high and low

For *who* and *what* details, ask for old and new values—representing customers who have become inactive versus brand-new customers, or products that have been discontinued versus those just released.

Repeat Stories

Ask for a *repeat* story to find out what makes an event story unique

Once you have collected a few different examples you ask for a *repeat* story—one that is as similar as possible to the typical story (the first row)—so you can discover what makes each event story unique. You do this by asking whether the typical values can appear again in the same combination; for example, you might ask:

Can *this* CUSTOMER order *this* PRODUCT again on the *same* day?

The third event story in Figure 2-6 shows that this is possible. Each time you add a new detail to the event you return to the repeat story to see if that detail can be used to differentiate the event, by adding it to the previous question; for example, "Can this CUSTOMER order this PRODUCT again on the same day, from the same SALES LOCATION?" If that's possible repeat the typical story values.

You might have uniqueness with the subject, object, and initial *when* details alone, or you might not have it until you discover a *how* detail with your very last question.

Repeat the *typical* story if it is not yet unique

Figure 2-6
Adding event stories

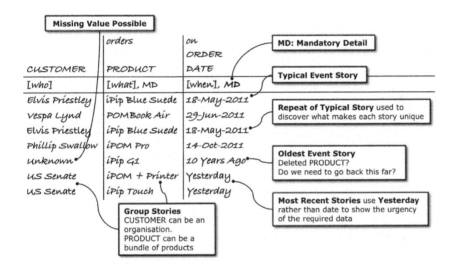

Missing Stories

You ask for a *missing* story to discover which event details can have missing values (e.g. unknown, not applicable, or not available) and which are mandatory (always present). You use a missing story to document how stakeholders want to see missing values displayed on their reports. When you fill out a missing story (such as the fifth story in Figure 2-6) you use normal values for mandatory details and the stakeholders' default *missing value* labels (e.g. "N/A", "Unknown") for the non mandatory details. For quantities you must find out whether missing data should be treated as NULL (the arithmetically correct representation of missing) or replaced by zero, or some other default value. You document the mandatory details by also adding the short code **MD** to their column type.

MD : *mandatory detail*. Event detail is always present under normal circumstances (no data errors).

Missing stories can be unrealistically sparse, containing missing values for *any* detail that might *ever* be missing. It's okay if there are more missing values than would ever be seen in a single real event story.

Missing stories document how missing values will be treated by BI applications. They also help to identify mandatory event details

It's OK for *missing* stories to be unrealistically empty

Occasionally you may have an event subject that is consistently missing. For example, a retail sales event might be described as "CUSTOMER buys PRODUCT in STORE", but the customer name is never recorded. When the event is implemented as a physical fact table this *virtual detail* will be dropped, but during event storytelling it focuses everyone on the atomic-level event. Perhaps the event stories should contain "Anon." or "J. Doe".

Evolving events will have many missing details.
For discrete and recurring events this is a warning that they may be too generic

Evolving events by their nature will have a number of validly missing details that are unknown when the event begins; for example, ACTUAL DELIVERY DATE for an order or FINAL PAID AMOUNT for an insurance claim. However, if you find discrete and recurring events with a lot of missing details it is often a clue that you are trying too hard to model a "one size fits all" generic event that is difficult for stakeholders to use and it may be better to model a number of more specific event tables where the details that really define distinct business events are always present.

Group Stories

Group stories highlight details that vary in meaning

You ask for example events containing *groups* to expose any variations in the meaning of a detail. For example, a typical order event consists of an individual customer ordering a product. But is this always the case? You should ask the stakeholders:

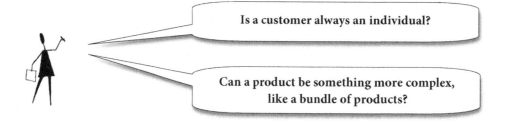

Is a customer always an individual?

Can a product be something more complex, like a bundle of products?

Mixed business models (B2B, B2C, products and services) are often discovered by *group* stories

The last two example events in Figure 2-6 are *group* themed. From these you learn that customers can be organizations as well as individuals and orders can be placed for multi-product bundles. The knowledge that there are different types of customer (B2B: business-to-business and B2C: business to consumer), and product/service bundles will make you think carefully about how you implement these details as dimensions. Chapter 6 covers mixed customer type dimensions, multi-level dimensions and hierarchy maps, while Chapter 9 covers multi-valued dimensions. These design patterns can be used to solve some of the more vexing modeling issues surfaced by *group* themed examples.

You should ask for just enough event stories so that everyone is clear about the meaning of each event detail. Don't get carried away trying to record every story — that's what the data warehouse is for — you want to concentrate on discovering all the event details.

Additional *When* Details?

After you have documented the initial *when* detail and collected the beginnings of several stories, you continue looking for *when* details. Discovering all the *when* details as early as possible is useful, because it helps you determine the *story type* which in turn helps you to ask more insightful questions as you look for further details. For now you ask:

Ask for more *when* details to discover the *story type*

> **Are there any other dates and times associated with a customer ordering a product?**

to which the stakeholders might reply:

> **Yes, orders are due for delivery on a delivery due date.**

You add this new *when* detail to the event table, as shown in Figure 2-7. With each additional *when* you also capture examples before proceeding on to the next *when* detail. As you do this you may want to adjust some existing example date/times to illustrate interesting time intervals (exceptionally short and long stories) between milestones.

Use *when* examples to describe long and short durations

Second *when* detail
Prepositional phrase contains a verb, may denote an evolving event

Figure 2-7
Adding a second
when detail

CUSTOMER	orders PRODUCT	on ORDER DATE	for delivery on DELIVERY DUE DATE
[who]	[what], MD	[when], MD	[when]
Elvis Priestley	iPip Blue Suede	18-May-2011	22-May-2011
Vespa Lynd	POMBook Air	29-Jun-2011	4-Jul-2011
Elvis Priestley	iPip Blue Suede	18-May-2011	22-May-2011
Phillip Swallow	iPOM Pro	14-Oct-2011	Not Applicable
Unknown	iPip G1	10 Years Ago	Not Applicable
US Senate	iPOM + Printer	Yesterday	3 Days from now
US Senate	iPip Touch	Yesterday	3 Days from now

Orders with no delivery due date
Customer collection or cancelled order?

If you have more than two *when* details, draw a simple timeline to help stakeholders describe the chronological sequence and name the most interesting durations between pairs of *whens*.

Determining the Story Type

Knowing the story type helps you to discover more details

After you have identified all the *when* details and documented them with example data, you use this information to determine the story type which in turn will give you strong clues about subsequent detail types you can expect especially the *how many* details.

Recurring Event

Recurring events contain a *when* detail with an **every** preposition

If the event contains a *when* detail with an **every** preposition and the example stories confirms that it occurs on a regular periodic basis then the event is *recurring*. If so, it will often contain balance measures. You should check for these when you ask your *how many* questions.

Evolving Event

If an event has at least one changeable *when* detail it is *evolving*

If you have two or more *when* details you may have an evolving event. If any of the *when* details are initially unknown and/or can change after the event has been created (and loaded into the data warehouse) then it is definitely an evolving event. If so, you should look out for changeable duration measures that make use of the multiple *whens*.

If an event is evolving you should ask the stakeholders for example stories that illustrate the initial and final states—the emptiest event story possible, and a fully completed one—to help explain how the event evolves.

Imagine for a moment that the stakeholders had responded to your additional *when* question with:

> **Orders are *delivered on* delivery date and *paid on* payment date.**

This would make the event evolving if the *actual* delivery dates and payment dates are unknown when orders are loaded into the data warehouse.

Evolving events contain *additional verbs* that may be modeled as discrete events in their own right

Notice that the *"on"* prepositions for these *when* details are preceded with the verbs *"deliver"* and *"pay"*. These verbs are events in their own right that occur some time after the initial order event. However, if stakeholders respond in this way they view them primarily as order event milestones. Therefore, you should continue to model them as *when* details of an evolving order event but you may also want to model delivery and payment as separate discrete events too: You would ask "Who delivers what?" and "Who pays what?" to discover if there are important details that will be lost if deliveries and payments are only available at the order level.

If stakeholders provide multiple *when* details, pay attention to the verbs used in prepositional phrases. The multiple verbs can identify a process sequence of related milestone events. These events can be modeled as part of the current evolving event and as discrete events in their own right if you suspect they have more details. See Chapters 4 and 8 for more details on modeling evolving events.

Discrete Event

By a process of elimination, if an event is neither recurring nor evolving, it must be discrete. You reconfirm this each time you discover a new detail by asking if its example values can ever change. If details never change, or changes are handled as new adjustment events, then the event remains discrete. In Figure 2-7 both the ORDER DATE and the DELIVERY DUE DATE (if applicable) are known at the time of an order and do not change, so the order events, as modeled so far, are discrete.

Discrete events contain details that do not change

Who?

Once you have identified the story type it's time to double-back (to the top of the 7Ws flowchart in Figure 2-2) and find out whether any other *whos* are associated with the event. The general form of a *who* question is "*Subject Verb Object* from/for/with **who**?" Using the current subject, verb and object you might ask:

Ask a who question to see if anyone else is involved

> **CUSTOMER orders PRODUCT from *whom*?**

To which the stakeholder might reply:

> **Salesperson**

If so, you add the new *who* to the table and ask for example salespeople to match the existing event stories. E.g., to continue a group themed story you might ask:

> **Is there always just one SALESPERSON responsible for the order?**

In Figure 2-8, the event stories introduce you to some of Pomegranate's finest sales personnel, but also shows that orders can be made without a salesperson, and that some orders are handled by sales *teams* rather than individual employees (continuing the *group* story theme).

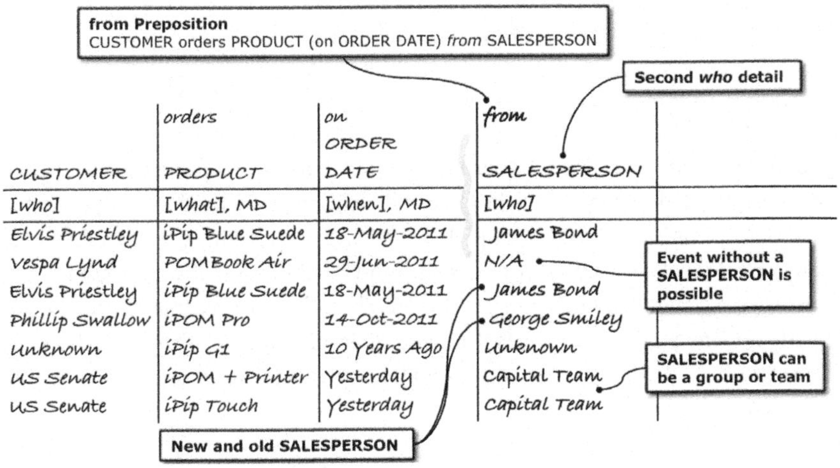

from Preposition
CUSTOMER orders PRODUCT (on ORDER DATE) *from* SALESPERSON

Second who detail

CUSTOMER	orders PRODUCT	on ORDER DATE	*from* SALESPERSON
[who]	[what], MD	[when], MD	[who]
Elvis Priestley	iPip Blue Suede	18-May-2011	James Bond
Vespa Lynd	POMBook Air	29-Jun-2011	N/A
Elvis Priestley	iPip Blue Suede	18-May-2011	James Bond
Phillip Swallow	iPOM Pro	14-Oct-2011	George Smiley
Unknown	iPip G1	10 Years Ago	Unknown
US Senate	iPOM + Printer	Yesterday	Capital Team
US Senate	iPip Touch	Yesterday	Capital Team

Event without a SALESPERSON is possible

SALESPERSON can be a group or team

New and old SALESPERSON

Figure 2-8

Adding a second *who* detail

Don't use real employee names in event stories. You may have to model stories where employees underperform—you don't want to point the finger at anyone in the room or elsewhere. Try using famous fictional characters instead. This side-steps any legal problems, and can be mildly entertaining, but don't overdo it: you don't want to distract everyone from the real event stories and details.

What?

Ask a *what* question, especially if you don't already have a *what* detail

Next you ask for any additional *whats* associated with the event. The general form of the question is: "*Subject Verb Object* with/for **what**?" *What* questions are particularly useful when the main clause doesn't already contain a *what* detail; for example:

> **CUSTOMER pays MAINTENANCE FEE for *what*?**

might give you the *what* detail: SOFTWARE PRODUCT that would be added to the table with a "for" preposition. You can keep repeating variations on the *what* question to see if there are any more *what* details, but be careful not to collect "*detail about detail*" (see sidebar: **Detail about Detail**)

Where?

Ask for a *where* next

The next detail type to look for is a *where*. You ask for this by using the event's main clause with a *where* appended:

> **CUSTOMER orders PRODUCT, *where*?**

You are trying to find out whether the event occurs at a specific geographic location (or website address). If the stakeholders respond:

> **Online, or at a retail outlet.**

Online and retail outlets could be generalized as sales locations. Generalizations should be clearly documented by examples

you would extend the table to record the website URL or retail store location as a *where* detail of the event. You might generalize the stakeholders' response to: CUSTOMER orders PRODUCT *at SALES LOCATION*. Naming the detail SALES LOCATION enables you to record websites and retail stores in the same column. If you define a generalization detail like this you should make sure that its meaning is clearly documented by examples. In Figure 2-9 the examples for the new *where* detail SALES LOCATION show three different types of location: store, website and call center.

Detail About Detail

A new event detail can sometimes turn out to be an additional characteristic of an existing detail, rather than a detail of the whole event itself. It is *detail about detail* instead of detail about the event. You can be given unnecessary details if you ask too many *what* questions as they can sound so open-ended. For example, the what question: "CUSTOMERS order PRODUCTS with what?" might give you an answer "with product type", but is PRODUCT TYPE a detail of the event that would be lost if it was not recorded in the event or does it belong elsewhere?

Spotting detail about detail is usually intuitive, but if you have any doubts you can test a detail to see if it is *position sensitive*. You do this by mentally swapping the new detail into the middle of the main clause, and reading it both ways: before and after swapping. If the event still makes sense, then the detail isn't position sensitive, and belongs to the event. However, if the event sounds like nonsense (even when you change the detail preposition), then the detail is really about another detail and will only make sense if placed directly to the right of the detail that it actually describes. For example:

> "CUSTOMER orders PRODUCT with PRODUCT TYPE"

This sounds okay, but try placing the new detail after the subject:

> "CUSTOMER with PRODUCT TYPE orders PRODUCT"

Oops, clearly this no longer makes sense. Customers don't have product types, products do. Product type only makes sense if it appears directly after (to the right of) PRODUCT. It is position sensitive. This tells you that product type describes PRODUCT, not the event itself, and is therefore detail about detail.

Stripping out any details that are not directly related to the event is important, so that the event can be used to define an efficient fact table. However, you do not want to completely discard the important finding that PRODUCT TYPE is a detail about products. It's obviously something that stakeholders want to report on. Instead of adding it to the table you can place it above the PRODUCT column in the space set aside for capturing *detail about detail*. You will use it shortly to define the PRODUCT dimension.

You can apply the same test to the SALESPERSON detail from the earlier *who* question: swap it around the event main clause and listen to yourself saying:

> "from SALESPERSON CUSTOMER orders PRODUCT"

or

> "CUSTOMER, from SALESPERSON, orders PRODUCT"

You sound strange (like Yoda in Star Wars) but it still makes sense. You can see that the additional *who* detail can be placed anywhere in the main clause and its meaning is not lost. Therefore SALESPERSON is not position sensitive, and this tells you that it is a detail about the event.

Check that each new detail belongs to the whole event and is not just *detail about detail* that only further describes a detail you already have

Detail about detail isn't discarded. It is used to define dimensions

If you find yourself generalizing several details you should ask questions about how similar the event stories really are. If stories have very different details you will probably want to model them in separate event tables, because highly generalized events rapidly become meaningless to stakeholders.

Figure 2-9

Adding *where* details

| | orders | on
ORDER | | where details |
CUSTOMER	PRODUCT	DATE	at SALES LOCATION	to DELIVERY ADDRESS
[who]	[what], MD	[when], MD	[where]	[where]
Elvis Priestley	iPip Blue Suede	18-May-2011	POMStore NYC	Memphis, TN
Vespa Lynd	POMBook Air	29-Jun-2011	store.POM.com	London UK
Elvis Priestley	iPip Blue Suede	18-May-2011	POMStore NYC	Memphis, TN
Phillip Swallow	iPOM Pro	14-Oct-2011	POMStore London	Not Applicable
Unknown	iPip G1	10 Years Ago	Amazon.com	Not Applicable
US Senate	iPOM		1-800-MY-POM	Washington, DC
US Senate	iPip T		1-800-MY-POM	Washington, DC

SALES LOCATION can be a retail store, website, or call center

Check that each *where* is a detail of "*who does what*" not just *who* or *what*

When you ask for additional *where* details emphasize that you are looking for locations that are specific to the whole event, *not* the existing *who* or *what* details. This helps avoid (for the moment) *detail about detail*—like customer address and product manufacturing address—that are not dependent on the event. These reference addresses will be modeled as dimensional attributes of CUSTOMER and PRODUCT once the event is complete (see Chapter 3).

Each time you finish collecting a *W-type*, it's good practice to quickly scan through the previous Ws to check for missing details. After you finish asking *where* questions check to see if any of the *where* details remind the stakeholders of additional *whos*, *whats* and *whens*.

Modelstorming with Whiteboards

Whiteboards are the agile practitioner's favorite collaborative modeling tool. They are ideal tools for modelstorming snippets of your design at a time but even the most generous whiteboards can be challenged by the width of a full BEAM✲ table. Here's some practical advice for using them and other tools for event modeling:

- Use "whiteboard on a roll" plastic sheets to extend/replace your finite white-board. Large post-it™ notes or flipchart paper and masking tape work too but are not so neat or forgiving for iterative design. Sheets with a 2.5cm grid work very well for event tables.

- Whatever material you use, go landscape rather than portrait.

- Put the *primary details*: the event main clause and initial *when* detail, on your main whiteboard or first sheet. If you can't fit those first three columns on your whiteboard, it's too small or your writing is too big. The primary details can stay front and center while you add or remove extension sheets for blocks of the other Ws. We suggest you divide up the details as we have the latter chapters of this book, with at least one sheet each for *who & what, when & where, how many,* and *why & how*.

- Have a *scribe* recording the model as you go. With traditional interactive modeling efforts, scribes are usually members of the data modeling team because of the technical nature of the information they record and modeling tools they use. With BEAM✲, the scribe can be anyone who can use a spreadsheet. This is an ideal role for the *on-site customer* or *product owner* (one of the stakeholders) on an agile team.

- If you are limited for whiteboard space and lacking a scribe because of the impromptu nature of your modelstorming, take pictures so you can erase as you go. Smartphone and tablet cameras are more than adequate for this and can take advantage of scanner apps that will automatically clean up whiteboard images (reduce glare, increase contrast, fix perspective) and email the results to your group. Don't forget to turn off the flash.

- If you have to erase as you go, leave the primary details and example data on the board. If room permits (or on a separate flipchart) keep a visible "shopping list" of the detail names you've had to erase.

- Use any color you like as long as its black! If you're going to take photos of your work, stick to black whiteboard markers to improve the results. BEAM✲ notation is deliberately non-color coded to help you here. Why do you see so many rainbow-colored whiteboard diagrams? Occasionally someone will have a well thought out color scheme (but did they remember 8% of the male population have color vision deficiency?). More often than not it's because black is the missing/dried-up pen. Go out and buy a box of black dry-wipe markers now! Right now!

- If you want to increase the level of interest, interactivity, contribution and energy when you're modelstorming give everyone a (black) marker. Get stakeholders on their feet writing their own event stories on the board as soon as they're used to BEAM✲. How well this works depends on your style, their style, everyone's handwriting and the number of modelstormers. Having everyone edit the whiteboard model together can work well for small groups of peers but no one wants to feel they're back at school being told to "Write that on the board".

- For more structured modeling sessions with larger groups of stakeholders you might want to use a data projector and model directly into a projected spreadsheet. If so, investigate the use of short throw, interactive projectors and annotation software. With these tools, modelstormers can huddle round a projected interactive whiteboard without casting shadows—but don't let gadgets get in the way of modeling.

- If you are using the BEAM✳*Modelstormer* spreadsheet you will find that the primary details (the subject, object, and initial *when* detail) of each table are frozen, so that you can scroll horizontally without losing the context of each event story. This spreadsheet also draws a pivoted ER table diagram in sync with the BEAM✳ table, so you can see a list of all the details at any time.

Appendix C provides recommendations for tools and further reading that will improve your collaborative modeling efforts.

How Many?

Ask "*how many?*" to discover facts, measures, KPIs

How many questions are used to discover the quantities associated with an event that will become facts in the physical data warehouse and the measures and key performance indicators (KPIs) on BI reports and dashboards. Again, you repeat the main clause of the event as a question to the stakeholders, but this time with "how many" and its variants: "how much", "how long" etc. inserted to make grammatical sense. For example:

> **CUSTOMER orders *how many* PRODUCTs?**
> ***How much* are PRODUCT orders worth?**

In both cases you want the name of the quantity. Likely answers to these questions—ORDER QUANTITY and REVENUE—have been added to the event table in Figure 2-10 along with examples that show a wide range of values. You should ask *how much/many* questions for each detail to see if it has any interesting quantities that should be associated with the event. So you could ask:

> ***How many* CUSTOMERs order PRODUCTs?**

The stakeholders would probably like to answer "thousands" but for each order event story it is always one customer. For details like this where the answer is always one, or zero if the detail is missing (not mandatory), there isn't a useful additional quantity to name and add to the event. When you have checked all the details for quantities, you should follow up with the general question:

> **How else would you measure this event?**

Figure 2-10
Adding quantities

	orders	on		How many/much details	
CUSTOMER	PRODUCT	ORDER DATE	ORDER QUANTITY	REVENUE	
[who]	[what], MD	[when], MD	[retail units]	[$, £, €, ¥]	
Elvis Priestley	iPip Blue Suede	18-May-2011		$249	
Vespa Lynd	POMBook Air	29-Jun-2011		£1,400	
Elvis Priestley	iPip Blue Suede	18-May-2011	1	$249	
Phillip Swallow	iPOM Pro	14-Oct-2011	1	£2,500	
Unknown	iPip G1	10 Years Ago	50	$20,000	
US Senate	iPOM + Printer	Yesterday	100	$150,000	
US Senate	iPip Touch	Yesterday	100	$25,000	

Different currency

High value product

High value order

Unit of Measure

When you ask the stakeholders for example quantity values, you should also discover their unit of measure. If you find that a quantity is captured in multiple units of measure it will need to be stored in a *standard* unit in the data warehouse to produce useful *additive* facts, so you should ask the stakeholders what that standard unit should be. (Chapter 8 provides details on designing additive facts.) You record the unit of measure in the quantity's column type using square brackets type notation; e.g., [$] or [Kg]. The unit of measure is a more useful descriptive type for a quantity than [*how many*].

Ask for the *standard* unit of measure for each quantity

> **[ ]: Square brackets denote detail type (e.g. *who*, *where*) and unit of measure for *how many* details.**

If a quantity needs to be reported in multiple units of measure you can record them as a list with the standard unit of measure *first*. Figure 2-10 shows examples events where REVENUE is captured in dollars and pounds. The column type [$, £, €, ¥] records that US Dollar is the standard unit for the data warehouse, but BI applications will also need to report REVENUE in Sterling, Euro and Yen.

Multiple units of measure can be listed in the column type

Durations

You discover durations by asking *how long* questions. For example, **"How long does it take a CUSTOMER to order a PRODUCT?"** If the stakeholders view the event as a point in time there will be no duration (not recorded or not significant). Asking for durations is another way of testing if the event should be modeled as evolving. Duration calculations can expose missing *when* details and highlight other events (verbs) that are so closely related to the current event that they should all be part of an evolving event.

Ask "How long?" to discover durations and evolving events

Derived Quantities

Some modelers may question the need for modeling duration quantities. If time-stamps are present then durations can be calculated rather than stored. This is true, but BEAM✳ tables are BI requirements models for documenting data *and reporting* requirements not physical storage models. By documenting durations and other derived measures as event details you have the opportunity to capture their business names and document their maximum and minimum values (in stories), which can be used as thresholds for dashboard alerts and other forms of conditional reporting.

BEAM✳ event tables do not translate column for column into physical fact tables. When an event table is physically implemented as a star schema the majority of its non numeric details will be replaced by dimensional *foreign keys*, and some of its quantities can be replaced by BI tool calculations or database views. This process is covered in Chapter 5.

Why?

Time to ask "Why?"

Capturing *why* details is the next step in modeling the event. As with the other "W" questions you ask a *why* question using the main clause of the event:

> **Why do CUSTOMERs order PRODUCTs?**

might be a little open ended but

> **Why do CUSTOMERs order PRODUCTs in these quantities on these dates at these locations?**

Why details often
explain quantity
variations

will focus the stakeholders on identifying the causal factors that specifically explain variations in event quantities. The *why* details you are looking for can include promotions, campaigns, special events, external marketplace conditions, regulatory circumstances or even free-form text reasons for which data is readily available. If the stakeholders respond with:

> **Product promotions.**

Try to discover
typical and
exceptional *why*
stories

you would expand the event table as shown in Figure 2-11, and add example stories that illustrate typical and exceptional circumstances. Notice that the typical promotion is "No promotion" and that the *why* detail has prompted the stakeholders to supply an additional DISCOUNT quantity. Chapter 9 provides detailed coverage on modeling *why* details as *causal* dimensions.

If event stories show wide quantity variations, point this out as you model *why* details. Ask stakeholders if there are any reasons that would explain these variations? If causal descriptions are well recorded they may also lead you to discover additional quantities.

Figure 2-11

Adding a *why* detail

> **Presence of *why* detail PROMOTION prompts additional quantity DISCOUNT**

> *why* detail

	orders	on ORDER	for	on	with
CUSTOMER	PRODUCT	DATE	REVENUE	PROMOTION	DISCOUNT
[who]	[what], MD	[when], MD	[$, £, €, ¥]	[why]	[$, £, €, ¥, %]
Elvis Priestley	iPip Blue Suede	18-May-2011	$249	No Promotion	0
Vespa Lynd	POMBook Air	29-Jun-2011	£1,400	Launch Event	10%
Elvis Priestley	iPip Blue Suede	18-May-2011	$249	No Promotion	0
Phillip Swallow	iPOM Pro	14-Oct-2011	£2,500	Star Coupon	£150
Unknown	iPip G1	10 Years Ago	$20,000	Trial Price	$2,500
US Senate	iPOM + Printer	Yesterday	$150,000	New Deal	$20,000
US Senate	iPip Touch	Yesterday	$25,000	New Deal	$1,000

How?

The final "W" questions discover any *how* details. *How* refers to the actual mechanism of the business event itself. You discover these details by asking a *how* question using the main clause of the event:

> **How does a CUSTOMER order a PRODUCT?**

You finish with *how* questions

Often *how* details include transaction identifiers from the operational system(s) that capture each event. If the stakeholders respond with:

> **A customer or salesperson creates an ORDER with an ORDER ID.**

then you would add ORDER ID to the table as in Figure 2-12. ORDER ID might be an equally good answer to other *how* questions such as: "How do you know that a customer ordered a product; what evidence do you have?" or "How can you tell one similar order from another?" With these questions you are explicitly asking for operational evidence that these event stories exist and can be differentiated from one another.

Transaction IDs (*how* details) help to differentiate events

Figure 2-12

Adding a *how* detail

> **How Detail** Order identifier provides evidence of the event. May identify the source system.

	orders	on ORDER		for	using
CUSTOMER	PRODUCT	DATE	ORDER QUANTITY	REVENUE	ORDER ID
[who]	[what], MD	[when], MD	[retail units]	[$, £, €, ¥]	[how]
Elvis Priestley	iPip Blue Suede	18-May-2011	1	$249	ORD1234
Vespa Lynd	POMBook Air	29-Jun-2011	1	£1,400	ORD007
Elvis Priestley	iPip Blue Suede	18-May-2011	1	$249	ORD4321
Phillip Swallow	iPOM Pro	14-Oct-2011	1	£2,500	ORD0001
Unknown	iPip G1			0	ORD0012
US Senate	iPOM + Print			00	ORD5466
US Senate	iPip Touch			0	ORD5466

> **ORDER ID + PRODUCT** resolves the search for uniqueness. Differentiates events where the same customer ordered the same product on the same day in the same quantity at the same price.

How details can be also be descriptive

You should ask further *how* questions to find out if there are any more descriptive *how* details. You are typically looking for methods and status descriptions. A suitably rephrased *how* question might be:

> **In what ways can a CUSTOMER order a PRODUCT?**

to which the stakeholders might respond:

> **Using a credit card or a purchase order. We'll call that PAYMENT METHOD.**

Multi-verb evolving events can have multiple transaction ID and/or descriptive *how* details; one for each verb. In Chapter 5, transaction ID *hows* are modeled as *degenerate dimensions* within fact tables. In Chapter 9, more descriptive *hows* are modeled as separate *how* dimensions.

Event Granularity

Event granularity is the combination of event details that guarantee uniqueness

Each event story must be uniquely identifiable (otherwise there would be no way to identify duplicate errors). Therefore you must have enough details about an event so that each example story can be distinguished from all others by some combination of its values. This combination of detail is called the *event granularity*. Discovering the event granularity is the job of the *repeat* story theme. If every detail in the repeat story matches the typical story you do not have enough details to define the granularity.

Transaction IDs (*how* details) can be used to define granularity

In most cases, event granularity can be defined by a combination of *who, what, when,* and *where* details, but occasionally details stubbornly refuse to be unique through most of the *7Ws*. While highly unlikely, perhaps the same customer really *can* order the same product at the same time at the same price from the same salesperson for delivery on the same date to the same location. In cases like this, the operational source system will have created a transaction identifier—such as Order ID (a *how* detail)—that can be used to differentiate these event instances.

Granular details are marked with the code **GD**

After you have discovered the event granularity you document it by adding the short code **GD** (granular detail) to the column type of each *granular detail* that in combination defines the granularity. Figure 2-12 shows that the order event granularity is defined by a combination of ORDER ID and PRODUCT. This would equate to order line items in the operational system.

GDn : *Granular Detail (or Dimension).* A detail that singularly or in combination with others defines the granularity/uniqueness of an event. Alternative combinations are numbered; e.g., GD1 and GD2 denote two alternative granular details groups.

Sufficient Detail

Just because you have enough details to define the event granularity does not mean you stop adding details. If the stakeholders are still providing relevant details, keep adding then. Event uniqueness is a *minimum* requirement. What you are aiming for is the complete set of details that tell the "full" story (or at least as much of it as is currently known).

Granularity is not enough, you want all the details

Naming the Event

It is now time to give the event a short descriptive name, one that the stakeholders will be comfortable with and that matches a recognized business process. The name can often be some variant of the event verb. If the verb is shared by other events (you may have to model other types of orders; e.g., wholesale orders or purchase orders) then a combination of subject and verb will be needed to make a unique name. By convention, event names are uppercase plural. In Figure 2-13 the completed event table, now named CUSTOMER ORDERS using the subject and a verb, has been transferred to a spreadsheet.

Event names often use the event subject and verb

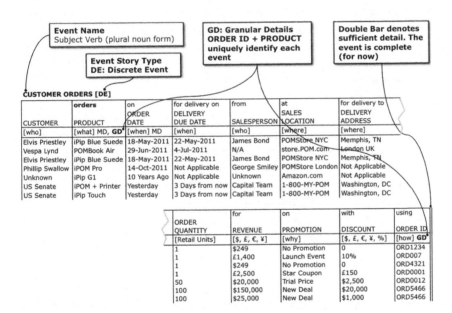

Figure 2-13

Documenting the event

If the event verb doesn't provide a good name try using one of the *how* details. For example, if the main clause was "Customer Buys Product" an event name of CUSTOMER BUYS might be replaced by CUSTOMER PURCHASES or CUSTOMER INVOICES using *how* details like PURCHASE ID, or INVOICE NUMBER.

If the verb doesn't sound right try a *how* detail

The subject of an event is actually *subjective*: it is based on the stakeholders' initial perspective. Different stakeholders can describe the very same event starting with a different subject. Once all its details have been discovered the initial event might be better described using one of those alternative points of view, by swapping around

Event subjects are *subjective!*

Before naming an event you may need to change its subject

its details to establish a better subject and/or event name. For example, the event "'SALESPERSON sells PRODUCT to DISTRIBUTOR'" might be reordered as "'DISTRIBUTOR orders PRODUCT from SALESPERSON'" and named DISTRIBUTOR ORDERS rather than SALESPERSON SALES. The initial subject (SALESPERSON) has helped to tease out the event stories, but its work here as a subject is now done.

If the subject-verb combination doesn't provide a good event name try using the *object* and a *how* detail.

Completing the Event Documentation

Add the story type to the table heading after the event name

Finally, now that you have all the event details you can define the story type with confidence. To recap, if the event has a *when* detail with an *every* preposition it is recurring. If the event has multiple *when* details that can change it is evolving. Otherwise it is a discrete event. You record the story type using one of the table codes: **DE**, **RE**, or **EE** which you place in the event name header. Table level codes follow the table name within square brackets as in Figure 2-13.

[DE] : Discrete event
[RE] : Recurring event
[EE] : Evolving event

Draw a double bar on the right edge to denote a completed table

When you finish documenting an event using a spreadsheet (as in Figure 2-13) draw a double bar on the right edge to signify that the table is complete (for now). This is a helpful visual clue because BEAM✲ tables grow wider than the screen or printed page. If you can't see the double bar you know you should scroll right or look for a continuation page to see more details.

The finished stories can now be told

By scanning the completed table stakeholders can now read their finished event stories, such as:

- *Elvis Priestly (is that really his name?) orders 1 iPip Blue Suede on the 18th May 2011, for delivery due on the 22nd May 2011, from James Bond at the POMStore NYC, for delivery to Memphis, TN, for $249, on no promotion with zero discount, using ORD1234.*

- *Vespa Lynd orders a POMBook Air on the 29 June 2011, for delivery on the 4th July 2011, from POMStore.com, for delivery to London, UK, for £1,400 with a launch event 10% discount, using ORD007.*

With a little tweaking of prepositions and reordering of details (mainly the *how manys*) you can now construct an event story archetype for CUSTOMER ORDERS from the examples. This final piece of documentation might say:

Customer orders a quantity of products, on order date, for delivery on delivery due date, from salesperson at sales location, for delivery to delivery address, for revenue, on promotion with discount using order ID.

The generic customer orders story

The Next Event?

Having fully described the details of your initial event, you should model the dimensions they represent before moving on to other events. This is exactly what stakeholders will want you to do because although they may find the details discovered so far to be fascinating, they will want to know that they can analyze events using many more descriptive attributes. If stakeholders provide you with lots of *detail about detail* this is a sure sign that they are keen to define the dimensional attributes they will need to aggregate and filter the atomic-level business events to produce interesting reports—and that is exactly what you learn how to do in Chapter 3.

Having modeled the first event you should model its matching dimensions next

In subsequent modelstorming iterations, when you have established a library of dimensions, stakeholders will want to move directly from event to event, rapidly telling event stories by reusing common details (dimensions) and examples. This is a habit that you want to encourage early on by using the *event matrix* techniques, described in Chapter 4.

When you already have a library of common dimensions you can quickly move to the next event

When you and your stakeholders get the hang of telling event stories, BEAM✲ can proceed at a storming pace, describing many events in quick succession but you should be careful not to model too many events at the story level. It is a balancing act. Stakeholders need to model multiple events, to describe their cross-process analytical requirements and be able to prioritize the most important event(s) for the next release—not necessarily the first event(s) you discover when modelstorming. However, telling many more detailed event stories than can be implemented in the next sprint is unnecessarily time consuming and can create unrealistic expectations of what will soon be available. It can also lead to the dreaded BDUF (Big Design Up Front) that does not reflect the business realties, changed requirements and available knowledge when it is eventually implemented.

You should reserve event stories for just-in-time (JIT) modeling of the detailed data requirements for your next sprint/iteration/release depending on your agile development schedule. Look to Chapter 4's JEDUF (Just Enough Design Up Front) techniques for *modeling ahead* to (even more rapidly) create higher-level models of the events in future releases. These models provide just enough information to help stakeholders decide the best events to model in detail now, and help you design more flexible versions of those events: ones that will require less rework in future DW iterations.

Summary

- Business events represent the measureable business activity that give rise to DW/BI data requirements. BEAM✻ uses data storytelling techniques for discovering business events by modelstorming with business stakeholders.

- BEAM✻ defines three event story types: discrete, evolving and recurring. They match the three fact table types: transaction fact tables, accumulating snapshots and periodic snapshots.

- Each BEAM✻ event consists of a main clause, containing a subject verb object, followed by prepositional phrases containing prepositions and detail nouns. Each subject, object and detail is one of the *7Ws*; i.e., a noun that potentially belongs in a dimensional database design.

- BEAM✻ modelers use the *7Ws* to discover a business event and document its type, granularity, dimensionality and measures—everything needed to design a fact table.

- BEAM✻ modelers avoid abstract data models. They "model by example": ask stakeholders to describe their BI data requirements by telling data stories. BEAM✻ modelers document these requirements using example data tables.

- Event stories are example data stories for business events.

- Event stories are sentences made up of main clause and preposition-detail examples.

- Event stories succinctly describe event details and clarify their meaning by providing examples of each of the five themes: *typical, different, missing, repeat and group*.

- *Typical* and *different* themed stories explore data ranges and exceptions.

- *Typical* and *repeat* stories describe event uniqueness (granularity).

- *Missing* stories help BEAM✻ modelers to discover mandatory details and document how BI applications should display missing values.

- *Group* stories uncover event complexities including mixed business models and multi-valued relationships.

- BEAM✻ short codes are used to document mandatory details, granular details and story type. Other elements of the BEAM✻ notation document *W-type*, units of measure and completed event models.

balanced
minor event
low cardinality group change
previous value Identity
dimensional fixed value
exclusive variable depth current value attributes
defining characteristic
ragged hierarchy charts single parent hierarchy
multi-parent mandatory
temporal change stories
historic value business key

3

MODELING BUSINESS DIMENSIONS

I keep six honest serving-men
(They taught me all I knew);
Their names are What and Why and When
And How and Where and Who.

— *Rudyard Kipling*, The Elephant's Child

Business events and their numeric measurements are only part of the agile dimensional modeling story. On their own, BEAM✲ event tables are not sufficient to design a data warehouse or even a data mart, because they do not contain all the descriptive attributes required for reporting purposes. For complete BI flexibility, stakeholders need both the atomic-level event details modeled so far *and* higher-level descriptions that allow those details to be analyzed in practical ways. The data structures that provide these descriptive attributes are dimensions.

> Business events need dimensions to fully describe them for reporting purposes

In addition to the *7Ws* and example data tables, BEAM✲ uses *hierarchy charts* and *change stories* to discover and define dimensional attributes. Hierarchy charts are used to explore the hierarchical relationships between attributes that support BI drill-down analysis, while change stories allow stakeholders to describe their business rules for handling *slowly changing dimensions*.

> BEAM✲ modelers draw *hierarchy charts* and tell *change stories* to define dimensions

In this chapter we describe how these BEAM✲ tools and techniques are used to model complete dimension definitions from individual event details. We will use the CUSTOMER and PRODUCT event story details from Chapter 2 for our example dimension modelstorming with stakeholders.

> This chapter shows you how to model dimensions from event story details

- Modeling the dimensions of a business event
- Using the *7Ws* and BEAM✲ tables to define dimensional attributes
- Drawing hierarchy charts to model dimensional hierarchies
- Telling change stories to describe dimensional history

> Chapter 3 Topics
> *At a Glance*

Dimensions

Dimensional attributes are the nouns and adjectives that describe events in familiar business terms

Dimensions are the significant nouns of a business or organization that form the subjects, objects, and supporting details of interesting business events. They are 6 of the 7Ws: the *who, what, when, where, why,* and *how* of every event story. Dimensional attributes further describe business events using terms that are familiar to the stakeholders. They represent the *adjectives* that make data stories more interesting. From a BI perspective, dimensions are the user interface to the data warehouse, the way into the data. Dimensional attributes provide all the interesting ways of rolling up and filtering the measures of business process performance. BI applications use dimensions to provide the row headers that group figures on reports and the lists of values used to filter reports. BI takes advantage of the hierarchical relationships between dimensional attributes to support drill-down analysis and efficient aggregation of atomic-detail measurements. The more descriptive dimensional attributes you can provide, the more powerful the data warehouse and BI applications appear. Consequently, good, richly descriptive customer and product dimensions can have 50+ attributes.

The data values of a dimension (or an individual dimensional attribute) are referred to as its *members*.

Dimension Stories

Dimensions data stories have weak narratives. They are subject and object heavy but verb light

Dimensions, because they represent descriptive reference data (adjectives and nouns), lack the strong narrative of business events. Events (and event stories) are associated with "exciting", active verbs such as "buy", "sell", and "drive" as used in: "customer buys product", "employee sells service" and "James Bond drives Aston Martin DB5". Dimensions, on the other hand, are associated with static verbs such as "has" and "is" that lead to weak narratives like "Customer has gender. Customer has nationality" and "Product has product type. Product has storage". These are *state of being* events, archetypes for many "is/has" data stories such as "Vespa Lynd is female. She is British" and "iPOM Pro is a computer. It has a 500GB disk". Important as these sentences are, we hardly think of them as stories because they lack the drama of "who does what, to whom or what, and when, and where" that propels you through all of the 7Ws to rapidly discover data requirements. Dimension stories are not exactly page-turners!

BEAM✲ modelers add *drama* and *plot* to help define dimensions

While data stories are highly effective at discovering dimensions and facts (as event details) and the 7Ws remain a powerful checklist at all times, additional techniques are needed to uncover the information hidden within the weaker narratives of dimension stories. BEAM✲ modelers have to add some *drama* to dimensions to help stakeholders tell more interesting stories that fully describe their attributes *and* business rules that affect ETL processing and BI reporting. To do this BEAM✲ modelers use two *plot devices*:

- **Hierarchy charts** are used to ask stakeholders questions about how they *organize* (an active verb) the members of a dimension (the values in event stories) into groups. These groups, because they generally have much *lower cardinality* than the individual members of the dimension, make good row headers and filters for reports—good starting points for telling fewer, higher-level event stories for BI analysis. Many of these groups have hierarchical relationships with one another. Exploring these hierarchies will prompt stakeholders for additional descriptive attributes and provides the information needed to configure BI drill-down and aggregation facilities.

  Hierarchy charts help you to ask questions about how dimensions are organized

- **Change stories** are data stories that document how each dimensional attribute should handle historic values. By asking stakeholders how dimension members *change* (another active verb) they not only describe which attributes can and cannot change (but can be corrected), but also state their reporting preferences for using current values or historical values. Getting stakeholders to think about change reminds them of additional attributes that behave in similar ways to existing ones and can lead to the discovery of auxiliary business processes that capture changes. Some of these auxiliary processes can be significant enough that they need to be modeled as business events in their own right.

  Change stories describe how dimensional attributes change, and how they should reflect history for reporting purposes

The *Cardinality* of an attribute or relation refers to the number of unique values. *High cardinality* attributes have a large number of unique member values, whereas *low cardinality* have a small number of unique members.

Discovering Dimensions

Having modeled an event, there is no elaborate discovery technique for dimensions because they naturally come out of the event details that you already have. Each event detail that has additional descriptive attributes will become a dimension. For most details there is, at the very least, an identity attribute—a business key—that uniquely identifies each dimension member. This is typically the case for the *who, what, when, where,* and *why* details. The candidate dimensions from Chapter 2's CUSTOMER ORDERS event are:

Dimensions are discovered as event details by telling event stories

- CUSTOMER [who]
- PRODUCT [what]
- ORDER DATE [when]
- DELIVERY DUE DATE [when]

- SALESPERSON [who]
- SALES LOCATION [where]
- DELIVERY ADDRESS [where]
- PROMOTION [why]

Event details with additional descriptions become dimensions

Missing from this list are the event quantities and any *how* details, such as ORDER ID, which do not have any additional descriptions that need to be modeled in separate dimension tables. When the event is converted into a star schema these details translate directly into facts and *degenerate dimensions* (denoted as DD) within the fact table. Chapter 9 covers instances where physical *how* dimensions are needed.

DD : Degenerate Dimension. A dimensional attribute stored in a fact table.

Documenting Dimensions

Dimensions are modeled using BEAM✳ tables

Dimensions are documented by taking each event detail (that has additional attributes), one at a time, starting with the event subject and modeling it as a BEAM✳ (example data) table. Figure 3-1 shows how CUSTOMER—the subject of CUSTOMER ORDERS—is used to define a dimension of the same name. Note that dimensions are singular whereas events are plural.

Dimension Subject

The event detail becomes the subject of the dimension

The event detail also becomes the first attribute of the dimension table—its *subject*. This mandatory attribute of the dimension is denoted by the code MD. You should ask the stakeholders for a suitable *subject* name. Typically, a dimension's subject is its "Name" attribute, such as CUSTOMER NAME, PRODUCT NAME, or EMPLOYEE NAME. After you have a name for the attribute you populate it with the unique examples from the event table: notice in Figure 3-1 that the repeated customer names have been removed.

Figure 3-1
Modeling the Customer dimension

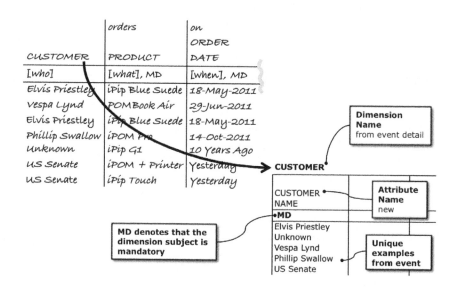

Dimension Granularity and Business Keys

The next step is to define the granularity of the dimension so that it precisely matches the event(s) it describes. The event stories modeled so far have used customer and product names for readability but you must now discover the *business keys* that uniquely identify these details. Business keys are the primary keys of source system reference tables. You discover a business key by asking "What uniquely identifies each [dimension name]?" or "How do you distinguish one [dimension name] from another?" For example:

> **What uniquely identifies each customer?**

To which stakeholders might reply:

> **A customer ID**

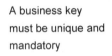

You check that this is what you need (a single, universal, reliable identifier) by confirming with the stakeholders that:

- **CUSTOMER ID is mandatory.** Every customer must have a value for this business key at all times. If this were not the case other business keys would be needed to augment this one.

- **CUSTOMER ID is unique.** There are no duplicate values. New customer are not assigned old lapsed customer IDs.

- **CUSTOMER ID is stable.** IDs are not changed or reassigned.

Assuming CUSTOMER ID passes these stakeholder tests (which should be confirmed by data profiling as soon as possible) you add this *identity* attribute to the dimension table with examples to match the existing customer names as shown in Figure 3-2. You also mark it with the column code **BK** to denote that it is a "Business Key" and because it is the only business key for CUSTOMER you also mark it as mandatory using **MD**. You can leave out the "has" preposition as it adds little value. When the relationship between an attribute and the dimension subject is more complex (and not apparent from the attribute name) you can add a preposition to help you read the dimension members as stories.

Ask for a business key to uniquely identify each dimension member

A business key must be unique and mandatory

Add the identity attribute immediately after the dimension subject

Figure 3-2

Adding a business key to a dimension

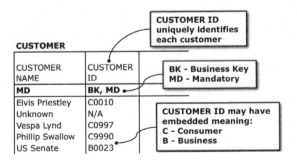

BK : Business Key. A source system key that can uniquely identify a dimensional member.

Discovering a suitable customer identifier can be difficult. There may be more than one

Asking for a customer business key can be a vexing question. If customer data comes from multiple sources, a single business key that identifies all customers uniquely across all business processes may simply not exist. If you are lucky, customers will have a single major source, or a master data management (MDM) application will have created a master customer ID that the data warehouse can use. If not, be prepared for some interesting discussions with the stakeholders. You may have to model several alternate business keys to have a reliable identifier for each customer.

Dimensional Attributes

Use any *detail about detail* that you have then ask for new attributes

Having defined the dimension's granularity, you are now ready to discover the rest of its attributes. You may already have a short list of candidate attributes that were identified as *detail about detail* while modeling an event. Figure 3-3 shows the PRODUCT TYPE *detail about detail* being added to the PRODUCT dimension. These candidate attributes are a good place to start, because the stakeholders are obviously keen to use them. If you don't have any candidate attributes then it's time to ask the stakeholders:

What attributes of [dimension name] are interesting for reporting purposes?

What attributes would you like to be able to sort, group, or filter [dimension name]s on?

This usually produces a list of attributes that should be tested, one at a time, to ensure they are in scope.

Attribute Scope

Check that the new attribute is in scope for your current project, iteration or release

Before you add an attribute to a dimension you need to check that it is within the scope of the dimension *and* the current project iteration. You check the initial feasibility of an attribute by asking stakeholders whether they believe that data for the new attribute will be readily available from the same sources as other attributes and event details. You should be wary of attributes that don't exist yet, or greatly expand the number of data sources you have to deal with in an iteration. Attempting to collect examples is a good way of weeding out attributes that are "nice to have if we had an infinite budget." If stakeholders struggle to provide any examples, or can't agree on common examples, the attribute may be of limited value.

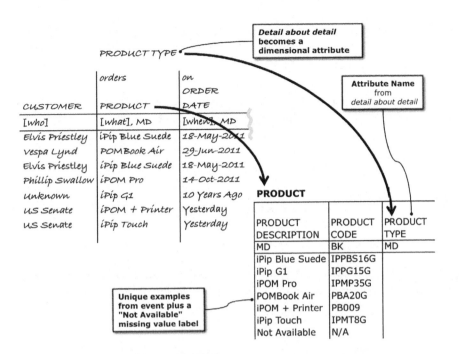

Figure 3-3
Product dimension
populated with *detail*
about detail

If you are modeling directly into (projected) spreadsheet BEAM✲ tables, as in the figure examples in this chapter, *freeze* the dimension subject and business key columns, as you would the primary details of events, to keep them visible as you scroll horizontally to add new attributes.

Assuming that most of the attributes that stakeholders suggest are within the current scope, your next task is to check that they belong in the current dimension. You are looking for attributes that have a single value for each dimension member at any one moment in time (including "now"): These are attributes that have a one-to-one (1:1) or a one-to-many (1:M) relationship with the dimension subject when you disregard history. You will consider historical values shortly when you ask for change stories. For now, you check each new attribute by asking the following "moment-in-time" question:

Check that the new attribute has only one value for each dimension member

> **Can a [*dimension name*] have more than one [*new attribute name*] at any one moment in time?**

The question is carefully phrased so that you are checking for the condition you don't want, so if the answer is **NO** then the attribute belongs. **NO** is good! It tells you that the attribute does *not* have a M:M or M:1 relationship with the dimension, both of which would rule it out. For example, you might ask:

> **Can a *customer* have more than one *customer type* at any one moment in time?**

If the stakeholders answer **NO**, you add CUSTOMER TYPE to the dimension as in Figure 3-4. Try this question on something which doesn't belong to CUSTOMER, like the *detail about detail* PRODUCT TYPE:

> **Can a *customer* have more than one *product type* at any one moment in time?**

The short answer is **YES**; the stakeholder's long answer might be:

> **Yes, a *customer* can buy or use several *products* with different *product types* at any moment.**

Product type obviously doesn't belong to Customer and the **YES** answer confirmed it. In reality, common sense would have prevented you or the stakeholders from considering this as a CUSTOMER attribute.

Figure 3-4

Adding
CUSTOMER TYPE
to CUSTOMER

> **CUSTOMER TYPE is mandatory.
> Every customer must have a type**

CUSTOMER

CUSTOMER NAME	CUSTOMER ID	CUSTOMER TYPE
MD	BK, MD	**MD**
Elvis Priestley	C0010	Consumer
Unknown	N/A	Unknown
Vesp Lynd	C0997	Consumer
Phillip Swallow	C9990	Consumer
US Senate	B0023	Government

> **but if CUSTOMER is
> missing then
> CUSTOMER TYPE
> will be displayed as
> "Unknown"**

Sometimes you will also have to exercise a little intuition to interpret a **YES** (multiple values are possible at any moment) answer. If you ask:

> **Can a *customer* have more than one *customer address*?**

The answer could be **YES** but you intuitively feel that CUSTOMER ADDRESS belongs to CUSTOMER. How you solve this problem depends on just how many interesting addresses a Customer has. You could ask:

> **Is there a single *primary* (easily identifiable) *address* for each *customer* that should be used for geographic analysis?**

If the answer is:

> **Yes, *billing address*.**

then you have found a single-valued attribute that belongs. You should also find out how many other address values a customer can have. If customers have only two additional addresses, for example, home address and work address, then you can define them as separate attributes in the dimension by being more precise about their meaning/name.

A small fixed number of values can be modeled as separate attributes

If customers can have multiple addresses (some might have hundreds) then you may have discovered a missing *where* detail of CUSTOMER ORDERS. Addresses might be delivery addresses; customers are ordering gifts for their family and friends or resellers are ordering products for their clients. If that is the case, the addresses in question don't belong to customers. They belong instead to the business event as a DELIVERY ADDRESS detail and subsequently as a separate dimension. This handles the genuine many-to-many (M:M) relationship between customers and these addresses.

If a proposed attribute has multiple values it may represent a separate dimension of the business event

If the answer to the question: "Can a [*dimension name*] have more than one [*attribute name*] (at one moment in time)?" is a resounding NO then the attribute belongs in the dimension. If the answer is a resounding YES it most likely doesn't belong but may warrant more investigation before you rule it out. If no one is happy to see the dimension without a particular attribute, you may have to qualify the attribute in some way (for example, *Primary* Address), or adjust the dimension's granularity to accommodate it.

A proposed attribute can be qualified (e.g. Main... or Primary...) to restrict it to a single value

If the multiple addresses do belong to a customer—they are the offices or stores of a corporate customer—you might need to change the CUSTOMER dimension granularity to customer location, if event activity is tied to specific locations and stakeholders treat each location as an individual customer. In which case you would redefine the granularity as one row per customer per location and define a composite business key to uniquely identify each member.

Alternatively the dimension granularity might need to be adjusted to match the vital attribute

The previous example treats customer address as a single attribute. In reality, address would be several dimensional attributes, such as Street, City, Region, Postal Code, and Country: attributes that represent a geographic hierarchy. If this is well understood by stakeholders, the individual attributes can be modeled later.

Attribute Examples

After you have established that an attribute belongs in the dimension you add it to the BEAM✲ table and ask the stakeholders for example values that match the dimension subject. The dimension subject will already contain typical and exceptional (*different* and *group* themed) examples copied from an event (that you captured using the *event story themes* in Chapter 2). These usually prompt the stakeholders to provide interesting values for each new attribute, too. Stakeholders will typically give you values that they want to see on their reports.

Ask for examples for each new attribute that match the dimension subject members

The goal of using examples is to ensure that everyone is in clear agreement about the definition of each attribute. If the meaning or use of an attribute is unclear or contentious ask for additional examples. If stakeholders can't agree on example values for an attribute it can indicate that you have discovered *homonyms*: two or more attributes with the same name but different meanings. If all the possible meanings are valid, then each set needs to be uniquely named, and modeled as a separate attribute with its own examples.

If stakeholders cannot agree on examples, you may have *homonyms*: multiple attributes with similar names

If stakeholders struggle to provide examples for an attribute you should be alerted to the possibility that the attribute doesn't exist yet, or is a "nice to have" attribute that isn't currently well understood enough to be useful.

Descriptive Attributes

When documenting examples for business keys and any other cryptic codes check if the values contain any hidden meaning. For example, the data in Figure 3-2 suggests that CUSTOMER ID is a "smart key" that can be used to differentiate business and consumer customers. How does this tally with CUSTOMER TYPE? You would investigate this further via data profiling. It might prove useful as an additional quality assurance test during ETL processing. For every code you are given you should ask the stakeholders:

Check if codes such as business keys are *smart keys*: contain hidden meaning

Do any existing reports or spreadsheets decode [*business keys / other cryptic codes*] into more descriptive labels?

If **YES**, you want to convert this *report logic* in to ETL code and define descriptive attributes for these labels in your dimensions, where they will be consistently maintained and available to everyone. Your motto should be **"No SQL decodes at query time!"** If BI applications need to decode dimensional attributes you and the stakeholders have not done a good enough job of defining the dimensions.

Model descriptive attributes that decode all cryptic codes. No decodes in BI queries!

Beware of "smart keys" with embedded meaning. They seldom remain smart over their lifetime, and often become overloaded with multiple meanings as business processes evolve. BI applications should not attempt to decode smart keys and other codes to provide descriptive labels. It is almost impossible for embedded report logic to keep up with these codes as their meaning morphs over time. It should be replaced by descriptive data in the data warehouse.

Codes provide consistent sort order for multi-language text

If you find more BI-friendly descriptive attributes for codes you can remove or hide the codes in the final version of a dimension, as long as stakeholders have no use for them on reports. However, if you are designing a multinational data warehouse that will translate descriptive attributes into several national languages, these otherwise cryptic codes are useful for consistently sorting reports that are re-run internationally. Chapter 7 covers techniques for handling national languages.

Boolean flag attributes that contain "Y" or "N", (e.g., RECYCLABLE FLAG) can usefully be augmented with matching report display-friendly attributes containing descriptive values, (e.g., "Recyclable" and "Non-Recyclable").

Mandatory Attributes

While you are filling out example data for an attribute ask whether it is mandatory. If the stakeholders believe it is, you should add **MD** to its column type. MD does not necessarily define attributes as NOT NULL in the data warehouse. MD may just represent the stakeholders' idealistic view, while the data warehouse has to cope with the actual operational system data quality. By documenting *allegedly* mandatory attributes you are capturing rules that the ETL process can test for, and identifying potentially useful attributes for defining dimensional hierarchies.

Use **MD** to record that stakeholders believe an attribute to be mandatory

Missing Values

One example you must fill in for every attribute is its "Missing" value. If the dimension subject has already been identified as possibly missing from an event story there will already be a missing subject copied from the event. If not you should add a missing row to the dimension just as you would to an event. You fill out this row by asking the stakeholders how they want "Missing" to be displayed for each attribute.

Every dimension needs x missing row to document missing display values

Paradoxically you need to ask for missing values even for mandatory attributes. For example, If CUSTOMER TYPE is a mandatory attribute of CUSTOMER then for all SALES events involving Customers you can rely on the Customer Type to be present. But if Customers are missing for certain SALES events (for example, anonymous cash transactions) then CUSTOMER TYPE will also be missing. Figure 3-4 shows that when CUSTOMER is missing, the stakeholders want CUSTOMER TYPE to be displayed as "Unknown."

Even mandatory attributes need a missing value

If stakeholders need the data warehouse to be able to differentiate between various types of "Missing" (e.g., "Not Applicable", "Missing in error", or "To be assigned later") the dimension will need additional special case missing stories with different descriptive values and ETL processes will have to work a little harder to assign the correct "missing" version to the events. The implementation of this is discussed in Chapter 5.

If there are different types of missing, you need multiple missing stories

Don't go overboard with examples. Dimensions usually have far more attributes than events have details, and you want to discover as many dimensional attributes as possible rather than exhaustively capture examples for only a few.

Exclusive Attributes and Defining Characteristics

Dimensions with mixed types often contain mutually exclusive attributes

As you explore missing and mandatory examples you may come across mutually *exclusive attributes*: attribute pairs or attribute groups that cannot both have values for the same member. Figure 3-5 shows examples of exclusive customer attributes. Customers can have a DATE OF BIRTH and GENDER *or* a SIC CODE and EMPLOYEE COUNT but not all 4 values. This is often an indication that you have discovered a *heterogeneous* dimension, one that contains a highly diverse set of members that are described in different ways (even if they are measured in similar ways by taking part in similar business events). In this case, the customer dimension contains businesses and consumers. Their mutually incompatible descriptions should be marked as exclusive attributes using the short code **X*n*** where *n* is an exclusive group number. In Figure 3-5, consumer attributes are exclusive group 1, marked **X1**, and business attributes are group 2, marked **X2**. Exclusive attributes are often a sign of mixed business models; e.g., business-to-business (B2B) and business-to-consumer (B2C), offering products and services.

Figure 3-5
Exclusive customer attributes

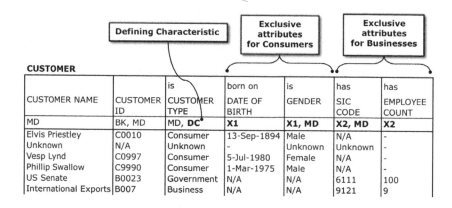

CUSTOMER						
CUSTOMER NAME	CUSTOMER ID	is CUSTOMER TYPE	born on DATE OF BIRTH	is GENDER	has SIC CODE	has EMPLOYEE COUNT
MD	BK, MD	MD, **DC**	**X1**	**X1, MD**	**X2, MD**	**X2**
Elvis Priestley	C0010	Consumer	13-Sep-1894	Male	N/A	-
Unknown	N/A	Unknown	-	Unknown	Unknown	-
Vesp Lynd	C0997	Consumer	5-Jul-1980	Female	N/A	-
Phillip Swallow	C9990	Consumer	1-Mar-1975	Male	N/A	-
US Senate	B0023	Government	N/A	N/A	6111	100
International Exports	B007	Business	N/A	N/A	9121	9

Exclusive attributes have at least one defining characteristic

If you discover exclusive attributes, you need to find their *defining characteristic(s)*: one or more attributes whose values control the validity/applicability of the exclusive attributes. For customer there is a single attribute, CUSTOMER TYPE, which dictates whether the attributes in **X1** or **X2** are valid. This is marked as a defining characteristic with the code **DC**. If a dimension contains multiple defining characteristics each **DC** code should be followed by a list of the exclusive group numbers controlled by the attribute. For example, if CUSTOMER TYPE was one of several **DC** attributes in CUSTOMER it would be marked **DC1,2** because it selects between **X1** and **X2** group attributes only.

DC*n,n* : Defining Characteristic, dictates which exclusive attributes are valid.

X*n*   : Exclusive attribute or attribute group

Good defining characteristics should be low cardinality, mandatory attributes. They should have a small number of unique values to match the small number of exclusive groups they control and they should always be present to provide controlling values. Because of these properties **DC** attributes are typically important levels in dimension hierarchies. If a **DC** attribute is optional and high cardinality and/or a dimension is awash with exclusive groups it may be a clue that you are struggling to model a 'one size fits all' generic dimension.

Defining characteristics should be low cardinality and mandatory

Exclusive attribute groups can be nested if required. For example, if "for profit" and "non profit" organizations were described differently, an additional defining characteristic BUSINESS TYPE marked **DC3,4** would govern their descriptive attributes marked **X3** and **X4**. As these are all business related attributes they would be nested within the "Business" exclusive group **X2** using the code combinations **X2, X3** and **X2, X4**. Their defining characteristic BUSINESS TYPE is also a business only exclusive attribute so it should be marked in full as **X2, DC3,4**.

Exclusive attribute groups can be nested with other exclusive groups

Some of the exclusive attributes in Figure 3-5 are marked as mandatory (**MD**) but are not always present because they are exclusive to a subset of the dimension members. The code combination **X*n*, MD** means *exclusive mandatory attribute: attribute is only mandatory when its exclusive group is valid.*

*An attribute can only be mandatory when its **X*n*** group is valid*

Defining characteristic and exclusive attribute groups allow you to model *subsets* within a single BEAM✲ table. Subsets can help you later to define restricted views (or *swappable dimensions,* see Chapter 6) to increase usability and query performance. They also provide important ETL processing rules and checks.

Exclusive attribute subsets can be implemented as separate tables

Using the *7Ws* to Discover Attributes

Every dimensional attribute, just like every event detail, is one of the *7Ws*. Therefore you can use the *7Ws* as a question checklist to help you ask stakeholders for additional attributes when their initial flood of attributes starts to dry up. Not every *W* question makes sense for every *W-type* dimension so you don't want to stick so rigidly to the BEAM✲ sequence you use to follow the narrative arch of an event. For *who, what, when* and *where* dimensions it is often useful to start with a question of the same *W-type* as the dimension. For *who* and *what* dimensions the answers are often example members for type attributes. For example, if you ask:

Use the 7Ws as a checklist for discovering attributes

> ***Who* or *what* is a customer or a product?**

Pomegranate stakeholders might reply with examples like:

> **Customers are consumers, businesses, charities…**
>
> **Products are computers, software, accessories…**
> **They can also be services.**

Answers like these would lead you to attributes such as CUSTOMER TYPE and PRODUCT TYPE (if you didn't already have them). Table 3-1 illustrates other *7W*-inspired questions and example answers for customer and products.

Table 3-1
Example *7W*
attribute questions
and answers

BEAM✲ MODELER QUESTION	STAKEHOLDER ANSWERS
Who else is associated with a customer?	Primary Contact, Spouse, Sponsor, Decision Maker, Owner (Parent Company), Referrer
Who is associated with a product?	Manufacturer, Distributor, Supplier, Marketer, Promoter, Product Manager, Inventor, Designer, Developer, Author
What dates (*whens*) are important to know about a customer?	Birth Date, Graduation Date, First Purchase Date, Last Purchase Date, Renewal Date
What milestone dates (*whens*) are there for a product?	Launch Date, Arrival of First Competitor, Patent Expiration Date, Discontinued Date
Where are customers?	Headquarters, Sales Region, Work Address, Home Address, Nearest Branch
What geographic (*where*) information describes a product or service?	Country of Origin, Manufacturing Plant, Language, Market, Voltage
Are there any single-valued quantities (*how many*) that describe or group customers?	Life Time Value, Loyalty Score, Current Balance, Number of Employees, Number of Dependents
What quantities (*how many*) describe products?	Weight, Size, Capacity, List Price
Why or *how* do customers become customers?	Channel, Prospect Source, Referral

When stakeholders give you examples (such as "Consumer" or "Business") instead of a suitable attribute name (Customer Type) try adding these examples to the dimension table in a new column against their matching members and then ask what that column should be called.

Dimensional Hierarchies

Hierarchies provide a mechanism for dealing with details that are too numerous or small to work with individually. Dimensional hierarchies describe sequences of successively lower cardinality attributes. They allow individual business events to be consistently rolled up to higher reporting levels, and subsequently drilled-down on, to explore progressively more detail. Without hierarchies, BI reporting would be overwhelmed by detail.

So how much detail is too much? In everyday life we all seem to agree that 365 (or 366) are too many! Too many days to always deal with individually—too short a period of time to complete large tasks and activities or see trends. So we group our days into longer periods: weeks, months, quarters, terms, semesters, seasons etc. so that we can plan bigger things and see patterns and trends in our lives. Figure 3-6 shows how the days in the first quarter of 2012 can be grouped hierarchically. Organizations naturally do this with the many fiscal time periods, geographic locations, people, products, and services that they work with. The clue is in the name: organizations *organize* things and if there are enough things (their *7Ws*) they typically organize them hierarchically. The majority of the *7Ws* that describe a business will have de-facto hierarchies in place, and it is vitally important that they are standardized and made available in the dimensions in the data warehouse.

Dimensional hierarchies support BI drill-down analysis

When dealing with lots of things, we naturally tend to organize them hierarchically into fewer and fewer groups

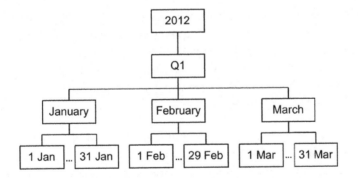

Figure 3-6
The calendar: a balanced hierarchy

Why Are Hierarchies Important?

Explicit hierarchies are not strictly necessary for drill-down or drill-up reporting. So long as dimensions contain the attributes that BI users want to drill on they can effectively drill-down by adding them to existing reports and drill-up by removing them. However, there are a number of significant modeling and implementation benefits in making at least one hierarchy in each dimension explicit:

Agile dimensional modelers take advantage of hierarchies for a number of reasons

Hierarchy definition provides a hook for catching additional attributes	▪ Hierarchies provide a necessary hook to catch dimensional attributes. When you ask stakeholders about hierarchies you are asking them how they (would like to) *organize* their data. Discussing this activity is one technique for adding some otherwise missing narrative to dimension stories and prompting stakeholders for the BI friendly attributes you need to model good dimensions. When stakeholders think about their *7Ws* hierarchically, they describe low level attributes that can be used as discriminators for similar dimensional members, and higher level attributes that can group together many dimensional members.

Hierarchies help expose "informal" stakeholder maintained data sources that can greatly enrich dimensions	▪ When stakeholders describe their favorite hierarchy levels they will frequently provide you with additional "informal" data sources (spreadsheets, personal databases) they own that contain this categorical information. These stakeholder maintained sources often contain hierarchy definitions, vital to BI, that are missing from "formal" OLTP databases because they are nonessential for operational activity. Many operational applications happily perform their function at the bottom of each hierarchy with no knowledge of the higher level groupings that are imposed upon their raw transactions for reporting purposes. For example, orders can be processed day in, day out without the order processing system knowing how a single date is rolled into a fiscal period. Similarly, items can be shipped to the correct street number/postal code without knowing how the business currently organizes sales geographically (or how they might have been organized differently last year).

Hierarchies help you discover planning processes	▪ Hierarchies exist so that organizations can *plan*. Discussing hierarchies with stakeholders will get them thinking about their planning processes, and will likely help you discover additional events and data sources that represent budgets, targets or forecasts. You must make sure the dimensions you design contain the common levels needed to roll up *actual* event measures for comparison against these *plans*.

BI users and BI tools require default hierarchies to enable simple drill-down	▪ BI users like default hierarchies and BI tool "click to drill" functionality that allows them to quickly drill-down on an attribute without having to manually decide each time what to show next. For example, if users drill on "Quarter" they usually want to see monthly detailed data by default. Explicit hierarchies establish predictable analytical workflows that are very helpful to (new) BI users exploring the data for the first time. "Clicking to drill" is less laborious and error prone than manually adding and removing report row headers.

Hierarchies are used to optimize query performance	▪ Everyone wants common drill-down and drill-up requests to happen quickly. Explicit hierarchies are needed to define efficient data aggregation strategies in the data warehouse. On-Line Analytical Processing (OLAP) cubes in multidimensional databases, aggregate navigation /query rewrite optimization in relational databases and prefetched micro cubes in BI tools, all take advantage of hierarchy definitions to maximize query performance.

Hierarchy Types

Data warehouses and BI applications have to deal with three types of hierarchies: balanced, ragged (unbalanced) and variable depth (recursive). Each of these can come in two flavors: simple single parent and more complex multi-parent. Of the six varieties shown in Figure 3-7, single parent balanced hierarchies are the easiest to implement and use and should be the main focus of your initial modeling efforts.

There are three hierarchy types: balanced, ragged and variable depth

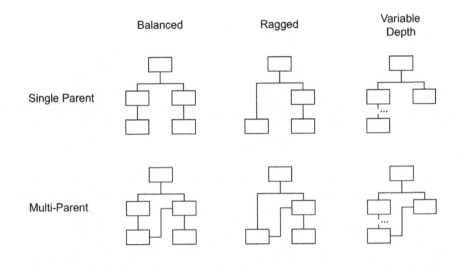

Figure 3-7
Hierarchy types

Balanced Hierarchies

Balanced hierarchies have a fixed (known) number of levels, each with a unique level name. Time (*when*) is an example of a balanced hierarchy, as the example calendar data in Figure 3-6 shows. This example has four levels: day, month, quarter, and year. The hierarchy is balanced because there are always four levels; days always roll up to months, months to quarters, and quarters to years—there are no exceptional dates that do not belong to a month and only belong to a quarter or a year.

Balanced hierarchies have fixed numbers of levels

Being *balanced* has nothing to do with the *number* of members (unique data values) at each hierarchy level. For example, even though the number of days in a month varies from 28 to 31, and days in a year can be 365 or 366, the calendar hierarchy is still balanced *in depth*. Figure 3-6 is not the only time hierarchy; alternative hierarchies of day → fiscal period → fiscal quarter → fiscal year and day → week → year may all exist in the same calendar dimension. Each of these is a separate balanced hierarchy.

The number of members at each level can vary

A hierarchy is implemented in a dimension by adding an attribute for each of its levels. For a balanced hierarchy each of its fixed levels must be a mandatory attribute with a strict M:1 relationship with the parent attribute one level above it and a 1:M relationship with the child levels below it.

Balanced hierarchy levels are mandatory attributes

Ragged Hierarchies

Ragged hierarchies have missing levels (with zero members) that unbalance them

Ragged (or unbalanced) hierarchies are similar to balanced hierarchies in that they have a known maximum number of levels and each level has a unique name, but not all levels are present (have values) for every path up or down the hierarchy—making some paths appear shorter than others. Figure 3-8 illustrates a ragged product hierarchy, where a product (POMServer) does not belong to a subcategory. This product is effectively a subcategory all of its own.

Figure 3-8
Ragged product hierarchy

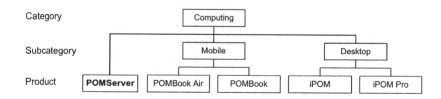

You can model ragged hierarchies in a dimension by using non-mandatory attributes for the missing levels, but these gaps (missing values) cause problems for BI drilling. If a hierarchy is only *slightly* ragged you can often redesign it with the stakeholders help as a balanced hierarchy, to improve reporting functionality. This can involve removing levels that are not consistently implemented for all members or creating new level values to fill in the gaps (e.g. a subcategory value of "Server" for the Figure 3-8 example). See Chapter 6 for more details on balancing ragged hierarchies.

Try to balance *slightly* ragged hierarchies by removing levels or filling in missing values

Variable Depth Hierarchies

Variable depth hierarchies often represent *recursive relationships*

Variable depth hierarchies have a variable (unknown) number of unnamed levels. The variable levels do not have unique names because they are typically all of the same type; for example, in human resource hierarchies that document the relationships between staff and managers, each level is an employee. Another example is the bill of material for a product comprised of components and subassemblies that are themselves decomposed into other components and subassemblies. Variable depth hierarchies are also know as *recursive hierarchies* because they are typically represented in source data by *recursive relationships*: tables that join to themselves.

Recursive relationships are used in operational database design for succinctly recording variable depth hierarchies but are very difficult to work with in a data warehouse. They are impractical for measuring business processes because they are impenetrable to stakeholders and BI tools alike. They must be "unfurled" for efficient reporting purposes using the hierarchy map technique described in Chapter 6.

Multi-Parent Hierarchies

The time hierarchy in Figure 3-6 is *single parent* hierarchy because each child level value rolls up to just one parent level value. In contrast, Figure 3-9 shows a *multi-parent* product hierarchy where a product (iPipPhone) belongs to more than one Product Type (it is part telephone, part media player). In a multi-parent hierarchy each child level can roll up to multiple parents. If a multi-parent product hierarchy is used to roll up sales to the Product Type level, something must be done to account for products that fall into multiple types. Their sales will need to be carefully allocated; otherwise revenue for products with two parents will be double-counted at the Product Type or Subcategory level.

Multi-valued hierarchies contain members with two or more parents at the same level

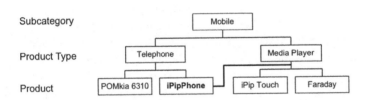

Figure 3-9
Multi-valued Product
hierarchy

Multi-parent hierarchies can also be ragged or variable depth. The latter are typically represented in source systems by M:M recursive relationships. Multi-parent hierarchies and variable depth hierarchies cannot be modeled directly in dimension tables. Chapter 6 covers additional structures (hierarchy maps) for coping with these complex hierarchies and handling fact allocation at query time across multiple parents. For the remainder of this chapter, assume hierarchies to be single parent hierarchies that are modeled within dimension tables.

Multi-parent, variable-depth hierarchies represent M:M recursive relationships

A dimension can contain multiple hierarchies of different types. You should model at least one balanced hierarchy for each dimension to help discover additional attributes and common levels for comparisons across processes, and to enable default BI drill-down facilities.

Hierarchy Charts

Hierarchy charts are simple, quick to draw diagrams used to model single or multiple hierarchies. On a hierarchy chart a dimensional hierarchy is represented by a vertical bar with the dimension name at the bottom and the highest-level attribute of the hierarchy at the top. The levels are represented as marks on the bar, in ascending order. Figure 3-10 shows three example hierarchy charts for Time and Product.

Hierarchy charts are a quick way to visualize hierarchies

Hierarchy charts are based on Multidimensional Domain Structures (MDS) described in *Microsoft OLAP Solutions*, Erik Thomsen et al., Wiley, 1999.

Figure 3-10a, b, c
Hierarchy charts for
Time and Product

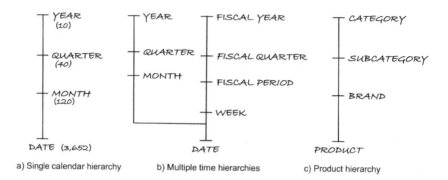

a) Single calendar hierarchy   b) Multiple time hierarchies   c) Product hierarchy

Levels can be
spaced evenly or
relative to the
aggregation they
provide

When you draw a hierarchy chart you can space out the level tics evenly, as in Figure 3-10a and 3-10c, or in rough approximation of their relative aggregation, as in Figure 3-10b where levels that expose more details are placed further below their parent than levels that reveal fewer details. Relative spacing gives stakeholders a visual clue as to how much more detail they can expect to drill down to at each level, or how selective filters would be placed at various levels. You can also annotate levels with their approximate cardinalities, as in Figure 3-10a. Large gaps or jumps in cardinality on a hierarchy chart can prompt stakeholders for missing levels that would give them 'finer grain' drill-down and even more interesting descriptions.

Hierarchy charts
can show single or
multiple hierarchies

In addition to providing a visual comparison of levels within a single hierarchy, a hierarchy chart can also be used to compare multiple hierarchies for a single dimension, as in Figure 3-10b, or all the dimensions associated with an event, as in Figure 3-11.

Figure 3-11
CUSTOMER
ORDERS
hierarchy chart

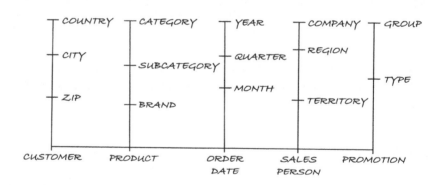

Hierarchy charts
can be annotated to
model ragged,
multi-parent and
variable depth
hierarchies

Modeling Hierarchy Types

Ideally, hierarchy charts are used to discover the attribute levels of simple balanced hierarchies, but they are capable of modeling ragged, multi-parent, and variable depth hierarchies when necessary. Figure 3-12a shows a hierarchy chart for the ragged product hierarchy of Figure 3-8. The missing/optional level is enclosed in brackets. In Figure 3-12b the multi-parent hierarchy (matching Figure 3-9) is denoted with a double bar between the product child level and its multiple product type parents. In Figure 3-12c the variable depth of a human resources (HR) hierarchy caused by the recursive relationship (see Chapter 6) between managers and employees is modeled by adding a circular path between the two levels. These annotations can be combined to model the most complex hierarchies.

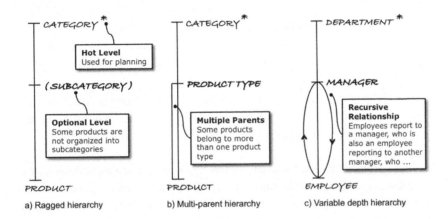

Figure 3-12a, b, c
Ragged,
multi-parent and
variable depth
hierarchy charts

a) Ragged hierarchy   b) Multi-parent hierarchy   c) Variable depth hierarchy

Modeling Queries

Event hierarchy charts which combine multiple dimension hierarchy charts for the same event can be used to model query definitions for report and dashboard design. One or more queries can be defined on an event hierarchy chart as lines connecting the referenced levels, as shown in Figure 3-13 where **X** marks levels that are used to filter the query (WHERE clause), and **O** marks those used to aggregate it (GROUP BY clause). In this way, event hierarchy charts can also be used to model the dimensionality of OLAP cubes and aggregate fact tables.

Event hierarchy charts can model the dimensionality of queries, OLAP cubes and aggregates

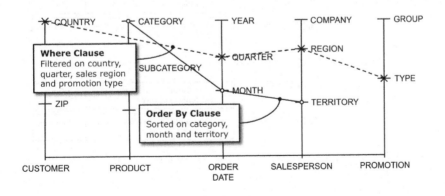

Figure 3-13
Query definition
hierarchy chart

Event hierarchy charts can be used *while* modeling events to help capture their major dimensional attributes. By drawing a hierarchy chart above an event table you can record *detail about detail* (dimensional attributes) in hierarchical order at the same time that you model event details (dimensions and facts).

Discovering Hierarchical Attributes and Levels

You discover hierarchies by asking stakeholders how they organize the members of a dimension. You could begin by drawing a hierarchy chart with PRODUCT at the bottom and asking:

How do you organize products (hierarchically)?

It's a leading question if you add "hierarchically", but stakeholders generally have a good idea about the hierarchies they need, and will usually offer you candidate levels in hierarchical order—which helps. If any are new attributes check that they belong in the dimension (have a M:1 relationship with it) and ask for examples before considering them as candidates.

Introduce stakeholders to hierarchy charts by drawing a simple version of the time hierarchy (Figure 3-10) on the whiteboard. Try using relative spacing for this well known hierarchy to get stakeholders thinking generally about additional useful levels that fill large hierarchical gaps. At some point, you will want to use this chart to model any custom calendar levels and design an explicit CALENDAR dimension (see Chapter 7).

Ask stakeholders to add their new levels to the hierarchy chart

Ask stakeholders where they think a candidate attribute sits on the hierarchy chart bar and add it to your diagram where they suggest, or better still get them to add it. Figure 3-14 shows SUBCATEGORY added to a PRODUCT hierarchy chart between BRAND and CATEGORY.

Figure 3-14
Adding SUBCATEGORY to the PRODUCT hierarchy at the correct level

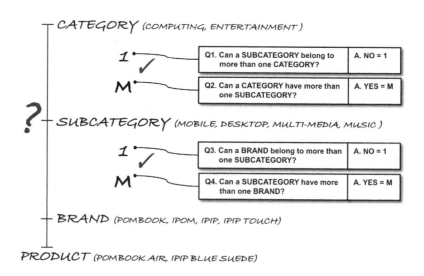

Check that each candidate level has the correct parent child relationships

As each new candidate is added, you need to check that it is in the right position relative to the existing levels. It must have a M:1 relationship with its parent (if present) and a 1:M relationship with its child. If you or any stakeholders are unsure, you can check the relationship by methodically asking the following "moment-in-time" questions and temporarily marking up the hierarchy chart with the cardinality results. Starting with the parent relationship, ask:

> **Can a [*Candidate*] belong to more than one [*Parent*] (at one moment in time)?**

- If the answer is **YES** put "M" just below the parent.
- If the answer is **NO** put a "1" just below the parent.

> **Can a [*Parent*] have more than one [*Candidate*]?**

- If the answer is **YES** put "M" just above the candidate.
- If the answer is **NO** put "1" just above the candidate.

For example, to test that SUBCATEGORY belongs below CATEGORY ask:

> **Can a SUBCATEGORY belong to more than one CATEGORY?**

then:

> **Can a CATEGORY have more than one SUBCATEGORY?**

If you finish with "M" above the candidate (SUBCATEGORY) and "1" below the parent (CATEGORY) (**NO, YES** answers) as in Figure 3-14 then you have the M:1 relationship you are looking for and the candidate belongs in the hierarchy below the parent. If the child below the new level is the dimension itself then the candidate is in the correct position (you already know that the new level has a 1:M relationship with the dimension). Otherwise you test that the child relationship is 1:M by asking a few more quick fire questions while pointing at the hierarchy chart (pointing always helps):

If a new level is M:1 with its parent, check that it is 1:M with its child

> **Can a [*Candidate*] have more than one [*child*]?**

- If the answer is **YES** then put "M" just above the child.
- If the answer is **NO** put "1" just above the child.

> **Can a [*child*] belong to more than one [*Candidate*]?**

- If the answer is **YES** put "M' just below the candidate.
- If the answer is **NO** put a "1" just below the candidate.

To test that SUBCATEGORY belongs above BRAND ask:

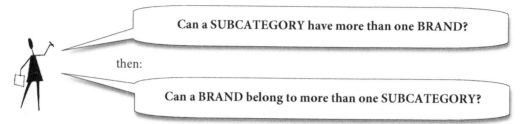

Can a SUBCATEGORY have more than one BRAND?

then:

Can a BRAND belong to more than one SUBCATEGORY?

If you finish with "M" above the child (BRAND) and "1" below the candidate (SUBCATEGORY) (**YES, NO** answers) you have the right M:1 child relationship, the candidate is in the correct position and you can move on to the search for another level in the hierarchy.

Hierarchy Attributes at the Same Level

A 1:1 relationship means that attributes are at the same level

If you have two "1"s between levels this indicates a one-to-one (1:1) relationship which means that the candidate is at the same level as the existing hierarchical attribute. As such it adds no additional drill-down functionality to the hierarchy, and you should not insert it. It may, however, replace the existing attribute, if it proves to be a better report label. For example, CATEGORY NAME is at the same level as CATEGORY CODE, but would be a more useful descriptive label on a drill-down report than the cryptic code. Remember that even if an attribute is not added to a hierarchy it will still be available in the dimension as an alternative for report formatting, so excluding CATEGORY CODE from the hierarchy does not preclude its use in custom drill-down reporting, just its use in default drilling.

Hierarchy Attributes that Don't Belong

M:M indicates that attributes do not belong in the same hierarchy

If you get two "M"s between levels this indicates a M:M relationship which means that the two levels do not belong in the same (balanced) hierarchy. If stakeholders want to define a hierarchy containing the candidate it must be a separate parallel hierarchy to the current one, just as Week and Month are in different time hierarchies in Figure 3-10b.

Hierarchy Attributes at the Wrong Level

Reverse relationships mean that attributes need repositioning on the hierarchy chart

If you finish with the reverse relationship from the one you are looking for the candidate is at the wrong level. If you get a 1:M with a parent (you're looking for an M:1), the candidate is too low and you should move it up a level. If you get an M:1 with a child (you're looking for a 1:M), the candidate is too high and you should move it down a level. After you move it, be sure to retest it against its new parent and child levels.

Follow each hierarchy level name with a few example values as a bracketed list as in the Figure 3-14 chart. This is especially useful if you are modelstorming a hierarchy chart with limited whiteboard space and stakeholders cannot see a copy of the dimension example data table.

Completing a Hierarchy

After you have found the correct position for the new level—or discarded it if it does not belong—you continue to find more levels by pointing at the existing ones and asking stakeholders whether any other levels exist above or below them. When they have finished providing new levels you should ask one more hierarchy related question:

> **Do you have plans, budgets, forecasts, or targets associated with [*dimension*]s? If so at what level(s) are they set?**

Check for "hot" planning levels before finishing each hierarchy

If stakeholders identify planning levels, mark these with an asterisk (*) to denote that they are *"hot"*, i.e., likely to be particularly important levels for many BI comparisons. You may need to design aggregates or OLAP cubes at these levels to improve query performance (see Chapter 8). You should definitely model the planning events themselves along with any additional hot level *rollup dimensions* they require. E.g., Month is typically a hot level in the *when* hierarchy that is implemented as a rollup dimension (a separate physical dimension derived from the base calendar dimension) to match the granularity of plan and aggregate facts. (See Chapters 4 and 8.)

Mark hot levels with an * and be prepared to model their additional matching events and rollup dimensions

Hot levels often appear at the points where different *W-type* hierarchies logically or physically intersect. For example, Category and Department are hot levels in the Product and Employee hierarchies (as denoted in Figure 3-12) because this is notionally where a *what* hierarchy of things (products) intersects with a *who* hierarchy of people (employees). At that point, a de facto 1:1 relationship exists between the HR and product hierarchies: a single employee (a product sales manager) responsible for a single group of employees (a department) is also responsible for a single group of products (a category). He or she will want many reports summarized to these levels.

Hot levels exist where different W-type hierarchies intersect

When you have finished modeling a hierarchy, check that each level is a mandatory attribute. If some are not mandatory then you may have a ragged hierarchy instead of your preferred balanced one. If data profiling confirms that certain level attributes contain nulls, then update the hierarchy chart to document the missing levels by putting brackets around their names (as in Figure 3-12a) prior to resolving the issue with stakeholders. It is especially important that hot levels are mandatory for successful cross-process analysis.

Check all levels are mandatory to avoid ragged hierarchies

When you have completed all the hierarchy charts for a dimension, rearrange the level attributes in hierarchy order in the dimension table with the low level attributes first followed by higher level attributes (reading left to right). Hierarchical column order increases readability and helps to roughly document the hierarchical relationships within physical dimension tables.

Dimensional History

You must define
how dimensional
attributes handle
history

When you have discovered all the attributes of a dimension, described them using examples, and modeled their hierarchical relationships, there is one more piece of information that stakeholders must tell you about each one: how to handle its history. This information is also known as a dimension's *temporal* properties or *slowly changing dimension (SCD)* policy.

*Slowly changing
dimensions*
dramatically affect
how historical
events are reported

Stakeholders instinctively feel the need to preserve *event* history—especially legally binding financial transactions—but may think of dimensions as (relatively static) reference data that simply has to be kept up to date when it does change. While it is true that dimensions are relatively static compared to dynamic business events, *slowly changing dimension* history, or rather the lack of it, can have a profound effect on a data warehouse's ability to accurately compare events over time and meet stakeholders' initial and longer-term needs. For example, Dean Moriarty, a customer who was based in New York, relocates to California at the beginning of this year. Should a BI query for "order totals by state, this year vs. last year" associate *all* of Moriarty's orders to his current location: California? Or should Moriarty's orders last year be associated with New York (last year's location), and only this year's with California? What if BI users want to look at the biggest spenders in California over the last two years, should their queries include Moriarty based on his high spending while he was still in New York last year or exclude him because he hasn't spent so much since moving to L.A.? Another way of asking these questions is "Should queries use the current or historical values of customer state?" Is there a simple answer?

Current Value Attributes

Operational systems
generally default to
current valued
reference data

Operational systems generally concentrate on the "here and now" with an understandable bias towards current values for reference or master data. For example, an order processing system will make sure that only "this year's model" products are available to be selected for shipping to customers' current locations. Because of this bias, operational database applications will often overwrite reference data when it changes. If the same updates are applied to dimensional attributes they will contain current values only.

Current value (**CV**)
attributes provide
"as is" reporting that
matches operational
reporting results

Dimensional attributes that only contain the current value descriptions provide "as is" reporting; i.e., they roll up event history using today's descriptions, making it seem as if everything has always been described as it is now. For the previous example, *current value* (**CV**) attributes would roll up all of Moriarty's orders to California (his current location) regardless of where, on the road, he was living when he placed them. This is typically the style of reporting that stakeholders are used to from their attempts to analyze history directly from operational systems.

CV attributes enable the data warehouse to produce the same results as existing operational reports—often an initial acceptance criteria for stakeholders.

Unfortunately problems arise when current values are the *only* descriptions available for DW/BI systems, which by definition, must support accurate historical comparisons. **CV** attributes may be capable of answering questions such as: "Where are the customers, now, who bought ... in the last three years?" or "What are the top selling products this year vs. last year?" But they cannot answer: "Where were those customers and what were they like when they bought our products?" or "Exactly what were products like (how were they described and categorized) at the time they were purchased?" These questions cannot be answered because dimensional history is lost when **CV** attributes are updated (overwritten).

With current values only, dimensional history is lost and many potentially important BI questions cannot be answered correctly

Another limitation of current value only solutions is that they cannot reproduce previous historical analyses. The same report with exactly the same filters will often yield different results when run later—even though every detailed event remains unaltered—because the reference data used to group, sort and filter the events has changed when it should not have. This is a common bane of reporting from operational sources that stakeholders do not want repeated in the data warehouse.

Current value only designs make it impossible to reproduce reports when dimensions change

It's not all bad news for **CV** attributes. Even though they are historically incomplete/incorrect, they can be useful for certain types of historical comparisons that *recast history*: deliberately pretend everything was described as it is now. For example, a sales manager who wants to compare channel sales for this year versus last year, may need to pretend that today's channel structures also existed last year, in order to make the comparison. This is exactly what **CV** channel description attributes will do.

Current value attributes can usefully *recast history*

Corrections and Fixed Value Attributes

Current values are also entirely appropriate when mistakes are corrected and previous erroneous values should never be used again. For example, when a customer or employee's date of birth changes in an operational database, we know it hasn't really changed (from one corrected date to another), it must be a correction. We assume that the most recent (current) value is correct as someone has gone to the trouble of making the update. Date of Birth is an example of a *fixed value* (**FV**) *attribute* that cannot change but can be corrected (fixed when it's not right). **FV** attributes have a strict 1:M relationship over time with the dimension. All other attributes have potentially a M:M relationship over time with the dimension, which is ignored (treated as M:1) in the case of **CV** attributes.

Current values are historically correct for *fixed value* (**FV**) attributes that do not change over time but can be corrected

Historic Value Attributes

Historical value (HV) attributes support "as was" reporting

Historic value (**HV**) attributes support "as was" reporting by providing the historically correct dimensional values to group and filter historical events and measures. Everything is reported "as it was" at the time of the event. Returning to the Moriarty example, an HV customer STATE attribute would roll last year's orders up to New York, and this year's up to California.

HV attributes require more ETL resources, but provide more flexible reporting

Preserving dimensional history requires more ETL work but data warehouses that are built using **HV** dimensions are more flexible. Not only can they correctly answer the "What were things really like when …?" questions by default, they can also be used with minimal effort to recast history to current values for "as is" reporting, or to a specific date, such as a financial year-end for "as at" reporting. **HV** dimensions techniques for supporting both "as is" and "as was" reporting are covered in Chapter 6.

Historic value dimensional attributes support the agile principle "Welcome changing requirements, even late in development." Stakeholders are able to change their mind about using current or historic values without ETL developers "tearing their hair out" and having to reload the data warehouse.

Telling Change Stories

You discover temporal properties by telling change stories

To discover exactly how a dimension handles descriptive history, you add an extra row to the dimension table, to hold a change story for each attribute and ask the stakeholders to help you fill it out. For each attribute, you start by asking if it can change; for example:

> **Can the PRODUCT NAME of a PRODUCT change?**

If the answer is **NO**, label the attribute as fixed value with the short code FV and copy its example value from the first row (the typical member) into its change story as in Figure 3-15 to illustrate that it is unchanging over time. Then move on to the next attribute.

If the answer is **YES,** the attribute's values are not fixed and you need to ask a follow-on question to discover if stakeholders want/need (not always the same thing) historical values. For example, if PRODUCT TYPE is not **FV** ask:

> **If the PRODUCT TYPE of a PRODUCT changes will you need its historic values for grouping and filtering your reports?**

Make sure you never ask: "Do you want current values *or* historic values?" The answer, which is invariably "current values", tells you nothing you shouldn't already know. Of course stakeholders want current values—that's a given: they are incredibly interested in current business events and want those events to be described properly using current values just as they are in the operational systems. You want to discover if attribute history is equally important. It is also highly misleading to present historic values and current values as an either/or choice: **HV** attributes must include current values because current values are the historically correct descriptions for the most recent events.

Ask about historic values: you know current values are important already

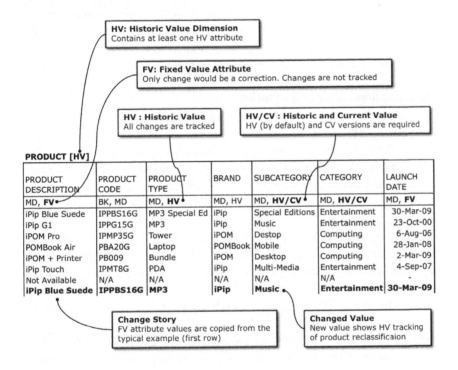

Figure 3-15
Modeling dimensional history using a change story

If the answer to your "Do you need historic values?" question is **NO**, double-check with the stakeholders that they will only ever care about current values and are fully aware of the BI limitations they are settling for. The problems of misstated history and unrepeatable reports caused by **CV** only attributes are best explained using examples (see **Documenting CV Change Stories** shortly), to any stakeholder making this decision for the first time.

Double-check that history really is unnecessary before defining a **CV** attribute

For many attributes it is a good idea to treat the stakeholders' **CV** answers as *reporting directives* rather than *storage directives*. They, quite rightly, are telling you how they want their (initial) BI reports to behave: often exactly like existing operational reports they know (and love), but not how to store information in the data warehouse—that's not their role. For all but the largest dimensions and most volatile attributes it is possible to efficiently store (compliance ready) **HV** attributes but provide **CV** versions by default for reporting purposes.

You may need to provide **CV** reporting behavior initially but store **HV** attributes to provide flexibility in the future

Documenting CV Change Stories

For **CV** attributes: copy their typical examples into the change story or better still (time permitting) ask for new values to fill out the change story row and then replace the typical example values

If stakeholders confirm that an attribute's history is never needed—perhaps they want an explicitly current value attribute such as CURRENT STATUS or LIFETIME VALUE—you label the attribute as **CV**. To fill out its change story, you can either copy the attribute's typical example (as you would if it was **FV**), for speed, or ask stakeholders for a changed value, for clarity. If you do the latter you must also change the typical example on the first row to this new value. Both the typical example and the change story of a **CV** attribute contain the same value, the new current value, to "show, don't tell" that there is no history. Figure 3-16 illustrates this for CUSTOMER NAME: if customer Elvis Priestley changes his name to J.B. Priestley both the first and the last rows in the BEAM✽ dimension are updated to J.B.; Elvis has left the building! The graphic demonstration of existing examples being overwritten, during modelstorming, hammers home the point that history is lost and may cause stakeholders to reconsider some of their **CV** attribute decisions.

Documenting HV Change Stories

For **HV** attributes ask for new examples for their change stories but leave their typical examples unaltered

If stakeholders say they do want the historical values of an attribute such as PRODUCT TYPE, label the attribute as **HV**, and ask for a new example value to place in the change story, as shown in Figure 3-15, but don't update the original typical example. Leaving different values in the first and last rows clearly document the attributes that can change and will hold different historical values over time for the same dimension member: product code IPPBS16G in the Figure 3-15 example.

You can document *hybrid* temporal requirements by combining **HV** and **CV** short codes

If you, or the stakeholders, decide that both **HV** and **CV** data is needed for an attribute you can label it as an **HV/CV** or **CV/HV** *hybrid* attribute, with its default reporting behavior listed first. In figure 3-15, SUBCATEGORY and CATEGORY default to **HV** but **CV** reporting will also be available. For both attributes their change stories reflect the more complex **HV** behavior.

Unless you are using specialist temporal database technology, the CV and HV values of a hybrid attribute will need to be stored as separate physical columns in the same dimension or in separate *hot swappable* dimensions. See Chapter 6 for the *hybrid slowly changing dimension* design pattern to implement this.

Use **CV/PV** to document requirements for previous values

For certain attributes, that change very infrequently, stakeholders may be content with the current value and one *previous value*: the value before the last change. These attributes can be labeled **CV/PV** in the BEAM✽ model and implemented as separate columns in a physical star schema. This design pattern is know as a *type 3 slowly changing dimension*.

FV : Fixed Value or type 0 slowly changing dimension.
CV : Current Value only or type 1 slowly changing dimension.
HV : Historic Value or type 2 slowly changing dimension.
PV : Previous Value or type 3 slowly changing dimension.

Business Keys and Change Stories

As a general rule, business keys that uniquely identify dimension members and define dimensional granularity should not change over time; they should be defined as fixed value (**FV**) and you should simply copy their typical values into the change story. If this is not the case and business keys have been known to change you will need to model their **CV** or **HV** rules and help design more complex ETL processes to identify these awkward changes and handle them appropriately when they occur.

Business Keys (**BK**) should be **FV** by default

Detecting Corrections: Group Change Rules

One of the ETL complexities of handling **HV** updates is how to distinguish between corrections that should overwrite errors and genuine changes that should preserve history. This is a non-issue for **FV** and **CV** attributes because they handle correction and change alike (**FV** attribute updates are always corrections). Being able to tell the difference between corrections, minor changes and major changes is especially important when designing the ETL for large, highly volatile dimensions such as customer because tracking every change may not even be possible, let alone necessary.

HV ETL processes must differentiate corrections from changes

Ideally, source systems should provide reason codes for the most important **HV** attribute updates. Unfortunately, explicit reason descriptions are not often available. One of the many benefits of proactive dimensional modeling is that ETL designers can take advantage of preemptive **HV** definitions to request that not only update notification but update *reason* notification is built into a new operational system while it is still in the early stages of development.

Source systems rarely provide update reasons to help detect corrections

If update reasons are not available, the next best thing is to define business rules that identify important changes based on groups of attributes that should all change at the same time. An example *group change rule* which tracks only "large" changes affecting several attributes at once, might be:

Group change rules can help detect corrections and minor changes

"If customer STREET Address changes but ZIP CODE is unchanged, then handle the update as a correction (or minor move in the same Zip code area): do not preserve the existing address. If STREET and ZIP CODE change together, track the customer's address history prior to this major relocation"

You can discover these rules by asking general questions like "What attributes change together?" or specific questions for each attribute such as "what other attributes must change when this changes?". You can also tie your questions to some activity; you might ask:

To discover these rules ask for attributes that change together

> **When customers really move—rather than just correct their address—which attributes should change?**

Asking for change groups can help find missed attributes

Questions like this, not only expose change dependencies between existing attributes, they can help uncover missed attributes too. They are another one of the BEAM✳ modeler's secret weapons for attribute discovery. Discussing the activity of change is another way of adding narrative to an otherwise static dimension and will get stakeholders thinking. They might respond:

> STREET, ZIP CODE and CITY should all change together. If only one or two of those change, its probably a correction or a move within the same zip or city. If customers move locally—in the same city—we don't need their old addresses. But if they move city, we will want to use those previous addresses.

Use **HV***n* to define a *conditional **HV** group* of attributes that must change together

You can model a group change rule like this one, very concisely, by using numbered **HV** codes to define *conditional **HV** groups*: attributes that only act as **HV** when every member of the same numbered group changes at the same time. In Figure 3-16, the stakeholders' rule has been documented by marking STREET, ZIP CODE, and CITY as **CV, HV1**. They are each **CV** by default (the first temporal short code in the list) so that individual changes will be treated as corrections. Additionally, they are all members of the conditional group **HV1** and will act as **HV** to preserve address history when a customer moves city (when all three attributes change) unless, that is, an exceptional customer manages to move to the very same street address in a different city. Perhaps ZIP CODE and CITY should be in a group of their own (**HV3**) to safeguard missing this rare type of relocation.

Figure 3-16

Modeling a **CV** change story and group change rules

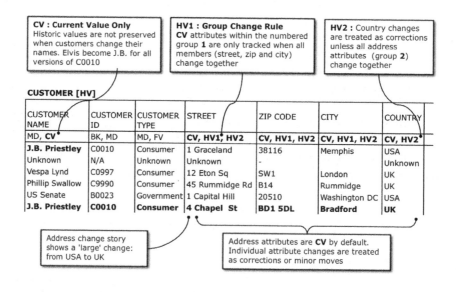

An attribute can belong to multiple **HV***n* groups and be **HV** by default

Notice that the three **HV1** attributes in Figure 3-16 are also in group **HV2** along with COUNTRY. This means that their history is tracked when all three (group **HV1**) change even if COUNTRY does not change, but COUNTRY itself will only be tracked when all four address attributes (group **HV2**) change. If an attribute is always **HV** but also triggers a conditional **HV** attribute: **HV3**, it would be marked **HV, HV3** rather than **CV, HV3**.

Effective Dating

When you have captured change stories and temporal business rules for each attribute, add three more attributes to the dimension table: EFFECTIVE DATE, END DATE, and CURRENT as in Figure 3-17. These additional administrative attributes enable ETL processes to track changes and flag the current version of each member. They effectively convert **HV** dimensions into *minor event* tables capable of recording numerous small events.

Add administrative attributes to each dimension for effective dating

Effective Dating
Records the date range that each historical version of a product is valid for. End date for current version is the maximum date allowed by the DBMS

PRODUCT [HV]

PRODUCT DESCRIPTION	PRODUCT CODE	PRODUCT TYPE	from EFFECTIVE DATE	to END DATE	is CURRENT
MD, **NC**	BK, MD	MD, **HV**	MD	MD	MD
iPip Blue Suede	IPPBS16G	MP3 Special Ed	30-Mar-09	1-Sep-2009	N
iPip G1	IPPG15G	MP3	23-Oct-00	1-Jan-3000	Y
iPOM Pro	IPMP35G	Tower	6-Aug-06	1-Jan-3000	Y
POMBook Air	PBA20G	Laptop	28-Jan-08	1-Jan-3000	Y
iPOM + Printer	PB009	Bundle	2-Mar-09	1-Jan-3000	Y
iPip Touch	IPMT8G	PDA	4-Sep-07	1-Jan-3000	Y
Not Available	N/A	N/A	-	-	-
iPip Blue Suede	**IPPBS16G**	**MP3**	2-Sep-09	1-Jan-3000	Y

Current Flag shows that the change story represents the current version for this product

Figure 3-17
Effective dating a dimension table

With the addition of effective dating, readers who are familiar with how *type 2 slowly changing dimensions* are implemented will notice how closely the change story row in a BEAM✲ dimension matches this ETL technique. This is intentional as BEAM✲ models are designed to be translated into physical dimensional models with minimal changes. It is also important that BEAM✲ modelers do not refer to **HV** attributes as type 2 SCDs or attempt to modelstorm the final piece of their puzzle: surrogate keys, with business stakeholders. Type *n* SCD terminology and surrogate keys (covered in Chapter 5) are appropriate star schema-level topics for discussion with ETL and BI developers not stakeholders.

Change stories demonstrate *type 2 slowly changing dimension* behavior but don't use this ETL jargon with stakeholders

Documenting the Dimension Type

When you have completed a dimension (for now), add a double bar to the end of the table just as you would for an event, and add its dimension type to the table header. To do this you use one of the temporal short codes. If the dimension contains at least one **HV** attribute mark the dimension as **[HV]**, otherwise mark it as **[CV]** to denote that it contains only **CV**, **FV** or **PV**, i.e., its members will not include multiple historic versions.

Mark dimensions that contain no **HV** attributes as **[CV]**

Minor Events

Not every event is a significant business process

Occasionally, you will discover events that do not seem to have enough details or occur frequently enough to represent significant business processes in their own right; they seem more like dimensions. For example, imagine the answer to your next "Who does what?" event discovery question is:

> **Customer moves (to a new) address.**

Minor events have few details. They often represent external activity

You model several event stories and end up with the CUSTOMER MOVES event table in Figure 3-18. This is a perfectly acceptable event, with a *subject-verb-object* main clause, containing a *who* subject (CUSTOMER), an active verb ("moves"), a *where* object (ADDRESS), and a *when* detail (MOVE DATE) but that's all. Despite asking all the *7Ws* questions, it lacks any other *who, what, why, how,* or *how many* details. Why customers move, how much it costs them, or who helps them are unknowns because the event is external to Pomegranate's business. In BEAM✲ terms CUSTOMER MOVES is a *minor* event (despite being quite a major event for the customer). Minor events represent activities that are not always interesting or detailed enough for standalone analysis. But the data values arising from them *are* important for correctly labeling, grouping, and filtering the other, far more interesting, *major* events of the organization.

Figure 3-18
Minor CUSTOMER
MOVE event

CUSTOMER MOVES [DE]

CUSTOMER	Moves to ADDRESS	on MOVE DATE
[who]	[where]	[when]
J.B. Priestley	Bradford	18-May-2009
Vespa Lynd	Venice	14-Oct-2009
Phillip Swallow	Rummidge	1-Jan-1983
Felix Leiter	Langley	Yesterday

HV Attributes: Dimension-Only Minor Events

Minor events can be modeled as **HV** attributes if they occur infrequently

If the verb provided by the stakeholders can easily be replaced with **"has"** without losing important information, this often indicates that the subject and object can be attributes of the same dimension. For example, "customer **moves to** address on **move** date" can be replaced with "customer **has** address on effective date" if the act of *moving*, itself, is unimportant and all that stakeholders care about is a history of customer locations. A customer dimension can model simple **"has"** events as **HV** attributes.

If the subject and the object of an event both describe the same thing (e.g., customers) and there are no other details except *when*, you can handle the event object as an HV attribute of the subject dimension, as long as the change represented by the event does not occur too often. Daily or monthly change would make it a *rapidly changing dimension*—better handled as an event.

Minor Events within Major Events

If no explicit business process captures customer relocation, how does Pomegranate know that it occurs? It must be recorded as a byproduct of some other significant business event(s). Customers typically inform you about new addresses when they order products. If customers move infrequently, these changes can be captured by an **HV** dimension. If moves are frequent—for example, some (perhaps undesirable) consumers provide a new address every time they apply for credit—then the new address is a detail of the credit application event and "moving" is also part of that event—a minor event within a major event. For Orders, a new or different customer address may, in fact, be a third party delivery address for gift purchases: a separate *where* detail of the event and therefore a separate *who/where* dimension rather than an attribute of the customer *who* dimension.

If you discover a minor event with a small number of details (typically three Ws, including *when*), ask how and when these details are captured. You may be able to model their capture within a far more interesting major event.

Figure 3-19 shows a very different version of the CUSTOMER MOVES event compared to the minor version of Figure 3-18. By reading the event stories in both tables you can see that these are actually the *same* events happening to the *same* people—but in Figure 3-19 they have been modeled in far greater detail for the data warehouse of a relocation company. This CUSTOMER MOVES is clearly a *major* event—for that company.

If minor events occur frequently they can be modeled as additional details of other, more interesting, major events

One organization's minor event may be another organization's major event

CUSTOMER MOVES [DE]

CUSTOMER	Moves to ADDRESS	on MOVE DATE	with TEAM LEADER	Sold by SALES AGENT	using CONTAINER TYPE	from PREVIOUS ADDRESS	with MOVING COSTS	with CONTRACT NUMBER
[who]	[where]	[when]	[who]	[who]	[What]	[where]	[£]	[how]
J.B. Priestley	Bradford	18-May-2009	DD	AL	Large	Memphis	2001.00	M3434
Vespa Lynd	Venice	14-Oct-2009	RTD	GS	Medium	London	2500.34	M2342
Phillip Swallow	Rummidge	1-Jan-1983	DL	JB2	Small	Euphoria	3000.99	M2122
Felix Leiter	Langley	Yesterday	IF	JB1	Small	Miami	1750.41	M5666

Figure 3-19
Major CUSTOMER MOVES event

Sufficient Attributes?

How do you know when you have sufficient attributes for a dimension or levels in a hierarchy? There is no magic test; stakeholders will simply run out of ideas. If you feel you have not discovered every possible attribute: don't worry, be agile, press on. As long as you have the major hierarchies and **HV** attributes, and a clear definition of granularity for each dimension, additional attributes can be added with relative ease in future iterations. That said, the great benefit of modelstorming with stakeholders is the ability to define common (*conformed*, see next chapter) dimensional attributes early on, so don't miss your opportunity while you have their initial attention.

Summary

- A dimensional data warehouse is only as good as its dimensions. Good dimensions contain *dimensional attributes* that describe business events using terms that are familiar and meaningful to the BI stakeholders. This is the best reason for asking stakeholders to modelstorm the dimensions they need using examples to clarify the terms they use.

- Dimensions themselves are discovered by event modeling; most *who, what, when, where* and *why* event details become dimensions. Dimensional attributes are discovered by modeling each of these details as the subject of its own BEAM✲ dimension table. *How* details can be dimensionalized in this way too but they typically do not have additional descriptive attributes. Non-descriptive *how* details become *degenerate dimensions*, stored in fact tables along with the *how many* details which become facts.

- The first additional attribute that must be modeled for a dimension subject is its *identity*. This is the *business key* (**BK**) which uniquely identifies each dimension member and defines the dimension granularity. If a dimension is created from multiple source systems there may be more than one **BK** for a dimension member. The unique **BK** for a dimension can be a composite of multiple source systems keys.

- Further dimension attribute requirements are gathered by asking stakeholders to provide example descriptive data for each dimension (using the *7Ws* as an attribute type checklist). Examples help to discover mandatory attributes (**MD**), and exclusive attribute combinations (**X***n*) together with their defining characteristics (**DC***n,n*).

- *Hierarchy charts* describe how stakeholders (want to) organize dimensional members hierarchically to support drill-down analysis and plan vs. actual reporting. Drawing these charts helps to prompt stakeholders for additional hierarchical attributes and data sources. Hot hierarchy levels, that represent popular levels of summarization, help to identify additional planning events, rollup dimensions and aggregation opportunities.

- Hierarchies can be balanced, ragged or variable depth. Each type can be single or multi-parent. Single parent, balanced hierarchies are the easiest hierarchies to implement dimensionally and the simplest to work with for BI. Additional techniques are needed to balance ragged hierarchies and represent multi-parent and variable depth hierarchies (See Chapter 6).

- *Change stories* describe how dimensional history is handled. The short codes **CV, HV, FV, PV** are used to document the *temporal properties* of each attribute. These temporal codes can be numbered to define *group change rules* involving multiple attributes.

- *Minor events* are events that occur infrequently and contain few details. They typically do not represent significant business processes that warrant modeling as separate events. Often they can be modeled as **HV** dimensional attributes, or as additional details of other major events (recognizable business processes).

MODELING BUSINESS PROCESSES

> The only reason for time is so that everything doesn't happen at once
>
> — *Albert Einstein*

Designing a data warehouse or data mart for business process measurement demands that you quickly move beyond modeling single business events. All but the simplest business processes are made up of multiple business events and BI stakeholders invariably want to do cross-process analysis. When you modelstorm these multi-event requirements you soon notice two crucial things:

BI Stakeholders need multiple events for process measurement

- **Stakeholders model events chronologically.** As you complete one event, stakeholders naturally think of related events that immediately follow or precede it. These event sequences represent business processes and value chains that need to be measured end-to-end.

Events sequences represent business processes and value chains

- **Stakeholders describe different events using many of the same *7Ws*.** When you define an event in terms of its *7Ws*, stakeholders start thinking of other events with the same details, especially events that share its subject or object. These shared details, known to dimensional modelers as *conformed dimensions*, are the basis for cross-process analysis.

Events share common dimensions that support cross-process analysis

In this chapter we describe how an *event matrix*, the single most powerful BEAM✲ artifact, is used to storyboard the data warehouse: rapidly model multiple events, identify significant business processes and conformed dimensions, and prioritize their development.

The event matrix is an agile tool for modeling multiple events

- **The importance of conformed dimensions for agile DW design**
- **Modelstorming event sequences with an event matrix**
- **Prioritizing event and dimension development using Scrum**
- **Modeling event stories with conformed dimensions and examples**

Modeling Multiple Events With Agility

Agile designers might be tempted to limit the modeling scope per release

Deploying an *agile* data warehouse that will eventually handle the multiple business events required for enterprise BI is especially challenging. To meet the agile principles of *early and frequent delivery of valuable working software*, agile designers may be tempted to limit their modeling scope per release in terms of business processes and/or stakeholder departments. Unfortunately this can quickly lead to the *silo data mart anti-pattern*, of Figure 4-1.

This can result in *silo data marts* that are unable to support cross-process analysis

With a tightly-controlled initial scope, BI users can receive their agile data marts early and obtain valuable insight from them individually on a department by department basis. So far so good, but when users want to step up to cross-department, cross-process analysis they find they cannot make the necessary comparisons due to incompatible or missing descriptions and measures. Rebuilding each data mart from scratch is unthinkable so data is re-extracted from the source systems so that each department can look at it "their way". The cost of this extra work and the inconsistent or conflicting answers that emanate from these "multiple versions of the truth" drive BI stakeholders crazy!

Figure 4-1
Silo data marts that cannot be shared: a data warehouse anti-pattern

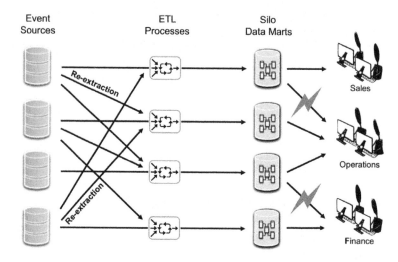

With too limited a scope data warehouse design incurs heavy *technical debt*

Silo data marts are examples of *technical debt*. Agile software development intentionally takes on technical debt when "just barely good enough" code is released. This makes good sense when the business value of early working software outweighs the interest on the debt: the extra effort involved in refactoring the code in future iterations. However, for DW/BI projects, the cost of servicing high interest technical debt: refactoring terabytes of incorrectly represented historical data, can be ruinously high.

Traditional BDUF does not match agile BI requirements

The especially high interest of database technical debt could be argued as a good reason for taking a traditional, non-agile, approach to data requirements gathering and data warehouse design itself and postponing agile practices for ETL and BI development. But the problem is this fallback to the "big design upfront" (BDUF) simply does not match the evolutionary nature of modern BI requirements nor their delivery timescales. Plus it is incredibly hard for a DW/BI project to become agile when it does not start off agile.

Instead, agile data warehouse modelers should stay agile (and dimensional), but lower their technical debt by balancing "just in time" (JIT) detailed modeling of business events for the next development sprint and "just enough design up front" (JEDUF) for cross-process BI in the future. To do so, modelers need to rapidly *model ahead* in just enough detail to discover which of the dimensions, needed for the next sprint, should also be *conformed dimensions* that will help to future proof their designs for enterprise BI.

Agile dimensional modelers lower their technical debt by modeling ahead *just enough to define* conformed dimensions

Conformed Dimensions

Figure 4-2 shows a *Promotion Analysis Report* that combines information from two events: CUSTOMER ORDERS and PRODUCT CAMPAIGNS to explore the connection between campaign activity and sales revenue. The report is possible because the two different events have identical descriptions of PRODUCT and PROMOTION. These *conformed dimensions* allow measures from both events to be aggregated to a compatible level and lined up next to one another on the report. Lining up the answers or *drilling-across* like this appears obvious but if the events are handled by different operational systems (an Oracle-based order processing application and a SQL Server-based customer relationship management system) then this report might be the first time that the two sets of data have actually met. If each source system describes products and promotions differently *and* the individual star schemas use these *non-conformed* descriptions, the analysis would not be possible because the measures would not align.

Conformed dimensions allow measures from different events to be combined and compared

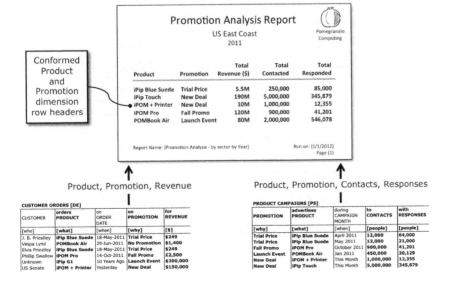

Figure 4-2
Conformed dimensions enable cross-process analysis

Conformed dimensions are shared by multiple fact tables

The simplest technical definition of a conformed dimension is a single physical dimension table shared by multiple fact tables or exact replicated copies of a master dimension, if fact tables are distributed on multiple database servers. Separate distinct dimensions can also be conformed at the attribute level if they contain *conformed attributes* with identical business meanings and identical contents that line up as common report row headers. Three types of dimension are conformed at the attribute level, they are:

Swappable, rollup and role-playing dimensions are conformed at the dimensional attribute level

- **Swappable dimensions [SD]** that are subsets of conformed dimensions. For example, a CUSTOMER dimension (1M people) and a subset EXTENDED WARRANTY CUSTOMER dimension (100K people) are conformed if they describe the same customer in exactly the same way. These two dimensions would allow product sales and extended warranty claims to be compared for all customers or just warranty holding customers. Swappable dimensions are covered in Chapter 6.

- **Rollup dimensions [RU]** with conformed attributes in common with their base dimensions. Figure 4-3 shows an example of the conformed *when* dimensions CALENDAR and MONTH. These two dimensions can be used to compare daily and monthly granularity measures at the Month, Quarter, or Year level. Rollup dimensions are typically used to describe planning events and aggregate fact tables.

- **Role-playing dimensions [RP]:** Single physical dimensions used to play multiple logical roles. For example, a CALENDAR [RP] dimension used to play the role of ORDER DATE and PAYMENT DATE.

Figure 4-3

When dimensions, conformed at the attribute level

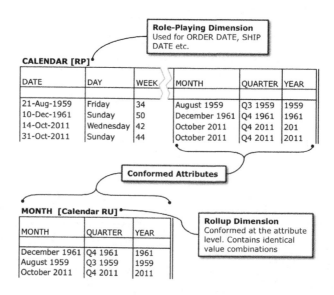

While dimensions are frequently shared across many business processes, facts are typically specific to a single process or event. However, they can be used to create *conformed measures* if they have compatible calculation methods and common units of measure that allow totaling and comparison across processes; for example, if sales revenue and support revenue are both pre-tax dollar figures they can be combined to produce region totals.

Conformed measures rely on compatible facts with common units of measure

Conforming data is not so much a technical challenge, as a political one, requiring consensus on data definitions across many departments within an organization as well as operational systems. By modelstorming with stakeholders you highlight the value of conformed dimensions to the very people who can make them happen. Modeling multiple events *by example,* as BEAM✲ encourages you to do, quickly reveals inconsistencies that would otherwise thwart conformance. Stakeholders will work to address these inconsistencies and conform dimensions when they see the potential business value they provide.

Conforming data is a political challenge. BEAM✲ tackles this by modeling with stakeholders who can make it happen

Homonyms are data terms with the same name but different meanings. They are the opposite of conformed dimensions and attributes. For example, both Pomegranate's Sales and Finance departments use the term "Customer Type" but Sales has five types of customer and Finance only three. If stakeholders cannot agree on a conformed customer type then you would have to define two uniquely named details: SALES CUSTOMER TYPE and FINANCE CUSTOMER TYPE. However, taking this approach for every homonym perpetuates incompatible reporting and weakens the analytical power of the data warehouse. Perhaps by discovering this problem through modelstorming examples, Sales and Finance stakeholders could agree on a new conformed version of Customer Type with four descriptive values.

Homonyms are nonconformed data terms with the same name but different meanings

Synonyms are data terms with the same meaning but different names. Organizations will often use different names across different departments/ business processes for what could be the same conformed dimension or attribute. For example, an insurance company might use the terms Customer Enrollee, Subscriber, Policy Holder and Claimant interchangeably, while a pharmaceutical company may refer to the same person as a Physician, Doctor, Healthcare Provider or Practitioner.

Synonyms are conformable data terms with the same meaning but different names

The value of *modeling with examples,* to help define conformed dimensions, cannot be overstated. Stakeholders often think they fully understand the meaning of their data terms, until ambiguities and differences of opinion are quickly exposed when they provide examples to their peers.

The Data Warehouse Bus

Conformed dimensions define a *data warehouse bus* standard for plug-in data marts

Figure 4-4 presents a very different data mart architecture to the silo data marts of Figure 4-1. This time, data marts are shareable by departments and do support cross-process analysis because they have been implemented using conformed dimensions. These valuable dimensions define a data mart integration standard referred to as *the data warehouse bus* because each data mart "plugs into the bus" of conformed dimensions, much like a USB (universal serial bus) device plugs into a computer.

Defining a data warehouse bus requires more initial work

Compared to standalone data mart projects or the silo data mart anti-pattern, the data warehouse bus requires some more initial work to:

- Model enough different business processes/events to identify potentially valuable conformed dimensions and expose conformance issues.

- Face, up front, the political challenges of getting stakeholders to conform inconsistent business terms.

- Build more robust ETL processes that actively conform dimensional attributes, from multiple operational data sources, not just the event source(s) currently in scope.

- Establish a conformed dimension (master data) management regime that promotes the use of conformed dimensions, not just by enforcing reuse but also refactoring (improving) the conformed dimensions on a regular basis. This removes the need for individual BI projects to develop their own "better" versions, that would inevitably dilute conformance.

The pay-back is reduced technical debt and greater long-term agility

The reward for conforming is less technical debt and rework and greater agility in the long run. Once the initial conformed dimensions have been defined, self-governing agile teams, that promise to use them, can work in parallel to develop data marts for individual business events or processes, becoming experts in their data sources and measurement.

Data mart teams can develop additional *local* (*non-conformed*) *dimensions* so long as they adhere to the data warehouse bus for conformed dimensions. Local dimensions will always be necessary to describe what is unique about an event. They are used in *addition* to conformed dimensions—never in place of.

While the inception costs of conforming are higher, the data warehouse bus is still an agile JEDUF technique: once the bus has been defined, only the conformed dimensions for the current development sprint need to be modeled in detail and actively conformed; i.e. you can conform incrementally.

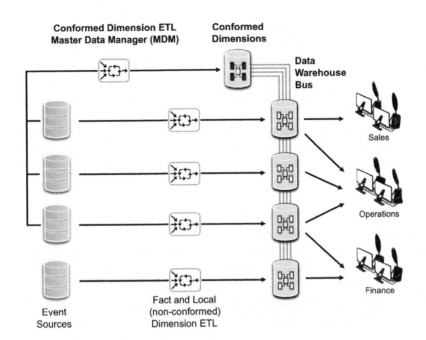

Figure 4-4
Data warehouse
bus design pattern

The most useful tool for planning conformance and designing a data warehouse bus is a *dimensional matrix*. This is a grid of rows representing business processes and columns representing dimensions with tick marks at the intersections where a dimension is a candidate detail of a process. Figure 4-5 shows an example dimensional matrix for Pomegranate's manufacturing process. The simplicity of this diagram belies the power of the single page overview it provides (even for a complex real-world design as opposed to this text book example). The clarity of this model, in a format readily understood by stakeholders and IT alike, compared to individual tables or data warehouse level ER diagrams, can be truly inspiring! Start scanning the matrix and see.

A dimensional matrix is the ideal conformance planning tool for designing a data warehouse bus

	EMPLOYEE	SUPPLIER	RESELLER	CARRIER	COMPONENT	PRODUCT	PROCESS	TEST	PLANT	WAREHOUSE	STORE	CONTRACT	SHIP MODE
MANUFACTURING PLANS						✓			✓				
PROCUREMENT	✓	✓			✓	✓			✓			✓	✓
COMPONENT INVENTORY						✓			✓				
MANUFACTURING	✓	✓				✓	✓	✓	✓	✓			
PRODUCT INVENTORY						✓				✓			
SHIPMENTS			✓	✓		✓				✓	✓	✓	✓

Conformed Dimensions
Used in multiple processes

Non-conformed Dimensions
Used in only one process

Figure 4-5
A dimensional
matrix

Scan down the matrix columns to identify potential conformed dimensions

Scanning down the dimension columns reveals the potential for dimensional conformance. Conformed dimensions that could form a data warehouse bus show up with multiple ticks. The contrast between these valuable dimensions that support cross-process analysis (Hurray!) and the non-conformed dimensions that do not (Boo!) should encourage everyone to work towards conformance.

Scan across the matrix rows to compare process complexity

Scanning across the process rows helps to estimate the complexity of a business process: generally, the more dimension ticks, the more complex a process is likely to be and the more resource needed to define its business events and implement them.

Start with a high-level matrix to help you plan dimensionally

It's a good idea to start your agile DW/BI project by creating a high-level matrix to help you plan your data warehouse design from a *conformed dimensional process measurement perspective* from the outset. You may want to add to it some of the additional features of the event matrix described below.

Use a high-level dimensional matrix to gain support from senior business and IT management for conforming dimensions.

The Event Matrix

The event matrix is a modelstorming version of the dimensional matrix

An event matrix is a more detailed version of the dimensional matrix. It is a business event-level modelstorming tool designed to be filled in by/with stakeholders, using the *7Ws* framework. Figure 4-6 shows an event matrix version of the Figure 4-5 manufacturing processes. The additional details on this matrix include:

It contains details for BEAM✻ event story telling and Scrum planning

- **Event Sequences**: Business events, including their main clause short stories, recorded in time/value/process order.

- **Dimensions in BEAM✻ story sequence** (*who, what, where, why,* and *how*). This helps you fill in the matrix using the *7Ws*, read summary event stories, spot opportunities to reuse dimensions of the same *W-type* and focus on conforming the most important *who* and *what* dimensions: typically customer, employee and product.

- **Stakeholder Group** columns for recording event interest and ownership. Ticks can be linked to attendee lists of who was involved in modelstorming the event details, or should be.

- **Importance and Estimate** rows and columns for prioritizing events and dimensions on a Scrum product backlog and estimating their ETL tasks for a sprint backlog.

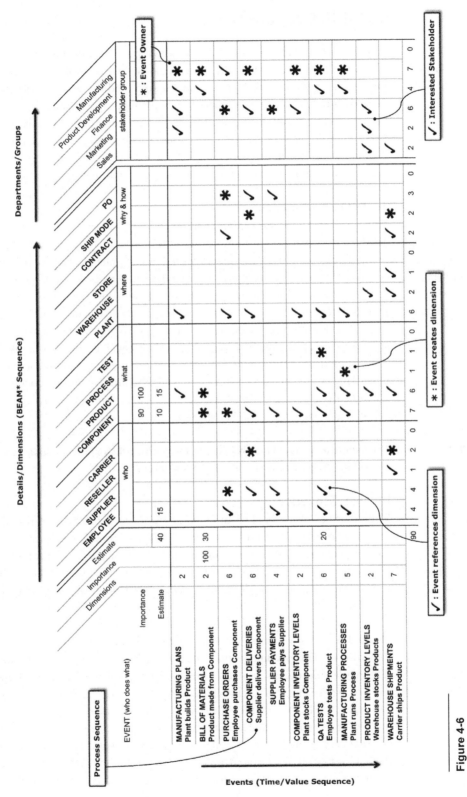

Figure 4-6
An event matrix

Event Sequences

Look back at the event rows on the matrix in Figure 4-6 and you will notice that events are not listed alphabetically. Instead, they are listed in *value sequence* beginning with MANUFACTURING PLANS, and ending with WAREHOUSE SHIPMENTS. This sequence orders the events by the increasing value of their outputs. In this example, the sequence starts with potentially valuable planning followed by the procurement of lower value components, and proceeds through the building and shipment of higher value products. When business activity is ordered in this way it is often referred to as a *value chain*.

Time/Value Sequence

Value sequence can also represent time sequence. Generally low value output activity occurs before high value output activity or at least that is how most of us think of business activity at a macro-level. For example, in manufacturing, procurement happens before product assembly, shipping, and sales. Similarly, in service industries, time and money is spent acquiring low value (high cost) prospects before converting them into potentially valuable customers and then into high value (low cost) repeat customers. In reality, value sequencing may not be a strict chronology because many of the micro-level business events described in a value chain occur simultaneously and asynchronously—not waiting for one another. However, time/value sequencing is highly intuitive and by documenting events in this way, the matrix helps stakeholders to think of *next* or *previous* events, and spot gaps (missing links) in their value chains.

Add events to an event matrix in the order in which they increase business value by asking "Who does what next that adds value?"

Process Sequence

Within the flexible chronology of value chains there will be stricter chronological sequences of events that must occur sequentially to complete a significant time consuming *process* such as order fulfillment or insurance claim settlement. These *process sequences*—which begin with a *process (initiating) event* and continue serially through a number of *milestone events*—are denoted on an event matrix by indentation.

Figure 4-6 shows a process sequence of PURCHASE ORDERS to SUPPLIER PAYMENTS. This documents that a delivery only occurs after a purchase order (PO) has been processed and a payment is only made after a delivery has been received. Notice that these events share a conformed PO dimension. This may only be a degenerate PO NUMBER dimension in each event table but it ties these events together at the atomic detail level and allows stakeholders to track the progress of each PO item through delivery and payment. Notice also that POs are created by PURCHASE ORDER events (denoted by a ✱ on the matrix): PO numbers are generated when an employee raises a purchase order. This confirms the strict process sequence of events: payments and deliveries reference PO numbers, they must occur after the event that creates them.

Modeling Process Sequences as Evolving Events

Identifying a process sequence highlights an opportunity to model an evolving event that will bring together all the individual milestone events of a process, allowing them to be easily compared at a detail level. For example, PURCHASE ORDERS to SUPPLIER PAYMENTS could be modeled as an evolving event containing order date, order quantity, order value, plus actual delivery time and quantity from COMPONENT DELIVERIES, and payment date and amount. This single evolving event would give stakeholders easy access to supplier performance measures such as: late deliveries, average delivery time, and outstanding order quantities.

> The milestone events of a process can be modeled as details of a single evolving event that provides additional duration measures

Using Process Sequences to Enrich Events

Process sequences also help to add missing details to milestone events. The matrix will often reveal dimensions on an initial triggering event that can be added to the subsequent milestone events. For example, in Figure 4-6 the CONTRACT dimension of the PURCHASE ORDERS event could be added to the COMPONENT DELIVERIES and SUPPLIER PAYMENTS milestone events. It is possible to add this dimension because of the strict chronology of the process sequence: everything about the originating purchase order is known at the time of a delivery or payment.

> Process sequences help you to find additional details for milestone events

Modelstorming with an Event Matrix

In their book "Gamestorming" (O'Reilly 2010), Dave Gray, Sunni Brown and James Macanufo describe the "shape" of every useful brainstorming game as a stubby pencil sharpened at both ends representing the acts of *opening* discussions, *exploring* alternative ideas and *closing* with decisions. Modelstorming, with BEAM✲ tables, hierarchy charts and an event matrix, maps to this shape as in Figure 4-7.

> Modelstorming is a three act play: *opening, exploring* and *closing*

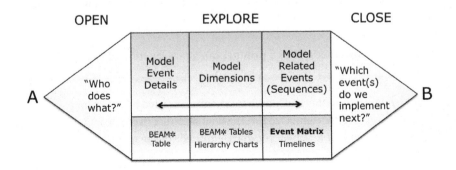

Figure 4-7
The "shape" of modelstorming from A to B

Time-box
modelstorming
meetings to four
hours (maximum)

Like most agile activity, modelstorming should be time-boxed. For an initial modelstorm use four hours as a guideline. Reserve two hours for modeling the first (most important?) event table and its dimensions tables. One hour for modeling related events on a matrix, and a further hour for prioritizing events and making sure the most important event(s) and dimensions are modeled in detail. Not enough time? Don't overrun. Schedule another.

Use an event matrix to
identify the most
important events and
conformed dimensions

So far, we have covered how to open a modelstorm, at point A, with the question "Who does what?", and use BEAM✲ tables and *7W* data story telling techniques to model the answer as *single* event and matching dimensions *in great detail*. Now we describe how you get to point B's implementation decisions using an event matrix to rapidly storyboard *several* more events, *in just enough detail*, to identify the most important events and conformed dimensions for the next sprint. To show how the matrix gets you there we shall continue modeling Pomegranate's order processing BI requirements.

Adding the First Event to the Matrix

Start an event matrix
by adding the main
clause and
dimensions of
your initial event

Start with a blank matrix—download the template from **modelstorming.com**—and add the initial CUSTOMER ORDERS event along with its main clause, leaving several rows above it for previous events and planning (importance and task estimate). Add its dimensions as columns in BEAM✲ sequence (*who, what, where, why,* and *how* order), leaving blank columns between *W-types* for additional dimensions. As you do so, explain to stakeholders that you are now modeling *when* events occur down the page (hence no *when* columns), and how events are described across the page but not how they are measured (hence no *how many* columns).

Include degenerate
dimensions: they can
be conformed too

Don't forget to add any degenerate *how* dimensions, such as ORDER ID. Even though these dimensions are not modeled as tables (because they have no additional descriptive attributes) they still need to be recorded on the matrix because they can be *conformed degenerate dimensions* appearing in multiple events. You will see shortly how important they are for identifying process sequences.

Ask if the event
creates any new
dimension values

Tick off the dimensions referenced by the event. As you do so, ask stakeholders if the event can create new values for any of its dimensions. For example, you might ask:

> **When a customer orders a product can a new customer be created?**

Mark any dimensions that can have new members created by the event (e.g. Customer, Delivery Address and Order ID) with a ✱ rather than a tick to record this significant dependency. When you have finished, the matrix should look like Figure 4-8.

CUSTOMER	SALESPERSON		PRODUCT		SALES LOCATION	DELIVERY ADDRESS		ORDER ID [DD]		PROMOTION	
		who		what			where			why & how	
CUSTOMER ORDERS customer orders product	*	✓		✓			✓	*		✓	*

Figure 4-8
Adding CUSTOMER
ORDERS to the
event matrix

Modeling the Next Event

Having safely documented the first event on the matrix, you now want to model as many related events as you can in the time available. You discover the next event, in exactly the same way as the first event, by asking: **"Who does what?"**. If, at any point, you sense hesitation, or you are intent on discovering events in *when* order, you might want to direct the stakeholders' attention to the last event on the matrix (so far, the only one) by pointing at it and asking a more leading question:

Ask for a new event to add to the matrix. Or ask for the next verb in sequence

> **What happens next?**

Stakeholders might say that **"*Packing* follows Orders"** or **"*Shipments* follow Orders."** If you were given both of these verbs at once, the next one in time sequence would be obvious but when you are modeling less familiar events the sequence many not be so apparent to everyone, in which case you can draw a simple timeline to help sort them chronologically. With a mixed group of stakeholders, the answer to "what happens next?" can vary depending on their individual departmental perspectives.

What happens next depends on the stakeholders' departmental perspective

Watch out for instances where multiple verbs refer to the same event. Stakeholders may use several verbs for the same activity, or multiple activities may be indivisible: captured as a single transaction by the source system. For example, if products are packed and shipped by the same person within a short period of time, the two tasks may be recorded as a single shipment event. If you have any doubts, model each verb as a separate event but if you uncover no extra details, or later discover they represent a single transaction, you can merge the events with no loss of information. Once you have a new verb (assume it is **"ship"**) you can use it to ask a more focused *"Who does what?"* question to get the next event's *subject-verb-object* main clause:

Watch out for verb synonyms that represent the same event

> **Who ships what?**

Remember, this question is designed to focus the stakeholders on identifying the *responsible subject* (*who*) and *object* (*what*) of the event, to model its atomic-level detail. If stakeholders respond with:

> **Warehouse worker ships product.**

Add the next event and any new dimensions. Tick off its conformed dimensions

You add this new main clause to the matrix below CUSTOMER ORDERS, as in Figure 4-9, leaving enough room to add an event name later. You then check the dimension columns to see if the new subject (WAREHOUSE WORKER) and object (PRODUCT) are potential conformed dimensions. PRODUCT is already on the matrix so you should tick its use on the new event row, once you have confirmed that stakeholders are talking about the *same* products described in the *same* way as before. Though it seems unlikely, you should also confirm that shipping does not create new products otherwise you would use a ✱ instead of a tick.

Figure 4-9
Adding "warehouse worker ships product" to the event matrix

	EMPLOYEE [RP] / CUSTOMER	PRODUCT	DELIVERY ADDRESS / SALES LOCATION	ORDER ID [DD] / PROMOTION
	who	what	where	why & how
CUSTOMER ORDERS customer orders product	✱ ✓	✓	✓ ✱	✓ ✱
Warehouse worker ships product	✓	✓		

Role-Playing Dimensions

Check each new dimension for synonyms among the dimensions already on the matrix

WAREHOUSE WORKER looks like a new dimension but before you add it you should check if it is a synonym for an existing dimension; *W-type* can help you here. WAREHOUSE WORKER is a *who,* and there are already two other *whos*: CUSTOMER and SALESPERSON. Are either of these similar to warehouse workers? Customers obviously aren't but warehouse workers and salespeople, while they're not the same people, they maybe a specific type of *who: employees* of the same organization. If so, they would share many common attributes (e.g., Employee ID, Department, Hire Date, etc.) and could be modeled as a single role-playing conformed dimension. You should confirm with stakeholders:

> **Are warehouse workers and salespeople employees?**

If the answer is **NO**, logistics could be handled by a contractor and warehouse workers are not Pomegranate employees. However if the answer is **YES** then you have discovered two different *roles* for a conformed EMPLOYEE dimension. You record this by renaming the SALESPERSON dimension to EMPLOYEE and adding the dimension type code **[RP]** to denote that it is a role-playing dimension. This change needs to be made to the matrix as in Figure 4-9 and the dimension table as in Figure 4-10. However, you should leave the subject of the new shipping event on the matrix as "warehouse worker" to record the specific employee role that stakeholders used to describe the event.

Use [RP] to identify role-playing dimensions

Role names such as WAREHOUSE WORKER and SALESPERSON are used as detail column headers in event tables, so the SALESPERSON column in CUSTOMER ORDERS does not need to be renamed but you do need to associate it with the EMPLOYEE dimension. You document an event detail, such as SALESPERSON, as a role of an existing dimension by adding the role-playing dimension name to its column type using the [ ] type notation as in Figure 4-10.

Roles are documented as event details with a [ ] type identifying their RP dimension

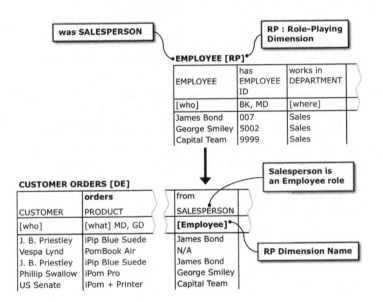

Figure 4-10

A role-playing dimension and an event detail role

[ ] type notation can be used to qualify the *type* of any event detail or dimensional attribute. Initially it can be useful to type every event detail with its *W-type*, such as [who], [what] or [where], to help everyone think dimensionally using the *7Ws*. Details that are dimension roles use this notation instead to document their role-playing dimension name; for example, [employee] or [calendar]. As other details are named after their dimension, they don't need this qualification. For quantities their type is their unit of measure, for example, [£], [$], or [miles] as described in Chapter 2, while Yes/No flags can be documented with a type of [Y/N] showing their permissible values.

[ ] type notation is used to record W-type, unit of measure, flag values and RP dimension names

RP dimensions can play multiple roles in the same event

A role-playing dimension can play multiple roles in the *same* event. For example, EMPLOYEE could appear twice in an evolving event containing both order and shipment details as both SALESPERSON and WAREHOUSE WORKER. Similarly, CALENDAR—the most commonly occurring role-playing dimension—would play the roles of ORDER DATE and SHIP DATE.

When using [ ] notation to document an event role you can drop its generic W-type (e.g., [who] or [what]) to save space, because this is already documented within the dimension table and on the matrix.

Define conformed role-playing dimensions as early as possible

Changing the name of a dimension (and its attributes) to make it more reusable at the design stage is painless compared to the refactoring and testing involved if the dimension had already been deployed. Hence the importance of modeling multiple events to identify conformed dimensions and their role-playing opportunities *before* the first star schema is deployed.

Don't implement any dimension until you have used an event matrix to check whether it should be conformed across multiple events.

Role-playing dimensions, while more conformed, may not initially appeal to stakeholders

Is a role-playing employee dimension the right approach? Stakeholders can often feel uncomfortable with *generalization* (see opposite) like this, if they cannot see any business benefit, i.e., cannot imagine ever wanting to group together the activities of salespeople and warehouse staff. If stakeholders do voice concerns, you should try to encourage them to see the "bigger picture" benefit of a conformed dimension beyond the current scope. You can also assure them that when they query sales or logistics they will have filtered lists of salespeople or warehouse staff to choose from, and will never have to search through all employees.

Use the new event's main clause with the 7Ws to ask for further details

Once you have added the new event to the matrix, you ask for the rest of its details almost exactly as you would if filling out an event table: by turning its main clause into a series of questions using the *7Ws*. The only difference being that you ignore *when* and *how many* questions as you don't need that level of detail for the matrix. Using the *who*, *what* and *where* column headings on the matrix as a checklist, you might ask:

Warehouse worker ships product for/to/using whom?
Warehouse worker ships product with what/in what way?
Warehouse worker ships product from/to where?

Add any new dimensions to the matrix and then tick off all dimensions used by the event

In response to these *who, what, where* questions the stakeholder might identify CUSTOMER (*who*) and DELIVERY ADDRESS (*where*) as potential conformed dimensions, and introduce new dimensions for CARRIER (*who*), SHIP MODE (more of a *how* than a *what*) and WAREHOUSE (*where*) as new dimensions. When you, or better still the stakeholders themselves, have added these to the matrix, it should look like Figure 4-11.

Figure 4-11
Adding shipment dimensions to the matrix

	CUSTOMER	EMPLOYEE [RP]	CARRIER	PRODUCT	SALES LOCATION	DELIVERY ADDRESS	WAREHOUSE	PROMOTION	ORDER ID [DD]	SHIP MODE	
	who			what		where		why & how			
CUSTOMER ORDERS customer orders product	*	✓		✓		✓	*		✓	*	
warehouse worker ships product	✓	✓	✓	✓			✓	✓			✓

Generalization: Model Spoiler Alert

Role-playing dimensions, such as EMPLOYEE [RP], are examples of generalization: a technique frequently used in data modeling to increase the flexibility of a model to represent more varied *things*, and in database design to reduce the number of database objects that need to be created and maintained.

Generalized data models work well for packaged application vendors, because they want to create databases that do not need to be changed for each new customer or industry. Generalization removes customer or industry-specific meanings and business rules from the data model and places them in reference data-driven application logic.

A common generalization design pattern is the use of a single Party entity to represent all *who* details (persons and organizations), with an associative entity Party Role to represent their various types, positions, titles, and responsibilities, (e.g. customer, employee, supplier, etc). This database pattern is capable of recording the multiple positions that people might hold throughout their lives or the multiple responsibilities they might have simultaneously, but is it a good generalization to make when modeling a data warehouse? If BI stakeholders are explicitly looking for people who change roles—such as spies and criminals who change identities, or government regulators who become political lobbyists—then a generic *who* dimension that plays multiple roles might be exactly what they need.

However, if stakeholders are not terribly concerned about role switchers, or the available data sources simply lack any reliable means of capturing role changes, then this design flexibility is wasted. Worse still, it can get in the way of what stakeholders really want to do. For example, a single dimension representing Customers and Employees containing every possible *who* related attribute would be very confusing to use compared to separate dimensions containing customer and employee specific attributes.

Generalization creates smaller more flexible data models that work well for packaged applications

Party and Party Role are common examples of generalized entities used to model all types of people and organizations

Stakeholders may not see any obvious BI benefit in generalization

Generalization produces data models that are difficult for BI users to understand and query

Agile data warehouse modelers must use generalization carefully. Data models that value flexibility over simplicity are notoriously difficult to understand and use for BI. They can work for transactional software products because their data structures are completely hidden from the users by application interfaces. But "universal data models" that rely on high levels of generalization or abstraction do not work so well for BI users who—despite the semantic layers provided by BI tools—need far simpler data warehouse designs to be able to construct and run ad-hoc queries efficiently.

Modelstorming data requirements specifically rather than generally promotes stakeholder design ownership

One of the great benefits of modelstorming is that stakeholders feel a sense of ownership in the resulting design. If they have abstractions forced upon them they start to lose that feeling: it's no longer their model, their data—it could be anyone's. The only Party Roles most stakeholders recognize are Host, Guest, or Gatecrasher—or maybe political ones if that's their specialist field. In extreme cases where generalization is taken too far, to the point where the data model can be used to represent almost anything, it will actually mean nothing to stakeholders. This defeats the goal of modelstorming, which is not to design data structures that merely store data but to design ones that stakeholders will use and cherish. Modeling each interesting *who*, *what*, *when*, *where*, *why* and *how* as specifically as possible helps to promote the data model understanding needed to construct meaningful queries and interpret their results.

Postpone 'technical benefit only' generalization until star schema design

Stakeholders are happy with "reasonable" levels of generalization if they can see an obvious business benefit such as a better understanding of the commonalities (conformance) between business processes that improves analysis. But if the benefits are purely technical—to cut down database administration or streamline ETL—then you should postpone generalization until you design your star schemas and ETL processes.

Discovering Process Sequences

Conformed *why* and *how* dimensions often indicate a process sequence

The last two Ws, *why* and *how*, are grouped together on the matrix because of their similarities and close relationships within processes. *Whys* and *hows* are the most common types of non-conformed dimension but when they are conformed they can often change type, from *how* to *why* and vice versa. This happens when events have a cause and effect relationship that often represents a process sequence. You discover just such a sequence if you ask:

> **Why does a warehouse worker ship a product?**

and get the answer:

> **Because a customer ordered the product.**

This sounds a lot like the main clause of the previous order event. The stakeholders have told you that orders are the reason for shipments. You can find the evidence for this: the conformed dimension that ties the two events together, by turning their answer into a *how* question:

> **How do you know that a customer ordered the product for shipment (what data tells you so)?**

The answer:

> **There is an order ID on each shipment.**

reveals that the order *how* detail (ORDER ID [DD]) is effectively a *why* detail of shipment, indicating that the two events are likely to be part of a process sequence with shipments treated as milestones of CUSTOMER ORDERS. You can check how strict this sequence is by asking, "What about free samples or replacement products and parts; how are shipments for these processed?" If the answer is, "We don't want to consider these when measuring our sales fulfillment processes," then perhaps they are events for a marketing or product support data mart, another sprint, another day. Alternatively, stakeholders might tell you "Pseudo orders are generated when we ship samples or replacements". Either way, all the in-scope shipments are milestone events of orders and ORDER ID is a conformed degenerate *how/why* dimension.

Conformed degenerate dimensions represent how details of process events and why details of milestone events

Figure 4-12 shows the completed shipment event, now named PRODUCT SHIPMENTS, with its final *how* detail a SHIPMENT NUMBER degenerate dimension. The new event name and main clause have also been indented under CUSTOMER ORDERS to document the process sequence. Note that this sequence, shipments follow orders and not the reverse, is confirmed by CUSTOMER ORDERS being an ORDER ID creator (denoted by the **✱** in the ORDER ID column). CUSTOMER ORDERS must occur first to create the ORDER IDs referenced by PRODUCT SHIPMENTS.

Document process sequences by indenting milestone events

	CUSTOMER	EMPLOYEE (RP)	CARRIER	PRODUCT	SALES LOCATION	DELIVERY ADDRESS	WAREHOUSE	PROMOTION	ORDER ID (DD)	SHIP MODE	SHIPMENT NUMBER (DD)	
	who			what		where			why & how			
CUSTOMER ORDERS customer orders product	✱	✓		✓		✓	✱		✓	✱		
PRODUCT SHIPMENTS warehouse worker ships product	✓	✓	✓	✓		✓	✓		✓	✓	✱	

Figure 4-12

Adding *why* and *how* dimensions to shipments

Ask for the next
event but don't
worry about strict
chronology

The presence of common degenerate dimensions (transaction IDs) often signifies that events are milestones in a process sequence.

After completing shipments, your search for the next event begins anew. This can be the next one in sequence, or simply the next one the stakeholders think of when they see popular dimensions like CUSTOMER and PRODUCT on the matrix. If their next event doesn't sound like the very next one chronologically, don't worry, just go with their train of thought—don't try and derail it. Missing 'next' events are much easier to spot as gaps on the matrix once you add the events you are freely given. Imagine that the Pomegranate stakeholders respond to your next **"Who does what?"** question with:

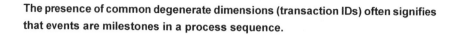

> **Customer returns product.**

Exceptional steps
within a process are
documented
by bracketing their
event names

Figure 4-13 shows the matrix after PRODUCT RETURNS have been added along with its new PROBLEM REASON dimension. PRODUCT RETURNS are dependent on PRODUCT SHIPMENTS because customers have to order and receive products to be able to return them, but this sequence of events is exceptional: only a small percentage of orders are returned. You can document an optional or exceptional event within a process by bracketing it. This acts as a visual clue that you might want to handle the event separately to mandatory/unexceptional process milestones. For example, order and shipment could be combined in a worthwhile evolving order event because almost every order leads to a shipment, but the much smaller number of returns might be better treated as part of a separate customer support process rather than complicate orders. Exceptional events often indicate that there may be missing events and other processes that need to be considered.

Figure 4-13
Adding PRODUCT
RETURNS to the
matrix

	CUSTOMER	EMPLOYEE (RP)	CARRIER	PRODUCT	SALES LOCATION	DELIVERY ADDRESS	WAREHOUSE	PROBLEM REASON	PROMOTION	ORDER ID (DD)	SHIP MODE	SHIPMENT NUMBER (DD)
	who	who		what	where	where	where	why & how	why & how	why & how	why & how	why & how
CUSTOMER ORDERS customer orders product	✱	✓		✓		✓	✱		✓		✱	
PRODUCT SHIPMENTS warehouse worker ships product	✓	✓	✓	✓			✓	✓			✓	✓	✱
(PRODUCT RETURNS) customer returns product	✓			✓			✓		✓	✓		

Stakeholders occasionally find it difficult to decide which of two events happen first. Problematic "chicken or egg" events can occur simultaneously, loop each other, or be mutually exclusive (e.g., payments or returns). Don't get hung up on perfect sequencing, just put them next to one another, above or below the events, on the matrix, that everyone can agree they precede or follow.

Using the Matrix to Find Missing Events

When PRODUCT RETURNS has been added to the matrix, you can check for a missing event in the sequence by asking the obvious question: "Does anything happen *after* PRODUCT SHIPMENTS but *before* PRODUCT RETURNS?" Alternatively, you can get stakeholders thinking about what might belong in the gap, if there is one, by asking:

> **Does anything difficult, costly, valuable, or time-consuming happen between shipments and returns?**

Check for missing events by looking for gaps on the matrix

This might prompt stakeholders to think of CUSTOMER COMPLAINTS. If they agree that this event represents the start of a new process you would add it to the matrix as in Figure 4-14, which now shows PRODUCT RETURNS indented as a milestone in that process. Notice that the exceptional step brackets have been removed from PRODUCT RETURNS. Not every complaint leads to a return; for example, a complaint might be that a product hasn't been *delivered* yet (another event: "Carrier *delivers* Product", to add to the matrix), but a high enough percentage of complaints do result in returns, enough for stakeholders to view return date as a standard milestone of this new customer support process.

Look for large time gaps or value changes. They often represent the start of a new process

	who			what			where		why & how				
	CUSTOMER	EMPLOYEE (RP)	CARRIER	PRODUCT	PRODUCT TYPE (RU)	SALES LOCATION	DELIVERY ADDRESS	WAREHOUSE	PROMOTION	PROBLEM REASON	ORDER ID (DD)	SHIP MODE	SHIPMENT NUMBER (DD)
SALES TARGETS salesperson has product type target	✓				✓	✓							
CUSTOMER ORDERS customer orders product	*	✓		✓	✓	✓	*			✓		*	
PRODUCT SHIPMENTS warehouse worker ships product	✓	✓	✓	✓	✓		✓	✓			✓	✓	*
CARRIER DELIVERIES carrier delivers product	✓		✓	✓	✓		✓				✓	✓	✓
CUSTOMER COMPLAINTS customer complains about product	✓	✓		✓	✓				✓	✓			
PRODUCT RETURNS customer returns product	✓			✓	✓			✓		✓	✓		

Figure 4-14
CARRIER DELIVERIES, CUSTOMER COMPLAINTS and SALES TARGETS added to the matrix

Trying to find the correct position for an event within a process sequence can often help to expose additional events that represent the end of one process and the start of another. In our example, deliveries are the final milestones for *most orders*. Complaints and returns, on the other hand, are thankfully *not part of many orders*. The indentation in Figure 4-14 shows how CARRIER DELIVERIES completes the order fulfillment process and CUSTOMER COMPLAINTS begins a new customer support process. Documenting the first and last events of a process is particularly important. They represent cause and effect, origin and outcome and are the most

Model the first and last events in a process. They are the basis for almost all process performance measurement basic events needed to measure process performance—stakeholders will not be satisfied until you have modeled at least some of these events.

Add rollup (**RU**) dimensions next to their base dimensions and tick all the events that can be rolled up to their level

Figure 4-14 shows another new event: SALES TARGETS. It is not part of the order or customer support processes, hence no indentation, but stakeholders believe that sales targets drive orders so they have placed the event before CUSTOMER ORDERS in time/value sequence. From its main clause "Salesperson has product type target" it is immediately obvious that it should take advantage of the conformed role-playing EMPLOYEE dimension. But it cannot reuse the conformed PRODUCT dimension because stakeholders have stated that targets are set for product types not for individual products. The good news is that the event can still be conformed with PRODUCT at the product type level because this is a conformed PRODUCT attribute. You record this by adding a rollup dimension PRODUCT TYPE [**RU**] (immediately to the right of PRODUCT, if possible, to denote that it is derived from it) and ticking it for each PRODUCT-related event to denote that they can be compared to SALES TARGETS at the PRODUCT TYPE level. There is no need to model the rollup any further, at the moment, because it will not contain any new attributes, just PRODUCT TYPE and any other conformed product attributes above it in the product hierarchy, such as SUBCATEGORY and CATEGORY already defined in PRODUCT.

Using the Matrix to Find Missing Event Details

Use your final set of dimensions to recheck events for missing details

Once you have added all the events that the stakeholders are currently interested in (or as many as time permits), it is well worth making one more quick pass of each event, now that you have built up a collection of potential conformed dimensions, to see if you can get any more reuse from them. For each event, point at each dimension it doesn't reference and ask:

> **Why isn't this dimension a detail of this event?**

Simply pointing at each empty cell in turn like this takes full advantage of the physical proximity of all the events and dimensions on the same spreadsheet or whiteboard that the matrix provides and can often jolt someone into spotting a valuable missing conformed detail at the last minute.

Playing the Event Rating Game

Ask stakeholders to rate the importance of each event

You now need the stakeholders help to decide which event(s) to implement in your next release. To do this add an extra column to the matrix (as in Figure 4-15) to record event *importance* and ask the stakeholders to rate each event based on a few simple rules:

- Higher rated events are more important and should be implemented sooner —if possible.

- *Every* event gets an importance rating.

- Every event gets a *different* importance rating, except…

- Events that have been completed have an importance of 0.

- Events that are truly unimportant (currently) can all have an importance of 100.

- Events are rated in 100 importance point increments, e.g. 100, 200 (you'll see why the gaps are useful shortly).

- The importance rating is only used to sort events by importance not measure their relative business value. If Event A has importance 100 and Event B has importance 500, B is simply more important than A, not five times more important.

Figure 4-15
Event importance
rating

	Importance	Estimate	CUSTOMER	EMPLOYEE (RP)	CARRIER
				who	
SALES TARGETS salesperson has product type target	400		✓		
CUSTOMER ORDERS customer orders product	600		✱	✓	
PRODUCT SHIPMENTS warehouse worker ships product	500		✓	✓	✓
CARRIER DELIVERIES carrier delivers product	300		✓		✓
CUSTOMER COMPLAINTS customer complains about product	100		✓	✓	
PRODUCT RETURNS customer returns product	100		✓		

If you are using the downloadable BEAM✲ matrix template, you can hide and unhide the built in planning columns (Figure 4-15) which include *event* importance and planning rows (Figure 4-16) which in turn include *dimension* importance. Before you use the importance column to actually sort the event rows make sure you fill in the event sequence column first, so that you can re-sort events back into time/value sequence when you have finished.

As soon as the importance rules are understood, start by rating the initial event that the stakeholders modeled. Theoretically, this should be the most important event so you might suggest an importance based on that starting position; for example, if the matrix describes 10 events that haven't been implemented yet

Start by rating the initial event highly. Then rate other events relative to it

suggest an importance of 1,000. This event may not stay the most important; stakeholders can easily give a higher importance to an event that was modeled in less detail at the last minute but this opening gambit gets the rating game going. In Figure 4-15 the initial CUSTOMER ORDERS event has remained the most important and is followed by PRODUCT SHIPMENTS rather than CARRIER DELIVERIES (perhaps stakeholders realize that data will not be readily available from carriers). Stakeholders have also rated the customer support events as currently unimportant!

You may not wish to ask all the modelstorming stakeholders to vote on importance. Arguments may ensue! If you are using Scrum to manage your agile DW/BI development, prioritizing requirements is the role of the *product owner* who manages the *product backlog*. A subset of the stakeholders can act as a proxy for the product owner and provide input to the product backlog prior to release and sprint planning meetings. At these meetings, event importance will be adjusted by the product owner in the cold light of source data profiling results and the DW team's ETL task estimates.

Add a dimension importance row and rate each dimension higher than its most important event

When all events have been rated and any tied positions resolved—remember important events should have unique importance ratings—add a dimension importance row to the matrix (as in Figure 4-16). Dimensions are rated after events because dimensions are only important if the events that use them are important. Now that the stakeholders have decided which events are important, you rate each dimension higher than its most important event, because it must be implemented before any fact table based on the event can be implemented (due to foreign key dependencies).

Dimension Rating Rules

Dimension importance rating follows the same rules as event rating with a few additions/variations:

- A dimension should be rated higher than its highest importance event, unless it has already been implemented, in which case it should be 0. E.g., if Event B with importance 500 is the highest rated event using Dimension C then C must have an importance between 505 and 595.

- A dimension should be rated lower than any higher importance events that do not use it.

- Dimensions are rated in 5 or 10 importance point increments, so they fit between events and BI functional requirements (report user stories). Hence the reason for the 100 point gaps between events.

- Rate conformed dimensions higher than non-conformed dimensions.

- If an event's importance is changed its dimensions must be re-rated.

In Figure 4-16, dimensions have been rated by first sorting events by importance. CUSTOMERS ORDERS and PRODUCT SHIPMENTS have come top so their importance points (600 or 500) are copied to their dimensions. Stakeholders have then rated order dimensions 610-670 and shipment dimensions 510-540. This numbering scheme allows dimensions and events to be sorted correctly when transferred to a single product backlog.

Dimensions and events are rated so they sort correctly on a single product backlog

	Importance	Estimate	CUSTOMER (who)	EMPLOYEE (RP) (who)	CARRIER (who)	PRODUCT (what)	PRODUCT TYPE (RU) / SALES LOCATION (what)	DELIVERY ADDRESS (where)	WAREHOUSE (where)	(where)	PROBLEM REASON (why & how)	PROMOTION (why & how)	ORDER ID (DD)	SHIP MODE	SHIPMENT NUMBER (DD)
Importance			660	650	510	670		620	630	530	610	100	640	520	540
Estimate															
CUSTOMER ORDERS customer orders product	600		∗	✓		✓		✓	✓	∗			✓		∗

Figure 4-16
Dimension importance rating

In subsequent sprints, the stakeholders/product owner will need to prioritize BI reporting requirements too. While these "report user stories" are more important to stakeholders than data models they must be rated below the star schemas backlog items they are used to query, as in Figure 4-17 which shows a product backlog containing prioritized reporting, dimension and event requirements.

BI reporting requirements must be rated lower than the events they measure

CALENDAR dimension	680
PRODUCT dimension	670
CUSTOMER dimension	660
CUSTOMER ORDERS event	**600**
LARGE ORDER report	595
YTD ORDERS report	590
CARRIER dimension	510
PRODUCT SHIPMENTS event	**500**
LATE SHIPPING report	495

Figure 4-17
A DW/BI product backlog

For more advice on Scrum, sprint planning and time-boxing read *Scrum and XP from the Trenches*, Henrik Kniberg (InfoQ.com 2007).

When you have finished rating all the events and dimensions on the matrix, if the most important events (top 1 or 2 usually) and all their dimensions have been modeled with examples, your modeling work is done, for now, and you can bring the modelstorm to an end. You have reached point B with enough information. However, if matrix only events have been rated highly important you may have one or two more events to model in detail before you can proceed to star schema design and sprint planning.

When you have modeled the most important events and dimensions *with examples*, the modelstorm is complete. If not...

Modeling the Next Detailed Event

Create a BEAM✱ table for the next important event and ask for its *when* detail

When you discover an event on the matrix, such as PRODUCT SHIPMENTS (with an importance of 500), which needs to be modeled in detail, you begin by creating a new BEAM✱ table and copying the event main clause to it. But before you copy any further details, ask for a new *when* detail to help tell interesting event stories. For PRODUCT SHIPMENTS you ask:

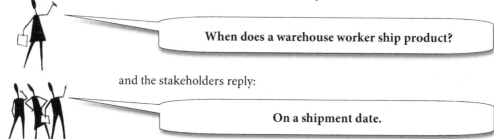

When does a warehouse worker ship product?

and the stakeholders reply:

On a shipment date.

Reuse conformed dimensions and examples wherever possible

Add this to the table, as in Figure 4-18, and ask for event stories just as you did with the initial CUSTOMER ORDERS event. The only difference this time is that you will be using candidate conformed dimensions that already have examples. You want to re-use these examples where possible, to illustrate the conformance.

Figure 4-18
New PRODUCT SHIPMENTS event table

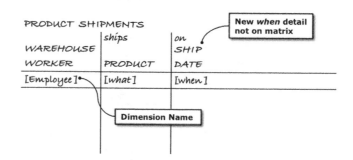

Reusing Conformed Dimensions and Examples

Conformed examples relate new event stories to existing stories

When you use conformed dimensions to describe new events, you should reuse their existing examples where applicable to help relate new event stories to existing ones. Once you get into the habit of using conformed examples to show that the same customers, products, employees, etc. are involved, you will soon want to minimize the drudgery of duplicating the same examples again and again.

Don't use cryptic business keys to speed up event story telling

You might be tempted to speed up the process by using shorter business keys rather than rewriting dimension subjects out in longhand. This may even appear to be good data modeling practice because event tables will then contain foreign key references to the dimension business keys that will surely make them easier to translate into physical tables. But this rush to physically model events is counterproductive. Business keys are mostly cryptic codes that will rob event tables and stories of their readability and descriptive power, and—as you will see in Chapter 5—business keys do not make the best foreign keys (or primary keys) in a dimensional data warehouse.

Using Abbreviations in Event Stories

Instead of business keys, use *abbreviated examples*: abbreviations or shortening of previously modeled examples, as in Figure 4-19 which shows shipment stories with abbreviated employee and product examples. The advantage of abbreviations over business keys is that they keep event stories readable while saving whiteboard space and speeding up story telling. You can also expand them to full examples later in your documented model relatively easily with a "replace all".

Use abbreviated *examples* to keep stories brief *and* readable

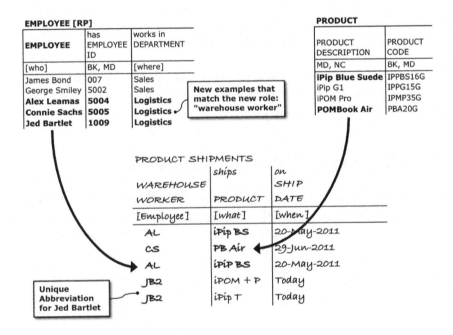

Figure 4-19
Using abbreviations to tell event stories

To avoid confusing abbreviated stories, keep abbreviations unique within dimensions. If an abbreviation is not unique, just add a sequence number to it. For example, if your two favorite employees are James Bond and Jed Bartlett, they can appear in stories as JB1 and JB2. Of course employee James Bond is exceptional; his business key, employee ID 007, is so well known that it is more descriptive than his initials, and could be used very successfully in many eventful stories.

Keep abbreviations unique by adding a sequence number if necessary

Provide stakeholders with handouts of previously modeled BEAM✲ dimension tables and an 'up to date' event matrix to help them reuse conformed examples and decode abbreviations. the dimension tables need not show every attribute; just the example dimension subjects (which get abbreviated) and one or two defining characteristics that identify role subtypes, such as warehouse employees and sales employees.

Adding New Examples to Conformed Dimensions

Ask for any new examples needed to cover the five event story themes and describe new dimensional roles

You not only want stories to relate new events to existing events, you also want them to tell you as much as possible about each new event detail. You make sure that they do by asking for *typical, different, repeat, missing,* and *group* themed stories, as described in Chapter 2. To cover all these themes and illustrate new roles for role-playing dimensions you will need examples that are not present in any BEAM✲ tables modeled so far.

Test conformed dimensions by adding new examples

When stakeholders give you new examples try adding them to the appropriate dimension before using them in event stories. Apart from allowing you to use the examples by abbreviation, filling out their dimensional attributes is also a great test of conformance that helps you to spot missing or non-conformed attributes. For role-playing dimensions, you may have to adjust some existing attributes to match new roles; e.g., COMMISSION is a mandatory (**MD**) attribute of SALESPERSON, but would be a non-mandatory exclusive (**X**) attribute of a conformed EMPLOYEE [RP] dimension that must play the role of warehouse worker as well as salesperson.

Asking for examples encourages everyone to define and use conformed dimensions. Why make up new example values when you can copy them from a conformed BEAM✲ dimension table?

Modeling New Details and Dimensions

Ask for additional *when* details before copying more dimensions from the matrix

After you have filled in the themed examples for *who* (WAREHOUSE WORKER), *what* (PRODUCT), and *when* (SHIP DATE), proceed through the *7Ws* in BEAM✲ order (see Figure 2-2) by asking for any other *when* details before moving on to *who,* and *what,* and *where.* For each of these *W-types* copy the relevant dimensions, one at a time from the matrix, and ask for examples.

Don't forget to check for additional *who, what, where, why* and *how* details too and add them to the matrix

Before you move on to the next *W-type* always check for additional details of the current type. Seeing the event stories build up will often prompt stakeholders to suggest additional details they couldn't think of when modeling at the matrix summary level. As soon as stakeholders confirm any additional *who, what, where, why* or *how* detail with relevant examples, add them to the matrix where they too might become conformed dimensions.

Mark new details with a [?] type as a reminder to model their dimensional attributes

Figure 4-20 shows four *who,* and *where* details added to the shipping event. CUSTOMER and DELIVERY ADDRESS, with their highly abbreviated examples, are conformed dimensions, while CARRIER and WAREHOUSE are new and have not been modeled as dimension tables yet. Any new details/dimensions, like these, can be marked as type [?] as a reminder that, while they maybe on the matrix, they still need to be modeled at the attribute level, with examples, when the event is completed.

Figure 4-20

Adding details to the
shipment event

PRODUCT SHIPMENTS

WAREHOUSE WORKER	ships PRODUCT	on SHIP DATE	to CUSTOMER	using CARRIER	from WAREHOUSE	to DELIVERY ADDRESS
[Employee]	[what]	[when]	[who]	[who ?]	[where ?]	[where]
AL	iPip BS	20-May-2011	JBP	Fedex	Baton Rouge	TN
CS	PB Air	29-Jun-2011	VL	UPS	Dublin	UK
AL	iPip BS	20-May-2011	JBP	Fedex	Baton Rouge	TN
JB2	iPOM + P	Today	US S	DHL	New Jersey	DC
JB2	iPip T	Today	US S	DHL	New Jersey	DC

? : new dimension, yet to be modeled in detail

Conformed dimensions using abbreviated examples

Following the *where* details, you ask for the *how manys*. These quantitative details do not feature on the event matrix, just like the *when* details, and are the main reason for modeling the event in table form; the matrix shows how events are described using (conformed) dimensions. The *how many* examples show how events can be measured.

Ask *how many?* to discover the event measures not modeled on the matrix

In Figure 4-21, two new quantity details: SHIPPED QUANTITY and SHIP-MENT COST have been added, along with the ORDER ID *why* detail. The quantity examples are new, supplied by stakeholders, but the order ids are copied from the previously modeled CUSTOMER ORDERS event because ORDER ID was identi-fied, on the matrix, as a conformed degenerate dimension linking the events. With that existing *why* filled in, you ask for additional *whys*, remembering to ask why quantities vary. If you know that an event, such as shipment, is a process milestone you should ask why similar details vary (or do not vary) within the process; for example, you might ask:

Add any existing *why* dimensions from the matrix and ask additional *why* questions to explain story variations in the measures

Why can SHIPPED QUANTITY differ from ORDER QUANTITY?

and get the answer:

Several partial order shipments can be made when product stock is too low to completely fulfil an order line.

This tells you there is a 1:M relationship between orders and shipment. It also tells you that you haven't yet found a combination of details that would make a ship-ment event unique. You record this by adding a new *repeat* story to the table, as in Figure 4-21, which demonstrates there can be multiple identical shipment events for the same order line item by duplicating the granular details (ORDER ID, PRODUCT) of an original order (ORD5466).

Why answers can represent the need for additional examples as well as new *why* details

Figure 4-21

Adding new quantities, a *why/how* detail from a previous event and an additional *repeat* story

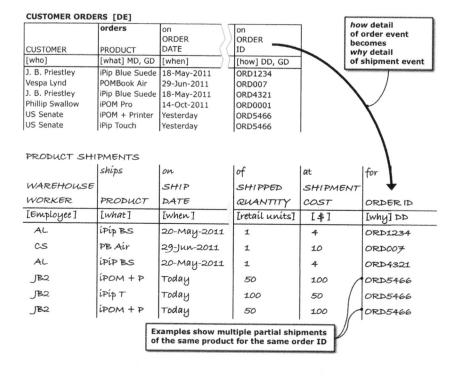

CUSTOMER ORDERS [DE]				
	orders	on ORDER DATE		on ORDER ID
CUSTOMER	PRODUCT			
[who]	[what] MD, GD	[when]		[how] DD, GD
J. B. Priestley	iPip Blue Suede	18-May-2011		ORD1234
Vespa Lynd	POMBook Air	29-Jun-2011		ORD007
J. B. Priestley	iPip Blue Suede	18-May-2011		ORD4321
Phillip Swallow	iPOM Pro	14-Oct-2011		ORD0001
US Senate	iPOM + Printer	Yesterday		ORD5466
US Senate	iPip Touch	Yesterday		ORD5466

> **how** detail of order event becomes **why** detail of shipment event

PRODUCT SHIPMENTS					
	ships	on	of	at	for
WAREHOUSE		SHIP	SHIPPED	SHIPMENT	
WORKER	PRODUCT	DATE	QUANTITY	COST	ORDER ID
[Employee]	[what]	[when]	[retail units]	[$]	[why] DD
AL	iPip BS	20-May-2011	1	4	ORD1234
CS	PB Air	29-Jun-2011	1	10	ORD007
AL	iPip BS	20-May-2011	1	4	ORD4321
JB2	iPOM + P	Today	50	100	ORD5466
JB2	iPip T	Today	100	50	ORD5466
JB2	iPOM + P	Today	50	100	ORD5466

> **Examples show multiple partial shipments of the same product for the same order ID**

Concentrate on completing the event with the *when*, *how many* and granularity details not recorded elsewhere

Thanks to its ORDER ID *why* detail you have the option to embellish PRODUCT SHIPMENTS with additional order dimensions, but because these dimensions are already well documented in the CUSTOMER ORDERS table and on the matrix, you can, if pressed for time, add them later without stakeholders involvement. Just make sure you let the stakeholders know you will be doing this. While you have their attention now you should concentrate the modelstorm on capturing brand new shipment details, especially the *when*, *how many* and granularity details not recorded on the matrix. You also need to allow time for modelstorming the attributes of any new dimensions (the details you temporally marked [?]).

You can add any useful order dimensions to shipments but you should avoid the *how many* details, such as ORDER QUANTITY or REVENUE, because the 1:M relationship between orders and shipments would cause these measures to be overstated when summarized; e.g., 2 partial shipments events that both record (i.e. duplicate) the original ORDER QUANTITY of 10 units will produce a total of 20 units with double the correct order REVENUE.

Don't copy measures from one event to another. This can lead to facts that double count

Order measures are better left in the order event and its subsequent order fact table at their true granularity (the order line item) rather than also stored at the shipped line item. In Chapter 8, we cover how you would instead combine shipments with orders to produce a single evolving order event and model the additional measures that provides. For now, we will press on and complete the shipment event with *how* details.

Completing the Event

Copy the *how* details SHIP MODE and SHIPMENT NUMBER from the matrix to the event table and ask for examples—as neither has been modeled in table form before. The SHIPMENT NUMBER examples should confirm that you have finally found a detail that can differentiate two partial order shipments of the same product to the same customer on the same day. With this final piece of the puzzle you can define the granularity and type of PRODUCT SHIPMENTS. The granularity is a combination of SHIPMENT NUMBER, ORDER ID, and PRODUCT, and is recorded by marking these details as **GD** (Granular Details/Dimensions). From a business perspective this granularity can be described as "Shipment note line items". This granularity makes the story type **DE** (discrete event). Figure 4-22 shows this information added to the final spreadsheet version of the event table.

When you finish modeling an event table don't forget to model dimension tables for any details that you have marked as [?]. You still need to define some dimensional attributes for these details, before ending the modelstorm.

Complete the event table by recording event granularity and type

PRODUCT SHIPMENTS [DE]

Completed event is discrete

WAREHOUSE WORKER	ships PRODUCT	on SHIP DATE	for CUSTOMER	using CARRIER	from WAREHOUSE	to DELIVERY ADDRESS
[employee]	[what] **GD**	[when]	[who]	[who]	[where]	[where]
AL	iPip BS	20-May-2011	JBP	Fedex	Baton Rouge	TN
CS	PB Air	29-Jun-2011	VL	UPS	Dublin	UK
AL	ipip BS	20-May-2011	JBP	Fedex	Baton Rouge	TN
JB2	iPOM + P	Today	US S	DHL	New Jersey	DC
JB2	iPip T	Today	US S	DHL	New Jersey	DC
JB2	iPOM + P	Today	US S	DHL	New Jersey	DC

of SHIPPED QUANTITY	at SHIPMENT COST	for ORDER ID	using **SHIP MODE**	with **SHIPMENT NUMBER**
[retail units]	[$]	[why] DD, **GD**	[How]	[How] DD, **GD**
1	4	ORD1234	Standard	SN001
1	10	ORD007	Standard	SN002
1	4	ORD4321	Standard	SN001
50	100	ORD5466	Express	SN003
100	50	ORD5466	Express	SN003
50	100	ORD5466	Express	SN004

GD - Granularity Detail
The event granularity is shipment line item – a combination of Shipment Number, Order ID and Product

Figure 4-22
Completed PRODUCT SHIPMENTS event

You might be tempted to start a modelstorming session by using a matrix to model and rapidly prioritize multiple events. While this can work well with stakeholders who are already familiar with the process, it can be too abstract for some brand new modelstormers. Remember many BI stakeholders would prefer to define reports rather than data models. Starting with an event table and example data (even if it is not for the most important event) that looks like a report can help stakeholders get the matrix and appreciate its value.

Sufficient Events?

Merge subject area matrices to provide a DW-wide overview of conformance

After the earlier manufacturing events in Figure 4-6 are added to the sales targets, order processing and customer support events of Figure 4-14, the matrix should look like Figure 4-23. If this matrix inspires you to reuse more dimensions, particularly dimensions from process initiating events such as PURCHASE ORDERS or CUSTOMER ORDERS that could be carried over to their dependent milestone events, then the matrix is doing its job. It should encourage you to maximize dimensional reuse to make each event as descriptive as possible. In addition, if the similarities of the dimensions of PRODUCT SHIPMENTS and WAREHOUSE SHIPMENTS makes you think that they might actually be the same type of event, then the matrix is also doing its job. It may turn out that wholesale shipments to resellers are quite different to retail shipments to consumers: These events might be handled by completely different systems. Even so, the matrix is again doing its job in highlighting an opportunity to conform the dimensions of both events, just in case there is business value in doing so.

The event matrix is a great technique for upholding the agile value of *working software over comprehensive documentation*. The event matrix is enough comprehensive documentation to help you create working software based on conformed dimensions but if you do need more documentation, link to it from your event matrix spreadsheet cells; e.g., events and dimensions can be hyper-linked to their BEAM✲ tables or star schema models.

A matrix may never contain every event and not every event it does contain will be implemented

Although the event matrix in Figure 4-23 might be complete enough for several DW/BI development sprints, is it the complete matrix for the Pomegranate Data Warehouse? What about customer invoicing and payment events after orders, or product configuration prior to shipments? What about events in other subject areas such as HR, finance, R&D? Many of these events may be out of scope for sometime, or will never capture sufficiently interesting additional details to be worth measuring.

The role of the matrix is to identify the conformed dimensions for the next release

Rather than initially modeling every possible event on a matrix, agile DW designers concentrate on making the matrix complete *enough* for the next release. When a matrix contains enough detail to help prioritize the right events for the next release and understand their conformed dimensions that will be used again in future releases, its job, *for now*, is done.

Put a large version of the event matrix on the wall where everyone can see it. Regardless of your preferred methods for modeling events and dimensions: BEAM✲ tables or ER notation, flipcharts, whiteboards, or projected spreadsheets, viewing more than a few details at once is impossible. When event and dimension tables cover all your walls, or are buried in spreadsheets, a matrix enables stakeholders and the DW team to see the entire design at a glance.

Figure 4-23
A complete event matrix?

The event matrix below plots each business event (row) against the dimensions it references (columns), grouped under **who**, **what**, **where** and **why & how**. A star (*) marks a primary/degenerate dimension and a check (✓) marks a participating dimension.

Dimension (group)	MANUFACTURING PLANS — Plant builds Product	BILL OF MATERIALS — Product contains Component	PURCHASE ORDERS — Employee purchases Component	COMPONENT DELIVERIES — Supplier delivered Component	SUPPLIER PAYMENTS — Employee pays Supplier	COMPONENT INVENTORY LEVELS — Plant stocks Component	QA TESTS — Employee tests Product	MANUFACTURING PROCESSES — Plant runs Process	PRODUCT INVENTORY LEVELS — Warehouse stocks Products	WAREHOUSE SHIPMENTS — Carrier ships Product	SALES TARGETS — salesperson has product type target	CUSTOMER ORDERS — customer orders product	PRODUCT SHIPMENTS — warehouse worker ships product	CARRIER DELIVERIES — carrier delivers product	CUSTOMER COMPLAINTS — customer complains about product	PRODUCT RETURNS — customer returns product
why & how — PO [DD]			*	✓	✓											
SHIPMENT NUMBER [DD]										*			✓	✓		
ORDER ID [DD]												*	✓	✓	✓	✓
SHIP MODE										*					✓	✓
PROBLEM REASON															✓	✓
PROMOTION			✓							✓						
where — CONTRACT												*	✓	✓		
DELIVERY ADDRESS										✓		✓	✓	✓		
SALES LOCATION											✓	✓		✓		
WAREHOUSE									✓	✓			✓			
PLANT	✓		✓			✓		*								
what — TEST							*									
PROCESS	✓		✓			✓	✓	✓	✓	✓	✓	✓	✓	✓	✓	✓
PRODUCT TYPE [RU]	✓	*				✓	✓	✓	✓	✓	*	✓	✓	✓	✓	✓
PRODUCT	*	*	✓	✓	✓	✓	✓	✓	✓	✓		✓	✓	✓	✓	✓
COMPONENT		*	*	✓	✓	*	✓	✓	✓	✓						
who — CUSTOMER										*		✓	✓		✓	✓
CARRIER										✓			✓	✓		
RESELLER																
SUPPLIER			✓	*	*											
EMPLOYEE [RP]	✓		✓	✓	✓	✓	✓	✓	✓		✓	✓	✓		✓	

EVENT (who does what)

Keep the event matrix up to date! It's not an initial planning tool or a one-time modeling technique. Use it to document the ongoing data warehouse design. Refer to it and update it whenever you are modelstorming. A well-maintained matrix acts as a constant reminder to everyone to reuse and enhance conformed dimensions.

Summary

- "Just barely good enough" dimensional modeling can lead to the early and frequent deployment of data marts that answer current departmental reporting requirements, but it also stores up *technical debt*, in the form of incompatible data silos that cannot support cross-process analysis and enterprise level BI. Due to the large data volumes associated with DW/BI, repaying this debt can be ruinous.

- To avoid silo data marts and reduce technical debt, agile DW designers need to *model ahead* of the current development sprints and release plans, just enough to identify and define *conformed dimensions*. These reusable components of a dimensional model enable drill-across reporting by providing the consistent row headers and filters needed to combine and compare measures from multiple business processes. A well documented, well publicized and well maintained set of conformed dimensions form a data warehouse bus architecture that supports the incremental development of truly agile data marts.

- Conformed dimensions are single dimensions tables or synchronized copies shared by multiple star schemas. They can also be *swappable* [SD] subsets or *rollups* [RU], derived from a base dimension, conformed at the attribute level with identical business meaning and contents. Generalized conformed dimensions that play multiple roles in the same or different events are referred to as *role-playing* [RP] dimensions.

- Agile dimensional modelers define conformed dimensions by modeling *with* examples, *with* business stakeholders. BEAM✲ example data stories highlight the value of conformance to the very people who can make it happen politically. Examples can quickly expose the inconsistent business terms that would hinder conformance.

- The *event matrix* is a modeling and planning tool that documents the relationship between events and dimensions. It acts as a storyboard for an entire data warehouse design showing just enough detail to help identify the most valuable conformed dimensions and prioritize their development.

- Listing events in *time/value sequence* on an event matrix helps you discover missing events by highlighting large time gaps or value jumps in process workflows. It also helps you identify strict chronological *process sequences*: candidate evolving events, that combine all the *milestone events* of a business process, to support end-to-end process performance measurement.

- When modeling new events, *abbreviated examples* allow you to quickly tell stories by reusing conformed examples where applicable. Unlike codes, abbreviations help to keep stories brief *and* readable for stakeholders. They also support the validation, reuse and enhancement of conformed dimensions.

5

MODELING STAR SCHEMAS

> We are all in the gutter, but some of us are looking at the stars.
> — *Oscar Wilde*

In this chapter we describe the star schema design process for converting BEAM✳ models into flexible and efficient dimensional data warehouse models.

The agile approach that we take begins with *test-first design*, by using *data profiling* techniques to verify the BEAM✳ model against the data available in source systems. This results in an *annotated model* which documents source data characteristics and issues. This is used for *model review* with stakeholders and development *sprint planning* with the DW/BI team.

Next, the revised BEAM✳ model is translated into a logical dimensional model by adding *surrogate keys*. The resulting facts and dimensions are documented by drawing *enhanced star schemas* using a combination of BEAM✳ and ER notation.

Finally, the star schemas are used to generate physical data warehouse schemas which are validated by BI prototyping and documented by creating a physical dimensional matrix.

This chapter is a guide to:

Verifying BEAM✳ models against available data sources

Converting BEAM✳ models into star schemas

Validating DW designs by prototyping

- Data profiling to verify stakeholder data requirements
- Annotating BEAM✳ models with data sources and profile metrics
- Reviewing annotated models and planning development sprints
- Converting BEAM✳ models into logical/physical dimensional models
- The importance of data warehouse surrogate keys
- Designing for slowly changing dimensions
- Defining additive facts
- Drawing enhanced star schema diagrams and creating physical schemas
- BI Prototyping to validate dimensional models
- Creating a physical dimensional matrix

Chapter 5 Topics
At a Glance

129

Agile Data Profiling

Profile candidate
data sources for the
prioritized events
and dimensions, to
discover their data
structure, content
and quality

The first step in translating a BEAM✳ model into a viable data warehouse design is
to use *agile data profiling* to identify candidate data sources for the model's prioritized events and dimensions. Data profiling is the process of examining data
sources to learn about their structure, content, and data quality. Agile data profiling (see Figure 5-1) is also:

- **Targeted** to the candidate data sources for the business events and conformed
  dimensions that the stakeholders have prioritized for the next release, rather
  than *all* available data sources.

- **Done early**, as a data modeling task to help define the dimensional model.

*Agile data profiling
is done early as a
modeling activity –
before a target DW
schema is created*

- **Done frequently**, to ensure that the model responds to change; this is especially important for new data sources that are being developed in parallel with
  the data warehouse.

- **Done by DW/BI team members** who will load the data, to give them a feel for
  its complexity that will help them with their ETL task estimates.

- **Recorded in the business model** so that data profiles can be used to review
  that BEAM✳ BI data requirements model with the stakeholders, before any
  technical data models are proposed.

Figure 5-1
Agile data profiling

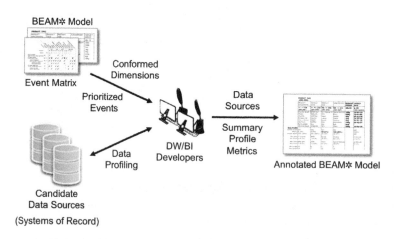

The most expensive and painful way to discover the data profile of an operational
source is to create an idealized target schema, attempt to ETL the source into the
target and record all the errors. Don't make this extremely late/non-existent data
profiling mistake. Agile data warehouse designers never create a detailed physical
model before profiling a source, unless they are deliberately doing *proactive
DW/BI design* to help define a brand new source.

Agile data profiling is a form of test-driven (or test-first) design (TDD). Profiling the source data provides you with metrics that can be used to test the fit of a data warehouse model and the content of a data warehouse database before you develop your SQL DDL (data definition language) and ETL code. When profiling isn't possible yet, a proactive DW/BI design can be viewed as an advanced test specification for the new operational system; a test that asks "can the system supply this data required for BI to this specification?"

Think of agile data profiling as a form of test-driven design

Identifying Candidate Data Sources

Data warehouses should be sourced from the most current and accurate data available, which, in practice, means identifying the *system-of-record (SoR)* for each fact and dimension. The system-of-record is the authoritative source for a particular type of data, such as The Payroll System for employee salary data. Data should be extracted directly from the system-of-record rather than downstream copies—from the original image of the data, rather than a "photocopy of a photocopy"—to reduce latency, system dependencies and data quality issues. The only exceptions should be where downstream systems explicitly improve data quality or unlock proprietary data formats.

Find the original system-of-record (SoR). Avoid downstream copies that introduce latency and data quality issues

For business events and the facts they provide, finding the system-of-record that creates and maintains the original transactions is relatively straightforward as there is often only one source system for a specific event type. For example, the claims processing system would be the obvious and possibly only choice for sourcing claim submission events. But where should claiming customers or insurance products be sourced from? Identifying the system-of-record for dimensions like these can be far more challenging.

Events/facts often have unique sources

Conformed dimensions are common to multiple business processes, which may themselves be implemented using a mixture of purchased enterprise software packages and bespoke in-house applications. It is not uncommon for several operational systems to independently maintain common reference data (sometimes called *master data*), such as Customers, Products, and Employees: the most valuable candidate conformed dimensions. You may need to profile systems that are outside of your present prioritized event scope to find the best source for a conformed dimension and spot any conflicts that would hamper conformance and reuse in the future. There may be no single best source for a dimension!

Conformed dimensions can have multiple sources that should be profiled to identify conformance conflicts

If you are fortunate, one system will have been declared as the system-of-record for each conformed dimension. But even then, facts (events) from other systems may use alternate business keys and carry additional dimensional attributes. If so, conforming ETL processes will need to match the keys from the systems-of-record and these other sources to create the "perfect" set of conformed dimensional attributes for the next sprint and ultimately to be able to load facts from these sources in the future.

Conforming ETL processes may have to merge sources to obtain all the necessary keys and attributes

Master data
management
systems help
dimensional
conformance

If you are *extremely* fortunate, you may have a *Master Data Management* (MDM) system that can help you identify the sources to profile for the most important conformed dimensions. MDM captures, cleanses, and synchronizes reference data across operational systems and can provide the cross-referenced business keys that ETL needs to conform multiple sources.

Profile early, before the data warehouse model exists or is updated, then any data quality issues you discover must be inherent in the established system-of-record not a problem with the newcomer database or ETL process used to build it. Do it the other way round and see who stakeholders (subconsciously) blame.

Data Profiling Techniques

Dedicated data
profiling tools are
incredibly powerful
but useful profiling
can be done using
SQL scripts and BI
tools

Data profiling has become common practice, and sophisticated profiling tools that can graphically visualize data sources are readily available as standalone applications and as modules of data modeling and ETL tools. But even without specialized tools, useful data profiling can be performed with simple SQL scripts, BI tools, and spreadsheets. A full discussion of data profiling techniques is beyond the scope of this book, but here are three basic checks for quickly assessing whether a data source is fit for purpose in the data warehouse:

Missing Values

The first, best test
for any source is
to count missing
values and calculate
the percentage
missing

Nothing (literally) illustrates the value of data profiling more than the early discovery of *missing* data that the stakeholders have deemed *mandatory*. Profile for missing values by counting the occurrence of Nulls or blanks in each candidate source column/field and calculating the percentage missing. Knowing how often the source data is Null is essential for any column—but especially for columns that have been identified as mandatory (**MD**) by the stakeholders. The SQL for counting Null values in a column is:

```
SELECT COUNT(*) FROM [SourceTable] WHERE [SourceColumn]
IS NULL
/*For character columns you should add:*/
or [SourceColumn] = ''
```

When you are working with non-database sources, such as flat files, you can map the source data as external tables, or perform basic ETL, with minimal transformations, to move it into DBMS tables, so that it can be profiled using SQL queries and BI tools.

Unique Values and Frequency

Another vital property of each candidate source is the number of *unique values* that it contains, and the frequency of each value. The SQL for counting unique values and calculating percentage unique is:

Check source columns for uniqueness to identify candidate keys, and hierarchy levels

```
SELECT COUNT(DISTINCT [SourceColumn]), COUNT(DISTINCT
[SourceColumn])/COUNT(*) * 100 FROM [SourceTable]
```

A source column with 100% unique values may be a good candidate for a business key while progressively lower percentage uniqueness can suggest that a set of columns represent a viable hierarchy. The SQL for ranking each value in a column by its frequency is:

```
SELECT [SourceColumn], COUNT(*) FROM [SourceTable]
GROUP BY [SourceColumn] ORDER BY 2
```

Source column value frequency can be graphed to help you spot columns that have no informational content in spite of not being Null. For example:

Graph source column values by frequency to discover poor quality content

- Columns where values are (almost) all the same (equal to the default)
- Empty or spaces only strings: the logical equivalent of Null
- Favorite dates for lazy data entry staff such as "1/1/01"

Data profiling requires full table scans, making some of the queries involved very resource intensive. You should avoid profiling a live operational system directly, because transactional performance can be adversely effected. This is clearly *not* the ideal first impression that any data warehouse team wants to make on operational support! Instead use snapshots (off-line copies) of the candidate data sources held on your own server or wait until after-hours.

Data Ranges and Lengths

The third category of simple data profiling tests identify source *data ranges* by querying the minimum, maximum and average values for numeric columns, the earliest and latest dates for datetime columns, and the shortest and longest strings for character columns. As well as helping you to define data types and set date ranges for the data warehouse these queries help you to spot outliers that often represent errors.

Query data ranges to help define data types and spot erroneous outlier values

If source data is reliably time-stamped, try grouping your data profiling queries by the Month, Quarter, or Year that the data was inserted/updated to see how data quality changes over time. The worst quality issues may be older than the historical scope of the warehouse—if you're lucky.

Automating Your Own Data Profiling Checks

Use SQL scripts
to generate data
profiling queries
that write their
results to a table

If you don't have a data profiling tool but you do have hundreds or thousands of source columns to check, you can use SQL-generated SQL to create data profiling tests that write their results to a table for analysis and presentation with BI tools. For example, the following SQL generates a set of INSERT statements that count Nulls for all columns in a schema, and write the results to a PROFILING _RESULTS table:

```
SELECT
'INSERT INTO PROFILING_RESULTS(TABLE_NAME, COLUMN_NAME,
MISSING_COUNT) SELECT '''
|| Table_Name
|| ''', '''
|| Column_Name
|| ''', COUNT(*) FROM '
|| Table_Name
|| ' WHERE '
|| Column_Name
|| ' IS NULL;'
FROM SYS.All_Tab_Columns
WHERE …
```

Search online for
ready-made
profiling scripts

Search online for "SQL data profiling script" and you should be able to find ready-made scripts that you can adapt for your database platform that will create all the tests recommended above and more and store the results in table form.

For in-depth coverage of data profiling, data quality measurement, and ETL techniques for continuously addressing data quality read:

- *Data Quality: The Accuracy Dimension*, Jack E. Olsen (Morgan Kaufmann, 2003)
- *The Data Warehouse ETL Toolkit*, Ralph Kimball, Joe Caserta (Wiley, 2004) Chapter 4, pages 113–147

No Source Yet: Proactive DW/BI Design

*Proactive DW/BI
designers* have to
cope without stable
data sources to
profile (yet)

What if there is no source to profile? This might not be a disaster, just a timing issue that needs to be anticipated. When agile BI systems are developed *in parallel* with new operational systems, a *proactive data warehouse design* can preempt operational system development or the installation of a packaged solution. Initially, there will be no indicative source data, possibly not even a source data model. Even when there is a well documented data model, as in the case of a packaged source, it can provide little useful information until the system has been configured and real data migrated to it.

Use *no source* as
an opportunity to
define the perfect
BI data source

ETL development is especially challenging when source data definitions are still fluid (non-existent), but this *does* present an opportunity for the agile data warehouse team to negotiate a better "data deal." The BEAM✲ model can be used to provide a detailed specification of business intelligence data requirements to the operational development team—while they are still in design mode. An agile operational team will welcome your early input to ensure their system will capture crucial business intelligence information needed by the data warehouse. If you have this level of cooperation you can press on with your dimensional design and ETL development.

When source database development lags behind data warehouse design, you can avoid delaying ETL development by defining extract file layouts, based on your BEAM✲ tables, and getting the operational development team to agree to their scheduled delivery. The agile ETL team can then get on with mapping these initially empty files to their star schema targets.

Once data take-on has begun for a new operational system you should profile the initial data *and* the previously agreed-upon extract files *as early as possible* to help the operational team keep to their promises. Trust no one!

Profile sources as soon as they are available

Annotating the Model with Data Profiling Results

The results of data profiling need to be presented to the stakeholders, so that they can review the data issues, decide on next steps, and if necessary reprioritize development based on the data realities. While data profiling tools can provide many useful graphical reports for the warehouse team, the profiling results for a BEAM✲ model are best delivered to the modelstorming stakeholders in a format that they are familiar with: the BEAM✲ model itself.

Present data profiles to stakeholders using the BEAM✲ format familiar to them

In Figure 5-2, the PRODUCT dimension has been extended with data profiling results showing counts and percentages for missing, unique, minimum and maximum values for each column. These simple profiling measures are a great start for highlighting potential issues, and can be augmented with more sophisticated measures and graphics generated by data profiling tools. The Figure 5-3 table has also been annotated to show data sources, unavailable details, new attributes and definition mismatches. The following sections describe the model review notation used.

BEAM✲ tables are extended to hold profiling metrics and annotated to highlight source data issues

Data Sources and Data Types

For each dimensional attribute and event detail, record its best candidate data source within braces ({ }); for example, {**ERP.Employee.Grade**} identifies the source system ERP, Employee table or file, and Grade column or field. If a single source table or file is the source for *all* columns in a BEAM✲ table you can add its name once to table header and only name the individual source column or field in each BEAM✲ column; For example, in Figure 5-2 the table header shows that the source for all PRODUCT attributes is the ERP system table PRD and the column type for SUBCATEGORY shows its source column to be PRD_SCAT. If a table or column will be derived from *multiple* sources, you can comma delimit them or use

For each column add its source name, data type and length

source reference numbers within the braces and expand upon the mapping rules in hyperlinked supporting documentation or footnotes. If there are conflicting sources for the same data, slash (/) delimit the choices. As well as identifying column sources you should also record their data type and length using the codes in tables 5-1.

Figure 5-2

Dimension table annotated with data sources and profiling results

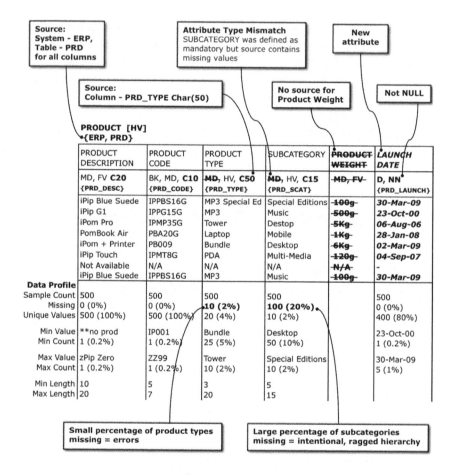

Place data source references on new rows in the table header and column type (as in Figure 5-2) so they can be hidden when not needed; e.g., during a model review, if the source names are not meaningful to the stakeholders.

Table 5-1

Data type codes

CODE	DATA TYPE
C(n)	Character(length)
DT	Date and Time
D	Date
N(n.n)	Numeric(digits, precision)
T	Text. Long character data used to hold free format text
B	Blob. Binary object used to hold documents, images, sound etc.

Additional Data

While profiling the candidate sources, it is extremely likely that you will discover relevant data that the stakeholder didn't request. If any of it looks like potential facts, or dimensional attributes for the currently prioritized events, you should add them to the model for review. Additional business keys that represent further reuse of conformed dimensions are especially interesting. Use **bold italics** to highlight new columns.

Use italics to highlight additional data

Unavailable Data

If you cannot find a data source, or the only available source conveys little or no information, use ~~**bold strikethrough**~~ on the unavailable column and its examples. Figure 5-2 shows that PRODUCT WEIGHT is unavailable. If an entire event or dimension is unavailable you should strikethrough the whole table and the appropriate row or column on the matrix (and inform the stakeholders as soon as possible). Figure 5-3 shows the (thankfully unlikely) situation that there is no reliable source for a product dimension. If this really was the case you would also strikethrough all PRODUCT details in event tables—making them non-viable.

Use ~~strikethrough~~ to highlight unavailable data. If an entire table is unavailable highlight this on the matrix too

~~PRODUCT [HV]~~			
~~PRODUCT DESCRIPTION~~	~~PRODUCT CODE~~	~~PRODUCT TYPE~~	~~BRAND~~
~~MD, FV~~	~~BK, MD~~	~~MD, HV~~	~~MD, HV~~
~~iPip Blue Suede~~	~~IPPB516G~~	~~MP3 Special Ed~~	~~iPip~~
~~iPip G1~~	~~IPPG15G~~	~~MP3~~	~~iPip~~
~~iPom Pro~~	~~IPMP35G~~	~~Tower~~	~~iPom~~
~~PomBook Air~~	~~PBA20G~~	~~Laptop~~	~~PomBook~~

Strikethrough of all information: no suitable data source was found for the required dimension

---

Figure 5-3
BEAM✲ diagram showing missing data source for an entire dimension

Nulls and Mismatched Attribute Descriptions

If you discover an attribute definition mismatch you should highlight these by using bold strikethrough on the appropriate column code. For example, PRODUCT SUBCATEGORY in Figure 5-2 was defined by the stakeholders as a mandatory (**MD**) description of all products (and would therefore be a good level in the default product hierarchy). However, data profiling shows that it is missing for 20% of products so it has been marked as ~~**MD**~~.

Highlight missing mandatory data using ~~MD~~. Strikethrough other mismatched column codes

It can be very useful to point out 'not Null' sources for any event details and dimensional attributes that the stakeholder did not explicitly identify as mandatory, by highlighting them as **NN**. These rare cases, where data is more reliably available than stakeholders thought, may open up new areas of analysis that they previously didn't consider.

Highlight mandatory source data as **NN**: Not Null

Use the following notation to annotate a model with source definitions:

{source} : Data source system, table, column, file or field name

~~**Value**~~ : Unavailable or incorrect data or conflicting definition

NN : Not Null. Column cannot contain null values

Model Review and Sprint Planning

Use the data profiling results to rank the data issues and estimate the ETL tasks

Once the profiling results are in and have been added to the model it's time to hold an initial planning meeting (Figure 5-4) with the DW/BI team prior to stakeholder model review. Armed with their new-found knowledge from running the data profile checks, the team should rank the data issues by severity (see Table 5-2) and provide ETL task estimates, in man-days, for loading the viable events.

Figure 5-4
Initial planning meeting

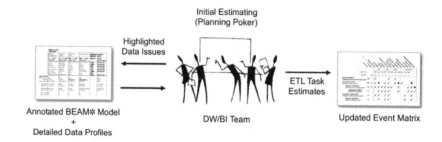

Annotated BEAM✳ Model
+
Detailed Data Profiles

DW/BI Team

Updated Event Matrix

Team Estimating

Estimating is an agile DW/BI team activity, every team member should be involved to bring them up to speed with the emerging design. Everyone can usefully contribute; e.g., BI developers can often help with ETL estimates if they are familiar with the data sources, from having had to report directly off them in the past.

Play *planning poker* to get unbiased team estimates

A downside of team estimating is that one person, who "knows best" or has the loudest voice, can influence everyone's estimate. A great way to avoid this is to play *planning poker*: using a special deck of cards, everyone reveals their estimate for a task simultaneously, and the team learns a lot from the differing opinions.

Dimension and event estimates are added to the event matrix

When task estimates have been agreed, the totals for each table are added to the event matrix so that *star schema estimates* can be calculated by summing the relevant dimension and event totals. These estimates, used in conjunction with the team's *velocity* (work delivered per iteration), will give stakeholders an idea of what could be prototyped after the next sprint or delivered in the next release.

For information on calculating *team velocity* and estimating by playing *planning poker* with agile teams, read *Scrum and XP from the Trenches*, Henrik Kniberg (InfoQ.com 2007) Chapter 4: How we do Sprint Planning.

Review the annotated data model and task estimates with stakeholders as soon as possible. Delaying the review can allow unrealistic expectations for the data warehouse to grow. Don't let the stakeholders dream for too long!

Running a Model Review

With the aid of the annotated tables and the event matrix estimates you are ready for the model review (Figure 5-5) with stakeholders. The purpose of this meeting is to make stakeholders aware of what could be achieved in the next release, based on the currently available data sources and task estimates. If the data sources are in good shape and the business priorities have not changed then it should be a short meeting. If not, you need to concentrate on the serious data issues and large task estimates that need the stakeholders' attention most.

Review the annotated model with stakeholders to make them aware of what is possible in the next release

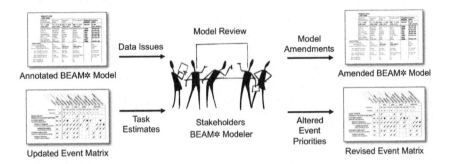

Figure 5-5
Model review

Start with the most severe issues (see Table 5-2) and work your way down by reviewing any major missing sources first. Completely missing event or dimension sources—strikethrough tables like Figure 5-3—may cause a serious rethink of priorities. Missing individual details are generally less disruptive, but some may be indispensable. Problems with conflicting conformed dimension sources are highly significant as they can have a knock on effect for future iterations and have the potential to build up the greatest technical debt.

Concentrate on severe data issues: missing sources and conflicting sources for conformed dimensions

SEVERITY	ISSUE	OUTCOME
1	Missing conformed dimension	**Stop**
1	Missing event	**Stop**
3	Missing or incorrect business key	**Stop**
3	Conflicting data for conformed dimension	**Stop**
5	Event granularity is different	**Stop/Pause**
6	Missing non-conformed dimension	**Pause**
6	Missing (or poorly populated) event detail	**Pause**
8	Missing mandatory values	**Pause**
8	Incorrect hierarchical relationship	**Pause**
10	Missing (or poorly populated) dimensional attribute	**Go**
10	Mismatched detail and attribute values	**Go**
12	Additional event details or dimensional attributes	**Go**

Table 5-2
Data source issues ranked by severity (1=highest, 12=lowest)

Stop : a major rethink or reprioritization is necessary.

Pause : provide feedback before you develop the physical database.

Go : proceed (with caution) but still provide feedback on the gaps in the model or the additional BI opportunities that may exist.

Revise the model
with the help of
the stakeholders

As you go through each table or column issue, update the model (the individual tables *and* the matrix) with the stakeholders assistance. Ask them to help you to decide:

> **Should we include, exclude, add or adjust this item?**
>
> **Which of these conflicting sources should we choose?**

If stakeholders want
to reprioritize
events, revise the
matrix accordingly

You should finish the review by asking the stakeholders if they want to reprioritize events in light of the data issues and task estimates—bearing in mind that the task estimates may also need to be adjusted based on the changes they have just agreed to. If the stakeholders do want to alter their priorities, revise the matrix by replaying the *event rating game* described in Chapter 4.

Sprint Planning

Use the revised
model, estimates
and priorities to
define the *sprint
backlog*

Following the model review, you hold a sprint planning meeting (Figure 5-6) where the DW/BI team will revise their estimates based on the model amendments and the product owner will decide on the data items that will make their way onto the *sprint backlog*: the list of data and user stories (tables and BI reports/dashboards) to be implemented in the next sprint. To help the team revise their estimates you may need to draw some quick star schemas. It is at this point you would introduce some of the design patterns described later in this book.

Figure 5-6
Sprint planning
meeting

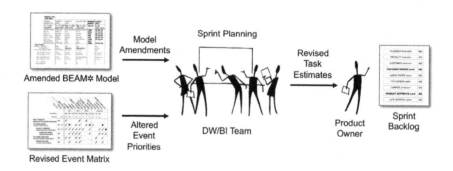

 Dimensions that have already been implemented should be given an estimate of zero. The estimate for all non-viable or low priority tables (that have not been profiled) should be left blank. The estimate for degenerate dimensions should also be blank—their development effort is included in fact table estimates. The total estimate for two star schemas that share conformed dimensions should not double count the conformed dimension estimates—the conformed dimension estimates should be high enough individually to include all the tasks involved in merging and conforming multiple attribute sources.

Star Schema Design

After you have updated the BEAM✲ model to reflect the data realities and altered priorities, you are ready to create a (logical) dimensional model and draw the star schemas that will be used by the DW/BI team to generate the physical data warehouse and design ETL and BI applications. This involves the purely technical steps shown in Figure 5-7, none of which require stakeholder input or participation.

The model is now ready to be drawn as star schemas

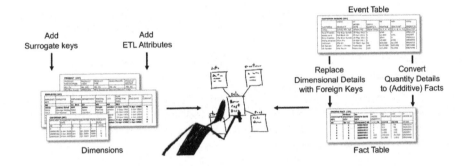

Add Surrogate keys

Add ETL Attributes

Event Table

Replace Dimensional Details with Foreign Keys

Convert Quantity Details to (Additive) Facts

Dimensions

Fact Table

Figure 5-7

Creating a (logical) dimensional model

If you are using the BEAM✲ *Modelstormer* spreadsheet, copy your BEAM✲ model to a graphical modeling tool for star schema layout by using the customizable SQL DDL it generates. If you haven't done so already, download the spreadsheet template and find full instructions for using it at modelstorming.com

Adding Keys to a Dimensional Model

The major difference between the BEAM✲ business model and a dimensional model that can be used to create a physical database schema is the addition of primary and foreign keys that define the relationships between the dimension and fact tables. There is no need to discuss these keys with the business stakeholders, because data warehouse key definition is purely a technical activity.

To convert the BEAM✲ model into a dimensional model just add keys

Choosing Primary Keys: Business Keys vs. Surrogate Keys

During modelstorming you defined at least one attribute in each dimension as a *business key* (denoted by the code **BK**) to uniquely identify each dimension member. Business keys, such as PRODUCT CODE or CUSTOMER ID, are the unique *primary keys* of source system reference tables. They may appear the obvious *candidate keys* for similar-looking dimension tables, but source system business keys never turn out to be as unique, stable, minimal or omnipresent across multiple business processes as a data warehouse needs them to be. Instead dimensional modelers use *(data warehouse) surrogate keys* (**SK**) as the primary keys for dimensions. These are integer sequence numbers assigned uniquely to each dimension table row, by ETL processes, and used by BI applications to join dimensions to fact tables—where they act as foreign keys.

Do not use *business keys* as dimension *primary keys*. Use *(data warehouse) surrogate keys* instead

Database Key Definitions

Primary key (PK): A column or combination of columns that uniquely identifies each row in a table. In addition to being unique, a primary key should ideally be:

- **Stable**: not change value over time.
- **Minimal**: be short, use as few columns as possible (ideally 1).
- **Not Null**: be present, have a value for all rows in the table.

Foreign key (FK): A column or combination of columns in one (child or referencing) table that relate to the primary key of another (parent or referenced) table. In a dimensional model, foreign keys within a fact table relate to the primary keys of its matching dimensions.

Composite Key: A key made up of two or more columns. Identified in a BEAM✳ model by numbering a group of key codes alike; e.g., two columns in the same table marked PK1 represent a two-part composite primary key.

Alternate Key: A column or combination of columns that can be used in place of a primary key. Identified by numbering alternatives differently; e.g., three columns in the same table marked PK1, PK2, PK2 represent a primary key and a composite alternate key.

Candidate Key: A column or combination of columns that could act as a key.

Natural key (NK): A key that is used to uniquely identify something in the "real-world" outside of a database; e.g., a barcode printed on a product package or a Social Security number on an ID card. Natural key values are sometimes known by stakeholders and used directly in reports and queries. The Employee ID 007 belonging to our favorite salesperson James Bond, has taken on a life of its own beyond the HR system and become a natural key.

Surrogate key (SK): A key with a "meaningless" or artificial value, typically a sequence number, generated by a database or application that is used instead of a natural key.

Business key (BK): A primary key from a source system. This can be a meaningful natural key or a meaningless system-generated surrogate within the source system, but by the time it reaches the data warehouse it has meaning to the business outside of the warehouse and so is referred to as a business key.

Benefits of Data Warehouse Surrogate Keys

Surrogate keys =
big DW/BI benefits

Data warehouse surrogate keys, referred to simply as surrogate keys, have the follow benefits over source system business keys:

Insulate the Data Warehouse from Business Key Change

Surrogate keys protect the data warehouse from changes or glitches in the way business keys are administrated. For example, if business keys change when a business process is migrated to a new packaged application they can be updated in a dimension without affecting millions or billions of facts. If business keys are reused when products are discontinued or customers depart, new dimensional rows with new surrogate keys can be assigned to these reused codes so they remain distinct from their previous use. Business key instability like this is often hidden because it may not cause a problem in the operational systems if older transactions are archived, but the problem surfaces when the data warehouse has to take a longer-term view.

When business keys are changed or reused, surrogate keys prevent facts from been affected

Cope with Multiple Business Keys for a Dimension

Surrogate keys allow the data warehouse to integrate events from multiple operational sources that store information about the same conformed dimensions using different business keys. By using a surrogate key, you can sidestep the question of which business key is *best* for a dimension—a politically sensitive issue within organizations that have grown by merger or acquisition. The safest answer is "there is no *best* business key." They are *all* important non-key attributes that should be stored in the dimension. The multiple business keys will be used by ETL processes to assign surrogate foreign keys to the facts derived from the multiple sources. They may also all have analytical value to various stakeholder groups, especially if some are *natural keys* that the stakeholders work with outside of their databases.

Surrogate keys provide a single primary key for conformed dimensions that have multiple business keys originating from multiple source systems

Track Dimensional History Efficiently

The data warehouse must provide history for the descriptive attributes of *slowly changing dimensions* (SCDs) as well as rapidly changing facts. Surrogate keys provide a simple mechanism for storing this history directly in dimension tables and efficiently joining the correct historical descriptions to the historical facts at query time.

Surrogate keys allow dimensional history to be tracked and joined efficiently to facts

Handle Missing Dimensional Values

Every dimension needs at least one special record that represents 'missing' or 'not applicable' to cope with errors or minor variations in business events. For example, in-store and telephone CUSTOMER ORDERS are handled by a SALESPERSON whereas online orders are not; they do not naturally have a SALESPERSON dimension. When online orders are loaded into the same fact table as other orders their Null or missing SALESPERSON IDs are replaced with a special surrogate key value that points to a "No Salesperson" record in the SALESPERSON dimension. This allows order queries that group by SALESPERSON to still include online orders but display them using "Missing" labels defined by stakeholders. If the SALESPERSON foreign key was left as Null, online orders would always be excluded. Having a special missing row in every dimension simplifies query joins; all joins can be inner joins as every fact will always find a matching dimension record.

Surrogate keys can represent special missing dimension values for which there are no business keys; e.g., "No Customer", "Missing Date"

Reserve the surrogate key value zero for the default *Missing* row in each dimension. You use this row zero to hold the stakeholders' *Missing* labels recorded in the BEAM✳ dimension table example data. If different types of *missing* are needed you can add additional special rows, using negative surrogate keys, to represent "Unknown", "Not Applicable", "Error" etc., leaving the normal dimension values to use positive integers. Being consistent in the use of special value surrogate keys can greatly simplify ETL processing.

Support Multi-Level Dimensions

Surrogate keys enable *multi-level* dimensions to describe *variable-level* business processes

Some business events have *variable-level* dimensional details. For example, tele-sales orders are normally attributed to individual salespeople, but occasionally an order is attributed to a sales *team*, when the salesperson is on probation or has left before the order is processed. Orders are a variable-level *who* event. By using an extension of the missing value SK technique, a number of additional special value rows can be added to the SALESPERSON dimension to represent teams, branches, regions, or other levels in the sales organization hierarchy, creating a *multi-level* dimension to which both normal and exceptional facts can be attached. The multi-level design pattern is covered in Chapter 6.

Protect Sensitive Information

Surrogate keys keep sensitive data anonymous. Unlike business keys they cannot be used to join sensitive data to source systems that might provide full disclosure

For data protection or security reasons you might need to create anonymous customer or employee dimensions for analyzing sensitive purchase habits or salary payment facts. Anonymized dimensions obviously must not contain name, exact address, date of birth, or other descriptive attributes that could be used in combination to identify individuals. However, if they use business keys (such as Customer ID or Employee Number) as primary keys, then fact tables will contain business key foreign keys that can be cross-referenced with other systems to provide full disclosure. You can prevent this by replacing business keys with surrogate keys, that do not exist outside of the data warehouse, and limiting access to the disclosing business key to surrogate key mapping tables, to secure ETL processes only.

Reduce Fact Table Size

Use integer surrogate keys instead of alphanumeric business keys to reduce the size of fact tables and indexes

Integer surrogate keys are more compact than datetime keys and most alphanumeric business keys—especially so called 'smart keys' that have embedded business logic. This can lead to significant reductions in the size of fact tables. For example, a typical detailed fact table has 10 dimensions and 5 measures. If the average length of a business key is 10 characters (bytes), replacing each foreign key with a 4-byte integer would halve the size of the fact table and its corresponding indexes. Even if savings can only be made on a few foreign keys, every byte counts when it comes to fact tables.

Adding surrogate keys to dimensions in addition to their business keys slightly increases the size of the dimensions, but this is insignificant. In general do not worry about the size of dimensions. Although dimension rows can be long with dozens of descriptive attributes, dimensions typically only contain hundreds or thousands of rows *in total*, whereas fact tables can record millions of rows *per day*. If you want to see where you should concentrate on saving storage take a look at the Figure 5-8 "scale" diagram of a star schema. In a dimensional data warehouse, fact tables along with their indexes and their staging tables account for 80%–90% of the storage requirements.

Don't worry about the size of dimension tables…

Of course not every dimension is small. Customer dimensions that contain individual consumers can contain tens or hundreds of millions of rows. These need to be treated with the same respect as fact tables and will benefit too from a primary key index based on a compact 4-byte integer rather than a longer "smarter' alphanumeric Customer ID that contains a check digit. Chapter 6 covers specific techniques for handling *very large dimensions* (VLDs), also known as "monster dimensions".

…except customer dimensions – they can be big!

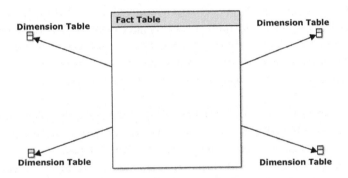

Figure 5-8

Scale diagram of a star schema by space used

For fixed length surrogate keys, a 4-byte integer is suitable for most dimension populations. If you are expecting a crowd (more than 2.1 billion *whos* or *whats*) or have specialized calendar dimension requirements (discussed in Chapter 7), you should use an 8-byte integer surrogate key.

Improve Query Performance

Because integer surrogate keys reduce the size of fact tables and indexes, they help to fit more records into each read operation. This in turn leads to improved star join processing and dramatic improvements in query performance.

Integer SKs join faster than date and character keys

Enforce Referential Integrity Efficiently

Surrogate keys do add an extra layer of complexity to ETL. It is true that fact records can be loaded quicker if business keys are not replaced by surrogates. But this overhead is more than outweighed by the benefits listed above and a byproduct of surrogate keys is efficient *referential integrity (RI)*.

SK lookups slow down fact loads but enforce *referential integrity* (RI)

RI prevents bad keys getting into good fact tables

Referential integrity means that every foreign key has a matching primary key. Without RI checks, facts could be loaded into fact tables with corrupt dimension foreign keys that do not match any existing dimensional values. If this happens, any query that uses these bad keys will fail to include those facts because they will not join to the appropriate dimensions. If these "bent needles" find there way into the giant haystack of fact tables the (SQL "NOT IN") queries needed to find them are prohibitively expensive.

DBMS constraints can enforce RI but ETL SK lookups can often do this more efficiently

RI can be enforced by defining foreign key constraints in the database. However, in practice, DBMSs can be too slow at loading data warehousing quantities of data with RI switched on. In contrast, ETL processes are optimized for performing the type of in-memory lookups required to check foreign keys against primary keys—this is exactly what ETL does when translating business keys into surrogate keys prior to loading fact tables. Effectively, the surrogate key processing provides "free" procedural referential integrity, which allows DBMS RI checking to be safely disabled.

DBMS query optimizers often benefit from having fact table RI constraints defined. You can retain these optimization clues but still boost ETL performance by setting the constraints to *unenforced* (you might call this "trust me I know what my ETL process is doing" mode). This tells the optimizer what it needs to know about the relationships between facts and dimensions to speed up queries, but avoids unnecessary insert and update checks that would slow down ETL.

Enable DBMS-enforced RI for fact tables during ETL development and initial data take-on to provide "belt and braces" data integrity assurance and test ETL surrogate key lookups. If no DBMS RI errors are raised, the ETL processes are assigning valid surrogate keys to facts and the additional DBMS checks are unnecessary. You can then disable the DBMS RI (drop the constraints or set them to unenforced), if it is having an adverse effect on load times.

Slowly Changing Dimensions

Change stories match the behavior of slowly changing dimensions

When you model dimensions with stakeholders you ask them how each dimensional attribute should handle change. You record their answers as change stories which illustrate the behavior of fixed value (**FV**) attributes that can only be corrected and have no valid history, current value (**CV**) attributes with no required history and historic value (**HV**) attributes that preserve their history. Figure 5-9 shows two Employee change stories for James Bond. The historical values of his MARITAL STATUS and CITY (his **HV** attributes) have been carefully tracked on each of his stories while his **CV** and **FV** attributes DEPARTMENT and DATE OF BIRTH show only the current or corrected single values for all his stories. This example data matches exactly how *slowly changing dimensions* (SCDs) are implemented by ETL processes in a dimensional data warehouse using surrogate keys.

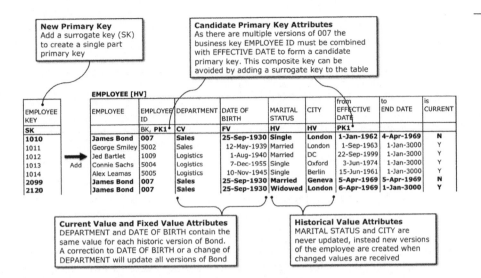

Figure 5-9
Slowly changing
EMPLOYEE
dimension

Overwriting History: Type 1 Slowly Changing Dimensions

CV and **FV** dimensional attributes are implemented as *Type 1 slowly changing dimensions*. When they are updated in the source system they are similarly updated in a dimension. For **FV** attributes such as DATE OF BIRTH this is entirely appropriate because an employee or customer can have only one date of birth, the update must be a correction and nothing of value is lost. For **CV** attributes, the stakeholders have decided that historically correct values are unimportant and current values are the only ones that matter. For both **CV** and **FV** attributes history is lost, making reports that use them "unrepeatable". They will give different answers if re-run because the reports will be grouped or filtered using "as is now" not "as was then" descriptions.

CV and FV
attributes are
implemented as
Type 1 SCDs.
Changes are
handled as
updates and
history is
overwritten

Tracking History: Type 2 Slowly Changing Dimensions

HV dimensional attributes are implemented as *Type 2 slowly changing dimensions*. They are *not* overwritten when they change in the source system. Instead new rows are inserted with the new values, just like the change stories in Figure 5-9 that show Bond's various statuses and locations.

HV attributes are
implemented as
Type 2 SCDs

Creating new rows to track change presents an issue for uniquely keying a dimension. For example, Bond's business key "007" no longer uniquely identifies a single Employee row and must be combined with the effective date of the change to provide a valid primary key. Unfortunately a composite key such as EMPLOYEE ID, EFFECTIVE DATE would ruinously complicate the joining of historical facts to the correct historical descriptions. Prior to tracking history a simple *equi-join* would locate Bond's expenses:

Tracking history
within a dimension
means you cannot
rely on the business
key alone as a
primary key

```
Employee.Employee_ID = Expenses_Fact.Employee_ID
```

Composite keys involving effective dates require *complex joins* to fact tables

With a composite key involving effective date this becomes a far more difficult to optimize *complex (or theta) join*:

```
Employee.Employee_ID = Expenses_Fact.Employee_ID and
Expenses_Fact.Expense_Date
between Employee.Effective_date and Employee.End_date
```

Without the *between* join on the dates, all of Bond's expenses would be joined to each historical version of him, triple counting his total based on the three versions of Bond in Figure 5-9. If the above join looks complex, imagine now that EMPLOYEE isn't the only **HV** dimension that must be joined to the facts, each join would be just as complex. This would not be a viable query strategy against typical data warehousing quantities of facts.

A Type 2 SCD surrogate key partitions history by using a simple equi-join

Instead, Type 2 SCDs use a surrogate key as an efficient minimal primary key that uniquely identifies each historical version of a dimension member. Figure 5-9 shows the surrogate key EMPLOYEE KEY being added to the dimension. This would become a foreign key in all employee related fact tables. For Bond, his earliest expense claims and sales transactions would have an EMPLOYEE KEY of 1010 while his most recent will be have 2120. A Type 2 SCD surrogate key guarantees that efficient equi-joins will automatically join historical facts to the correct historical descriptions and the most recent facts to current descriptions. They also have the effect of making reports "repeatable"; for example, Bond's 1968 expenses will always be reported as incurred by a single man never a widower.

Surrogate keys should be hidden from stakeholders wherever possible. BI tools use them as the *mechanical way* of joining facts and dimensions only. Surrogate keys are never to be used for sorting, grouping or filtering data. For example, you cannot rely on the highest surrogate key for an employee being the most recent version. A late-arriving employee change will be assigned a higher sequence number surrogate key than the current version. BI tools also have to be careful to count distinct employee IDs rather than employee version rows and show distinct lists of Employees so that so that stakeholders don't see "Bond, Bond, Bond, …"

Current Values or Historical Values? Why Not Both?

Define attributes as **HV** if you think their full history will be needed in the future. Refactoring "late arriving" history is expensive

You should carefully consider current value only (**CV**) dimension definitions. If you suspect that historical values *might* be needed at some point you should define these attributes as **HV** and design your dimensions and ETL processes accordingly to record historical values from the outset. Refactoring an attribute as **HV** and adding its "late arriving" dimensional history to an established warehouse is complex and expensive, and can involve updating the foreign keys of hundreds of millions of existing facts.

Treat **CV** as a reporting default rather than an ETL instruction

As discussed in Chapter 3, you should often treat **CV** codes added to the model by stakeholders as *reporting directives* rather than storage decisions. **CV** tells you that the stakeholders would prefer their reports to initially default to current values (because that is what they are used to). When their analysis requirements become more sophisticated they may change their minds. With modern DW/BI hardware you have the luxury of storing and processing dimensional history for most dimensions as standard practice. And just because you track history you don't have to give it to BI users who don't want it (yet). Chapter 6 covers the *hybrid SCD* pattern for providing *both* current value ("as is") reporting and historic value ("as was") reporting without further complicating the model or ETL processes.

The Data Warehouse ETL Toolkit, Ralph Kimball, Joe Caserta (Wiley, 2004), Chapter 5, pages 183–196 provides information on the ETL processing needed to support slowly changing dimensions. Pages 194–196 describe the complexities of handling late-arriving dimensional history.

Store dimensional history if possible. Enable **CV** reporting by providing a *hybrid SCD*

Updating the Dimension Definitions

You complete each dimension by adding a surrogate key primary key, and additional ETL administrative attributes to support SCD processing and audit requirements. Because you are only adding columns there is no need to create separate spreadsheet versions of dimensions. The extra columns can easily be hidden when you use the tables again for modelstorming with stakeholders.

You complete a dimension by adding a primary key and audit columns

Adding Surrogate Keys

Add a leading surrogate key column marked **SK** to each dimension, using a naming convention of [Dimension] KEY; e.g., PRODUCT KEY. This usually works well as the suffix "KEY" is seldom used for business keys (ID, CODE, and NUM are far more common). Fill in the example *missing* row in each dimension with a zero surrogate and use simple sequential integers for other examples to make it obvious that they are surrogate keys. Figure 5-10 shows a surrogate key added to the PRODUCT dimension.

Add a surrogate key (**SK**) with examples including zero for the missing row

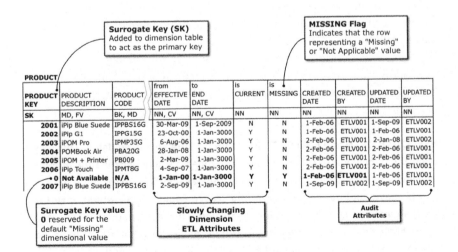

Figure 5-10
Updated PRODUCT dimension

Use unique example ranges for the most common surrogate keys; e.g., 1–1000 for customers, 2000–3000 for products. This can help the DW team read the foreign key examples in fact tables (stakeholders would never look at these values). This convention is just for human readability; reserving value ranges for specific dimensions keys in the physical database is *not* recommended.

ETL and Audit Attributes

Add effective dating attributes for managing SCDs

If you have already modeled how the dimension should track history and discovered its **CV** and **HV** attributes, you may already have the following SCD ETL administrative attributes in your dimensions (if not you should add them now):

- EFFECTIVE DATE
- END DATE
- CURRENT

Effective dating attributes support point in time dimension queries

EFFECTIVE DATE and END DATE define the valid date range for each dimension row. For example, in Figure 5-9 employee Bond's three MARITAL STATUS (**HV**) changes have unique effective date ranges—with no overlaps or gaps. For the current version of each EMPLOYEE there is no END DATE. But rather than leaving END DATE as Null, make sure ETL processes set it to the maximum date supported by the database. This allows query tools to use simple BETWEEN logic when asking questions about the dimension population at a specific point in time. For example, a query to count the number of employees in each city at the close of 2011 would be:

```
SELECT city, count(*)
FROM employee
WHERE TO_DATE('31/12/2011','DD/MM/YYYY') BETWEEN
effective_date AND end_date
GROUP BY city
```

Queries should use a CURRENT flag rather than the max DBMS date

The CURRENT flag indicates whether a row version is current (Y). This could be inferred from the value of END DATE but this saves stakeholders and query tools from remembering the otherwise meaningless maximum date value, which can vary by DBMS.

SCD administrative attributes should be Not Null

SCD administrative attributes should all be defined as Not Null. END DATE should have a default value of the maximum database date, and CURRENT should default to "Y".

EFFECTIVE DATE and END DATE in Figure 5-10 are shown as dates. This would allow the dimension to track one set of changes per day because the minimum effective range for a historical version is one day. Multiple changes on the same day (if they could be detected from the source system feed) would have to be batched into a single update to the dimension. This is a reasonable approach if multiple changes to the same attribute on the same day are corrections. If inter-day changes are more significant and must be tracked to match inter-day facts, EFFECTIVE DATE and END DATE need to be stored as full timestamps.

If a dimension contains only CV and FV attributes, effective dating attributes are unnecessary. Implement them anyway and you will be ready for the day when a new HV attribute is added, or stakeholders finally realize they needed historically correct attributes all the time. The cost of redundantly maintaining these attributes initially is insignificant compared to the cost of refactoring ETL processes.

There are five additional administrative attributes in Figure 5-10 that you should also consider adding to every dimension:

Additional ETL attributes can be useful...

- MISSING
- CREATED DATE
- CREATED BY
- UPDATED DATE
- UPDATED BY

The MISSING flag "Y" indicates that the row is a special "Missing" dimensional record (usually with a zero or negative surrogate key). "N" indicates a normal dimension record. This can be useful for filtering out all forms of missing (e.g. "N/A" and "Error") without exposing their surrogate key values to BI users.

...for identifying special "missing" rows...

The CREATED and UPDATED attributes provide basic ETL audit information on the date/time and ETL version used to create and update the dimension. Chapter 9 provides more details on audit techniques.

...and providing dimension audit information

When you present existing BEAM✲ dimension tables as spreadsheets to stakeholders, hide surrogate keys and other ETL-only columns to limit the discussion to business attributes.

Time Dimensions

If you haven't already done so you should model *when* dimensionally—just like any other *W-type*. A CALENDAR dimension is essential to the data warehouse because it provides the conformed time hierarchies (discussed in Chapter 3) and descriptions that stakeholders need to analyze every business process. You should also model *time of day* to discover if stakeholders have custom descriptions for periods during a day, such as peak/off peak or shift names. If so, these should be implemented as attributes of a separate minute granularity CLOCK dimension to avoid a single monster TIME dimension that would contain 2.6 million minutes for every 5 years of warehouse history.

Model time dimensionally as separate CALENDAR and CLOCK dimensions

Figure 5-11 shows how a single time of day granularity *when* event detail: CALL TIME is replaced by two surrogate keys: CALL DATE KEY and CALL TIME KEY in a fact table. Both CALENDAR and CLOCK are role-playing (**RP**) dimensions that will be used to replace the *when* details of every event. Chapter 7 provides full details on time dimensions and their special property surrogate date keys.

Datetime details become separate date and time surrogate keys

Figure 5-11

Splitting a *when*
detail into separate
Calendar and
Clock dimensions

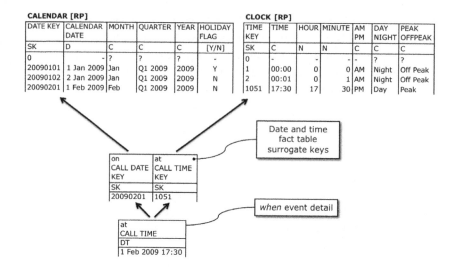

Figure 5-11

Splitting a *when* detail into separate Calendar and Clock dimensions

Modeling Fact Tables

Save copies of
event tables before
you convert them
into fact tables

Once all the dimensions have been updated with surrogate keys, you can then convert the event tables into fact tables by replacing their *who, what, when, where,* and *why* details with dimension foreign keys, while leaving quantities (*how many*) and degenerate dimension (**DD**) *how* details in place. Because you are changing columns, not just adding new ones, you should save copies of the original event tables for future modelstorming. The fact table versions will be used for creating star schemas and communicating design techniques within the DW/BI team.

Rename fact tables
and record their fact
type

With the event table copies saved you can replace event names with fact table names and change story types to fact table types. In Figure 5-12 the CUSTOMER ORDERS discrete event has been renamed ORDERS FACTS and its story type **DE** replaced with the fact table type **TF** for transaction fact. Chapter 8 describes each of the fact table types in detail.

The following table codes are used to identify fact table type:
    [TF] : **Transaction Fact table, the physical version of discrete events**
    [PS] : **Periodic Snapshot, the physical version of recurring events**
    [AS] : **Accumulating Snapshot, the physical version of evolving events**

Replace Event Details with Dimension Foreign Keys

Change dimensional
details to surrogate
keys by marking
them as **SK**

Replace all of the dimensional details with surrogate keys by renaming the columns and changing their type to **SK**. In Figure 5-12 CUSTOMER, PRODUCT, ORDER DATE, SALESPERSON and PROMOTION have been replaced by the appropriately named surrogate keys, and their examples changed to surrogate key integer values.

Replacing the examples is an optional step; you might change them to integer sequence numbers, as we have here, if you are using a BEAM✳ table to explain a surrogate key technique to the team. Alternatively, you can leave the descriptive examples from the original event modeling unaltered so that you don't have to keep referring to the separate dimension tables to understand the event stories behind the facts. Regardless of what you do to the examples, a column type of **SK** documents that a fact column is an integer dimension foreign key in the physical database schema.

Leave descriptive examples for readability or change them to integers to explain **SK** techniques

ORDERS FACT [TF]								
CUSTOMER KEY	Orders PRODUCT KEY	on ORDER DATE KEY	from SALESPERSON KEY	on PROMOTION KEY	in ORDER QUANTITY	for REVENUE	with DISCOUNT	on ORDER ID
SK	SK GD	[Calendar] SK	[Employee] SK	SK	[unit] **FA**	[$] **FA**	[$] **FA**	DD GD
1	1	20090518	1	1	1	249	50	ORD1234
1	1	20090518	1	1	1	249	50	ORD4321
2	2	20091014	2	2	1	5,000	150	ORD0001
3	3	20009101	0	3	1	1,400	140	ORD007
4	4	20090810	9	4	100	150,000	20,000	ORD5466
4	5	20090810	9	4	100	25,000	1,000	ORD5466

TF: Transaction Fact Table

Details replaced with dimension Surrogate Keys (SK)

Quantities converted to Fully Additive (FA) facts

Figure 5-12
Creating the ORDERS FACT table

Modeling Degenerate Dimensions

Degenerate dimensions (**DD**) such as ORDER ID are not replaced by a surrogate key because they have no additional descriptive attributes that need to be referenced. Degenerate transaction IDs allow stakeholders and ETL processes to tie facts back to their original operational transactions. They also provide useful ways of uniquely counting business events, especially in the presence of *multi-valued dimensions* (covered in Chapter 9). If a fact table contains a large collection of degenerate dimensions you should consider moving these to a new *how* dimension (sometimes referred to as a *junk* dimension) to reduce fact table size. *How* dimensions are also covered in Chapter 9.

Degenerate dimensions (**DD**) remain in fact tables to tie facts back to source transactions and provide unique counts

Modeling Facts

The remaining quantity columns in the fact table are defined as facts. Facts should be modeled in their most *additive* form, so that they can be easily aggregated at query time. Additivity describes how easy or possible it is to sum up a fact and get a meaningful result. The ideal facts are *fully additive* (**FA**) ones that can be summed using any of their dimensions.

The remaining *how many* details are converted into facts that can be aggregated

The three order facts in Figure 5-12 have all been defined as fully additive (**FA**). To convert the raw *how many* details to (fully) additive facts they must be stored using *consistent additive units of measure (UOM)*. ORDER QUANTITY can use the product units from the original business events, but REVENUE and DISCOUNT which originally showed examples in numerous currencies must be transformed

Full additive (**FA**) facts are ideal because they can be summed using any dimension

into dollars during ETL otherwise they would be *non-additive* (**NA**) facts. In the case of DISCOUNT some of the source figures were percentages. You could create a consistent UOM by transforming all discounts into percentages but that would not be an additive UOM. Additive fact design is covered in detail in Chapter 8.

[FA] : Full Additive fact, can be summed by any dimension
[NA] : Non-Additive fact, cannot be summed
[SA] : Semi-Additive fact, can be summed by certain dimensions only

Percentages make great measures and key performance indicators (KPIs) on reports and BI dashboards but they make for poor inflexible NA facts in fact tables. You should define facts that represent the additive components of percentage measures and calculate the percentages in BI applications.

Drawing Enhanced Star Schema Diagrams

Star schemas represent facts and dimensions using ER notation

When all the dimension surrogate keys are in place and the facts defined it is time to draw star schemas: ER diagram versions of the dimensional model that ETL and BI developers will find useful and familiar. The best way to create and maintain star schemas is to use a graphical data modeling tool that will also generate physical schema definitions for your chosen data warehouse platform.

The SQL DDL generated by the BEAM✳ *Modelstormer* spreadsheet allows you to transfer your model directly into graphical modeling tools that support SQL import. Alternatively, the DDL can be used to create default physical database tables, which can then be reverse engineered by many modeling tools.

Create a Separate Diagram for Each Fact Table

Display one fact table per star schema ER diagram

Once you have imported the dimensional model into a graphical modeling tool, arranging the tables into readable star schemas is usually straightforward. Most modeling tools support multiple ER diagram views for a single model. Use this feature to create one diagram for each fact table and add their relevant dimensions, making sure you are not duplicating the underlying dimensions as you do.

Don't attempt to create one single ER diagram showing *all* the fact tables and dimensions in the data warehouse. Even for a small subset of stars this quickly becomes a mess of overlapping lines. ER notation is best restricted to viewing one star at a time. Instead, develop a *data warehouse matrix* (covered shortly) to provide a more useful overview of multiple stars or the entire model.

Enhanced star schema = star + consistent layout + BEAM✳ codes

You can do two simple things to turn a standard star schema into an *enhanced star schema*. The first is to consistently place dimensions based on their *W-type*. The second is to add BEAM✳ short codes to the tables and columns to describe their dimensional properties.

Use a Consistent Star Schema Layout

Drawing star schemas with a consistently dimensional layout may seem trivial but as the number of stars grow with every release, the DW/BI team will find it tremendously helpful when they scan multiple stars every day. Figure 5-13 shows the recommended layout for star schemas designed using the *7Ws* framework. The four corners are reserved for the four major *W-types*: *who*, *what*, *when* and *where* with top left reserved for the most common *W*: *when*. Think of this as the dimensional modeling equivalent of drawing maps "north up".

Consistent star schema layout helps developers to speed read multiple stars

Figure 5-13
Consistent dimensional layout based on *W-type*

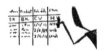

Discover the *BI Model Canvas* at **modelstorming.com** to help you model collaboratively using this layout

Display BEAM✳ Short Codes on Star Schemas

Enhancing a star schema with BEAM✳ codes allows you to document dimensional properties and design decisions not supported by standard ER modeling tools. Figure 5-14 shows an enhanced star schema for the CUSTOMERS ORDERS event (as described in Chapter 2). BEAM✳ codes are used to describe ORDERS FACT as a transaction fact (**TF**) table and the CALENDAR, and EMPLOYEE as role-playing (**RP**) dimensions. Table level codes (**FV, CV, HV**) describe the default slowly changing policy for each dimension. Column level codes identify surrogate keys (**SK**) degenerate dimensions (**DD**), and fully additive facts (**FA**).

Star schema BEAM✳ codes document dimensional properties not supported by standard ER notation

If your modeling tool allows you to include table and column comments or extended attributes on ER diagrams you can use these to display BEAM✳ codes. Alternatively, if this feature isn't available you may be able to display the codes by appending them to the business or logical table and column name in your model and setting the tool's model view to conceptual or logical. The BEAM✳ *Modelstormer* spreadsheet contains configurable options for export names and codes as comments or extended database attributes that can be imported by many modeling tools.

Figure 5-14

Enhanced star
schema for
customer orders

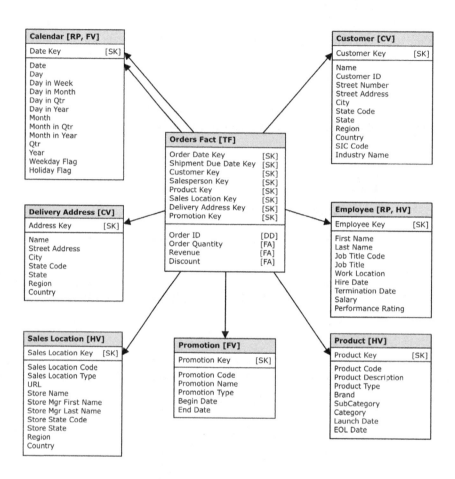

Avoid the Snowflake Schema Anti-pattern

A snowflake
schema is a star
with normalized
dimensions

A snowflake schema is a dimensional model where one or more dimensions have
been normalized, producing additional lookup tables known as *outriggers*. If this is
done to each of the dimensions that surround a fact table, the simple star begins to
look more like a snowflake, as in Figure 5-15.

Resist the urge to
snowflake. For most
dimensions there
are no advantages

Once the model is in a familiar ER modeling tool you (or the DBAs) may be
tempted to introduce *snowflaking* to reduce data redundancy and simplify dimension maintenance. However, snowflake schemas are not generally recommended.
They are too complex for user presentation (if required by your BI tool), offer no
significant space savings (see Figure 5-8), exhibit poor dimension browsing performance, and negate the advantages of bitmap indices. There are legitimate
reasons for snowflaking *very large dimensions*, covered in Chapter 6, but resist any
3NF (third normal form) urges brought on solely by using an ER modeling tool.

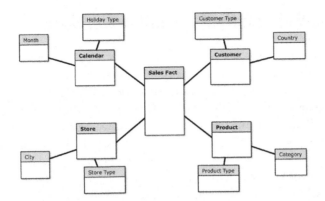

Figure 5-15
Snowflake schema

Do not use snowflake schema outriggers to document hierarchies if your database or BI toolset doesn't need them explicitly defined as 1:M relationships—most don't. Draw hierarchy charts instead. Do be pragmatic, if your toolset works better with snowflake schemas, create them as a physical optimization.

Use hierarchy charts rather than snowflakes to define hierarchies

Do Create Rollup Dimensions

Conformed rollup dimensions (**RU**), such as the product rollup PRODUCT TYPE [RU] or the Calendar Rollup MONTH [RU] described in Chapter 4, can look similar to outriggers and have similar relationships with their base dimensions (their surrogate keys are often carried in the base dimension). The important difference is that rollup attributes are not normalized out of the base dimensions.

Rollup dimensions (**RU**) look similar to outriggers but do not normalize their base dimensions

Rollup dimensions are often not explicitly modeled as BEAM✱ tables because they do not contain any attributes or values that are not present in their base dimensions. If a rollup dimension is as yet undefined you should create it at the star schema level by copying its base dimension and removing all the attributes below the rollup level in the base dimension hierarchy. This is analogous to the ETL process that should build the rollup from its base dimension data, rather than source data, to keep the two in sync and guarantee conformance.

Define rollups by copying and editing their base dimensions

Creating Physical Schemas

Dimensional modeling does not make a strong distinction between logical and physical modeling. Aside from the addition of DBMS-specific storage and indexing options there is very little difference between logical and physical star schemas. These database-specific additions are best defined in a data modeling tool that can apply them consistently to each table and column type, eliminating the need to directly edit *Data Definition Language* (DDL) scripts by hand.

Logical and physical star schemas are very similar

If you are using the BEAM✱*Modelstormer* spreadsheet, you can edit its DDL template to generate custom SQL for your DBMS.

Choose BI-Friendly Naming Conventions

Use business
friendly names for
physical facts and
dimensions to
reduce BI tool
metadata

What's in a name? Database object naming is a strangely emotive subject and naming conventions for facts and dimensions vary greatly. The convention used in this book is *singular* nouns for dimensions (for example, CUSTOMER and PRODUCT) and *plural* nouns with a FACT suffix for fact tables (for example, SALES FACT and ORDERS FACT). Doubtless you will have your own table name standards, but before you *adopt* any semi-cryptic standard that exists for traditional database application development consider the BI users who will use these tables and how they will interact with them. *Adapt* naming standards to work well with your BI tools. The closer you can name dimensions and facts to the labels stakeholders want to see on their reports—the terms they used during modelstorming—the less BI tool metadata the DW/BI team will have to maintain.

A common naming convention is to prefix all dimension tables with DIM_ so that they sort together. What do stakeholders and developers (subconsciously) think every time they see DIM_CUSTOMER or DIM_EMPLOYEE? Instead, reserve a common schema or owner name, perhaps "DIMENSION", for creating dimensions, to achieve the same grouping and avoid such pejorative table names.

Use Data Domains

Data domains
enable consistent
translation into
database-specific
data types

Many database modeling tools allow you to create data domains (or user-defined data types) to help standardize physical column properties for similar column types. If your modeling tool supports domains take advantage of them to translate the default data types imported from the BEAM✳ model into database-specific data types with appropriate constraints. Data domains are especially useful for making a data warehouse design portable across different database management systems. Table 5-3 shows a starter list of recommended domains for a dimensional model.

Table 5-3
Example data
domains for a
dimensional model

DOMAIN	USAGE	DATA TYPE	NULLS	DEFAULT VALUE
Surrogate Key	Dimension primary keys, Fact table foreign keys	Integer	Not Null	0
Flag	Yes/No flags	Char(1)	Not Null	"?"
Code	Short codes, Business keys	Varchar(20)	Not Null	"Unknown"
Name	Longer names	Varchar(60)	Not Null	"Unknown"
Description	Full descriptions	Varchar(99)	Not Null	"Unknown"
Count	Count facts	Integer	Nullable	
Amount	Monetary facts	Currency or Number	Nullable	
Duration	Duration facts	Integer	Nullable	

Prototyping the DW/BI Design

You cannot know how well your data warehouse design matches the available data until you try to load it, nor how well it matches the stakeholders' actual BI requirements until they use it. That is why the agile principle of early delivery of working software is vital for reducing DW/BI risk. So, as soon as you have a physical schema (some working software)—don't postpone the moment of reality any longer—validate the design by prototyping the reports and dashboards that stakeholders have wanted to talk about all along.

Validate the design by prototyping with *real* data, *real* BI tools, and *real* stakeholders

Turn end of sprint demos into prototyping workshops; have BI developers help the original modelstormers (real stakeholders) get their "hands dirty" using *their* design with real data and real BI tools, as in Figure 5-16. These workshops can be remarkably productive because the stakeholders—having used the *7Ws* to model-storm their data requirements—will already be thinking about their business questions and report layouts in terms of these *7W* dimensional interrogatives.

Stakeholders will be ready to define their reports using the *7Ws*

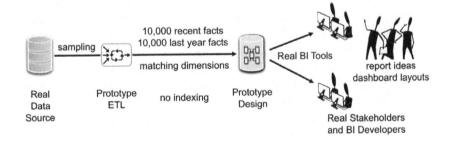

Figure 5-16
DW/BI Prototyping

You should value *working software over comprehensive documentation* and *maximize the work you don't have to do*: Don't waste time mocking up reports or dashboards specifications using spreadsheets or word-processors when you have a database schema, sample data and the stakeholders' BI tools of choice.

For prototypes, avoid test data generation—it proves nothing. Instead, validate the ETL process by sampling small amounts of real data, extracted from the actual sources documented in the model. 10,000 recent facts with matching dimensional descriptions plus similar samples from one or two previous years is usually just enough representative data for stakeholders to get a true feel for what the final solution will be like. Use data profiling to set realistic expectations of the prototype before any queries are run. Make sure stakeholders understand that counts and totals will be low because a small percentage of the data has been sampled.

Load prototype stars with 10,000 recent facts and similar samples from previous time periods

Speed up ETL prototyping by not indexing the data. BI prototyping with un-indexed sample data on modest hardware will also help to set realistic expectations for query performance against complete data, fully-indexed on specialist DW/BI hardware.

The Data Warehouse Matrix

A *data warehouse matrix* documents the actual relationships between fact and dimension tables

A *data warehouse matrix* is a version of the dimensional matrix that documents the relationships between physical fact tables (or OLAP cubes) and physical dimension tables. You can create an initial physical matrix by copying your event matrix and editing its row and columns to show the actual physical tables. When you do, you should also add additional technical details that will be useful to the DW/BI team. Figure 5-17 shows an example matrix with additional columns for data sources, fact table type, primary time dimension granularity and fact volumetrics.

The event matrix is for planning. The physical matrix documents the current live model

This physical matrix and the event matrix should be kept in sync as much as possible but will diverge at times because of their distinct functions. The event matrix is a modeling and planning tool that reflects the stakeholders' requirements, whereas the data warehouse matrix is a management tool that reflects the current state of the data warehouse—including any *conformance failures*.

Document *conformance failure* on the matrix by using *dimension version numbers*

If you have to compromise within a sprint and postpone conforming a dimension, or you inherit a warehouse that has evolved without conformed dimensions, you should record these conformance failures on the data warehouse matrix by using *dimension version numbers*. Rather than create a separate column for each non-conformed version of a dimension, continue to use a single column for each planned conformed dimension but number each different version in use, rather than just tick usage. Reserve the highest number for the best version of each dimension (usually the most recently developed). For example, Figure 5-17 shows that Pomegranate has failed to conform product across manufacturing, sales and customer support, instead there are three different versions of PRODUCT (perhaps it really should be called DIM_PRODUCT). Thankfully, PRODUCT is *partially conformed*; the best version is already the most widely used and only two stars (Customer Orders and Customer Complaints) need to be refactored.

If you need to document conformance failure, hyperlink each dimension version number to its non-conformed dimension table definition.

Update the event matrix with any conformance issues and address them with stakeholders

After each sprint, the event matrix should be updated with conformance failures (planned conformance that did not happen) and non-conformed realities (planned conformance that could not happen because it was wrong) so that these issues can be addressed with the stakeholders during the next modelstorm. Use the updated event matrix to plan the refactoring of older stars with newer more conformed dimensions as part of your iterative development approach.

A live version of the matrix, showing up-to-date volumetrics and the current ETL status for each star, is the ideal dashboard for a DW/BI team. You could develop one by using BI tools to summarize ETL and DBMS catalogue metadata.

When: Records the granularity of primary time dimension of each fact table

Conformance Failure: Three different versions of the PRODUCT dimension

FACT TABLE/CUBE	SOURCE App.Db.Schema.Table	FACT TYPE	Initial	Increment	Max	When	EMPLOYEE [RP]	SUPPLIER	RESELLER	CARRIER	CUSTOMER	COMPONENT	PRODUCT	PRODUCT_TYPE [RU]	PROCESS	TEST	PLANT	WAREHOUSE	SALES_LOCATION	DELIVERY_ADDRESS	CONTRACT	PROMOTION	PROBLEM_REASON	SHIP_MODE	ORDER ID [DD]	SHIPMENT NUMBER [DD]	PO [DD]
				VOLUMETRICS			who					what						where				why & how					
MANUFACTURING_PLANS	ERP.PROD.MFG.MFG_PLAN	PS	100K	10K / Month	500K	Month							✓	3				✓									
BILL_OF_MATERIALS	ERP.PROD.MFG.BILL_MAT	TF	100K	5K / Qtr	1M	Day		✓	✓				✓	3				✓				✓					
PURCHASE_ORDERS	ERP.PROD.INV.PO	AS	500K	10K / Day	2M	Minute		✓	✓				✓					✓									✓
COMPONENT_DELIVERIES	ERP.PROD.LOG.DLVRY	TF	500K	5K / Day	1.5M	hour		✓	✓				✓					✓							✓		✓
SUPPLIER_PAYMENTS	ERP.PROD.GL.SUP_PMT	TF	100K	1K / Day	1M	Day		✓	✓				✓								✓						✓
COMPONENT_INVENTORY	ERP.PROD.INV.COMP_STK	PS	100K	100K / Day	0.5M	Day		✓					✓	3				✓									
QA_TESTS	ERP.PROD.MFG.QA_TEST	TF	100K	10K / Day	1M	Minute		✓					✓	3		✓		✓									
MANUFACTURING_PRODUCTION	ERP.PROD.MFG.AUDIT	TF	5M	1M / Day	700M	Minute							✓	3	✓		✓										
PRODUCT_INVENTORY	ERP.PROD.INV.PRD_STK	TF	100K	10K / Day	0.5M	Day							✓	3				✓				✓					
WAREHOUSE_SHIPMENTS	ERP.PROD.LOG.SHIPMENT	TF	100K	10K / Day	1M	hour				✓			✓	3				✓						✓		✓	
SALES_TARGETS	EXCEL.SPLAN.CURRENT	PS	10K	1K / Month	100K	Month		✓					✓	1	✓												
CUSTOMER_ORDERS	POS.PROD.SALES.ORDER	AS	500K	100K / Day	2M	Minute		✓			✓	✓	✓	3	✓				✓	✓	✓	✓			✓		
PRODUCT_SHIPMENTS	ERP.PROD.LOG.SHIPMENT	TF	400K	100K / Day	1.5M	Hour		✓		✓	✓	✓	✓	3	✓					✓	✓			✓	✓	✓	✓
CARRIER_DELIVERIES	ERP.PROD.LOG.DELIVERY	TF	200K	50K / Day	1M	Hour				✓	✓	✓	✓	3	✓					✓				✓	✓	✓	✓
CUSTOMER_COMPLAINTS	CRM.PROD.CRM.CONTACT	AS	50K	1K / Day	0.5M	Minute		✓			✓	✓	✓	2									✓		✓	✓	
PRODUCT_RETURNS	ERP.PROD.LOG.RETURN	TF	10K	1K / Day	0.3M	Day					✓	✓	✓	3	✓					✓			✓	✓	✓	✓	✓

Figure 5-17
Data warehouse matrix

Summary

- *Agile data profiling* targets the data sources implicated by the BEAM✲ model. It is done early as a data-driven modeling activity to validate the stakeholders data requirements before detailed star schemas are designed. When data sources don't yet exist, proactive DW/BI designs based on the BEAM✲ model can help define better BI data feeds from new operational systems.

- *Annotated models* present data profiling results in a format stakeholders are familiar with. An annotated table contains source names, data types and summary data profiling metrics. Data source issues such as missing data and mismatched definitions are highlighted using ~~strikethrough~~. Additional data is highlighted using *italics*.

- The DW/BI team uses the annotated model and detailed data profiling results to provide initial task estimates for building and loading the proposed facts and dimensions. These ETL estimates are added to the event matrix for use during model review and sprint planning.

- During a model review, stakeholders use the annotated model and the DW/BI team estimates to agree amendments to the design and reprioritize their requirements in light of the data realities and available development resources.

- BEAM✲ models are easily translated into logical dimensional models and star schemas. Dimension tables are updated by adding primary keys and administrative attributes. Event tables are converted into fact tables by replacing dimensional details with foreign keys and changing quantities (*how many* details) into fully-additive (**FA**), semi-additive (**SA**), or non-additive (**NA**) facts with standardized (conformed) units of measure.

- *(Data warehouse) surrogate keys* are used as dimension primary keys to insulate the data warehouse from business keys, provide dimensional flexibility (manage SCDs, missing values, multi-levels, etc.) and improve query efficiency.

- *Enhanced star schemas* convey additional dimensional information. Consistent dimensional layout documents dimensions by *W-type* and increases multi-star schema model readability. BEAM✲ short codes document table and column level dimensional properties not handled by standard ER notation.

- In addition to the standard documentation provided by modeling tools, a *data warehouse matrix* provides an overview of all the star schemas and OLAP cubes in the data warehouse. Similar in layout to an event modeling and planning matrix, this physical matrix provides additional information about the actual warehouse for a technical audience. It is a vital tool for managing the warehouse and must be kept up to date along with the event matrix and star schema diagrams as the data warehouse design evolves.

PART II: DIMENSIONAL DESIGN PATTERNS

DIMENSIONAL MODELING TECHNIQUES FOR PERFORMANCE, FLEXIBILITY, AND USABILITY

> Computers are to design as microwaves are to cooking.
> — *Milton Glaser*

Chapter 6: Who and What: People and Organizations, Products and Services

Chapter 7: When and Where: Time and Location

Chapter 8: How Many: Facts and Measures

Chapter 9: Why and How: Cause and Effect

shortcut join
micro-level change
recursive key
macro-level change

mini-dimension
swappable dimension
multi-level dimension
hierarchy map
hybrid SCD

WHO AND WHAT

Dimensional Design Patterns for People and Organizations, Products and Services

Who's on first?
— *Bud Abbott and Lou Costello*

What's next?
— *President Jed Bartlet, "The West Wing"*

Who and *what* dimensions such as CUSTOMER, EMPLOYEE and PRODUCT represent some of the most interesting, highly scrutinized, and complex dimensions of a data warehouse. Modeling these dimensions and their inherent hierarchies presents a number of challenges that can be addressed by design patterns.

Who and *what* are the most important dimensions

In the first of our *W*-themed design pattern chapters we begin by describing *mini-dimensions and snowflaking* for handling large, volatile customer dimensions, *swappable dimensions* for mixed customer type models and *hierarchy maps* for recursive customer relationships. We then move on to employee dimensions to cover *hybrid SCD views* for current value/historic value (**CV/HV**) reporting requirements and *multi-valued hierarchy maps* for multi-parent HR hierarchies with dotted-line relationships. We finish by looking at product and service dimension issues and introduce *multi-level dimensions* for variable detail facts and *reverse hierarchy maps* for component analysis.

This chapter describes design patterns for defining flexible, high performance *who* and *what* dimensions

- Large, rapidly changing customer populations
- Mixed business models: businesses and consumers, products and services
- Simultaneous current and historic value reporting requirements
- Variable-depth hierarchies, recursive relationships
- Multi-valued hierarchies
- Business processes with variable levels of dimensional detail
- Product bill of materials

Chapter 6 Design Challenges At a Glance

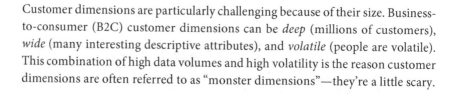

Customer Dimensions

Customer dimensions are particularly challenging because of their size. Business-to-consumer (B2C) customer dimensions can be *deep* (millions of customers), *wide* (many interesting descriptive attributes), and *volatile* (people are volatile). This combination of high data volumes and high volatility is the reason customer dimensions are often referred to as "monster dimensions"—they're a little scary.

Customer dimensions are typically *very large dimensions* (VLDs)

How large is a very large dimension (or table of any type)? Everything is relative. Any absolute figure we quote will be trumped by future hardware and that trumped again by unimagined requirements for capturing big data. The only definition that stands the test of time is: "a very large table is one that does not perform as well as you wish it to."

Mini-Dimension Pattern

Problem/Requirement

Stakeholders are very interested in tracking descriptive changes to the customer base to help to explain changes in customer behavior. So they have defined many historic value (**HV**) customer attributes. Unfortunately using the Type 2 SCD technique for each **HV** attribute is likely to cause explosive growth in the customer dimension; for example, a 10 million row CUSTOMER [HV] dimension with an AGE [HV] attribute will grow by 10 million rows per year. Obviously AGE is a poor choice as an **HV** attribute; it alone would turn CUSTOMER into a *rapidly changing dimension*. This issue is quickly solved by replacing AGE in the dimension with the fixed value (**FV**) attribute DATE OF BIRTH [FV] and calculating the historically correct age, at the time of the facts, in the BI query layer. Sadly, very few customer dimension historical value requirements are as easy to solve as age.

Customer attributes can be too volatile to track using the Type 2 SCD technique

If AGE is in constant use—perhaps with medical data—it can be treated as a non-additive fact (NA) and stored with other facts in a fact table.

It only takes 5 **HV** attributes (that cannot be calculated) that change on average once every two years for each customer, for an initial 10M row CUSTOMER dimension to grow by up to 25 million rows per year. With growth like that, you will have to be careful about which attributes you define as **HV**, and what types of change you track. You don't want to track attributes that have no historical significance—they should be defined as current value (**CV**). Nor do you want to track a history of corrections that should be handled as simple updates. Corrections are easy to spot for **FV** attributes, such as date of birth (cannot change, can only be corrected), but may require group change rules (described in Chapter 3) that look for combinations of **HV** and **CV** attributes changing together to detect genuine change. You may also want to avoid tracking *macro-level changes*.

Customer **HV** attributes must be carefully chosen. Not every change should be tracked, can be tracked, or is worth tracking

Micro and Macro-Level Change

Dimension members can experience two different types of change which will impact how well ETL processes handle HV attributes:

- **Micro-level change** occurs when individual dimension members experience change that is unique to them; for example, a customer changes CUSTOMER CATEGORY and goes from being a "Good Customer" to a "Great Customer". If CUSTOMER CATEGORY is an HV attribute, one row will be updated to give the old value an end date and one row will be inserted with the new value. Hierarchically, this is "change from below".

- **Macro-level change** occurs when many dimension members are changed at once; for example, every "Great Customer" becomes a "Wonderful Customer". Rows affected: 1,000,000 updated, 1,000,000 inserted. Hierarchically, this is "change from above": it's not customers who have changed but CUSTOMER CATEGORY itself. The category "Great Customer" has changed to "Wonderful Customer".

For most dimensions with moderately volatile HV attributes, micro-level changes can be easily and usefully tracked, but it is much harder to justify macro change tracking. A single macro-level change can cause millions of historical versions of customers to be created for little or no analytical value. In the case of every "great customer" becoming a "wonderful customer" should this be tracked using normal HV attribute behavior? You many need to define separate ETL processes that treat certain macro-level changes as one-time corrections.

Most Type 2 SCDs can cope well with individual *micro-level* changes

Macro-level, global changes are more challenging. Should they be handled as changes or corrections?

Solution

Rapidly changing **HV** customer attributes have a *high cardinality many-to-many* (M:M) relationship with customer. One possible solution for tracking these attributes is to model them just as you would model other customer M:M relationships, such as the products they consume, or the sales locations they visit. Products and locations are of course modeled as separate dimensions and related to customers through fact tables. The same can be done with volatile customer attributes by moving them to their own *mini-dimension*.

Volatile HV attributes have a *high cardinality* M:M with their dimension

Figure 6-1 shows CUSTOMER DEMOGRAPHICS, a customer mini-dimension formed by relocating the volatile HV CUSTOMER attributes relating to location, family size, income, and credit score. This mini-dimension has its own surrogate key (DEMO KEY) which is added to customer-related fact tables to describe the historic demographic values at the time of each fact. With fact relationships used to track history, all the problematic **HV** attributes can be removed from CUSTOMER, or changed to **CV** only. This would leave you with an entirely **CV** CUSTOMER dimension that only grows as new customers are acquired.

They can be stored in a separate *mini-dimension* with its own surrogate key and related to the dimension through fact tables

Figure 6-1

Removing volatile attributes from CUSTOMER

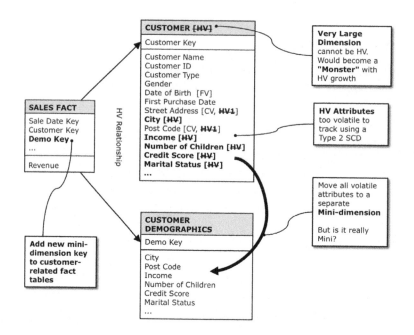

Poorly designed mini-dimensions can be almost as large and volatile as the original dimension

So, problem solved? Unfortunately, it might just be a case of problem moved. If the mini-dimension contains several high cardinality attributes, the number of unique demographic profiles may be almost as high as the number of customers and customer changes will create new profiles rather than reuse existing ones because they are too specific. The **CV** customer dimension might not grow but the so-called "mini-dimension" will, to become the new "monster dimension".

Create stable mini-dimensions by removing high cardinality attributes or reducing their cardinality by banding

Mini-dimensions need to be mini and stay mini if they are to solve the VLD HV problem. Figure 6-2 shows a redesign of CUSTOMER DEMOGRAPHIC where some of the original high cardinality attributes (CITY, POST CODE) have been removed and the continuously valued attributes (INCOME, CREDIT SCORE) have been converted into low cardinality discrete bands. This dramatically reduces the number of unique profiles and increases the chances of reusing them when customers change.

When you have defined a small stable customer mini-dimension you may be able to add additional frequently queried, low cardinality (GENDER, AGE BAND) attributes without significantly increasing its size. These would increase the filtering power of the mini-dimension and reduce the need for many queries to access the much larger CUSTOMER dimension at all.

Add mini-dimension keys to their main dimensions, to support efficient ETL processing

Figure 6-2 also shows that CURRENT DEMO KEY, a **CV** foreign key to CUSTOMER DEMOGRAPHICS, has been added to CUSTOMER. This creates a single table containing the customer business key: CUSTOMER ID and the two customer surrogate keys: CUSTOMER KEY and CURRENT DEMO KEY needed to load customer facts. ETL processes would use this to build an efficient lookup.

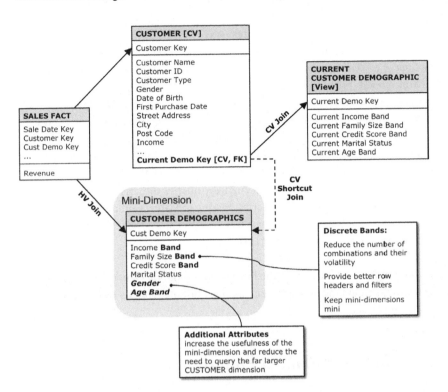

Figure 6-2
Creating a
mini-dimension

The CURRENT DEMO KEY also allows queries to ask questions using current demographic descriptions; for example, the stakeholder question "how many high income customers are there?" (with no further qualification it must mean *currently high income*) can be answered by joining CUSTOMER and CUSTOMER DEMOGRAPHICS directly without having to go through the fact table. This uses a *shortcut join* which is not compatible with fact related queries. For BI tools that do not support shortcut joins or for queries that need both current and historic demographics, a view can be created on the mini-dimension to play the role of CURRENT DEMOGRAPHICS as in Figure 6-2. This customer dimension outrigger could be used to answer interesting questions like "How many customers who are currently married, last purchased from us when they were single?"

A mini-dimension foreign key (**CV, FK**) allows the mini-dimension to be used to answer current value questions

A mini-dimension surrogate key should be added to all fact tables associated with the main dimension, where it represents a *historical value* foreign key (HV, FK). The mini-dimension surrogate key should also be added to the main dimension as a *current value* foreign key (CV, FK) to support ETL processing and CV "as is" reporting.

Consequences

Mini-dimensions increase the size of fact tables by adding foreign keys. If many high cardinality **HV** attributes must be tracked, they may need to be separated into multiple mini-dimensions, to control both main and mini-dimension size. Each mini-dimension that you create will contribute an extra foreign key and index to the fact tables.

Mini-dimensions create additional fact table keys

Banding causes some loss of dimensional detail but creates better attributes for report grouping and filtering

Banding continuous valued attributes, such as INCOME or CREDIT SCORE, causes historical detail to be lost. Having said that, these high cardinality details do not make *good dimensional attributes*. Remember, the role of a dimensional is to provide good report row headers and filters. A high cardinality INCOME attribute is a poor report row header. Precise income figures (if you actually knew them) are virtually unique to customers and would group very little data, resulting in unreadable long reports—more like database dumps than BI reports. Low cardinality banded attributes, such as INCOME BAND make far better row headers, just so long as the bandings are carefully designed with the stakeholders. When stakeholders give you examples of high cardinality dimensional attributes you should ask them for the rollup descriptions or bands they would like to see on their reports. When they define their favorite numeric bandings make sure the bands are contiguous—no gaps and no overlaps.

If stakeholders need access to the history of continuous valued customer details, you should model these *not* as dimensional attributes, but as *facts* in a customer profile fact table.

Large numbers of low cardinality attributes can waste space in very large dimensions

Sensible Snowflaking Pattern

Problem
Stakeholders want to use customer first purchase date in conjunction with commercially available geodemographic information to segment the customer base for marketing purposes. Adding all the necessary descriptive attributes related to first purchase date (first purchase quarter, first purchase on a holiday indicator etc,) and geodemographic code would greatly increase the size of an already very large customer dimension. Stakeholders are worried that existing queries, that don't need the new marketing attributes, will be adversely affected.

"Snowflake" the CUSTOMER dimension. Move large collections of low cardinality attributes to outriggers

Solution
Generally, it's a good idea to denormalize as many descriptive attributes as possible into a dimension to simplify the model and improve query performance. But CUSTOMER dimensions, because of their size, are exceptional and can often benefit from sensible normalization or "snowflaking". The FIRST PURCHASE DATE and GEODEMOGRAPHICS outriggers, shown in Figure 6-3, represent sensible snowflaking because they avoid a large number of much lower cardinality date and geodemographic attributes being embedded in the CUSTOMER dimension. Keeping these attributes separate will make a worthwhile storage saving that will improve query performance—especially for all the queries that are not interested in the first purchase dates or geodemographics. In this specific case the use of an outrigger for FIRST PURCHASE DATE makes even more sense as it can be implemented as a role-playing view of the standard CALENDAR dimension.

For commercially supplied geodemographic information there may be additional administrative or legal reasons for snowflaking. It may be supplied on a periodic basis and updated independently of customer data, or there may be licensing restrictions on the number of users who can access it, therefore it cannot be held in a customer dimension available to the entire BI user community.

Attributes that are administered differently may need to be snowflaked

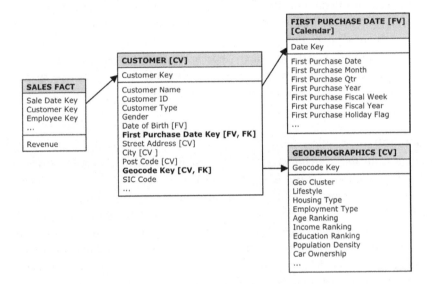

Figure 6-3
Useful customer "snowflaking"

The outriggers in Figure 6-3 do not track history. This is not a problem for first purchase attributes as they are fixed values that can only be corrected. For geodemographic attributes, history could be tracked by defining CUSTOMER as HV but this would lead to uncontrolled growth in the dimension. Alternatively, the GEODEMOGRAPHICS outrigger could be used as a mini-dimension by adding GEOCODE KEY to existing fact tables or a newly created customer demographics fact table.

Consequences

Outriggers complicate dimensional models and are generally unnecessary for most dimensions. Once you have introduced useful outriggers to one dimension, your colleagues, especially those with a 3NF bias, may be tempted to define less useful outriggers in other dimensions that might not have such a positive effect.

You should only model outriggers that have far fewer records than the monster dimensions they are associated with. If any attributes of a proposed outrigger have a cardinality that approaches that of the dimension, leave them there.

Mixed business
model customer and
product dimensions
can contain many
sparsely populated
exclusive attributes

Swappable Dimension Patterns

Problem

For organizations with mixed business models, selling heterogeneous products and services to both consumers and businesses, customer and product dimensions can quickly become complex and unwieldy. Each different type of customer or product can have its own set of exclusive attributes (X) that are not valid/relevant for the other types. This can lead to wide, sparsely populated dimension records. For very large customer populations this can lead to performance and usability issues. Although product populations rarely approach the size of customer populations, for heterogeneous products and services, the number of product type specific attributes can be very large indeed, causing similar problems.

Solution

Dimensions that contain large groups of exclusive attributes (based on one or more *defining characteristic* (**DC**) attributes) can be modeled as sets of *swappable dimensions* to improve usability and performance. Swappable dimensions are so named because they can be swapped into a query in place of (or in addition to) another swappable dimension that shares the same surrogate key. Figure 6-4 shows swappable sets of customer and product dimensions that would be useful for a mixed business model data warehouse. The main CUSTOMER dimension contains attributes that are common across the entire customer population, this includes the defining characteristic CUSTOMER TYPE [DC1,2] which identifies which of two exclusive groups of attributes are relevant: **X1** consumer attributes or **X2** business attributes. The swappable CONSUMER and BUSINESS CUSTOMER dimensions contain these common attributes and the exclusive attributes relevant to just their customer type.

More efficient
*swappable subset
dimensions* can
be created based
on defining
characteristics

Swappable subset dimensions are easier for many BI users to navigate because they contain only the rows and columns that are relevant to them. For example, BI users working in corporate sales would use the BUSINESS CUSTOMER version of CUSTOMER—using database synonyms, it can be renamed to be their default CUSTOMER dimension. Because BUSINESS CUSTOMER only contains corporate customers they would see only the business attributes they want, and would not have to add `where Customer_Type='Business'` to every query. If businesses made up only 10% of the customer base, the corporate sales analysts would see a significant performance boost too.

Hot swappable
dimensions can be
used in place of
each other without
rewriting queries

Swappable dimensions that have identical column names are referred to as *hot swappable,* because they can be used in place of each other without rewriting any queries. Hot swappable dimensions can be used to implement restricted access (row-level security), study groups, sample populations, national language translation and alternative **CV/HV** reporting views (See the *Hybrid SCD* pattern covered later in this chapter).

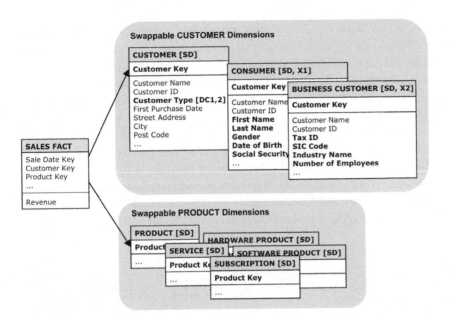

Figure 6-4
Swappable
dimensions

Swappable Dimension Consequences

Swappable dimensions increase the number of database objects that need to be maintained. You should only create them as physical tables if they improve performance. For databases that support variable length column types, sparsely populated exclusive attributes can take up very little space and cause less of a performance issue. In which case, swappable dimensions that are needed only to improve usability can be implemented as database views.

Customer Relationships: *Embedded Whos*

The stakeholder's specification for the CUSTOMER dimension, in Figure 6-5, contains attributes that relate each business customer to two other *whos:* an employee playing the role of ACCOUNT MANAGER [HV], and another customer playing the role of PARENT COMPANY [CV]. Both of these embedded *whos* need to be fully described with **HV** or **CV** attributes for reporting purposes.

Who dimensions can often contain references to other whos that need to be fully described

Figure 6-5
CUSTOMER
dimension with
embedded *who*
attributes

CUSTOMER [HV]

CUSTOMER NAME	CUSTOMER ID	CUSTOMER TYPE	CUSTOMER CATEGORY	ACCOUNT MANAGER	PARENT COMPANY
CV	BK	FV	HV	[EMPLOYEE] HV	[CUSTOMER] CV
Pomegranate	BC2349	Business	Good	LC	None
iPip Design	BC2570	Business	Great	JS	POM Computing
PicCzar Movies	BC2571	Business	Good	LC	Pomegranate
POM Computing	BC2565	Business	OK	LC	Pomegranate
POM Store	BC2567	Business	Great	JS	POM Computing
POMstore.co.uk	BC2569	Business	OK	LC	POM Store

Embedded *whos*

Embedded *whos* can be remodeled as separate *who* dimensions

ACCOUNT MANAGER, should be modeled as a separate dimension using a combination of the *mini-dimension* and *sensible snowflaking* patterns, as shown in Figure 6-6. The ACCOUNT MANAGER attribute is implemented as a foreign key to the EMPLOYEE dimension. This makes all the account manager's descriptive attributes available without bloating the CUSTOMER dimension. To prevent this potentially volatile relationship between account managers and customers from turning CUSTOMER into a rapidly changing dimension, the foreign key is defined as **CV**, so that it represents the *current* account manager. The stakeholder's requirement for reporting by the **HV** account manager is handled by fact table relationship. As with the mini-dimension pattern, the direct relationship can be defined as a shortcut join, or a second view can be created on EMPLOYEE to act as an outrigger playing the role of CURRENT ACCOUNT MANAGER.

Figure 6-6

Modeling an embedded *who* as a separate HV dimension and a CV outrigger

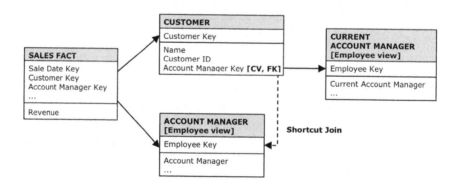

Recursive Relationship

A *who* within a *who* of the same type is a recursive relationship

Looking at the PARENT COMPANY examples, in Figure 6-5, you can see that it contains companies that are present as customers in the CUSTOMER dimension. This represents a *recursive relationship* which would be drawn in ER notation, as in Figure 6-7, with a M:1 relationship between the customer entity and itself. The relationship documents that each customer may **own** one or more customers and each customer may be **owned by** one customer.

Figure 6-7

M:1 recursive relationship or "head scratcher"

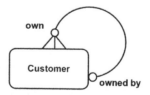

This relationship can be implemented in CUSTOMER by replacing the remaining embedded *who* with another foreign key. But this time the new foreign key: PARENT KEY will *not* refer to a different dimension, instead it will point back to the primary key of CUSTOMER itself. This makes PARENT KEY a recursive foreign key, denoted by the code **RK** in Figure 6-8.

Figure 6-8

BEAM✲ recursive
relationship

HV - dimension contains historical versions of
customers. (No HV attributes shown in this table snippet)

CUSTOMER [HV]

CUSTOMER KEY	CUSTOMER NAME	CUSTOMER ID	PARENT KEY
SK		BK	RK, CV
100	Pomegranate	BC2349	-
101	iPip Design	BC2570	104
102	iSongs Store	BC2572	106
103	PicCzar Movies	BC2571	106
104	POM Computing	BC2565	106
105	POM Store	BC2567	104
106	Pomegranate	BC2349	-
107	POMSoft	BC2566	104
108	POMstore.co.uk	BC2569	105
109	POMstore.com	BC2588	105
110	PicCzar Movies	BC2571	106

RK - Recursive Foreign Key
points to the primary key of
the same table.
Represents a M:1 recursive
relationship.

CV - We are tracking the
current parent only.
(See later for full HV solution)

Several customers are
owned by 106 - the current
version of Pomegranate

Recursion is a very efficient way of storing parent-child relationships. However merely storing the information is only a fraction of the DW/BI story—stakeholders have to be able to use it for analysis. Because a parent customer can in turn be owned by another customer and that in turn owned by another, the recursive relationship can represent a *variable-depth hierarchy*. Wherever a hierarchy exists stakeholders will invariably want to use it to explore the facts. An ownership hierarchy offers the possibility of rolling up individual customer activity to the topmost owners to see who becomes significant when all their indirect sales revenue is consolidated. This would be quickly followed by drill down analysis on ownership to see a breakdown of sales revenue by subsidiaries.

Recursive relationships are often used to represent variable-depth hierarchies

Variable-Depth Hierarchies

Customer ownership is a classic example of a variable-depth hierarchy. Some business customers will be self-contained or privately-owned companies, representing a hierarchy of only a single level. But other customers may be the top, middle, or bottom of a deep hierarchy of corporate ownership (stretching all the way to Liechtenstein or Delaware!). The Figure 6-9 organization chart reveals that all the Figure 6-8 examples customers are ultimately owned by Pomegranate.

Customer ownership is a classic example of a variable-depth hierarchy, best illustrated by an organization chart

If you have difficulty giving meaningful names to the levels in a hierarchy, it is a strong clue that you need to model it as a variable-depth hierarchy. The levels in a balanced or ragged hierarchy normally have distinct names because they represent different things or concepts; for example, day and month in a balanced time hierarchy or street and country in a ragged geographic hierarchy. The levels in a variable-depth hierarchy do not have distinct names, because they typically represent things of the same type; for example, each level in a variable-depth customer ownership hierarchy is a customer.

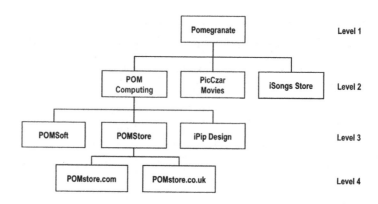

Hierarchy Map Pattern

Problem/Requirement

A consulting firm, that has billed each one of the customers in Figure 6-9 separately, wants to use company ownership information to aggregate all billing facts by parent companies. The data is available in the billing system, stored as a recursive relationship, referred to as a "pig's ear" or "head scratcher" by its designers—because of its shape (see Figure 6-7). Unfortunately, both terms are also very accurate descriptions of how difficult it is to query recursive relationships. The problem is, recursive relationships cannot be navigated using the standard non-procedural SQL generated by most BI tools. Although some databases have recursive extensions to SQL (for example, Oracle's CONNECT BY), they are not supported by BI tools, and seldom perform adequately against data warehousing volumes of fact data.

Because of the challenges involved in making recursive relationships report-friendly, the first thing to do, when you spot one, is to profile the data to see whether it actually represents a variable-depth hierarchy or not. If the data itself represents a balanced hierarchy with a fixed number of levels, or a hierarchy that is only "slightly" ragged, then the design can be kept simple by flattening (denormalizing) the data into a fixed number of well-named hierarchical attributes within a standard dimension.

If data profiling confirms that there is a variable-depth hierarchy, it is worth double-checking that the variable-depth is truly required for analysis purposes. If it is and it cannot be simplified then the following *hierarchy map* techniques will help, but they should also motivate you to, whenever possible, balance and fix the depth of all hierarchies that are under your control! For customer ownership analysis, there is no opportunity to simplify the hierarchies involved. You cannot tell a customer like Pomegranate that its ownership hierarchy is more complex than your other clients and ask it to sort itself out. This hierarchy is external—beyond your control—and must be represented as is.

Solution

A *hierarchy map* is an additional table that resolves a recursive relationship by storing all the distant parent-descendent relationships it represents. Recursive relationships record only immediate parent-child relationships, whereas a hierarchy map stores *every* parent-parent, parent-child, parent-grandchild, parent-great-grandchild relationship, and so on, no matter how distant. Its structure is best explained by looking at the BEAM✱ diagram Figure 6-10 which shows COMPANY STRUCTURE, a hierarchy map for the Figure 6-9 Customer owner-ship hierarchy. It is documented as **CV, HM** to denote that it is a current value hierarchy map: it records only the current ownership hierarchy because it is based on the **CV** definition of PARENT COMPANY in Figure 6-5.

Hierarchy maps store variable-depth hierarchies in a BI-friendly format

COMPANY STRUCTURE [CV, HM]

PARENT KEY	owns SUBSIDIARY KEY	COMPANY LEVEL	SEQUENCE NUMBER	LOWEST SUBSIDIARY	HIGHEST PARENT
SK, PK, CV	SK, PK, HV	N, CV	N, CV	[Y/N], CV	[Y/N], CV
Pomegranate	Pomegranate	1	1	N	Y
Pomegranate	Pomegranate	1	1	N	Y
Pomegranate	POM Computing	2	2	N	Y
Pomegranate	POMSoft	3	3	Y	Y
Pomegranate	POM Store	3	4	N	Y
Pomegranate	POMstore.com	4	5	Y	Y
Pomegranate	POMstore.co.uk	4	6	Y	Y
Pomegranate	iPip Design	3	7	Y	Y
Pomegranate	PicCzar Movies	2	8	Y	Y
Pomegranate	PicCzar Movies	2	8	Y	Y
Pomegranate	iSongs Store	2	9	Y	Y
POM Computing	POM Computing	1	1	N	N
POM Computing	POMSoft	2	2	Y	N
POM Computing	POM Store	2	3	N	N
POM Computing	POMstore.com	3	4	Y	N
POM Computing	POMstore.co.uk	3	5	Y	N
POM Computing	iPip Design	2	6	Y	N
PicCzar Movies	PicCzar Movies	1	1	Y	N
PicCzar Movies	PicCzar Movies	1	1	Y	N
iSongs Store	iSongs Store	1	1	Y	N
POMSoft	POMSoft	1	1	Y	N
POM Store	POM Store	1	1	N	N
POM Store	POMstore.com	2	2	Y	N
POM Store	POMstore.co.uk	2	3	Y	N
iPip Design	iPip Design	1	1	Y	N
POMstore.com	POMstore.com	1	1	Y	N
POMstore.co.uk	POMstore.co.uk	1	1	Y	N

Figure 6-10

Hierarchy map table

The first thing you notice about COMPANY STRUCTURE is that it contains far more rows than the original CUSTOMER dimension. This may explain why the technique is sometimes referred to as a *hierarchy explosion*. But don't worry—it's not a very big bang! The row count is rarely an order of magnitude higher, and hierarchy maps are quite narrow—made up of a pair of surrogate keys and just a few useful counters and flags. Table 6-1 describes these attributes for COMPANY STRUCTURE.

Hierarchy maps explode all the hierarchical relationships (it's not a big bang)

A hierarchy map treats each dimension member as a parent and records all its child, grandchild etc. relationships

COMPANY STRUCTURE contains 11 rows where Pomegranate is the parent: one for each subsidiary customer on the organization chart in Figure 6-9. Explicitly storing a relationship between *all* Pomegranate subsidiaries and their topmost parent makes it easy to answer any Pomegranate-related parent questions. If they were the only questions, these would be the only rows needed in the map but to support fully flexible ad-hoc reporting to *any* level of ownership, the map needs to contain additional rows where *each of the subsidiary customers is treated as the parent of its own small hierarchy.*

Table 6-1
COMPANY STRUCTURE Attributes

ATTRIBUTE	TYPE	USAGE
Parent Key	Surrogate Key	Foreign key to the CUSTOMER dimension playing the role of parent company. Part of the primary key.
Subsidiary Key	Surrogate Key	Foreign key to the CUSTOMER dimension playing the role of subsidiary company. Part of the primary key.
Company Level	Integer	The level number of the subsidiary company. Level 1 is the highest company in a hierarchy
Sequence Number	Integer	Sort order used to display subsidiaries in the correct hierarchical order.
Lowest Subsidiary	[Y/N] Flag	Y indicates that the Subsidiary Key is the lowest company in an ownership hierarchy, it is not the owner of any other customer.
Highest Parent	[Y/N] Flag	Y indicates that the Parent Key is the highest company in an ownership hierarchy, it is not owned by any other customer.

PARENT KEY and SUBSIDIARY KEY in Figure 6-11 are documented as SK. They contain company names for model readability (in true BEAM✳ fashion). The physical database columns will contain integer surrogate keys.

If you know how many members there are at each level you can calculate the size of a hierarchy

You can calculate the number of hierarchy map rows needed for a complete hierarchy by summing the number of members at each level times their level. For the data shown on the organization chart in Figure 6-10 that would be $1\times1 + 3\times2 + 3\times3 + 2\times4 = 24$ rows. COMPANY STRUCTURE has three more rows to handle slowly changing customer descriptions for customers (Pomegranate and PicCzar Movies) in the HV CUSTOMER dimension (Figure 6-8). They make the calculation $2\times1 + 4\times2 + 3\times3 + 2\times4 = 27$ rows.

A quick estimate of the number of rows in a hierarchy map is:

dimension members × (max levels − 1)

For the 11 Pomegranate related dimension members (only 9 customers but there are 2 additional versions of the slowly changed customers) with 4 levels the estimate would be 33. This simple formula always gives you an overestimate, which is good! You will be pleasantly surprised when the map is populated.

Hierarchy Maps and Type 2 Slowly Changing Dimensions

The observant reader may have noticed three seemingly duplicate records in COMPANY STRUCTURE (Figure 6-10) relating to Pomegranate and PicCzar Movies as subsidiaries. These are revealed to be subtly distinct when you see the surrogate key values in Figure 6-11 which show that the hierarchy map contains each *current* parent key to *historic* subsidiary key combination. This is necessary even though the hierarchy map is defined as **CV** (records the current hierarchy *shape* only) so that the current hierarchy can still be used to roll up all the fact history. To do this it must contain every historical subsidiary surrogate key so that it can be joined to all the historical facts just like the Type 2 SCD Customer dimension that it is built from. This design requirement is documented by modeling the SUBSIDIARY KEY as **HV**—even though the PARENT KEY and all other hierarchy map attributes are **CV**.

CV hierarchy maps must contain all the **HV** surrogate key values to join to every historic fact, even though they do not track hierarchy history

COMPANY STRUCTURE [CV, HM]

PARENT	SUBSIDIARY	PARENT KEY	owns SUBSIDIARY KEY
		SK, PK, **CV**	SK, PK, **HV**
Pomegranate	Pomegranate	106	100
Pomegranate	Pomegranate	106	106
Pomegranate	PicCzar Movies	106	103
Pomegranate	PicCzar Movies	106	110
PicCzar Movies	PicCzar Movies	110	103
PicCzar Movies	PicCzar Movies	110	110

HV: contains all the historical values for the Type 2 SCD surrogate key so it can join to all facts

CV: contains only the current surrogate key value for parents. Joins to current parent descriptions only. Does not track hierarchy history

Figure 6-11

Hierarchy map with Type 2 SCD surrogate keys

When HV customer attributes change, their new surrogate key values must also be inserted into the company ownership hierarchy map, as new SUBSIDIARY KEY values even if their ownership remains unchanged.

Using a Hierarchy Map

Joining the customer dimension directly to a fact table in the normal way allows queries to report the facts by the customers *directly* involved. To report the same facts rolled up to *parent* customer levels you insert the hierarchy map between the customer dimension and the fact table, and join on the parent and subsidiary keys as shown in Figure 6-12. To make the business meaning of joining through the hierarchy map more explicit you should create a role-playing view of the CUSTOMER dimension called PARENT CUSTOMER and use that to define the join path in a BI tool.

Parent totals are queried by joining a dimension to the facts through a hierarchy map

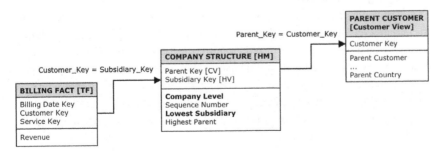

PARENT CUSTOMER [Customer View]
Customer Key
Parent Customer
...
Parent Country

Parent_Key = Customer_Key

COMPANY STRUCTURE [HM]
Parent Key [CV]
Subsidiary Key [HV]
Company Level
Sequence Number
Lowest Subsidiary
Highest Parent

Customer_Key = Subsidiary_Key

BILLING FACT [TF]
Billing Date Key
Customer Key
Service Key
Revenue

Figure 6-12

Using a hierarchy map table to rollup revenue to the parent customer level

Once PARENT CUSTOMER, COMPANY STRUCTURE and BILLING FACT are correctly joined, it becomes simple for stakeholders to ask:

> **What is the total revenue for Pomegranate,**
> **including *all of its subsidiaries*?**

Rolling up descendent facts is straightforward once the hierarchy map is joined correctly

By constraining a query on `Parent_Customer = 'Pomegranate'`, one row from PARENT CUSTOMER joins to the hierarchy map, finding 11 matching subsidiary records. These 11 subsidiary keys are then presented to the fact table, and their revenue is aggregated accordingly. Thanks to the parent-parent rows, where both the parent *and* subsidiary keys represent Pomegranate, the total revenue automatically includes any work done for Pomegranate directly. To exclude this from the total you simply add `Company_Level <> 1` to the query constraint, and only nine keys will be presented to the fact table.

Descendent levels can be filtered using the LEVEL and LOWEST columns in the hierarchy map

Queries can be further refined using COMPANY LEVEL and LOWEST SUBSIDIARY. For example:

- To get the total revenue just for customers that are directly owned by Pomegranate, change the constraint to `Company_Level = 2`

- To get the total revenue for only the Pomegranate companies that do not own other customers, add `Lowest_Subsidiary = 'Y'`

One of the strengths of the hierarchy map is that all of these questions can be answered without knowing (or caring) how many subsidiaries or levels there are.

A CV hierarchy map such as COMPANY STRUCTURE that does not track parent history is not symmetrical for query purposes if its matching dimension contains Type 2 SCD surrogate keys. You cannot reverse the joins in Figure 6-12 and use it to roll up *all* the historical revenue for the parents of a selected subsidiary, because the map only contains the current surrogate key values for each parent. If there is a requirement to roll up historical parent facts using current subsidiary descriptions a different version of the hierarchy map must be built that contains the full history of parent surrogate keys.

Displaying a Hierarchy

A hierarchy map can be used to display a hierarchy by joining a parent view of a dimension to the dimension

The example queries described so far use the hierarchy map to aggregate facts to the parent level. But the hierarchy map can also be used to *display* all the levels of a hierarchy on a report. To do this you join the customer dimension to the parent customer view through the hierarchy map, as shown in Figure 6-13. This gives you both a parent customer name *and* a (subsidiary) customer name to group on and display in your reports—allowing reports to display facts for each level in the hierarchy. However, to make sense of the hierarchy itself on such reports, the subsidiaries have to be displayed in the correct hierarchy sequence.

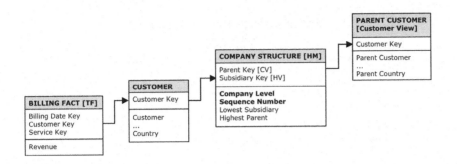

Figure 6-13
Using a hierarchy
map to browse a
customer hierarchy
and report facts at
the subsidiary level

Hierarchy Sequence

Sorting on company name would destroy the hierarchical order. But sorting by hierarchy level is no better, because this would display all the level 1 customers, followed by all level 2 customers, then all level 3 customers, and so on. You would not be able to tell which level 2 customer owns which level 3 customers. To solve this problem the hierarchy map needs a *Sequence Number* attribute that sorts the nodes in the hierarchy correctly "top to bottom before left to right" as shown in Figure 6-14. The Sequence Number can then be used to sort the decedents of a customer (top to bottom) ahead of the next customer (left to right) at the same level; i.e., ensures that all the level 3 subsidiaries of a level 2 customer will be displayed before the next level 2 customer is displayed.

To display a
hierarchy correctly
the hierarchy map
must contain a
hierarchy *sequence
number* that sorts
top to bottom before
left to right

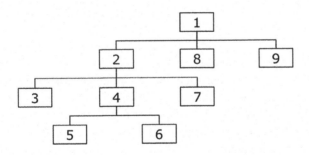

Figure 6-14
Hierarchy
sequence
numbers

The report in Figure 6-15 shows how you use SEQUENCE NUMBER with COMPANY LEVEL to display the hierarchy, by sorting down the page on SEQUENCE NUMBER, and indenting across the page on COMPANY LEVEL. The following snippet of Oracle SQL shows how an indenting Company Name could be defined in a BI tool:

Sort hierarchy
reports by sequence
number and indent
using level

```
LPAD( ' ', 3*(Company_Level-1)) || Customer_Name
```

This will indent each level 2 customer name by three spaces, each level 2 by six spaces, and so on. A level 1 customer would display on the left margin (indented by zero spaces).

To allow new nodes to be added to a hierarchy without updating the existing sequence numbers you can create the initial sequence numbers in increments of 10 or 100 depending on the growth you expect.

Figure 6-15
Hierarchy report,
indented to show
subsidiary level

Pomegranate Revenue Report
YTD 2011

Customer	Total Revenue (£)
Pomegranate	2M
POM Computing	3M
POMSoft	3.5M
POM Store	1M
POMstore.com	2M
POMstore.co.uk	4M
iPip Design	7M
PicCzar Movies	5M
iSongs Store	2.5M
	30M

Report Name: {Big Customer Revenue - YTD }   Run on: {6/9/2011}   Page {1}

Sequence Number

Company Level

Consequences

To populate the sequence number column correctly you have to build the hierarchy map in hierarchy sequence order. This precludes the use of SQL techniques that populate the table "a whole level at a time". It also means that maintenance is more complicated—if nodes are moved their sequence numbers and the sequence numbers of many others around them need to be updated. Because this involves complex coding it is often easier (time permitting) to rebuild (truncate and reload) the hierarchy map than update it.

Drilling Down on Hierarchy Maps

Drill down analysis on a hierarchy map can be implemented using recursive hyperlinks within browser-based reporting interfaces

The default drilling features of most BI tools have difficulty working with hierarchy maps, because they expect a fixed number of levels to drill to. However, drilldown can still be achieved by using report hyperlink features available in browser-based BI interfaces. You could create a report similar to Figure 6-15 that only shows the immediate level 2 subsidiaries for a selected owner with the subsidiary names formatted as hyperlinks. When BI users click on a link the *same report* is called again, passing the selected subsidiary as a parameter to the report. The newly invoked report will then show the next level down in the hierarchy—the subsidiary's level 2 subsidiaries. Even though hierarchy maps remove recursion from the data model to keep queries simple, you can still take advantage of *procedural recursion* to implement efficient variable-depth drilling by recursively calling the same report.

Querying Multiple Parents

Queries that do not constrain to a single parent have to be careful not to over-count descendent facts

Care must be taken when queries do not constrain to a single parent company. A revenue query that simply groups by Parent Customer and returns Pomegranate £30M and PicCzar £5M must not sum these to a grand total of £35M. As you can see from the report in Figure 6-16 the Pomegranate total of £30M already includes the £5M PicCzar revenue because it's a subsidiary. Perhaps what the consulting firm would prefer is a report that showed Pomegranate £30M, EyeBeeM £15M,

MegaHard £27M, and so on; i.e., a report showing total revenue for all the top level clients without listing any of their subsidiaries. This is where the HIGHEST PARENT flag (see Figure 6-10) is useful. By constraining on `Highest_Parent = 'Y'` a query will include only the full hierarchy for each top most customer, and the revenue figures for each of its subsidiaries will be summarized only once.

Use the HIGHEST PARENT flag to filter out partial hierarchies and avoid over-counting

Queries that include multiple parent customers without constraining on highest parents only, must fetch subsidiaries distinctly to avoid overstating the facts. For example, a query that asks for the total revenue for all customers with any parents in California must present a distinct list of SUBSIDIARY KEYs to the fact table before summing revenue, otherwise the revenue will be double counted for any subsidiary that has both a parent and grandparent in California.

For example SQL that handles subsidiaries distinctly while querying multiple parents see: *The Data Warehouse Toolkit, Second Edition*, **Ralph Kimball, Margy Ross (Wiley, 2002) page 166.**

Building Hierarchy Maps

Earlier we stated that proprietary recursive extensions to SQL are not suitable for ad-hoc BI queries against recursive relationships, but they can be used very successfully during ETL processing to unravel recursive relationships and populate hierarchy maps.

Recursive SQL can be used by ETL to load hierarchy maps

You can download an Oracle PL/SQL stored procedure for loading the COMPANY STRUCTURE hierarchy map from modelstorming.com. You will also find SQL for creating the map and a CUSTOMER dimension populated with the Pomegranate example data which you can use to test it or your own ETL hierarchy map loader.

Tracking History for Variable-Depth Hierarchies

When you are designing a hierarchy map to record history, you have to decide which of three histories you are going to track inside the map:

Parent History: tracking changes to the **HV** dimensional attributes of a parent level; for example, when a parent company is reclassified or a manager's salary grade changes. This involves populating the hierarchy map with every surrogate key value for a parent and adding new rows with the new parent key value for every level in its hierarchy every time a parent **HV** attribute changes.

Parent history is tracked by adding every **HV** parent key value to the hierarchy map

Hierarchy History: tracking changes to the hierarchical relationships; for example, a parent company sells a subsidiary or an employee starts reporting to a new manager. This involves the effective dating of all the rows in the hierarchy map. New rows are added to the hierarchy map with the appropriate effective date when new children are added to a hierarchy and end dates are adjusted on existing hierarchy relationships when they are changed or deleted. A change/move—for

Hierarchy history can be tracked by adding effective dates to each hierarchy map record

example, when an employee reports to a different manager—is handled as a logical deletion and a new relationship.

Child history is tracked by adding every HV child key value to the hierarchy map. This should be the default for most hierarchy maps

Child History: tracking changes to **HV** attributes of a child level; for example, the location of a subsidiary company or an employee's marital status changes. This involves populating the hierarchy map with every surrogate key value for a child and adding new rows with the new child key value for every parent level above it, every time a child's HV attribute changes. For a hierarchy map built from an **HV** dimension, such as COMPANY STRUCTURE, it must at least track child history to correctly join to child level facts and rollup all their history.

Tracking the historical version (HV) of a variable-depth hierarchy is a particularly vexing design challenge, not to be undertaken simply because all other attributes of a dimension have been defined as HV.

Historical Value Recursive Keys

To track full history a recursive key in the dimension must be defined as **HV**

If you want to expand COMPANY STRUCTURE to track full hierarchy history so that the historically correct ownership hierarchies could be rolled up or filtered using historically correct parent company values, the PARENT KEY [RK] in the CUSTOMER dimension must first be redefined as **HV** and the dimension populated accordingly with the historically correct recursive data.

The Recursive Key Ripple Effect

HV RK attributes cause a *ripple effect*. A change to a parent **HV** attribute will cause *all* its descendants to be changed and new records to be added to the hierarchy map

Figure 6-16 shows what happens to the CUSTOMER dimension when a change occurs to a high level parent company, such as Pomegranate if PARENT KEY is defined **HV RK**. When Pomegranate is upgraded from "Good" to "Great" a new record—with a surrogate key value of 106—is created to record the change to the HV attribute CUSTOMER CATEGORY. This new CUSTOMER KEY value of 106 must be reflected in the PARENT KEY of all of Pomegranate's children. As PARENT KEY is also **HV**, new child customer records must also be created to preserve its history. This causes a *ripple effect* as each new CUSTOMER KEY must in turn be reflected in the PARENT KEY of its children right down to the bottom of the ownership hierarchy. What would have been a micro-level change to a single customer (Pomegranate) becomes a macro-level change to 9 customers in total—Pomegranate and all of its 8 subsidiaries. This is startling enough, but these 9 new rows in the Customer dimension translate to 25 new rows in the COMPANY STRUCTURE hierarchy map.

Ripple effect growth can be manageable if a dimension contains a small number of small hierarchies

Using an **HV** recursive key to track every parent or child change will cause a dimension to grow more quickly, but the technique is still viable if hierarchies make up a small amount of the data. For example, if only a small percentage of customers are owned by another customer (PARENT KEY is mainly NULL) and ownership hierarchies are typically only a couple of levels deep, the resulting additional growth would be manageable.

CUSTOMER [HV]

CUSTOMER KEY	CUSTOMER NAME	CUSTOMER ID	CUSTOMER CATEGORY	PARENT KEY	CURRENT
SK		BK	HV	RK, **HV**	[Y/N]
100	Pomegranate	BC2349	Good	-	N
106	**Pomegranate**	**BC2349**	**Great**	-	**Y**
102	iSongs Store	BC2572	OK	100	N
110	**iSongs Store**	**BC2572**	**OK**	**106**	**Y**
103	PicCzar Movies	BC2571	Good	100	N
111	**PicCzar Movies**	**BC2571**	**Good**	**106**	**Y**
104	POM Computing	BC2565	OK	100	N
112	**POM Computing**	**BC2565**	**OK**	**106**	**Y**
101	iPip Design	BC2570	Great	104	N
113	**iPip Design**	**BC2570**	**Great**	**112**	**Y**
107	POMSoft	BC2566	Good	104	N
114	**POMSoft**	**BC2566**	**Good**	**112**	**Y**
105	POM Store	BC2567	Good	104	N
115	**POM Store**	**BC2567**	**Good**	**112**	**Y**
108	POMstore.co.uk	BC2569	OK	105	N
116	**POMstore.co.uk**	**BC2569**	**OK**	**115**	**Y**
109	POMstore.com	BC2588	Great	105	N
117	**POMstore.com**	**BC2588**	**Great**	**115**	**Y**

Figure 6-16

Recursive key ripple effect

Ripple Effect Benefits

Using surrogate keys to track every type of change ensures that **HV** hierarchy maps will correctly join the correct historical facts to the correct historical hierarchies using simple SQL. Each new surrogate key will automatically join the historical facts to the correct historical parent version through the correct hierarchical path using simple inner joins with no additional date logic—just like a normal slowly changing dimension. So although the **HV** hierarchy map requires additional rows to record each historical version of a hierarchy, thanks to the ripple effect, its structure and usage remains the same.

The surrogate key ripple effect keeps the correct **HV** joins between parent, hierarchy map and fact table, simple and efficient

Small and relatively stable variable-depth hierarchies can be tracked using an HV recursive key, just like any other HV attribute. While the HV recursive key will cause some additional growth in the dimension, it keeps the joins between hierarchy maps and fact tables simple and efficient.

Ripple Effect Problems

Unfortunately some variable-depth hierarchies are too large or too volatile to be tracked using an **HV** recursive key. A human resources hierarchy is a classic example of this, because it is one single hierarchy which contains *all* the employees in the employee dimension. A minor **HV** change at the highest level would result in the *entire* active employee population being issued with new recursive keys as the change ripples down to the 'shop floor'.

HR hierarchies are too large and volatile for their **HV** recursive keys to be stored in employee dimensions

Avoid tracking history for large or volatile variable-depth hierarchies by using an HV recursive key, because it will cause explosive growth in the dimension. Instead, track hierarchy history outside of the dimension by adding effective dating attributes to hierarchy maps. See the HV MV HM pattern shortly.

Employee Dimensions

HV Employee dimensions are typically Type 2 SCDs

After customers, employees are the next most interesting *who* for BI. Thankfully, because there are usually far fewer employees than customers, the Type 2 SCD technique can work well for tracking the majority of employee **HV** attributes. But employee dimensions are not without their challenges. More descriptive information may be known and recorded about employees and the departments they work in. If that information is tracked historically it can lead to additional BI requirements to analyze the organization, as represented by its employees, using current, previous, historical and year-end descriptions.

In *The Data Warehouse Toolkit, Second Edition,* Ralph Kimball, Margy Ross (Wiley, 2002) Chapter 8, "Human Resource Management" covers many of the basic issues involved in supporting Type 2 SCD Employee dimensions.

Hybrid SCD View Pattern

Problem/Requirement

HV/CV attribute requirements

Employee attributes have been defined as **HV/CV** so that stakeholders can use the historically correct values for "as was" reporting by default but can also use current values for "as is" reporting; for example, the stakeholder question

> **What were the annual expenses by employee location for the last 5 years?**

requires the HV location where employees were based when they incurred the expenses. Whereas the question

> **What are the total expenses over the last 5 years for every employee currently based in the London office?**

doesn't care where employees were based in the last 5 years, it only needs their CV location to filter on.

Solution

Create separate HV and CV swappable dimensions

Create and maintain an HV version of EMPLOYEE using Type 2 SCD ETL processing to satisfy the default reporting requirements. Create a separate *current value swappable dimension* (**CV SD**) from the HV employee dimension. Figure 6-17 shows how a **CV** swappable version of EMPLOYEE can be defined by joining the HV EMPLOYEE dimension to a copy of itself constrained to current employee definitions. In the example every version of James Bond is joined to the current James Bond. The resulting **CV SD** dimension initially appears rather wasteful, containing 3 identical Bonds but on closer examination you notice that each Bond has a different surrogate key value.

The self-join, in Figure 6-17, picks the historical EMPLOYEE KEYs and the current descriptive values. When this identical-looking EMPLOYEE dimension is used instead of the original HV version it will roll up all of Bond's facts from his 3 different era's (EMPLOYEE KEY 1010, 2099 and 2120) to a single location of London or a single status of "Widowed". Because the **CV** and **HV** swappable dimensions are identically described they can be "hot swapped" for each other to change the temporal focus of a query without rewriting any SQL.

A **CV** hot swappable dimension can be built as a self-join view of an **HV** dimension

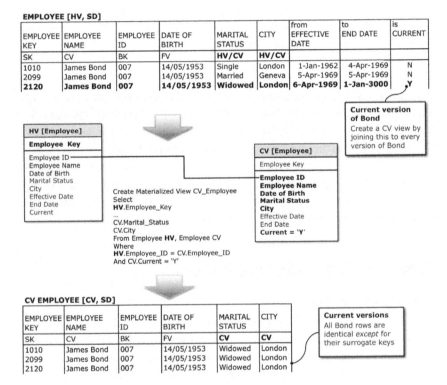

Figure 6-17
Defining a **CV** swappable dimension

CV swappable dimensions can be built as views but for better query performance store them as real tables or materialized views. The small amount of "wasted" space avoids having to do the self-join inside every query.

The **HV** and **CV** swappable dimensions are not mutually exclusive, both can be joined to a fact table in the same query, to group or filter on current and historical values simultaneously. If this is a common requirement, you can build a more query efficient hybrid **HV/CV** dimension by selecting both the **CV** and **HV** versions of attributes and co-locating them in the same swappable dimension to provide side by side attributes for easy comparisons and more ambitious queries; for example, a hybrid EMPLOYEE dimension would allow a query to group by HISTORICAL CITY while filtering on CURRENT CITY.

HV and **CV** swappable dimensions can be used in the same query to provide current and historical values

The self-join pattern can be used to create *Year-End dimensions* for "as at" reporting

As well as creating **CV** swappable dimensions the self-join view technique can be used to create *Year-End* dimensions for "as at" reporting; for example, a Year-End dimension for 4 April 2011 can be created by replacing the CV.Current = 'Y' constraint in the view definition with:

'4/4/2011' between CV.Effective_Date and CV.End_Date

Consequences

The **CV** swappable dimension is a "gold star" agile design pattern. As long as you have tracked history for a dimension from day one, a **CV** view can be added at any time, when **CV** reporting requirements emerge, without increasing ETL programming effort (if implemented as a materialized view) or rewriting any existing queries, because the view is hot swappable.

Don't trust CV only requirements. Build HV dimensions and deliver CV views

Having said that, it is often the case that **CV** reporting is the first choice. Stakeholders will define attributes as **CV/HV** rather than **HV/CV** (with the **CV** default first) because they initially want BI solutions to mimic the **CV** only perspective of existing operational reporting systems. Or perhaps, stakeholders just define **CV** attributes because they simply cannot see a need for history—yet. Either way, unless you are dealing with a very large dimension (customer), you should default to **HV** ETL processing, hide the **HV** dimension and make a **CV** view available. That way, when stakeholders finally demand **HV** reports, you can simply swap views rather than reload the entire warehouse.

Previous Value Attribute Pattern

Problem/Requirement

CV/PV attribute requirements

Occasionally, BI users will simply need the previous value of a dimensional attribute rather than its full history. This can be sufficient when there is a "one off" macro-level change such as the renaming/relocating of branch offices. Previous values can also be necessary when BI users want to look at "alternative realities". By running "as previously" reports they can see what things would be like if a change had not occurred. Stakeholders can define previous value requirements by documenting an attribute as **CV/PV**.

Solution

Implement separate **CV** and **PV** attribute columns

CV/PV attributes are implemented by defining additional PV columns (also known as *Type 3 SCDs*). Figure 6-18 shows PREVIOUS TERRITORY PV1 added to the EMPLOYEE dimension. This is marked **PV1** to link it to the current value TERRITORY attribute marked **CV1**. During ETL processing, whenever TERRITORY is updated its existing value is saved into PREVIOUS TERRITORY prior to storing the new value. **PV** attributes work well for small numbers of attributes that must be tracked but do not change frequently, because they only allow users to go back one version. Multiple PV attributes would allow for more versions; for example TERRITORY LAST YEAR PV1, TERRITORY 2YR AGO PV1, all linked to the current TERRITORY CV1 but can soon become unwieldy.

CV/PV : Current and previous value requirement.

CVn : Current Value attribute linked to a PVn previous value attribute.

PVn : Previous Value attribute. Always linked to a CVn attribute.

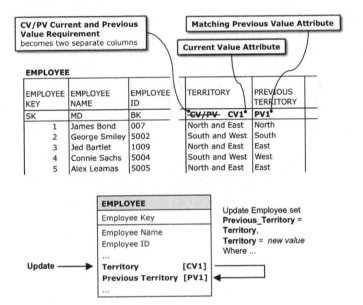

Figure 6-18

Implementing a
previous value
attribute

PV attributes can be used to hold initial or "as at specific date" values; for example, INITIAL TERRITORY PV1 or YE2011 TERRITORY PV1.

Previous Value Attribute Consequences

Defining a small number of hard-coded PV attributes can work well but maintaining large sets of hard-coded PV attributes within a dimension is cumbersome for both ETL and BI. Instead, define an **HV** only dimension and provide **PV** (and **CV**) attributes through hot swappable dimension views.

Human Resources Hierarchies

Organization reporting structures are another example of variable-depth hierarchies. These human resources (HR) hierarchies can be even more challenging than customer ownership hierarchies due to their high level of interconnection. Employees are far more related to one another than customers are: *all* employees ultimately work for the same parent, the CEO. This results in a HR hierarchy map containing a single large volatile hierarchy, rather than thousands or millions of small relatively stable ones. This, coupled with greater availability of data, and requirements to track history more precisely, can make HR hierarchies the most difficult hierarchies to implement in the data warehouse.

HR hierarchy maps
can be challenging
because employees
are highly
interconnected

Multi-Valued Hierarchy Map Pattern

HR hierarchies with dotted-line relationships must rollup employee activity to multiple managers

Problem/Requirement

The Pomegranate organization chart, in Figure 6-19, shows one of the main complexities of HR hierarchies: employees can report to more than one manager. When employee activity is rolled up to a manager or department level these multiple relationships needs to be taken into account. The problem is illustrated by James Bond, who reports to M, but also has a dotted-line relationship with George Smiley. This dotted-line represents a temporary or part-time posting with a full-time equivalence (FTE) of 20%. One must therefore assume, as Smiley might say, that M receives 80% of Bonds efforts. The dotted-line makes this a *multi-parent variable-depth hierarchy* as defined in Chapter 3, with the possibility of multiple immediate parents (managers) for any child (employee).

Figure 6-19
HR hierarchy with a dotted line relationship

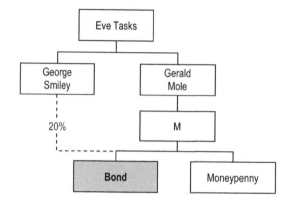

A *multi-parent hierarchy* is represented by a M:M recursive relationship

A multi-parent hierarchy is another example of a variable-depth hierarchy that can be represented in a source system by a recursive relationship, only this time it is a many-to-many (M:M) recursive relationship, as shown in Figure 6-20. The M:M relationship requires an additional association table containing a pair of employee foreign keys.

Figure 6-20
M:M recursive relationship

Solution

M:M recursive relationships can be recorded in a *multi-valued hierarchy* map (**MV, HM**) simply by storing additional rows for the multiple parent relationships but will require additional attributes (Role Type and FTE) to describe the meaning and value of each parent-descendent relationship correctly. Figure 6-21 shows the multi-valued hierarchy map REPORTING STRUCTURE [CV, MV, HM] populated with all the employee relationships documented on the Figure 6-19 organization chart. The first notable thing about this hierarchy map is the number of Bond records. Hierarchy maps always contain more records for the lowest levels because they are repeated for all the parent levels above them. But in the case of Bond the number is inflated by his *dual* roles. The easiest way to understand why this occurs is to imagine that there are two Bonds, one directly under each of his managers. This gives you an idea of how the hierarchy map for a large organization with highly interconnected staff and a deep reporting structure can grow (especially if you were to track its history).

A *multi-valued hierarchy map* (**MV, HM**) is used to represent a multi-parent hierarchy

MV: Multi-Valued dimension or multi-valued hierarchy map (when used in conjunction with HM). Typically contains a weighting factor.

Multi-Valued Hierarchy Map

LOWEST EMPLOYEE Flag denotes that the employee does not manage any other employees

Additional attributes for the type and value of the relationship

Figure 6-21
HR hierarchy map

REPORTING STRUCTURE [CV, MV, HM]

MANAGER KEY	manages EMPLOYEE KEY	at EMPLOYEE LEVEL	in SEQUENCE NUMBER	LOWEST EMPLOYEE	HIGHEST MANAGER	with ROLE TYPE	with WEIGHTING FACTOR
SK, PK, CV	SK, PK, HV	N, CV	N, CV	[Y/N], CV	[Y/N], CV	CV	N, CV
Eve Tasks	Eve Tasks	1	100	N	Y	Permanent	1
Eve Tasks	George Smiley	2	200	N	Y	Permanent	1
Eve Tasks	Bond	3	300	Y	Y	Temporary	0.2
Eve Tasks	Gerald Mole	2	400	N	Y	Permanent	1
Eve Tasks	M	3	500	N	Y	Permanent	1
Eve Tasks	Bond	4	600	Y	Y	Permanent	0.8
Eve Tasks	Moneypenny	4	700	Y	Y	Permanent	1
George Smiley	George Smiley	1	100	N	N	Permanent	1
George Smiley	Bond	2	200	Y	N	Temporary	0.2
Gerald Mole	Gerald Mole	1	100	N	N	Permanent	1
Gerald Mole	M	2	200	N	N	Permanent	1
Gerald Mole	Bond	3	300	Y	N	Permanent	0.8
Gerald Mole	Moneypenny	3	400	Y	N	Permanent	1
M	M	1	100	N	N	Permanent	1
M	Bond	2	200	Y	N	Permanent	0.8
M	Moneypenny	2	300	Y	N	Permanent	1
Bond	Bond	1	100	Y	N	Permanent	1
Moneypenny	Moneypenny	1	100	Y	N	Permanent	1

Additional Multi-Valued Hierarchy Map Attributes

REPORTING STRUCTURE contains two additional attributes to cope with the dotted-line HR relationships:

MV hierarchy maps contain additional rows to represent the multiple parent relationships and additional columns to describe their type and value

Role Type allows the HR map to record whether a manager-to-employee relationship is permanent line management (solid line) or temporary project management (dotted line).

Weighting Factor allows queries to allocate an employee's activity to his multiple managers based on the FTE of his role. For example, a weighted revenue measure would be defined as: Sum(Revenue × Weighting_Factor).

Multi-parent *who* hierarchies are by no means limited to HR. The earlier customer relationship hierarchy would also be multi-parent if it had to support fractional company ownership or joint ventures. Family trees are multi-parent hierarchies!

Weighting factors
become more
complex when there
are multiple dotted-
line relationships

All multi-parent hierarchies—even balanced ones with a fixed number of named levels—require hierarchy maps to store their multiple parent relationships, together with their appropriate weighting factors.

Handling Multiple Weighting Factors

The weighting factors in Figure 6-21 are relatively straightforward, because there is only one part-time employee (Bond) and he does not manage anyone else. However, if circumstances were to change, the allocations become more complicated. For example, if Moneypenny permanently divides her time equally between M and Bond, a new solid-line needs to be drawn between her and Bond worth 50% FTE, as shown in Figure 6-22.

Figure 6-22
Rolling up
weighting factors

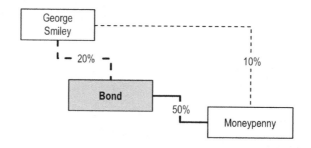

Distant relationship
weighting factors
are calculated by
multiplying the
weighting factors
of the intermediate
direct relationships

In the recursive source data this change would create one new association record in the EMPLOYEE_EMPLOYEE table (Figure 6-20) for Bond-Moneypenny, and update the existing M-Moneypenny record to 50% FTE. In the unraveled hierarchy map more work is required, because records for *each* new distant relationship need to be inserted and *all* the existing distant relationships need to be updated with the appropriate weighting factors. Figure 6-22 shows how the new direct Bond-Moneypenny permanent relationship also creates an distant *temporary* relationship between Smiley and Moneypenny, with a weighting factor of 10%. This is calculated by multiplying all the weighting factors of the direct relationships between the two distant employees: $0.2 \times 0.5 = 0.1$ or 10%.

Updating a Hierarchy Map

If hierarchy history is
not required, it is
often easier to drop
and rebuild hierarchy
maps rather than
update them

Figure 6-23 shows 6 new rows and 9 updated rows in the REPORTING STRUCTURE hierarchy map after all the necessary processing has been performed. Given that the table was initially 18 rows, dealing with only one new relationship has updated 50% of the original table, and caused it to grow by 33%. Because seemingly small changes can cause a large number of complex updates to a hierarchy map, dropping and rebuilding the map is often easier than updating it—if you do not need to track history.

Figure 6-23

Updating a
hierarchy map

REPORTING STRUCTURE [CV, MV, HM]

MANAGER KEY	manages EMPLOYEE KEY	at EMPLOYEE LEVEL	in SEQUENCE NUMBER	LOWEST EMPLOYEE	HIGHEST MANAGER	with ROLE TYPE	with WEIGHTING FACTOR
SK, PK, CV	SK, PK, HV	N, CV	N, CV	[Y/N], CV	[Y/N], CV	CV	N, CV
Eve Tasks	Bond	3	300	N	Y	Temporary	0.2
Eve Tasks	*Moneypenny*	*4*	*310*	*Y*	*Y*	*Temporary*	*0.1* (0.2 x 0.5)
Eve Tasks	Bond	4	600	N	Y	Permanent	0.8
Eve Tasks	*Moneypenny*	*5*	*610*	*Y*	*Y*	*Permanent*	*0.4* (0.8 x 0.5)
Eve Tasks	Moneypenny	4	700	Y	Y	Permanent	0.5
George Smiley	Bond	2	200	N	N	Temporary	0.2
George Smiley	*Moneypenny*	*3*	*210*	*Y*	*N*	*Temporary*	*0.1* (0.2 x 0.5)
Gerald Mole	Bond	3	300	N	N	Permanent	0.8
Gerald Mole	*Moneypenny*	*4*	*310*	*Y*	*N*	*Permanent*	*0.4* (0.8 x 0.5)
Gerald Mole	Moneypenny	3	400	Y	N	Permanent	0.5
M	Bond	2	200	N	N	Permanent	0.8
M	*Moneypenny*	*3*	*210*	*Y*	*N*	*Permanent*	*0.4* (0.8 x 0.5)
M	Moneypenny	2	300	Y	N	Permanent	0.5
Bond	Bond	1	100	N	N	Permanent	1
Bond	*Moneypenny*	*2*	*200*	*Y*	*N*	*Permanent*	*0.5*

6 new Moneypenny records for her new relationships: 2 Temporay, 4 Permanent

All Bond records are updated because he is now a manager

All existing Moneypenny records are updated with a weighting factor of 0.5

Historical Multi-Valued Hierarchy Maps

Earlier, we described how the customer ownership hierarchy map was able to track full hierarchy history without schema modification if it was populated from an HV version of its recursive key held in the customer dimension. This is not an option for the multi-parent HR hierarchy because multiple MANAGER KEYs cannot be stored in an employee dimension. Even if HR was a single parent hierarchy, it is too large and too volatile for an **HV** recursive key to be viable—the ripple effect would cause uncontrollable growth in the dimension. Instead the HR hierarchy map must be modified to use effective dating to track history.

*To track history, large volatile, multi-valued hierarchy maps cannot rely on **HV** recursive keys. Instead effective dating must be used*

Figure 6-24 shows an **HV** version of the REPORTING STRUCTURE hierarchy map that includes the effective dating attributes EFFECTIVE DATE, END DATE and CURRENT typically found in **HV** dimensions. These attributes allow BI Users to browse both the current hierarchy (Where CURRENT ='Y') and any point in time hierarchy (e.g., where '31/3/2011' Between EFFECTIVE_DATE and END_DATE). To understand how this hierarchy map records changes to an employee, a manager and their relationship, take a look at the timelines in Figure 6-25 for Bond, M and Bond's HR relationships during the first six months of 2011.

*Effective date, end date and a current flag should be added to **HV, MV, HM** tables*

Consequences

With its effective dated relationships, the REPORTING STRUCTURE [HV] map can be used to rollup employee facts using historically correct hierarchy descriptions, but its join to fact tables is more complex than before. When the hierarchy map did not contain historical relationships the join to SALES FACT was simply:

```
Where Reporting_Structure.Employee_Key = Sales_Fact.Employee_Key
```

Figure 6-24

HV hierarchy map with effective dating

Bond starts working for M

REPORTING STRUCTURE [HV, MV, HM]

HR HM KEY	MANAGER	EMPLOYEE	MANAGER KEY	manages EMPLOYEE KEY	with WEIGHTING FACTOR	from EFFECTIVE DATE	to END DATE	is CURRENT
SK			SK, PK1, HV	SK, PK1, HV	N, HV	D, PK1	D	[Y/N]
1	Smiley	Smiley	999	999	1	1-Dec-1960	1-Jan-3000	Y
2	Bond	Bond	1001	1001	1	1-Dec-1960	28-Feb-2011	N
3	M	M	1002	1002	1	1-Dec-1960	31-Jan-2011	N
4	**M**	**Bond**	**1002**	**1001**	**1**	**1-Jan-2011**	**31-Jan-2011**	**N**
5	M	M	1003	1003	1	1-Feb-2011	31-May-2011	N
6	M	Bond	1003	1001	1	1-Feb-2011	28-Feb-2011	N
7	M	Bond	1003	1004	1	1-Mar-2011	31-Mar-2011	N
8	Bond	Bond	1004	1004	1	1-Mar-2011	31-Mar-2011	N
9	**M**	**Bond**	**1003**	**1004**	**0.8**	**1-Apr-2011**	**30-Apr-2011**	**N**
10	**Smiley**	**Bond**	**999**	**1004**	**0.2**	**1-Apr-2011**	**30-Apr-2011**	**N**
11	M	Bond	1003	1005	0.8	1-May-2011	31-May-2011	N
12	Smiley	Bond	999	1005	0.2	1-May-2011	1-Jan-3000	Y
13	Bond	Bond	1005	1005	1	1-May-2011	1-Jan-3000	Y
14	M	M	1006	1006	1	1-Jun-2011	1-Jan-3000	Y
15	M	Bond	1006	1005	0.8	1-Jun-2011	1-Jan-3000	Y

Bond begins working
20% for Smiley
80% for M

Effective dating must be used to correctly join the hierarchy map to fact tables

Now the multiple historically correct versions of the hierarchical relationships must be joined to the correct historical facts to avoid over-counting. This requires a complex (or theta) join involving the hierarchy map effective dates and the primary time dimension of the fact table:

```
Where Reporting_Structure.Employee_Key=Sales_Fact.Employee_Key
and
Sales_Date is Between Reporting_Structure.Effective_Date and
                Reporting_Structure.End_Date
```

To avoid this, the hierarchy map can be given its own surrogate key which is then added to HR fact tables

This is likely to be a very expensive join. To get round this problem for HR fact tables that must be constantly joined to the hierarchy map, a surrogate key must be added to the hierarchy map such as HR HM KEY in Figure 6-24. This surrogate key works like any other dimensional surrogate key to avoid effective dated joins. It can be added to any specialist HR fact tables to simplify the join to:

```
Where Reporting_Structure.HR_HM_Key = Salary_Fact.HR_HM_Key
```

This creates a new dependency: the hierarchy map must be built and updated before any HR fact tables

Implementing this surrogate key would require the REPORTING STRUCTURE table to be built and updated ahead of the SALARY FACT table, like any normal HR dimension, because the HR HM KEY values must be ready before the fact table load begins. The simpler **CV** version of REPORTING STRUCTURE without its specialist surrogate key does not require this dependency and can be maintained independently of the facts.

Alternatively, large HR hierarchies could be split into a number of smaller hierarchies that can be tracked using surrogate keys

An alternative approach, to avoid effective dating joins or a hierarchy map surrogate key, is to break the single organization hierarchy into a number of far smaller departmental hierarchies by removing the executive level(s) from the hierarchy map; in this case: Eve Tasks. The smaller hierarchies would be less susceptible to macro change from above and its resulting ripple effect, which would enable the employee surrogate key to be used to track all **HV** changes to employees *and* their HR relationships.

Figure 6-25
HR timelines

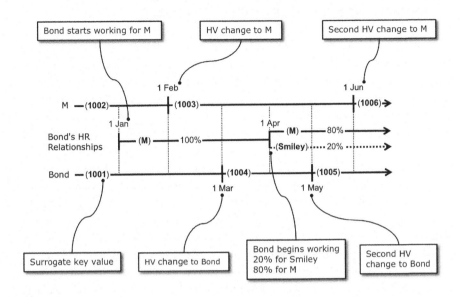

Product and Service Dimensions

Product dimensions have their own unique design challenges. Though not as large or volatile as *who* dimensions, these *what* dimensions can be just as complex to model because products can be described in so many different ways, by so many different stakeholder groups. While stakeholders never know enough about their customers, they know almost too much about their products and services!

Product hierarchies are important for BI reporting because businesses are often closely organized around them. Yet despite their importance, they may not be well designed from a BI perspective. Thankfully, product hierarchies are fixed-depth rather than variable-depth, but they can still be difficult to define. Established product hierarchies often represent the single biggest conformance issue for agile data warehouse design, because they have become ragged and full of conflicting definitions, through years of ad hoc growth and redefinition by many different departments.

Another challenge unique to *what* dimensions is the need to ask BI questions about what is going on *inside* a product or service. This is rare for *who* dimensions—unless you are dealing with medical data. For products, "what is going inside" may be other products and services, in the case of product bundle sales, or components and parts, in the case of design and manufacturing. To answer questions about these, a data warehouse design must handle "bill-of-materials" information—and that is another example of a variable-depth hierarchy.

Product dimensions are complex because stakeholders know too much about their products and services

Product hierarchies are typically the most important hierarchies but they can often be ragged and difficult to conform

Product "bill-of-materials" is another type of variable-depth hierarchy that the data warehouse may need to support

Describing Heterogeneous Products

Heterogeneous products and services can have too many specialist dimensional attributes to fit comfortably into a single product dimension

Product dimensions can become very complex when an organization like Pomegranate deals with very different types of products—such as hardware, software, third party accessories, consulting services, licenses and support subscriptions—that all need to be described in very different ways. These heterogeneous descriptions can lead to wide sets of dimensional attributes that are only valid for certain product types. This is the same mixed business problem as dealing with multiple customer types but greatly compounded by the fact that organizations usually know a lot more about their products than their customers and have many more specialist ways of describing them. Even though product dimensions rarely approach the row count of customer dimensions, the row length of product dimensions, that attempt to describe every radically different product type can cause just as many performance, usability and manageability problems. With large sets of specialist attributes for heterogeneous products and services, BI users will have to scroll through pages of attributes to find the ones that interest them and will be daunted when trying to find correlated attributes. You may even exceed the maximum number of columns in a single table supported by your DBMS.

Large sets of specialist attributes should be grouped together in their own swappable subset dimensions, based on a defining characteristic such as product type

For both query performance and usability, you may want to break a monolithic product dimension into several swappable subset dimensions (**SD**), as in Figure 6-4, based on defining characteristics (**DC**) such as product type or subcategory. Each swappable dimension would contain exclusive (**X**) attribute groups that require specialist knowledge to use or interpret correctly. For example, a retailer may have more than 300 attributes that describe clothing products—in minutia. These would be fascinating to clothing buyers but of little interest to finance or logistics. If query performance is not an issue, swappable subsets can be delivered as views, otherwise materialized views or separate tables may be needed to overcome poor performance or column number limitations.

Balancing Ragged Product Hierarchies

Product hierarchies can sometimes look like variable-depth hierarchies but they are in most cases ragged hierarchies

Product hierarchies can sometimes appear to be of variable-depth, especially when source data is held in recursive structures within an Enterprise Resource Planning (ERP) package, or when every department seems to have a different number of levels on the product hierarchy charts pinned to their walls. However, what is most often thought of as "the product hierarchy" is not a true variable-depth hierarchy—a hierarchy of products within products—but actually a ragged hierarchy of products within groups that are based on the physical, organizational, or geographic properties of products. Many of the attributes used to assign products to these groups are not mandatory, or are exclusive to certain subsets, leading to raggedness when you try to create a single conformed hierarchy of all products, across all business processes and departments.

Ragged hierarchies, as described in Chapter 3, can look similar to variable-depth hierarchies but the important distinction that makes them easier to deal with is that they have a known maximum number of named levels. This means that they can be implemented in a dimension by simply defining the missing or unused levels as nullable. Figure 6-26 shows an example of a product dimension containing a ragged hierarchy (that matches the hierarchy chart of Figure 3-8). It contains the product "POMServer", which does not have a subcategory, perhaps because it is the only product of its type. This simple "flattening" of the hierarchy, into a fixed number of columns within the dimension, is in stark contrast to the complexity of building a separate hierarchy map, but it can result in a "Swiss cheese" dimension, full of "NULL holes" that show up as gaps on reports. Even if these holes are filled in with the stakeholders' preferred label, such as "Not Applicable", they can cause problems for drill-down analysis: all the "Not Applicable" values are grouped together and cannot be further drilled on. Also, it does not inspire stakeholder confidence in the data warehouse when BI applications use such a common level as a product subcategory and return "Mobile," "Desktop," and "Not Applicable" .

Ragged hierarchies have a fixed number of uniquely nameable levels. They can be implemented in a dimension by defining non-mandatory attributes for the hierarchy levels that have missing values

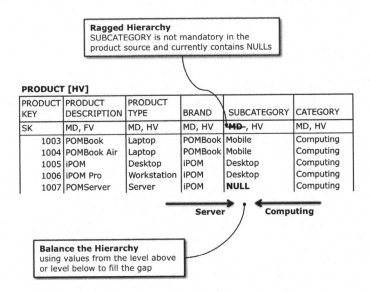

Figure 6-26
Balancing a ragged hierarchy

In most cases, the best approach is to *balance* a ragged product hierarchy by filling in the missing values with the stakeholders during a modelstorming workshop as part of conforming these dimensional attributes. Where filling in the gaps with the stakeholders is not possible—stakeholders cannot agree on the appropriate new or existing values or there are just too many missing values to tackle in the available time—there are three methods for automatically generating usable interim values for the missing levels (that will induce the stakeholders to create their own):

Balance *slightly* ragged hierarchies with the help of stakeholders: by asking them to fill in the missing values

Temporary balancing can be achieved by filling in a missing level with values from the level directly above or below

Top down balancing: A value is copied down into the missing level from the level directly *above* it. For example, the POMServer CATEGORY value "Computing" is copied into SUBCATEGORY.

Bottom up balancing: A value is copied up into the missing level from the level directly *below* it. For example the POMServer PRODUCT TYPE value "Server" is copied into SUBCATEGORY.

Top down and bottom up balancing: Gaps are filled with new unique values created by concatenating the values directly above and below the missing level. For example, "Computing/Server" might be used to fill the SUBCATEGORY gap for "POMServer".

When a ragged hierarchy is discovered during data profiling, if only a very small percentage (1-2%) of it is ragged (skips a level) this usually indicates errors in the data rather than intentional design. The errors should be corrected and a simple balanced hierarchy defined.

Multi-Level Dimension Pattern

Problem/Requirement

A business event needs to be described using various levels of a dimensional hierarchy

Having *different* business processes associated with *different* levels of the Product hierarchy is common. For example, sales plans are set on a monthly basis at the brand level, whereas sales transactions are recorded daily for individual products. These different business processes are handled by separate fact tables, and the different levels of product detail should be handled by separate dimensions too: a full PRODUCT dimension for sales facts and a BRAND [RU] rollup dimension for sales plans. Attaching the appropriate dimension to each fact table clearly documents its fixed product granularity. However, there are circumstances where a *single* business process can be associated with *different* levels of the Product hierarchy. For example, a web page event on a Pomegranate website can describe a visitor viewing a single product, multiple products of the same product type, a product category description or no product information at all.

Solution

It is possible to attach a product description to the majority of page visits recorded on the Pomegranate's websites, especially the online store pages. But not every page refers to products; some pages describe multiple products: whole product categories, subcategories, or specific brands. You can easily handle non-product pages by using the "special" zero surrogate key that represents "missing product", as discussed in Chapter 5. In a similar way, you can use other "special" surrogate key values to help you describe the page visits that relate to the higher levels in the product hierarchy by designing a *multi-level dimension*.

Multi-level dimensions contain additional rows that represent all the multiple levels within their hierarchies that are needed to describe mixed-level facts. For example, a multi-level product dimension contains records for each product *and* additional records for each brand, subcategory, and category if facts need all these levels. Figure 6-27 shows a multi-level PRODUCT dimension, denoted by the code **ML,** that contains example additional rows that represent entire categories (**SKs** -1 and -2), a subcategory (**SK** -3), and a brand (**SK** -4). The complete table would contain one additional row for every value at every level needed.

A *multi-level dimension* (**ML**) contains additional rows that represent level values within its hierarchy

Multi-Level (ML) Dimension
contains additional records representing higher levels in the product hierarchy

LEVEL TYPE
Majority of rows will be **Product**

Figure 6-27
Multi-level
Product
dimension

PRODUCT [ML]

PRODUCT KEY	PRODUCT DESCRIPTION	Weight	PRODUCT TYPE	BRAND	SUB CATEGORY	CATEGORY	LEVEL TYPE
SK	MD, FV	MD	MD, HV	MD, HV	MD, HV	MD, HV	NN
1002	iPip G1	500g	MP3	iPip	Music	Entertaiment	Product
1004	POMBook Air	1Kg	Laptop	POMBook	Mobile	Computing	Product
1008	iPOM + Printer	6Kg	Bundle	iPOM	Desktop	Computing	Product
1009	iPip Touch	120g	PDA	iPip	Multi-Media	Entertainment	Product
0	Not Available	N/A	N/A	N/A	N/A	N/A	Missing
-1	Not Applicable	N/A	N/A	N/A	N/A	Computing	Category
-2	Not Applicable	N/A	N/A	N/A	N/A	Entertainment	Category
-3	Not Applicable	N/A	N/A	N/A	Desktop	Computing	Subcategory
-4	Not Applicable	N/A	N/A	iPOM	Destop	Computing	Brand

Category Level Row
representing all **Entertainment** products

ML: **Multi-Level dimension that contains additional members representing multiple levels in its hierarchy. Also used to document an event detail or dimensional foreign key that represents a multi-level dimension.**

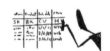

Multi-level dimensions also contain an additional attribute LEVEL TYPE that documents the meaning of each row in the dimension. The majority of rows will be normal members that represent individual products (or employees in the case of a multi-level employee dimension). Their LEVEL TYPE defaults to the name of the dimension itself, whereas the additional rows will be labeled after the level attribute in the hierarchy they represent. LEVEL TYPE is useful for ETL processes that manage the use of these additional records, and can also be used by queries that want to constrain on specific level facts only. LEVEL TYPE can be ignored by most queries that simply want to roll up all the facts to a particular level. For example, a query using PRODUCT [ML] could group by CATEGORY and count web page visits to get the total pages viewed for each category; the figures would automatically include pages for individual products, brands, and subcategories within each category, as well as pages for the categories themselves.

Multi-level dimensions contain a LEVEL TYPE attribute which documents the meaning of each row

You capture multi-level dimension requirements when stakeholders tell *group* themed event stories using example values that normally appear at higher levels in hierarchies; e.g., they give you "MI6" when you were expecting "Bond".

A multi-level employee dimension would allow you to handle events where *groups of employees* occasionally act like individual employees. For example, sales transactions are normally assigned to individual employees but when several members of staff are involved or the employee is unavailable (perhaps the individual has left the company or the transaction was customer self-service) sales facts can be assigned an EMPLOYEE KEY that represents a team, branch or division. In Chapter 9, we will combine multi-level and multi-valued employee dimensions to describe *how* joint sales commissions can be calculated.

Do not use a multi-level dimension to describe fixed-level facts

The additional flexibility of multi-level dimensions can be confusing, so they should never be used where their flexibility is unnecessary. Create separate single and multi-level versions of a dimension to make their usage explicit. If a star schema has a fixed level of dimensional detail, use normal (single-level) dimensions with no LEVEL TYPE attributes. The presence of a LEVEL TYPE in the star implies that facts are multi-level when that is not the case. If a fact table truly needs a multi-level dimension you should explicitly document it by marking the dimensional foreign key as **ML** in the fact table, as in Figure 6-28.

Figure 6-28
Documenting single and multi-level fact tables

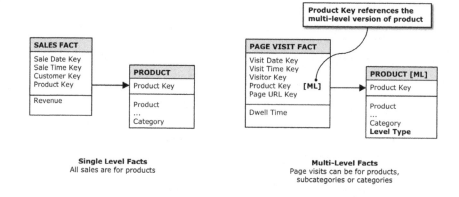

Single Level Facts
All sales are for products

Multi-Level Facts
Page visits can be for products, subcategories or categories

Never use a multi-level dimension to create facts with mixed meanings

Consequences

You should never use a multi-level dimension to change the meaning of a fact. For example, do not store target revenue at the brand level and actual sales revenue at the product level in the same fact table. Sales and planning are two very different business processes, two different verbs. How would you name and easily describe the resulting fact table? Even sticking to a single business process, do not store summary sales for a category in a product sales fact table. Performance enhancing summaries require their own aggregate fact tables (described in Chapter 8). If you used a multi-level dimension to store targets, summaries and actuals, the resulting revenue fact would not be additive across LEVEL TYPE. To avoid over-counting, every query would have to remember to constrain to a single LEVEL TYPE—a recipe for disaster. The multi-level product dimension works perfectly with the page visit fact table, in Figure 6-28, because it does not change the meaning of the facts; they are all page visits no matter if they are for a product or a category. That is why dwell time and total pages viewed remain additive across LEVEL TYPE.

Parts Explosion Hierarchy Map **Pattern**

Problem/Requirement

Stakeholders need to analyze product sales down at the level of the components that went into the products using product *bill of materials* (BOM) data. The bill of materials for a product can be represented as a variable-depth hierarchy of components within components; for example, Figure 6-29 shows the BOM hierarchy for a new product sold by employee James Bond. It reveals that the "POMCar" is made up of an "off the shelf" Aston Martin DB5 and an enhanced safety pack, that is itself made up of a number of interesting gadgets. A bill of materials like this is typically stored in an operational system using M:M recursive structures that allow the components of a product or service to be made up of other products and services.

A product bill of materials represents a variable depth hierarchy of components

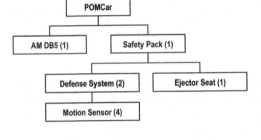

Figure 6-29
Bill of materials
for a POMCar

Solution

A BOM can be represented by the PARTS EXPLOSION hierarchy map in Figure 6-30. This is a *reverse hierarchy map* which joins to product facts (and the product dimension) by its parent key (PRODUCT KEY) as in Figure 6-31, allowing the facts to be *rolled down* to or *filtered on* child components. It contains a SUB ASSEMBLY flag that indicates "Y" if a component is made up of other identifiable components and QUANTITY, which records the number of components that go into the finished product. This is similar to a distant weighting factor in that it needs to be adjusted in the hierarchy map based on its parent quantities. For example, a single defense system contains 4 motion sensors, but a POMCar contains 2 defense systems, so the quantity of motion sensors it contains is 8.

A reverse hierarchy map joins to fact tables by its parent key and allows facts to be allocated to child levels

PARTS EXPLOSION [HV, MV, HM]

PRODUCT KEY	contains COMPONENT KEY	at PART LEVEL	in SEQUENCE NUMBER	SUB ASSEMBLY	QUANTITY
SK, PK, HV	SK, PK, HV	N, HV	N, HV	[Y/N], HV	N, HV
POMCar	AM DB5	1	10	N	1
POMCar	Safety Pack	1	20	Y	1
POMCar	Defense System	2	30	Y	2
POMCar	Motion Sensor	3	40	N	8 (2 x 4)
POMCar	Ejector Seat	2	50	N	1

Figure 6-30
PARTS
EXPLOSION
hierarchy map

Add a cost or revenue recovery weighting factor to a BOM hierarchy map to allocate revenue facts to product components (or the sub-products of a bundled offering) based on their quantity and unit value.

Figure 6-31
Component
Analysis

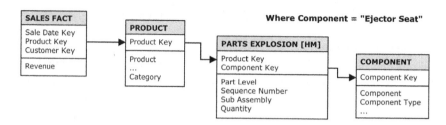

Consequences

Don't try to use the PARTS EXPLOSION hierarchy map pattern to describe the bill of materials for anything as complex as a real car, submarine or aircraft—unless you are prepared for a very large table.

Summary

- **Mini-dimensions** track historic values for very large volatile dimensions, like CUSTOMER, that cannot use the Type 2 SCD technique. Volatile **HV** attributes are moved to a separate mini-dimension to keep the size of the main dimension under control and the historical values are related back to the main dimension via fact table relationships. Mini-dimensions typically band high cardinality values to control their size and volatility and to provide better report row headers and filters.

- **Snowflaking** makes sense for very large dimensions when a large set of lower-cardinality, seldom used attributes can be normalized into outriggers. The calendar dimension can be a particularly useful outrigger for any dimension that contains embedded dates.

- **Swappable dimensions (SD)** are used to break up large mixed type dimensions into specialist subsets that are easier to use and faster to query. Swappable dimensions can be swapped into a star schema in place of one another because they share a common surrogate key.

- **Hybrid SCD** requirements for current value and historical value reporting are best handled by creating separate hot swappable **CV** versions of HV dimensions. These **CV** dimensions can be created as material views using simple self-joins of **HV** dimensions.

- **Hierarchy maps (HM)** are used to store variable-depth hierarchies in a report-friendly format and avoid recursive structures that cannot easily be queried by BI tools.

- **Multi-valued hierarchy maps (MV HM)** are used to represent multi-parent hierarchies that are typically stored in source systems as M:M recursive relationships.

- **Multi-level dimensions (ML)** describe business events that vary in their level of dimensional detail. A multi-level dimension will contain additional special value members that represent higher levels in the dimension's hierarchy.

fact-specific epoch time key
date key
YTD location-specific
calendar month
national language dimensional overloading
time zone ISO date
clock

WHEN AND WHERE

Dimensional Design Patterns for Time and Location

The past is a foreign country: they do things differently there.
— L.P. Hartley, The Go-Between

Every business event happens at a point in *time* or represents an interval of time. Time is the primary way that BI queries group ("show me monthly totals"), filter ("show me sales for Financial Q1"), and compare business events ("How are we doing year to date, versus last year?"). That is why *every* fact table has at least one time (*when*) dimension.

Most business events occur at a specific geographical or online *location*. Many interesting events represent changes of location. Hence, a large number of fact tables have distinct *where* dimensions in addition to the location attributes that can be found in *who* and *what* dimensions, such as customer and product.

Although *when* and *where* are separate dimensions, they can influence one another: Time zones, holidays and seasons, are all examples of *location-specific time attributes* that are affected by *event geography*. Similarly, analytically significant locations such as the first and last locations in a sequence of events are *timing-specific location dimensions*, affected by event chronology.

In this chapter, we describe dimensional design patterns for efficiently handling time and location, in particular, patterns for correctly analyzing year-to-date facts, and journeys—facts that represent changes in space and time, that are all about *where* and *when*.

- **Efficient date and time reporting**
- **Correct year-to-date analysis**
- **Time zones, international holidays and seasons**
- **National language support**
- **Trip and journey analysis**

Side notes:

Time is the most frequently used dimension for BI analysis

Location dimensions and attributes are frequently used too

Time and location are separate dimensions but can affect one another

This chapter describes *when* and *where* design patterns

Chapter 7 Design Challenges *At a Glance*

Time Dimensions

When details
are modeled as
physical time
dimensions

Every event contains at least one *when* detail, which should always be modeled as a time dimension, rather than left as a timestamp in the fact table. But why do you need a time dimension when you have datetime data types, date functions and date arithmetic built into data warehouse databases and BI tools?

Physical date
dimensions help to
simplify the most
common grouping
and filtering
requirements of BI
queries

Descriptive time attributes, such as day of week, month, quarter and year, are constantly used to group and filter the information on BI reports. Deriving them from raw timestamps in every query is woefully inefficient and puts an unnecessary burden on BI users and BI tools, that cause mistakes and inconsistencies. Why decode the month or day of week every time they are needed, when they could be stored *once* in a dimension and reused consistently and efficiently, like any other dimensional attribute? Also, many commonly used time attributes—such as fiscal periods, holidays, and seasons of the year—simply cannot be derived from timestamps alone because they are organization or location specific.

You should build a physical time dimension to:

- Avoid duplication of calendar logic in each report or BI application
- Remove date arithmetic from constraints to increase index use
- Insulate queries from DBMS-specific date functions
- Support organization-specific fiscal periods
- Define conformed time hierarchies
- Provide consistent time-related business labels and definitions

Date and time of
day are modeled
as separate
dimensions to
match their
dimensional usage,
manage their size
and make the time
granularity of facts
explicit

Time is actually best modeled dimensionally by splitting it into *date* and *time of day*. This may seem odd at first, but it does reflect how time is queried. Almost every query will group or filter on *sets of days* (Years, Quarters, Months or Weeks). Many queries will do the same with *periods within a day* (AM/PM, work shift, peak periods). But very few queries will use arbitrary periods that span dates and times (e.g., "sales totals by periods of 2 days and 8 hours"). Financial queries are grouped by the date-related fiscal calendar, ignoring time of day all together, while operational and behavior queries can group months of data together by time of day to see peak and average activity levels. In recognition of these query schisms, *when* details (logical time dimensions) should be implemented as two distinct and manageable physical dimensions: a *calendar* date dimension, and a *clock* time of day dimension, each with its own surrogate key. Separating date and time, like this, also makes the time granularity of facts explicit. If time of day is not significant (or not recorded) for a business event, its fact table design simply omits the clock dimension, and includes only the calendar dimension.

Calendar and clock
are role-playing
dimensions

Figure 7-1 shows typical examples of Calendar and Clock dimensions related to an order fact table. Each of these dimensions play *two* roles: representing distinct *Order* and *Delivery* dates and times. Although only one physical instance of each dimension will exist, BI tools should present the two roles as separate dimensions using views that rename each time attribute based on its role. For example, ORDER TIME, ORDER DATE, ORDER MONTH and DELIVERY TIME, DELIVERY DATE and DELIVERY MONTH.

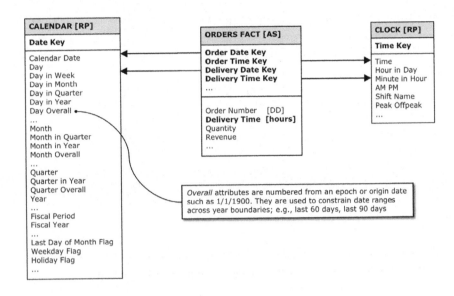

CALENDAR [RP]
Date Key
Calendar Date
Day
Day in Week
Day in Month
Day in Quarter
Day in Year
Day Overall ●
...
Month
Month in Quarter
Month in Year
Month Overall
...
Quarter
Quarter in Year
Quarter Overall
Year
...
Fiscal Period
Fiscal Year
...
Last Day of Month Flag
Weekday Flag
Holiday Flag
...

ORDERS FACT [AS]
Order Date Key
Order Time Key
Delivery Date Key
Delivery Time Key
...
Order Number [DD]
Delivery Time [hours]
Quantity
Revenue
...

CLOCK [RP]
Time Key
Time
Hour in Day
Minute in Hour
AM PM
Shift Name
Peak Offpeak
...

Overall attributes are numbered from an epoch or origin date such as 1/1/1900. They are used to constrain date ranges across year boundaries; e.g., last 60 days, last 90 days

Figure 7-1
CALENDAR and CLOCK dimensions used to play two roles with ORDER FACT

The ORDERS FACT table in Figure 7-1 documents Delivery Time (duration) as a fact. This is the elapsed time in hours taken to fulfill the order. This duration would be difficult to calculate and aggregate using the separate time dimensions alone, and is best stored as a fact.

Calendar Dimensions

Calendar dimensions should support all the groupings of day, week, month, quarter, year, fiscal period, and season that are needed as report row headings and query filters; for example, CALENDAR in Figure 7-1 contains the commonly used calendar attributes: DAY (Sunday–Saturday), DAY IN WEEK (1–7), MONTH (January–December), MONTH IN YEAR (1–12), and YEAR. It also contains several "Overall" attributes such as DAY OVERALL and MONTH OVERALL. These are *epoch counters* that increment for each new Day, Week or Month from the earliest date in the data warehouse (*the epoch date*). Overall values are used for calculating interval constraints that can cross year boundaries, such as: "last 60 days" or "last 4 weeks". The BEAM✱ excerpt of Pomegranate's CALENDAR, in Figure 7-2, shows that the company has 13 fiscal periods per year, and that its fiscal year runs February to January—not January to December. The full dimension would make *all* of Pomegranate's calendar information available for reporting, so that BI users do not have to decode any dates or remember which fiscal periods contain 29 days rather than 28 or even the name of the current period.

A good calendar dimension should include all the date-related attributes that stakeholders need. Ideally BI tools should never have to decode a date to provide a good report row header or filter

Figure 7-2
Pomegranate
CALENDAR
dimension
(excerpt)

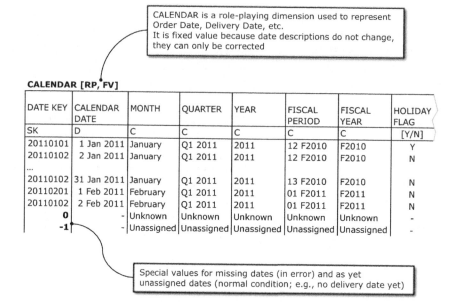

CALENDAR is a role-playing dimension used to represent Order Date, Delivery Date, etc.
It is fixed value because date descriptions do not change, they can only be corrected

CALENDAR [RP, FV]

DATE KEY	CALENDAR DATE	MONTH	QUARTER	YEAR	FISCAL PERIOD	FISCAL YEAR	HOLIDAY FLAG
SK	D	C	C	C	C	C	[Y/N]
20110101	1 Jan 2011	January	Q1 2011	2011	12 F2010	F2010	Y
20110102	2 Jan 2011	January	Q1 2011	2011	12 F2010	F2010	N
...							
20110102	31 Jan 2011	January	Q1 2011	2011	13 F2010	F2010	N
20110201	1 Feb 2011	February	Q1 2011	2011	01 F2011	F2011	N
20110102	2 Feb 2011	February	Q1 2011	2011	01 F2011	F2011	N
0	-	Unknown	Unknown	Unknown	Unknown	Unknown	-
-1	-	Unassigned	Unassigned	Unassigned	Unassigned	Unassigned	-

Special values for missing dates (in error) and as yet unassigned dates (normal condition; e.g., no delivery date yet)

The Data Warehouse Toolkit, Second Edition, **Ralph Kimball, Margy Ross (Wiley, 2002) pages 38–41 provide further examples of useful calendar attributes.**

Date Keys

Date keys are integer surrogates but they should be in calendar date order

Calendar dimensions, like every other dimension, should be modeled with integer surrogate keys. But *unlike* other surrogate keys, date keys should have a *consistent sequence* that matches calendar date order. Sequential date keys have two enormous benefits:

- Date key ranges can be used to define the physical partitioning of large fact tables. Chapter 8 discusses the benefits of doing this.

- Date keys can be used just like a datetime in a SQL BETWEEN join to constrain facts to a date range.

Historic value hierarchy maps (HV, HM) that use effective dating to track history can use sequential date keys (EFFECTIVE DATE KEY and END DATE KEY) rather than datetimes to improve efficiency when joining to fact tables. For example,

```
Where Reporting_Structure.Employee_Key = Sales_Fact.Employee_Key
and
Sales_Date is Between Reporting_Structure.Effective_Date_key and
                      Reporting_Structure.End_Date_key
```

This will join the historically correct version of the reporting structure HR hierarchy to the salary facts. Joins like this are complex (or theta) joins that are hard to optimize and need all the help they can get.

ISO Date Keys

Something else is unusual about the DATE KEYs in Figure 7-2: they are based on the ISO date format YYYYMMDD, which breaks the rule that surrogate keys should not be "intelligent." For date keys—and *only* for date keys—the benefits for breaking this rule outweigh any negatives:

ISO date keys are in the format YYYYMMDD

- **ETL benefits:** Date keys can be derived from the source date values directly, rather than with a surrogate key lookup table. This can be significant when processing events that contain many *when* details that all need to be converted into fact table date keys.

ISO keys are easy to generate

- **DBMS benefit:** The readable ISO format makes it easier to set up fact table partition ranges.

ISO keys are easy to read, which can be good (for ETL) and bad (for BI)

- **BI benefits:** None! BI queries should not use the YYYYMMDD format as a quick way of filtering facts and avoiding joins to the Calendar dimension with its consistent date descriptions. Best not to tell BI developers or users—keep this little secret between the ETL team and the DBAs.

Epoch-Based Date Keys

Epoch-based date keys are generated by subtracting an epoch or origin date from the date; for example, the DATE KEYs in Figure 7-5 have been generated using an epoch of 1/1/1900. Epoch keys can be a good alternative to ISO format if your ETL toolset is faster at date arithmetic than date reformatting. Epoch keys are also small contiguous numbers that may work better with some DBMS query optimizers than ISO keys, which are much larger—with a gap of 8770 between every December 31st and January 1st. The downside of epoch keys is that they are harder to read when setting up partition ranges. However, this may also be a BI benefit, because epoch keys are far less likely to be abused by queries using them directly as filter or decodes (instead of using the appropriate calendar dimension attributes). Which is the best approach ISO or epoch? If performance is paramount, you should speed test both with your ETL toolset and DBMS platform. You should also wait until you have read **Date Version Keys**, later in this chapter. before you decide on your date surrogate key strategy.

Epoch date keys are based on an origin date; e.g., 1/1/1900

Epoch keys are also easy to generate

Epoch keys are more compact than ISO keys but less easy to read

Create a version of your CALENDAR dimension that is keyed on a date rather than a surrogate key (as a materialized view). This can be useful as an outrigger that can be joined to date data type dimensional attributes such as FIRST PURCHASE DATE in CUSTOMER or HIRE DATE in EMPLOYEE. This allows them to be grouped and filtered using all the rich CALENDAR attributes for very little extra ETL effort. A date-keyed CALENDAR can also be useful for prototyping BI queries using sample data that has not yet been loaded into fact tables and converted to DATE KEYs. But it should never be used in place of a surrogate key-based CALENDAR for querying fact tables.

Populating the Calendar

CALENDAR dimensions often need to cover wider date ranges than you think: to cope with birth dates and future maturity dates

Because the CALENDAR dimension is relatively small and static, it is often pre-populated with all the dates needed for the foreseeable future. For example, loading the calendar with 20 years of data—enough to cover 10 years of history and 10 years into the future—would create a modest dimension of only 7,308 records. Having said that, calendars often need to cover a wider date range than first anticipated. For example, a financial services data warehouse might only hold 10 years of transactions, but may need a CALENDAR dimension that can cope with customer dates of birth up to 120 years ago and policy maturity dates 50 years into the future. For many of these future dates holiday information will not be available and will need to be left as null.

Spreadsheets, database functions, stored procedures, and ETL tools are all appropriate for populating the calendar—any of these can quickly generate the standard calendar attributes from any origin date. Search online for "date dimension generator" to find SQL code and spreadsheets that you can reuse. Table 7-1 includes additional, less automated, sources for enriching the calendar.

Table 7-1

Calendar attribute sources

ATTRIBUTE	EXAMPLE	SOURCE
Standard calendar	Day, Month, Quarter	Spreadsheets, SQL functions/stored procedures, ETL tools, online date dimension generators
Fiscal calendar	Fiscal Period, Fiscal Year	Finance department
Holiday schedule	Holiday Flag	HR, manufacturing, national calendar
Seasonal information	Sales Season	Sales, marketing, national calendar

BI Tools and Calendar Dimensions

Design the CALENDAR dimension to take advantage of your BI tool features

You should design your CALENDAR dimension with the features and limitations of your BI toolset in mind. For example, some BI tools require specific date columns to help calculate time series measures and make efficient time comparisons. Many BI tools have the ability to define a default display format for each column; for example, DISCOUNT can be defined to always display as a two-digit percentage. You can use this feature, if available, to create a "correctly sorted month" report item by defining MONTH as a date column that stores the first (or last, just be consistent) day of each month, with a BI display format of "Mmm YYYY". Even though MONTH is represented as a date, it will *group* the facts correctly because it contains only 12 distinct values for each year and it will *display* the month name correctly thanks to the default display format, and most importantly: it *sorts* correctly in calendar order because it is a date. This saves BI users from having to pick two columns: MONTH NAME to display and MONTH NUMBER to sort by. Holding the month as a date also enables automatic national language translation of month names, if your BI toolset supports localization.

Period Calendars

A day granularity calendar is not the only calendar you will need. Periodic snapshots and aggregate fact tables hold weekly, monthly, or quarterly facts and will require rollup (**RU**) calendar dimensions. Theoretically you could attach the CALENDAR dimension to these higher granularity fact tables by using the last date of the period that the facts represent; for example, a monthly sales snapshot could join to the CALENDAR using the last day of the month—the date on which the snapshot was taken. However, this is not a good idea, because it does not explicitly document the time granularity of the facts, and could lead BI users to incorrectly believe they can analyze the monthly sales facts using *any* calendar attribute, including day-level attributes like DAY OF WEEK or WORKDAY flag.

Do not use the standard day CALENDAR dimension with higher level periodic snapshots and aggregate fact tables

Month Dimensions

Instead of using a day calendar with monthly fact tables you should create a MONTH rollup dimension similar to the one shown in Figure 7-3, and define monthly fact tables using MONTH KEY foreign keys. This makes the granularity of these fact tables explicit, and limits queries to using only the valid monthly attributes. You can build the MONTH dimension from the CALENDAR dimension using a materialized view. MONTH KEY can be created using the DATE KEY for the last day of each month: the MAX(DATE_KEY) if the materialized view groups by month.

Monthly fact tables should use a MONTH dimension to make their time granularity explicit

Even though CALENDAR and MONTH dimensions have different time granularities they are still conformed dimensions because they use common attribute values: they are conformed at the attribute level.

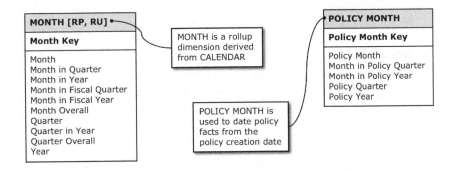

Figure 7-3
Period calendars

Some BI tools find it difficult to cope with separate day and month calendar tables and prefer all common date dimension attributes to be defined using a single table. If this is the case, having a MONTH KEY that matches the last day of the month DATE KEY can be useful. In that way, BI tools that need to, can use the CALENDAR dimension instead of MONTH at query time.

Offset Calendars

An offset calendar dates facts from a fact-specific origin date; e.g. policy facts are dated from a policy start date

Events such as insurance claims or policy payments can benefit from having their own specialized calendar dimension in addition to the standard calendar. A POLICY MONTH dimension like the one shown in Figure 7-3 would be used to offset the facts from the creation date or last renewal date of the policy rather than January 1 or the first day of the financial year as the normal calendar dimension would. For example, if a policy renews on April 1, an August claim fact for that policy would be labeled as MONTH "August" or MONTH NUMBER 8 by CALENDAR but POLICY MONTH 4 by the POLICY CALENDAR.

An offset calendar, like POLICY MONTH, can be used in conjunction with a standard MONTH dimension to define a MONTHLY POLICY SNAPSHOT with a granularity of POLICY by MONTH by POLICY MONTH. This fact table will contain exactly twice as many rows as a standard monthly snapshot but it will allow the facts to be queried by either calendar or policy month or a combination of both.

Year-to-Date Comparisons

Problem/Requirement

What is the "year to date" date for valid comparisons with previous years

To perform year-to-date (YTD) comparisons—such as YTD Sales 2011 versus YTD Sales 2010—the following needs to be known about the date range:

- **The "from date" when the year began.** This seems obvious but are we talking about the beginning of the calendar year, or the organization's fiscal year or the tax year?

- **The "to date."** Are you running the YTD calculation up to *now* or some specific date in the past. If you are defaulting to "up to now", what does "now" mean? Do you have complete data loaded right up to today or yesterday?

- **Which days to include.** Should YTD figures from previous years include facts up to the same "to date" in those years, or the same *number of days* (this copes with the extra day caused by the February 29 in leap years)? If it is based on the number of days, is that calendar days or workdays (for example, the same number of weekdays excluding public holidays)?

CALENDAR dimensions support YTD comparisons by providing conformed definitions of workday and fiscal year

The CALENDAR dimension can support consistent year-to-date (YTD) calculations by providing conformed definitions for the beginning of each year (calendar and fiscal) and which workdays to include. The attributes needed to do this are:

- DAY (NUMBER) IN YEAR
- DAY (NUMBER) IN FISCAL YEAR
- WORKDAY IN YEAR
- WORKDAY IN FISCAL YEAR
- WORKDAY FLAG

While these calendar attributes help tremendously, there is still the question of what date the "year to date" should be. For data warehouses that are loaded nightly, common sense might suggest a "year to date" of *yesterday* (SYSDATE −1). However, not every business process runs on the same schedule, and therefore not every fact table is loaded nightly. Some fact tables may be loaded weekly, monthly, or on-demand when source data extracts becomes available—a common requirement for external data feeds. This causes problems when trying to compare YTD figures for this year with YTD figures for last year. YTD figures for this year may not contain data up to yesterday whereas the YTD figures for last year will contain data right up to yesterday minus one year.

Even when fact tables are loaded nightly, they may not be loaded *completely*. ETL errors *will* occur from time to time, and complete data will not be available for reporting until these errors are fixed. It may also be quite normal for some ETL processes to encounter "late-arriving data" where the complete set of events for a particular date will not be fully available until several days (or weeks) *after* that date; for example, roaming call charges from international mobile networks, or medical insurance claims submitted long after treatments were given. Comparisons between the current year and last year are inaccurate whenever data is complete for last year and the current year is still a work in progress.

> You need to know when the YTD facts were last loaded to make valid comparisons with previous years

> Because of ETL errors or "late-arriving data", you also need to know the last complete load for YTD facts

Solution

Information about the status of each fact table—when it was last loaded and the last complete day's worth of data it contains—should be stored in the data warehouse rather than in the heads of ETL support staff or BI users. It should be available as data in a format that BI tools can readily use.

The FACT STATE table (shown in Figure 7-4) supports valid YTD comparisons by storing the recency and completeness of each fact table in a format that can easily be used with the CALENDAR dimension. It contains the *most recent load date* and the *last complete load date* of each fact table. The most recent load dates should be updated automatically by all fact-loading ETL processes. For ETL processes that are subject to unpredictable late-arriving data you may have to manually set the LAST COMPLETE LOAD DATE.

> A FACT STATE table holds the *most recent load date* and the *last complete load date* of each fact table

---

Figure 7-4

FACT STATE table

Values derived from the CALENDAR dimension using the MOST RECENT and LAST COMPLETE dates for each fact table

FACT STATE [CV]

FACT TABLE	MOST RECENT LOAD DATE	LAST COMPLETE DATE	MOST RECENT LOAD DAY IN YEAR	LAST COMPLETE DAY IN YEAR	MOST RECENT LOAD WEEK IN YEAR	LAST COMPLETE WEEK IN YEAR
C, PK	D	D	N	N	N	N
SALES_FACT	12-Nov-2011	10-Nov-2011	316	314	46	45
COMMISSION_FACT	31-Oct-2011	15-Oct-2011	304	288	44	41
CLAIMS_FACT	16-Nov-2011	16-Oct-2011	320	289	47	46

A FACT STATE table contains all the necessary YTD information but it can be difficult to use for BI queries

To use FACT STATE information, you add FACT STATE to your fact table query and filter it on the fact table name you are using. You can then use any of its attributes in place of a SYSDATE-based calculation. Unfortunately, because the FACT STATE table is not "properly" joined to any other table in the query, many BI tools complain about a possible Cartesian product. Even if your BI tool doesn't complain, using FACT STATE in this manner can be confusing for both BI users and developers, not to mention dangerous—if it is not properly constrained to the correct fact table. To overcome this issue, you can provide the FACT STATE information as part of a *fact-specific calendar* dimension.

Fact-Specific Calendar Pattern

FACT STATE information can be repackaged in easy to use *fact-specific calendars*

A fact-specific calendar is built by merging the dynamic FACT STATE row for a fact table with the static rows of the standard CALENDAR dimension. This creates a version of the calendar that is "aware" of the YTD status of the facts that it is designed to work with. Figure 7-5 shows an example fact-specific calendar SALE DATE, built by joining the one row in FACT STATE (where FACT_TABLE = "SALES_FACT") to every row in CALENDAR.

Figure 7-5
SALE DATE:
a fact-specific
calendar
with added
FACT STATE
information

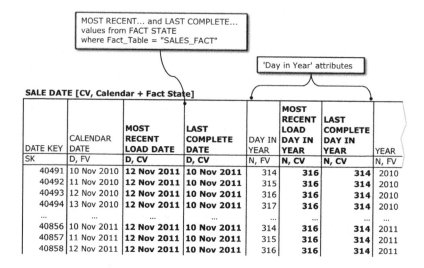

SALE DATE [CV, Calendar + Fact State]

DATE KEY SK	CALENDAR DATE D, FV	MOST RECENT LOAD DATE D, CV	LAST COMPLETE DATE D, CV	DAY IN YEAR N, FV	MOST RECENT LOAD DAY IN YEAR N, CV	LAST COMPLETE DAY IN YEAR N, CV	YEAR N, FV
40491	10 Nov 2010	12 Nov 2011	10 Nov 2011	314	316	314	2010
40492	11 Nov 2010	12 Nov 2011	10 Nov 2011	315	316	314	2010
40493	12 Nov 2010	12 Nov 2011	10 Nov 2011	316	316	314	2010
40494	13 Nov 2010	12 Nov 2011	10 Nov 2011	317	316	314	2010
...	...	...	...	...	...	...	...
40856	10 Nov 2011	12 Nov 2011	10 Nov 2011	314	316	314	2011
40857	11 Nov 2011	12 Nov 2011	10 Nov 2011	315	316	314	2011
40858	12 Nov 2011	12 Nov 2011	10 Nov 2011	316	316	314	2011

A fact-specific calendar makes ETL load dates as easy to use as SYSDATE

At first sight, it seems wrong or at the very the least wasteful, to repeat the same FACT STATE information on every row in the new calendar, but remember this calendar is still tiny by fact table standards and now it is simple to compare its attributes to their equivalent FACT STATE attributes. Because the fact-specific calendar will *always* be present in every meaningful query involving its specific fact table, the MOST RECENT and LAST COMPLETE attributes can be used just as easily as the DBMS system variable SYSDATE, without having to worry about constraining FACT STATE on the right fact table or a BI tool (or developer) complaining about a missing join. For example, to compare 2011 (the current year) YTD sales with 2010, based on the most recent load date, a query would contain the following simple SQL:

```
SELECT Year, SUM(Revenue)as Revenue_YTD
WHERE Year = 2010 or Year = 2011
AND Day_In_Year <= Most_Recent_Load_Day_in_Year
GROUP BY Year
```

To select the last three complete weeks of facts, the constraint would be:

```
WHERE Week_Overall BETWEEN (last_complete_week_overall - 3
                      AND   last_complete_week_overall)
```

You should create a fact-specific calendar for each fact table that is used for YTD comparisons, ideally as (materialized) views so that they will be updated automatically whenever the FACT STATE table is updated. If a fact table has a single time dimension, its fact-specific calendar can be given a unique role-specific name, such as SALE DATE (shown in Figure 7-5). If a fact table has multiple date dimensions, each one must use the same (more generically named) fact-specific calendar as its role-playing (**RP**) time dimension. It is possible for all fact-specific calendars to share the same conformed dimension name if each one is defined within a separate fact-specific database schema (that also contains its matching fact table). The naming approach you can adopt will depend on how your BI toolset qualifies tables when accessing multiple star schemas simultaneously.

Create a fact-specific calendar view for each fact table used for YTD analysis

To help keep the SQL that builds fact-specific calendars simple, the YTD comparison attributes within CALENDAR should be mirrored in FACT STATE; for example, if there is a QUARTER IN FISCAL YEAR attribute in CALENDAR there should be a MOST RECENT LOAD QUARTER IN FISCAL YEAR and a LAST COMPLETE QUARTER IN FISCAL YEAR in FACT STATE.

FACT STATE attributes should mirror calendar attributes to keep view building simple

You can expand fact-specific calendars to hold additional Y/N indicator flags— such as MOST RECENT DAY, MOST RECENT MONTH, PRIOR DAY, and PRIOR MONTH—that are based on the MOST RECENT LOAD DATE. Some BI tools may also find it useful to have a MOST RECENT DAY LAG column that numbers every date in the calendar relative to the MOST RECENT LOAD DATE; i.e., the most recent date is 0, the previous day is −1, the following day is +1.

Using Fact State Information in Report Footers

The system date (SYSDATE) is often used in report headers or footers to provide basic time context of a report. You can add FACT STATE information to produce a more descriptive report footer, such as:

FACT STATE information can be used to provide descriptive report footers that explain the data available

```
Report run on 23ʳᵈ March 2011. Report reflects data available up to
17th March 2011. The last complete week's data is for week 10,
data up to week 12 is included but is incomplete.
```

The bold values above are derived from SYSDATE, MOST RECENT LOAD DATE, LAST COMPLETE WEEK IN YEAR, and MOST RECENT LOAD WEEK IN YEAR, respectively. FACT STATE tables can be expanded to hold additional audit and data quality information, such as whether the latest facts have been signed off or not. This information, too, is handy stuff to print in a report footer.

Conformed Date Ranges

FACT STATE information helps define conformed date ranges for comparing business processes using multiple star schemas

In addition to defining meaningful date ranges for YTD comparisons on a single fact table, a FACT STATE table can help define the set of sensible comparisons that can be performed across fact tables. For example, you can't meaningfully compare current YTD sales with YTD commissions based simply on current year totals if SALES FACT contains data until the end of May and COMMISSION FACT only contains data up until the end of April. However, the two processes can be compared on a "year to end of April" basis. You derive this *conformed date range* from FACT STATE using the earliest LAST COMPLETE DATE among all the fact tables involved in the analysis.

Clock Dimensions

A clock dimension contains time of day descriptions, typically at the minute granularity

A clock dimension contains useful time of day descriptions, such as Hour of Day, Work Shift, Day Period (Morning, Afternoon, Evening, Night), Peak and Off-Peak periods. Its granularity is typically one row per minute, half hour, or hour of the day—whatever level of detail is needed to provide the row headers and filters that BI users need. Figure 7-6 shows a typical CLOCK dimension with minute granularity. It contains 1,440 rows—one for each minute in a day—plus a zero Time key row for *unknown* or *not applicable* time of day. You should avoid defining clock dimensions with a granularity of one row per second unless there really are useful rollups of less than a minute. For most business processes, time at the precision of a second or less is not useful as a *dimension* (as a report row header or filter), but it may be useful as a *fact* for calculating exact durations. Storing precise timestamps as facts allows the time dimensions to remain small and concentrate on being good dimensions—sources of good descriptions for report row headers and filters.

Time down to the second is best treated as a fact

Figure 7-6
CLOCK dimension

CLOCK [RP, HV]

TIME KEY	TIME	HOUR	MINUTE	AM PM	MINUTE IN DAY	DAY NIGHT	WORK SHIFT	PEAK OFFPEAK
SK	C, FV	N, FV	N, FV	C, FV	N, FV	C, FV	C, HV	C, HV
1	00:00	0	0	AM	1	Night	Graveyard	Off Peak
2	00:01	0	1	AM	2	Night	Graveyard	Off Peak
3	00:02	0	2	AM	3	Night	Graveyard	Off Peak
...	...	...	...	...	...	...	...	...
1051	17:30	17	30	PM	1051	Day	Drivetime	Peak
1440	23:59	23	59	PM	1440	Night	Evening	Off Peak
0	-	-	-	-	-	Unknown	Unknown	?

CLOCK in Figure 7-6 is an HV dimension because work shifts and peak time can change but their historical names and times must still be used to describe historic facts. A standard CALENDAR is an FV dimension because date descriptions are fixed and do not change. A fact-specific calendar is a CV dimension because it must contain the current ETL status dates for its specific fact table.

Day Clock Pattern - Date and Time Relationships

Problem/Requirement

The standard attributes of time—such as Hour, Minute, AM/PM, and Minute in Day—are independent of date; for example, 11:59 a.m. is always 11:59 a.m. no matter what the date or day of the week is. This is why you model a clock dimension separately from a calendar dimension. But as you embellish the clock with additional attributes—such as the peak/off peak and work shift name—you often find that some of these time descriptions *vary by date*. For example, 11:59 a.m. might be classified as "Work Time" on Friday March 27, 2010, and "Play Time" on Saturday March 28, 2010. Does this mean that you have to recombine time and create a dimension at a granularity of one minute for every day in the data warehouse?

Certain time of day descriptions vary based on date attributes

Solution

Thankfully not! Date and time *don't* have to be combined to solve this problem. Time of day descriptions, like work shift or peak/off peak, are seldom dependent on the actual date (March 27 or March 28) but on the *day type* (weekday, weekend, holiday, or *unusual day*.) You can handle this level of variation in the CLOCK dimension by using the TIME KEY to represent *versions* of a minute. Figure 7-7 shows a DAY CLOCK dimension, with a granularity of one record per minute, per day of the week, per day type. It holds 14 versions of each minute—one for each day of the week, *plus* an additional version for each day of the week when it falls on a holiday. This results in 20,160 rows in total. If CLOCK attributes vary only by weekday, weekend, and holiday then you would just need three versions of each minute, cutting the table down to 4,320 rows.

A DAY CLOCK contains a version of each minute for each day type; e.g. weekday, weekend

DAY CLOCK [RP, HV]

TIME KEY	TIME	HOUR	MINUTE	DAY	DAY TYPE	WORK SHIFT	PEAK OFFPEAK
SK	C, FV	N, FV	N, FV	C, FV	C, FV	C, HV	C, HV
1	00:00	0	0	**Monday**	**Weekday**	Graveyard	Off Peak
481	08:00	8	0	**Monday**	**Weekday**	Drivetime	**Peak**
841	14:00	14	0	**Monday**	**Weekday**	Normal	**Peak**
1051	17:30	17	30	**Monday**	**Weekday**	Drivetime	**Peak**
1052	17:31	17	31	**Monday**	**Weekday**	Evening	Off Peak
1440	23:59	23	59	**Monday**	**Weekday**	Evening	Off Peak
...	...	...	...	**...**	**...**	...	...
7201	00:00	0	0	**Saturday**	**Weekend**	Graveyard	Off Peak
7681	08:00	8	0	**Saturday**	**Weekend**	Weekend	**Off Peak**
8251	17:30	17	30	**Saturday**	**Weekend**	Weekend	**Off Peak**
10981	15:00	15	0	**Monday**	**Holiday**	Special	**Off Peak**
0	-	-	-	**Missing**	**Missing**	Unknown	?

Peak run 8:00am to 5:30pm weekdays

Weekends and holidays are off peak and have different work shift names

Figure 7-7
DAY CLOCK dimension with weekend and holiday variations

Resist any temptation to combine CALENDAR and CLOCK dimensions into one. The resultant dimension would be unnecessarily large and difficult to maintain, having 525,600 records (365×1440) for each year at the granularity of minute. Don't even think about it down to the second.

Time of day attributes that vary based on actual dates can be handled by a seasonal or **HV** CLOCK dimension

If work shift start times, or any other CLOCK attributes, change on a specific date rather than "on Saturdays", infrequent change can be handled by defining CLOCK as an **HV** dimension with a Type 2 SCD TIME KEY. If date-specific change is occurring on a more regular basis it may be seasonal; e.g., summer descriptions and winter descriptions. Check that values don't cycle back before you treat them as normal **HV** changes that would grow the dimension year on year. You may just need a few seasonal versions of a minute as well as day versions.

Day Clock **Consequences**

HV clock dimensions which contain special versions of a minute, like DAY CLOCK, keep the dimensional model simple and easy to query, but fact loading ETL processes must be designed to assign the correct TIME KEY value based on time of day and:

Clock dimensions that contain special versions of minutes require more complex TIME KEY ETL lookups

- **Day type**, which can be looked up from the CALENDAR dimension.

- **Location type**, which can come from an explicit *where* dimension such as STORE, or the implicit *where* details embedded within *who* or *what* dimensions such as CUSTOMER, EMPLOYEE, or SERVICE.

- **The current version of the minute**, where CLOCK.CURRENT='Y' unless the ETL processes are loading late-arriving facts and older versions of the time descriptions would be valid.

Time Keys

TIME KEYS are normal surrogate keys that are not based on time sequence. This allows them to cope with change and variation when it arrives

TIME KEY in Figure 7-7 is a normal surrogate key with no implicit time meaning. Unlike DATE KEY it is not derived from time and is not in time sequence (though the first 1440 are). By keeping time keys "meaningless" you can start with a simple clock dimension and expand it (by creating new rows) to cope with attribute variations as they arise. For example:

- **Time of day attributes that vary by location.** For example, certain branch types may have longer operating hours than others or different TV channels may have different advertising slot names and lengths.

- **Time of day descriptions may simply change.** The standard attributes of time such as hour and minute cannot change (unless everyone gets new decimal watches) and are defined as fixed value (**FV**) attributes. But an organization may decide to change the start time of its peak service. You can define the Peak/Off Peak attribute as HV to preserve the peak/off peak status of historical descriptions. The TIME KEY can act like any other **HV** surrogate key and allow an ETL process to create new versions of the minutes that are moving from peak to off peak and vice versa.

International Time

Problem/Requirement

To analyze global business events, a data warehouse needs to handle international time correctly. For customer (or employee) behavioral analysis, *local* time of day, weekday status, holiday status, and season are important. While an organization-wide *standard* time perspective—*irrespective of event location*—is equally important, for measuring simultaneous operational activity and accounting for financial transactions in the correct fiscal period.

Regardless of how events are originally recorded—using local time or the standard time of a central application server set to Greenwich Mean Time—converting between the two requires an understanding of event geography, time zones, and "daylight saving" that is beyond individual queries. Just how many time zones are there? It's not 24!

International events must be analyzed by local and standard time

Converting between time zones is not trivial

Solution

If standard organization and local customer time are important, the data warehouse should provide both as readily available dimension roles to avoid inconsistent and inefficient time zone calculations within reports. For consistency, a shared ETL process should perform all time zone conversions, and the results should be used to overload international facts with additional time dimension keys. Figure 7-8 shows how local time is modeled in a star schema—by *overloading* a global sales fact table with extra date and time of day keys (LOCAL DATE KEY and LOCAL TIME KEY) so that the CALENDAR and CLOCK dimensions can play the dual roles of *Standard Sale Time* and *Local Sale Time*.

Overload the facts with additional time dimensions to provide dual time perspectives

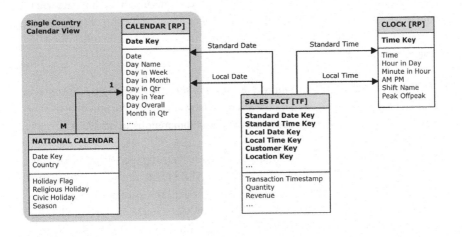

Figure 7-8

Sales fact table overloaded with local and standard time dimensions

Consequences

All *dimensional overloading* patterns require additional ETL processing and make fact tables larger but the trade off is faster, simpler, more consistent BI queries.

Multinational Calendar Pattern

Problem/Requirement

Holiday and season descriptions are *geopolitical time attributes* that vary by location as well as date

For a single-country data warehouse, adding holiday schedules and season descriptions to the calendar dimension is relatively straightforward. But when a data warehouse goes global, these attributes become problematic, because holidays and seasons are *location-specific* or *geopolitical time attributes* that vary by location, just as time zones do. If the number of countries to be covered is small—and will *remain* that way—then their holiday variations can be handled dimensionally by a small repeating group of attributes; for example, if a company operates only in the UK, a single SEASON and the following holiday attributes may be sufficient:

- ENGLISH HOLIDAY FLAG
- WELSH HOLIDAY FLAG
- NORTHERN IRISH HOLIDAY FLAG
- SCOTTISH HOLIDAY FLAG

A national calendar table holds geopolitical time attributes keyed on a combination of date key and country which can lead to over-counting

However, if the data warehouse is expected to cover more than a few countries, you will need a more robust solution. NATIONAL CALENDAR in Figure 7-8 attempts to solve the geopolitical attribute problem by using a composite key of date *and country* to record holiday information for each date and country combination as separate rows. Unfortunately, this design demands that BI users and developers remember to constrain NATIONAL CALENDAR to a *single country* when querying the facts, otherwise their answers will be overstated by the number of countries they "let into" the query. For example, if NATIONAL CALENDAR holds holiday information for ten countries and a busy sales manager forgets to correctly constrain the calendar, an ad-hoc analysis of holiday sales revenue will be overstated ten times. The figures would be wrong even if the query filters sales to just one branch for one holiday, because even a single sales transaction on that date will be joined to, and over-counted by, the multiple countries that observe that holiday. Commissioned sales staff may be happy by this oversight—few other BI stakeholders will be so enthusiastic.

NATIONAL CALENDAR, in Figure 7-8, is a *multi-valued dimension*. It contains multiple date values for each fact. If not used carefully it has the potential to over-count the facts. Chapter 9 covers multi-valued dimensions in detail.

Country-specific calendar views are safer to use but they limit analysis to one country at a time. They are not a good match for international facts

A safer solution for ad-hoc queries is to provide country-specific calendar views that pre-join CALENDAR to NATIONAL CALENDAR constrained to a single country. BI users can then choose (or be defaulted to) the most appropriate calendar view. Unfortunately, this solution limits analysis to one country at a time, and even then, BI users must still take care to constrain the geography of their queries to precisely match their chosen calendar, otherwise the geopolitical time attributes they use will not actually match the facts. Country-specific calendar dimensions are an international data warehousing anti-pattern: they do not match international fact tables.

Solution

To overcome the "one country at a time" query limitation and prevent calendar and fact mismatch you need a different calendar design that truly matches multinational fact tables. MULTINATIONAL CALENDAR in Figure 7-9 looks remarkably like a standard calendar dimension, but it handles date descriptions that vary geographically by storing multiple *versions* of the dates that have varying descriptions, each with a unique DATE KEY; for example, Figure 7-9 shows the three versions of March 17, 2010 needed to support the different combinations of SEASON and HOLIDAY in the UK, U.S., South Africa, and Ireland on that date.

UK, USA version

MULTINATIONAL CALENDAR [RP]

DATE KEY	CALENDAR DATE	MONTH NAME	QUARTER	SEASON	HOLIDAY	DAY TYPE
SK	D	C	C	C	[Y/N]	C
4061800	17 Mar 2011	March	Q1 2011	Spring	N	**Normal**
4061801	17 Mar 2011	March	Q1 2011	Spring	Y	**Holiday**
4061802	17 Mar 2011	March	Q1 2011	Autumn	N	**International**
4061800	18 Mar 2011	March	Q1 2011	Spring	N	**Normal**

Versions **00, 01** and **02** of March 17th

Irish version (St. Patrick's Day)

South African version

Figure 7-9
Multinational calendar dimension showing 3 versions of March 17th 2011

But how do these multiple versions of a date behave in fact queries? The answer is "just like a single version of the date" when you ignore multinational attributes. For example, all sales for March 17, 2011 will roll up to a single line on a report if they are grouped solely on CALENDAR_DATE. Only if sales are grouped by SEASON or HOLIDAY (attributes that vary internationally) will the report contain any additional lines, which is exactly what you want. In this way, the multinational calendar is similar to an **HV** employee dimension that uses surrogate key values to represent historical versions of an employee, except here the surrogate keys represents *geopolitical versions* of a date.

A multinational calendar uses a date key that represents a geopolitical version of a date to match multinational facts

The benefit of the multinational calendar is that it keeps both the model and queries simple while handling the complexity of the geopolitical attributes. BI users are totally unaware of the multiple versions of a date, they do not have to think about which national calendar to use, their queries can cross national boundaries, and they can use whatever calendar attributes interest them.

With a multinational calendar, simple queries can safely cross national boundaries

Consequences

BI user interfaces that provide date lists driven from a multinational calendar must do a `Select Distinct.` But that should be the default for all value lists anyway! ETL fact loading processes must know how to assign the correct DATE KEYs based on the *when and where* details of business events. You also need to think carefully about how ETL processes create DATE KEYs for multiple versions of a day, in the first place.

Date Version Keys

Problem/Requirement

Multiple DATE KEYs for a date must still sort in date order for efficient partitioning and join processing

When creating surrogate key values for multiple versions of a day it is important to preserve their date order sequence so that, for example, all versions of March 17, 2011 are sorted together, ahead of all versions of March 18, 2011 (as shown in Figure 7-9). This is vital for efficient fact table partitioning and date range join processing that uses SQL BETWEEN logic.

Solution

Maintain DATE KEY sort order by appending a fixed length version number

You can maintain surrogate key date order sequence by appending a version number *to the end* of the standard sequential date key—effectively scaling it by the number of version digits. Figure 7-9 shows an epoch date key (generated using a reference date of January 1, 1900) with a two-digit version number appended. Two-digits allow the calendar to support up to 100 versions (0-99) of each date. The same technique can also be applied to ISO format date keys, in which case YYYYMMDD would become YYYYMMDD**VV**, where **VV** is the version number.

Building version numbers into your date keys is a good idea even if your data warehouse or data mart will never go international. You never know when an extra version of a date will come in handy.

You can create a date version for every country or just one for each variation on a date

The number of date versions needed depends on your multinational business requirements. You can create a date version for every country (200+). This might be appropriate if there are many geopolitical attributes and the combination of possible values is greater than the number of countries. Alternatively, if the only attribute that varies by location is HOLIDAY (Y or N), then you need only *two* versions of a day: one for HOLIDAY = 'Y' and one for 'N'. Only one version would be needed for any date that is globally a holiday or non-holiday. A financial organization might use a calendar with six versions of each day, one for each of its global markets.

Needing a date version for each country is unlikely, because many will share common geopolitical attribute values. Create a single "00" standard version for each day, and then add versions as needed when you encounter regional or international variations.

Consequences

Because CALENDAR is the most commonly occurring role-playing dimension, it is important to keep DATE KEYs small when modeling for multinational versions. If you really need more than ten versions of a date and you have chosen YYYYMMDD format date keys, adding a two digit version number will require an 8-byte integer. If you can live with ten versions or less—or use an epoch-based date key—a 4-byte integer will suffice. Smaller date keys are always a good thing—especially for larger fact tables!

International Travel

To enable BI carbon footprint analysis, Pomegranate stakeholders have modeled the national and international flights taken by their global sales and consulting force. The resulting EMPLOYEE FLIGHTS event table, Figure 7-10 contains 6 event stories—6 flights taken by employee Bond during July 2011. These are typical movement stories containing pairs of *when* and *where* details that give rise to interesting *when* and *where* related measures, such as distance, duration and speed, in addition to other explicit facts such as their associated costs; e.g., CO_2 emissions.

Events with pairs of *when* and *where* details are typically movements with interesting distance, duration and speed measures

Figure 7-10
Flight events for employee James Bond

6 Flights but only 3 Journeys

from and **to** prepositions denote movement

EMPLOYEE FLIGHTS [DE]

EMPLOYEE	takes FLIGHT	at DEPARTURE TIME	arriving at ARRIVAL TIME	from DEPARTURE CITY	to ARRIVAL CITY	MILES	CO2	REASON
[who]	[what]	[when]	[when]	[Airport]	[Airport]		[lbs]	[why]
Bond	KL1000	18-Jul-2011 06:35	18-Jul-2011 09:05	London	Amsterdam	230	77	Conference
Bond	KL6241	18-Jul-2011 10:20	18-Jul-2011 12:40	Amsterdam	Minneapolis	4154	1078	Conference
Bond	NW2125	18-Jul-2011 14:45	18-Jul-2011 17:12	Minneapolis	Phoenix	1275	384	Conference
Bond	DL746	21-Jul-2011 07:10	21-Jul-2011 01:59	Phoenix	New York	2147	550	Consulting
Bond	AF0007	23-Jul-2011 19:10	24-Jul-2011 08:35	New York	Paris	3618	895	Return Home
Bond	AF1280	24-Jul-2011 10:00	24-Jul-2011 10:20	Paris	London	215	105	Return Home

Journey 1:
London to Phoenix

Journey 2:
Phoenix to New York

Journey 3:
New York to London

Movement doesn't have to be from one geographic location to another; it can be between virtual locations, such as the URLs of a website, or between members of a social network. Many of the same questions apply: How long does it take to navigate from page A to B or pass intelligence from James Bond to Jason Bourne and how far apart are they (measured in page links or people rather than miles)?

Figure 7-11 shows the flight events modeled as a star schema using the CALENDAR, CLOCK, and AIRPORT dimensions to play multiple roles of departure and arrival times and locations. This design can easily be used to answer many of the stakeholders' questions:

Which Employees travel the most frequently and furthest?

Which Airlines are used most often?

Which Airlines have the lowest CO2 figures on the routes we use?

But it makes one rather important question surprisingly difficult:

Where do our employees need to travel to on business?

The default *from* and *to* details may not answer the most important *where* questions

ARRIVAL AIRPORT will tell you where airlines are flying employees to—but that's not quite the same thing. Figure 7-10 shows that Bond took three flights on July 18th, each with the REASON of attending a conference. He did not, of course, attend three conferences in one day, nor did he actually have to go to Amsterdam or Minneapolis. He simply chose that route from London to the one conference he needed to attend in Phoenix. Apparently that routing had lower CO2 emissions per passenger than a direct alternative because it used a larger, newer aircraft.

Figure 7-11
Flight star schema

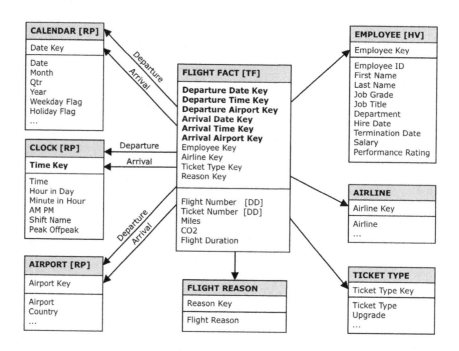

The most interesting *where* details are typically the *first* and *last* points in a journey

Bond's first multi-flight journey can be worked out manually by browsing all his flights and spotting the short gaps between the connecting flights and the longer gap that precedes his flight on July 21—which represents a different journey from Phoenix to New York for a consulting engagement. But getting a journey-level perspective on all of the flights in a large fact table via BI queries is difficult, because it involves comparing pairs of flights in the correct order on a per-employee basis. DW/BI designers don't want to hear that a query is difficult.

If stakeholders use the prepositions "from" and "to" to connect *where* details to the main clause of an event, it is an obvious clue that the event represents movement. Ask stakeholders for related stories such as those in Figure 7-10 to discover if individual movement events are part of a sequence that describes a greater journey from an origin to a final destination.

Solution

The FLIGHT FACT table, shown in Figure 7-12, has been modified to contain two extra airport foreign keys, representing the journey origin and journey destination locations not found in the original EMPLOYEE FLIGHT event details. With these additional AIRPORT roles, it suddenly becomes trivial to answer questions about where frequent flyer employees are located (Journey Origin) and where they really have to go to (Journey Destination). These incredibly useful *first and last* locations are hidden amongst all the flight information but can be found by applying a time-based business rule: *"all flights taken by the same employee, no more than four hours apart, are legs of the same journey"*. This test would be difficult for BI tools using non-procedural SQL but relatively simple for ETL processes with access to full procedural logic.

Overload every fact with the *first and last* locations within a meaningful sequence

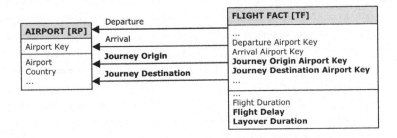

Figure 7-12
Flight fact table with dimensional overloading

Often, the location of first and last events represent something even more interesting than additional *where* dimensions; they represent *why* and *how*; for example, the *first* web log entry for a visitor arriving at a website contains the URL previously clicked on—this is usually a search engine or banner ad. In which case it represents *why* the visit took place and contains referral information, such as the advertising partner or search string. Similarly, the *last* URL visited is significant because it can describe the outcome of the visit—*how* it went. For example, if the last URL is a purchase checkout confirmation page then the visit was a successful sales transaction and each click leading up to the purchase can be labeled as such.

First and last events often contain *why* and *how* details that describe the cause and effect of all the movements within a sequence

Because *Timing-specific* first and last locations are so significant they should be attached to all the events in a sequence to help describe events more fully. Do this by overloading the fact table with additional location foreign keys or brand new *why* and *how* dimension keys.

Consequences

Adding useful dimensions from related events is another example of *dimensional overloading* that requires extra ETL processing and additional fact table storage. In this case, ETL must make multiple passes of the input data to read ahead, decide which events are related and then go back and load the facts with this extra information. However, this is well worth doing, so that common BI questions can be answered without resorting to complex and inefficient SQL.

Time Dimensions or Time Facts?

Flight facts could be overloaded with *actual* departure and arrival time dimensions, but would they be useful dimensions?

In addition to overloading the flight fact table with *where* dimensions, you might consider overloading it with *when* dimensions too—documenting the *actual* departure and *actual* arrival times of each flight, if these were available. This would allow Pomegranate to measure the on-time performance of airlines. But should these additional *when* details be modeled as dimensions? Would they provide useful new ways of grouping the data in addition to the existing scheduled time dimensions?

If actual and scheduled dates vary by very little there may be no value in defining the actuals as dimensions

If stakeholders asked for flights to be summarized by ACTUAL ARRIVAL DATE dimension rather than the SCHEDULED ARRIVAL DATE dimension, it would make little difference to the answers they saw, unless many flights arrive a day (or more) late. Even then comparing the two sets of dates dimensionally would produce skewed measures of airline performance; for example, a flight scheduled to arrive at 23:59 on March 31st could be only two minutes late but would be reported as arriving in a different fiscal quarter. In contrast, a flight scheduled to arrive at 8:55 a.m. could be just over 15 hours late and still roll up to the same day, when compared using ACTUAL ARRIVAL DATE and SCHEDULED ARRIVAL DATE. It would appear that the actual arrival and departure dates separated from their time of day components have no value as dimensions. Creating and indexing additional foreign keys for them in the fact table would be a waste.

Actual timestamps make good facts that can be used to calculate additional delay and duration facts

However the actual timestamps values themselves could be held in the fact table because they are valuable for calculating delays that can used to measure airline performance (perhaps filtering to ignore two-minute delays but looking for anything over two hours). Better still, the FLIGHT DELAY could be calculated during ETL and stored as an additive fact along with FLIGHT DURATION, as shown in Figure 7-12. Both of these facts should be pre-calculated—rather than force the BI users to perform the time arithmetic, especially because the timestamps involved are in different time zones!

Fact tables can be usefully overloaded with facts calculated using the next event

Figure 7-12 shows one more time-related fact called *Layover Duration*, which is the time spent at the arrival airport (or city) before taking the next flight. This is an example of *fact overloading*, again performed by ETL reading ahead and picking up details from the next related event.

The actual departure and arrival dates do not make good additional time dimensions in this particular example because they do not vary significantly from the scheduled dates—they are usually the same date or one day later. For many other business processes where actuals do vary significantly from targets or schedules, actual dates would make very useful time dimensions indeed.

National Language Dimensions

Data warehouses that have to deal with international locations and time zones will also have to provide national language support (NLS). Stakeholders will want to ask business questions in their own language and have the results translated.

International data warehouses need to be multilingual

National Language Calendars

Multilingual calendar presentation styles can often be handled by the localization features built into database management systems and/or BI tools; for example, you can configure language and default date presentation format (MM/DD/YYYY for USA and DD-MM-YYYY for Europe) at the database schema level or in the BI tool metadata layer to reformat dates into the appropriate local language for presentation. Changing the presentation format at the database or BI tool level preserves the correct date sort order of the underlying queries.

Use the localization features of your BI tools and DBMS to support local date formats and month name translation

If BI users and developers require national language support for reporting element names while constructing ad-hoc queries (for example, Italian users want to select "Mese Fiscal" and "Motivo per il Volo" rather than "Fiscal Month" and "Flight Reason"), attribute name translation should be handled by the BI tool semantic layer rather than database views. This keeps the SQL or OLAP query definitions portable across boarders.

Swappable National Language Dimensions Pattern

Problem/Requirements

Pomegranate has BI users in the UK, U.S., France, and Italy who want their reports to use the local language for descriptive labels—such as full product descriptions or flight reasons. One possible design is to create additional dimension columns for each of the required languages (for example, FRENCH FLIGHT REASON and ITALIAN FLIGHT REASON). But this approach overcomplicates the dimensions, especially if many attributes need localization, and many languages have to be supported. It also requires reports to be rewritten to use each new language column as other countries come on line.

Stakeholders want reports in English, French and Italian

Solution

Instead, a more scalable design is to create separate *hot* swappable dimensions (**SD**) for each language. Each language version would be identical in structure (identical table name, identical column names, and identical surrogate key values) but with its descriptive column contents translated as required. These language-specific dimensions would then be selected based on the schema the BI user logs into. For example, Italian user IDs would default to the schema with Italian versions of the PRODUCT and FLIGHT REASON dimensions.

Use hot swappable dimensions

Create separate
hot swappable
dimensions for
each reporting
language

With this approach standard reports can be developed once and run unaltered (as long as they do not filter on translated descriptions) in multiple offices with localized results. For example, a CO_2 footprint report in the London office that categorizes travel reasons as "Conference," "Consulting," and "Return Home", would display "Congresso," "Consulto," and "Casa di Ritorno" when in Rome.

Using separate hot swappable dimensions for national languages means that you can add new languages at any time without affecting the existing schemas and reports. This allows you to deliver an agile solution with a single language initially and then go global, without incurring technical debt.

Consequences

When translating dimensional attributes, care must be taken to preserve their cardinality; for example, 50 distinct product descriptions in English must remain 50 distinct product descriptions in French and Italian—so that reports contain the same number of rows with the same level of aggregation when translated.

Preserve sort order
and cardinality

National language versions of a dimension sort differently. Cryptic business keys (**BK**) are often stripped from dimensions if they are never required for display purposes. However, they can be used (without being displayed) to provide consistent sort order when standard reports are delivered in multiple languages.

Summary

- Time is modeled dimensionally by separating date and time of day into CALENDAR and CLOCK dimensions which should contain all the descriptive time attributes BI users need.

- Period Calendars, such as MONTH are built as rollups of the standard CALENDAR. They are used to explicitly define the time granularity of higher level fact tables.

- *Fact-specific* calendars, built using ETL fact state information, are used to ensure valid YTD comparisons.

- International facts should be *overloaded* with additional time keys to support standard and local time analysis.

- Location-specific date descriptions and day-specific time descriptions can be handled by using the time surrogate keys DATE KEY and TIME KEY to represent *versions* of a date or minute.

- Journey analysis can be enhanced by *overloading* movement facts with additional location keys and *why* and *how* dimensions based on the first and last locations in a meaningful sequence.

- Separate *hot swappable language-specific* dimensions are used to support national language.

HOW MANY

Design Patterns for High Performance Fact Tables and Flexible Measures

> How many times must a man look up…
> — *Bob Dylan, Blowin' in the Wind*

> Everything that can be counted does not necessarily count;
> everything that counts cannot necessarily be counted.
> — *Albert Einstein*

In this chapter we describe how the three fact table patterns—*transaction fact tables, periodic snapshots, and accumulating snapshots*—are implemented to efficiently measure discrete, recurring and evolving business events. We particularly focus on the agile design of accumulating snapshots, by describing how the requirements for these powerful but complex fact tables can be visually modeled as evolving events using *event timelines*, our final BEAM✲ modelstorming tool. We also describe the BEAM✲ notation for capturing *fact additivity* and fully documenting the limitations of *semi-additive facts*, such as balances. We conclude with techniques for optimizing fact table performance and multi-fact table reporting by concentrating on design patterns for *aggregates* and other *derived fact tables* that accelerate and simplify BI queries

This chapter covers techniques for incrementally designing and developing high-performance fact tables and flexible measures

- Point in time event measurement
- Periodic measurement
- Evolving process measurement
- Modeling evolving event milestones and duration measures
- Incremental development of complex fact tables
- Flexible fact definition
- Fact table performance
- Correctly querying multiple fact tables at once
- Cross-process analysis using simple BI tools

**Chapter 8 Design
Challenges
*At a Glance***

Fact Table Types

There are three *fact table types*. They vary in how they represent time

Facts are stored in three types of fact table: *transaction fact tables*, *periodic snapshots*, and *accumulating snapshots* that correspond to the three event story types: discrete, recurring, and evolving. Table 8-1 shows how each type represents time, and how it is maintained by ETL.

Table 8-1
Fact table types

Fact Table Type	BEAM✲ Code	Story Type	Time	Time Dimension(s)	ETL Processing
Transaction fact table	[TF]	Discrete	Point in time or short interval	Transaction date (and time)	Insert
Periodic snapshot	[PS]	Recurring	Regular predictable interval	Period (e.g., Month) or period end date (and time)	Insert (and update if period-to-date)
Accumulating snapshot	[AS]	Evolving	Irregular unpredictable longer interval	Multiple milestone dates (and times)	Insert and update

Transaction Fact Table

Transaction fact tables store point in time or short duration facts

Transaction fact (**TF**) tables are used to store point-in-time events, such as retail sales purchases, or short duration events, such as phone calls, that are completed by the time they are loaded into the data warehouse. These discrete events are the atomic-level details of business processes—the individual transactions captured by the operational system. Point in time facts have a single time dimension representing when the facts occurred. For short duration facts, the time dimension usually represents start time and can be accompanied by a second end time dimension, or simply a duration fact, if end time will not be used for grouping or filtering. If date *and* time of day are significant, each logical time dimension will be split into physical CALENDAR and CLOCK dimensions as described in Chapter 7. Figure 8-1 shows a BEAM✲ transaction fact table SALES FACT [TF] with a granularity of receipt line item: one record for each different product on a customer's sales receipt.

Figure 8-1
Transaction fact table

TF: Transaction Fact Table

FA: Fully Additive Fact

SALES FACT [TF]

CUSTOMER	Buys PRODUCT	on SALE DATE	in STORE	in QUANTITY	for REVENUE	with DISCOUNT	on RECEIPT NUMBER
SK	SK, GD	SK	SK	[units] FA	[$] FA	[$] FA	GD
Unknown	iPip Blue Suede	9-Dec-2010	POMStore NYC	1	249	20	NYC1014
Phillip Swallow	iPOM Pro	1-Apr-2011	POMStore London	1	1700	100	LON1212
Morris Zapp	POMBook Air	1-Apr-2011	POMStore LA	1	1400	0	LA90210
Martha Jones	iPip Touch	5-Jun-2011	POMStore London	1	289	10	LON1983

Financial transaction fact tables often have an additional "book date" or applicable financial period dimension to handle late-arriving transactions and adjustments. The generic version of this is an *audit date dimension*, which can be added to any fact table to record when facts are inserted.

Transaction fact tables are *insert only* because all the information about their transactional facts is known at the time they are loaded into the data warehouse, and does not change—unless errors occur. Even then, if the errors are operational rather than ETL, they are often handled as additional adjustment transactions that must be inserted. This helps to keep ETL processing as simple and efficient as possible—an important consideration when loading hundreds of millions of rows per day. Although transaction fact tables can be extremely deep, they are generally *narrow*—containing only the small numbers of facts captured by operational systems on any one transaction.

Transaction fact tables are insert only – which speeds up their ETL processing

Consequences

Transaction fact tables are the bedrock of dimensional data warehouses. Because they do not summarize operational detail, they provide access to *all* the dimensions and facts of a business process. In theory, this means they can be used to calculate any business measure. However, in practice—due to their size and the complexity of many business measures—they can't be used directly to answer *every* question. For example, transaction fact tables are impractical for repetitively calculating running totals over long periods of time. For efficiency, cumulative facts, such as balances, are best modeled as recurring events and implemented as periodic snapshots.

Transaction fact tables often need to be supplemented with snapshots for BI usability and query performance

Periodic Snapshot

Periodic snapshots (**PS**) are used to store recurring measurements that are taken at regular intervals. Recurring measurements can be atomic-level facts that are only available on a periodic basis (such as the minute by minute audience figures for a TV channel), or they can be derived from more granular transactional facts.

Periodic snapshots store regularly recurring facts

Most data warehouses use daily or monthly snapshots to store balances and other measures that would be impractical to calculate at query time from the raw transactions. For example, compare the cost of calculating product revenue and product stock level for April 1st 2011 using atomic-level sales and inventory transactions. Product revenue is calculated by summarizing that one day's worth of sales transactions, whereas the product stock level calculation requires *every* inventory transaction prior to April 1st 2011 to be consolidated. To efficiently answer stock questions you need a periodic snapshot, such as STOCK FACT shown in Figure 8-2. This is a daily snapshot of in-store product inventory that records the net daily effect of inventory transactions, rather than the transactions themselves.

Periodic snapshots can contain atomic-level facts but are typically used to hold measures derived from more granular transactions

Figure 8-2
Periodic snapshot
fact table

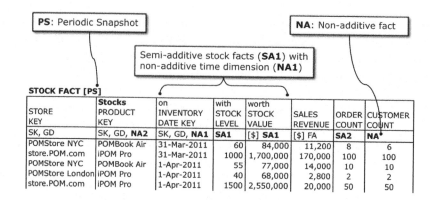

STORE KEY	**Stocks** PRODUCT KEY	on INVENTORY DATE KEY	with STOCK LEVEL	worth STOCK VALUE	SALES REVENUE	ORDER COUNT	CUSTOMER COUNT
SK, GD	SK, GD, **NA2**	SK, GD, **NA1**	**SA1**	[$] **SA1**	[$] FA	**SA2**	**NA**
POMStore NYC	POMBook Air	31-Mar-2011	60	84,000	11,200	8	6
store.POM.com	iPOM Pro	31-Mar-2011	1000	1,700,000	170,000	100	100
POMStore NYC	POMBook Air	1-Apr-2011	55	77,000	14,000	10	10
POMStore London	iPOM Pro	1-Apr-2011	40	68,000	2,800	2	2
store.POM.com	iPOM Pro	1-Apr-2011	1500	2,550,000	20,000	50	50

STOCK FACT [PS]

PS: Periodic Snapshot

Semi-additive stock facts (**SA1**) with non-additive time dimension (**NA1**)

NA: Non-additive fact

Periodic snapshots have fewer dimensions than transaction fact tables but more facts

Although periodic snapshots share many dimensions with their corresponding transaction fact tables, they will generally have fewer of them—because some will be lost when transactions are rolled up to a daily or monthly level. Periodic snapshots will typically have more facts than transaction fact tables. Their design is more open-ended—limited not by what is captured on a transaction, but only by the imagination of the BI stakeholders. Adding new facts to a transaction fact table is rare—the operational systems would have to be updated to capture more information. But periodic fact tables are more frequently refactored with additional facts as BI stakeholders become more creative in defining measures and key performance indicators (KPIs).

Periodic snapshots are typically loaded on an insert-only basis

Like transaction fact tables, periodic snapshots are typically maintained on an insert-only basis. For example, daily stock levels for each product at each location, shown in Figure 8-2 will be inserted into the STOCK FACT table at the end of each day. Most monthly snapshots are maintained the same way—with new facts inserted at the end of each snapshot period (month). However, for some monthly snapshots, such as a customer account snapshot for a bank, there are benefits in updating them on a *nightly* basis:

Some monthly periodic snapshots can be updated on a daily basis, to improve ETL processing and provide period-to-date measures

- **Stagger the ETL Workload:** If ETL processing waits until the end of the month it has to aggregate a whole month's worth of transactions for each account. This makes the last night of the month a particularly heavy night: if ETL fails, information for the whole of the last month will be unavailable. However, if ETL is run nightly for the snapshot, it has only to insert or update a day's worth of transactions for only the accounts that had activity on that day and if it fails the table is only one day out of date.

- **Provide Month-to-Date Facts:** Although a monthly snapshot can be useful for trending historical customer activity, it is on average 15 days out of date. If it contains an extra month-to-date row for each customer account it can be used to support additional operational reporting requirements.

Load monthly (and quarterly) snapshots on a nightly basis to improve ETL performance and support period-to-date reporting.

Consequences

Many end-of-period measures are complex and time consuming to calculate from raw transactional facts. If the necessary measures are already available from a reliable operational system it is often better to load a periodic snapshot directly from an additional source rather than attempt to reproduce the operational business logic with ETL processing by loading from a transaction fact table.

For case studies describing the use of periodic snapshots, see:
***Data Warehouse Design Solutions**, Christopher Adamson, Michael Venerable (Wiley, 1998) Chapter 6, "Inventory and Capacity", and Chapter 8, "Budgets and Spends"*
***The Data Warehouse Toolkit, Second Edition**, Ralph Kimball, Margy Ross (Wiley, 2002) Chapter 3, "Inventory", and Chapter 15, "Insurance"*

Accumulating Snapshots

Accumulating snapshots (**AS**) are used to store evolving events: longer running events that represent business processes with multiple milestone dates and facts that change over time. They are so named because each evolving event accumulates additional fact and dimension information over time, typically taking days, weeks, or months to become complete.

Unlike transaction fact tables, and most periodic snapshots, accumulating snapshots are designed specifically to be updated. Facts are inserted into an accumulating snapshot shortly after events begin and are updated whenever event statuses change. This leaves the fact table containing the final status of every completed event and the current status of all open events.

Figure 8-3 shows an accumulating snapshot for library book lending. It contains examples of books that have been borrowed and returned (completed events), books that are overdue (evolved events), and books that just been borrowed (new events). LENDING FACT has multiple time dimensions—like all accumulating snapshots—representing the milestones that a book loan can go through. Only two of these (LOAN DATE and DUE DATE) are available when a loan is created.

Accumulating snapshots store evolving events

Accumulating snapshots are updated with ongoing event activity

Accumulating snapshots have multiple milestone time dimensions

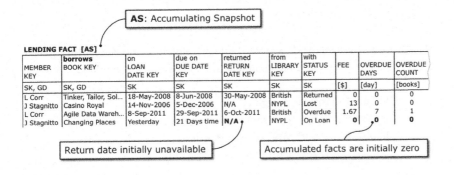

LENDING FACT [AS]

MEMBER KEY	borrows BOOK KEY	on LOAN DATE KEY	due on DUE DATE KEY	returned RETURN DATE KEY	from LIBRARY KEY	with STATUS KEY	FEE	OVERDUE DAYS	OVERDUE COUNT
SK, GD	SK, GD	SK	SK	SK	SK	SK	[$]	[day]	[books]
L Corr	Tinker, Tailor, Sol...	18-May-2008	8-Jun-2008	30-May-2008	British	Returned	0	0	0
J Stagnitto	Casino Royal	14-Nov-2006	5-Dec-2006	N/A	NYPL	Lost	13	0	0
L Corr	Agile Data Wareh...	8-Sep-2011	29-Sep-2011	6-Oct-2011	British	Overdue	1.67	7	1
J Stagnitto	Changing Places	Yesterday	21 Days time	N/A	NYPL	On Loan	0	0	0

AS: Accumulating Snapshot

Return date initially unavailable

Accumulated facts are initially zero

Figure 8-3
Accumulating snapshot fact table

Accumulating snapshots can usefully contain duration and state count facts that match their milestone time dimensions

LENDING FACT also contains a duration (OVERDUE DAYS) and a state count (OVERDUE COUNT). Durations are typical accumulating snapshot facts. If there are a small number of interesting durations, they can be stored as explicit facts. If there are many possible durations because there are a number of milestone dates, the fact table should physically store the milestones as timestamp facts and BI applications should access it through a view that calculates the durations. State counts are another characteristic of an accumulating snapshot fact. They typically match the milestones dates and simply record a 1 if a milestone has been reached or 0 if it has not. They allow queries to quickly sum the number of events at each milestone in a single pass without decoding dates or applying complex filters. LENDING FACT could be extended with additional state counts for returned, lost and on loan books.

Consequences

Accumulating snapshots are difficult to build, especially when they merge events from multiple source systems

Accumulating snapshots that support end-to-end business process measurement are some of the most valuable fact tables, and are very popular with stakeholders, but they can be extremely difficult to build. Many ETL nightmares are caused by trying to merge multiple operational sources and transaction types in one pass into the perfect accumulating snapshot. The code involved is complex and difficult to quality assure, often resulting in delays. And when the snapshot is finally delivered, while it may answer the initial questions perfectly, all too soon stakeholders can hit a BI brick wall when they need to drill into missing details. This happens because accumulating snapshots typically summarize a process from the perspective of the initial event and only record the current status of the overall event. For example, an order processing snapshot that summarizes deliveries for each order line would help to spot problems with fulfillment performance, but would lack the delivery details needed to explain why the problems are occurring.

Develop accumulating snapshots incrementally by modeling evolving events and delivering milestone star schemas

The agile approach to successfully delivering an accumulating snapshot is to build it *incrementally*. Using BEAM✲, snapshot requirements are captured by modeling an evolving event (described shortly) that is implemented over a number of short development sprints by remodeling its milestones as simpler discreet events. The resulting transactional star schemas are far easier to build and test individually and can provide *early BI value* ahead of the accumulating snapshot, which is incrementally created by the relatively straightforward merging of facts that already use conformed dimensions. The added bonus of this approach is reduced technical debt: the atomic-level transaction stars contain all the details stakeholders will need for drill down analysis in the future.

The Data Warehouse Toolkit, Second Edition, **Ralph Kimball, Margy Ross (Wiley, 2002) contains four interesting accumulating snapshot case studies:**

> **Chapter 5, "Order Processing"**
> **Chapter 12, "Education" (college admissions)**
> **Chapter 13, "Healthcare" (billing tracking)**
> **Chapter 15, "Insurance" (claims processing)**

Fact Table Granularity

A fact table's *granularity* is its level of detail: the meaning of each fact row in the table. Granularity can be stated in *business terms* and/or *dimensionally*. For example, the business definition of granularity for an order fact table is "one record per order line item", while the dimensional granularity is "orders by date, time, customer, and product". Transaction fact table and accumulating snapshot granularity tends to be defined in business terms while periodic snapshot granularity is defined dimensionally. Whichever approach you choose (often both, for the benefit of stakeholders *and* the DW team), stating and clearly documenting the granularity, is an essential step in fact table design. Fact tables that have fuzzy or mixed granularity definitions are impossible to build and use correctly.

Granularity describes a fact table's level of detail: the meaning of each fact row. It must be clearly documented

Granularity is documented in the model by recording the combination of *granularity dimensions* (**GD**) that uniquely identify each fact. For most transaction fact tables and accumulating snapshots the list of **GD** columns will include a degenerate transaction ID dimension; for example, a call detail fact table with a business granularity of "one row per phone call", can use a degenerate CALL REFERENCE NUMBER [GD] to uniquely identify each row. This succinct granularity definition is very useful for ETL processing, but for BI purposes it can be helpful if the granularity can also be defined using dimensions that are more likely to be queried—such as customer and call timestamp (assuming a customer can only make one call at a time). These alternative granularity definitions can be documented using numbered **GD** codes. For example, CALL REFERENCE NUMBER [GD1] and CUSTOMER KEY [GD2], CALL DATE KEY [GD2], CALL TIME KEY [GD2].

Granularity can be stated in *business terms* or *dimensionally* by listing **GD** columns

For accumulating snapshots and period-to-date snapshots that must be updated, GD columns, especially degenerate IDs, are used to define unique *update indexes* for fast ETL processing. For advice on fact table indexes see Indexing later in this chapter.

Modeling Evolving Events

Evolving events represent business processes that are complex enough or take enough time to complete that they are described as sequences of smaller milestone events. You can think of them as *multi-verb* events because each milestone can represent a discrete event (verb). These multiple verbs can be modeled as a single evolving event in two ways:

Related events that represent a process sequence can be modeled as multi-verb evolving events, initially or retrospectively

- **Initially as evolving:** An evolving event can emerge directly in response to a modelstorming "Who does what?" question when stakeholders think of an event as only the beginning of a time-consuming process that needs to be

measured end-to-end. If this happens stakeholders will instinctively tell *process stories* with multiple *when* details, as described in Chapter 2, that represent the milestones that must be reached to complete the process.

- **Retrospectively as evolving:** You can remodel an evolving event from multiple discrete events, when you discover, with the help of an event matrix, that they represent a process sequence (as described in Chapter 4).

Adding milestone details is straightforward when there is a 1:1 relationship between events

Whichever route you come to it, modeling an evolving event involves adding multiple milestone details to an event table, as in the Figure 8-4 example which shows shipment, and delivery milestones added to CUSTOMER ORDERS. Adding these milestone details is straightforward when there is a 1:1 relationship between all the events, because their granularity is unchanged by merging them; for example, if each order is associated with exactly one shipment, followed by exactly one delivery, all the details would naturally align and no information is lost by aggregating multiple events, or "made up" by allocating portions of events.

When an evolving event can have *repeating milestones*, the most recent or total milestone details are stored as part of the event

However, if an evolving event story can have *repeating milestones* (multiple occurrences of a specific milestone) there is a 1:M relationship between events, and something has to be done to bring everything to the same granularity. For example, if a single order line item for 100 units results in 4 staggered shipments from the warehouse that are then batched up in 2 deliveries by the carrier, the 4 shipment events and 2 delivery events need to be reduced to a single record to match the order event. The simplest way to align the multiple milestones is to record the totals for their additive quantities and the most recent values for all other details. For example, DELIVERY DATE and CARRIER, in Figure 8-4, hold the *last* delivery date and the last carrier (if more than one carrier was used) and DELIVERED QUANTITY holds the *running total* number of items delivered, so far, for each order line item.

Ask *how many* questions to discover repeating milestones

You discover the cardinality of milestones by asking *how many* questions about each *milestone verb*—these are *hidden* in the prepositions for the milestone details, particularly in the milestone *when* details. For the evolving CUSTOMER ORDERS event you would ask the following questions based on SHIP DATE:

> **How many shipments can there be for an ordered product ?**

If the stakeholders' answer is **"more than one"**, you should ask:

> **When there is more than one ship date for an order, which one will you use to measure the order process?**

The best way to ask this type of question, about multiple milestone values, is to get stakeholders to fill out the evolving event table with example stories.

Figure 8-4
Evolving orders event

CUSTOMER ORDERS [EE]

Event Type: EE – Evolving Event

CUSTOMER	Orders PRODUCT	on ORDER DATE	from SALESPERSON	at SALES LOCATION	in ORDER QUANTITY	for REVENUE	on PROMOTION	with DISCOUNT	on ORDER ID
[who]	[what] GD	[when]	[who]	[where]		[$]	[why]		[how] GD
J. B. Priestley	iPip Blue Suede	18-May-2011	James Bond	POMStore NYC	1	249	Trial Price	$50	ORD1234
Vespa Lynd	POMBook Air	29-Jun-2011	N/A	store.POM.com	1	1,400	Launch Event	10%	ORD007
J. B. Priestley	iPip Blue Suede	18-May-2011	James Bond	POMStore NYC	1	249	Trial Price	$50	ORD4321
Phillip Swallow	iPOM Pro	14-Oct-2011	George Smiley	POMStore Lon	1	5,000	Star coupon	£150	ORD0001
US Senate	iPOM + Printer	10-Aug-2011	Capital Team	1-800-MY-POM	100	150,000	New Deal	$20,000	ORD5466
US Senate	iPip Touch	10-Aug-2011	Capital Team	1-800-MY-POM	100	25,000	New Deal	$1,000	ORD5466

Order with no shipment (Customer Collection)

Shipment event details

for delivery by DELIVERY DUE DATE	packed by WAREHOUSE WORKER	to DELIVERY ADDRESS	shipped on SHIP DATE	shipped from WAREHOUSE	SHIPPED QUANTITY	with SHIPMENT COST	using SHIP MODE
[when]	[employee]	[where]	[when]	[where]	[units]	[$]	[How]
22-May-2011	AL	Memphis, TN	20-May-2011	New Jersey	1	6	Standard
4-Jul-2011	CS	London UK	14-Oct-2011	Dublin	1	20	Standard
22-May-2011	AL	Memphis, TN	21-May-2011	Baton Rouge	1	4	Standard
N/A	N/A	N/A	N/A	N/A	-	0	N/A
20-Aug-2011	JB2	Washington, DC	16-Aug-2011	New Jersey	70	500	Express
20-Aug-2011	JB2	Washington, DC	18-Aug-2011	New Jersey	50	35	Express

Delivery event details

delivered on DELIVERY DATE	delivered by CARRIER	DELIVERED QUANTITY
[when]	[who]	[units]
22-May-2011	Fedex	1
Not Yet	UPS	0
23-May-2011	USPS	1
N/A	N/A	-
18-Aug-2011	Fedex	70
20-Aug-2011	Fedex	50

If all the repeated milestone values are needed they must be modeled as discrete events

Typically, BI queries will use the most recent values for a repeating milestone but if stakeholders say they need all the values then you will have to model the milestone as a separate discrete event at its atomic-level of detail. If you have already done so you can point the stakeholders at its event table. Either way, you still want to push for a single value definition for each repeating detail so that you can add it to the evolving event. To help stakeholders to understand why the most recent value would be useful, remind them that the role of the new event table is to summarize the current progress or final state of each evolving event story.

If milestone events have a M:M relationship it may not be appropriate to combine them in the same evolving event

If stakeholders continue to struggle to give you a single value definitive answer for a detail, then it probably does not belong in the evolving event. This can happen where there is a M:M relationship between milestones and more complex allocations are needed. In which case, it may not be appropriate to combine *any* of the details from the milestone. If the initial event and a milestone turns out to have a M:1 relationship, this is not so problematic but some allocation of additive quantities will be needed. For example, if 2 different orders for 100 units are partially fulfilled by a single shipment of 190 units, a SHIPPED QUANTITY of 100 must be assigned to the first evolving order event and 90 assigned to the second.

Tell process stories that describe the typical, min and max intervals between milestones

If you determine that a milestone' detail belongs in the event, you should use its examples to tell interesting process stories. For milestone dates, ask stakeholders to give you examples that will represent typical, minimum, and maximum intervals between milestones. If a detail has already been modeled as part of a discrete event, you may be able to reuse values from its event table, but these must make sense *in combination* with the examples already present in the evolving event. For example, if you have used a relative time value like "Today" for ORDER DATE you might leave SHIP DATE as missing to show that initially there is no shipment yet for an order loaded into the data warehouse today.

Use missing values to describe the initial state of an event. You also want to describe its final states, completed or otherwise

As you add new details, you may have to alter some of the existing examples dates to bring out interesting scenarios, such as the initial and final states of the event. The initial state will have missing values for all the milestone details that have not happened yet. This means some details that are mandatory in discrete events must become optional in the evolving event. For example, CARRIER is always present on a CARRIER DELIVERY event but will be "Unassigned" in the evolving CUSTOMER ORDERS event if an order has not been shipped yet. If there can be more than one final state, try to capture additional process stories for each possible outcome; for example, ask stakeholders to give you stories of successfully completed orders and cancelled orders.

When you have finished modeling an evolving event, it is a good idea to reorder the details after the main clause in *W* and process order—keeping all the *whens*, *whos*, *whats*, *wheres*, and so on together in the order they appear chronologically. Doing so can make a complex evolving event much easier to read.

Evolving Event Measures

Evolving events are implemented as accumulating snapshots. These are fact rich fact tables because they typically combine several events, each of which brings its own facts. These combined facts can then be used to calculate additional *evolving measures* such as *event counts*, *state counts* and *durations* that are worth storing in the accumulating snapshots to simplify process performance reporting.

Accumulating snapshots are fact rich. They contain additional evolving measures

Event Counts

When an evolving event has a 1:M relationship with its milestone events, define additional event measures—such as (number of) SHIPMENTS or (number of) DELIVERIES, in Figure 8-5—to record the number of aggregated/repeated events.

Event counts record the number of repeated milestones

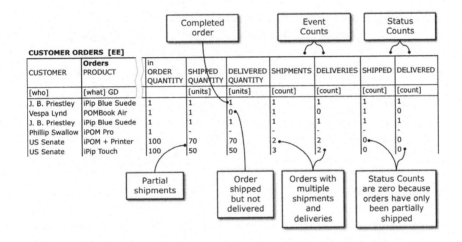

Figure 8-5
Event and status counts

State Counts

Each milestone date or embedded verb within an evolving event represents a state that the event can reach. Stakeholders will often have questions about how many orders, applicants, claims, etc. have reached a particular state. Answering these questions can be greatly simplified by adding *state counts*, such as SHIPPED and DELIVERED in Figure 8-5. These counts are 1 or 0 depending on whether a state has been achieved or not. They can be incredibly useful because state logic can often be more complex that you think; for example, you might imagine that count(DELIVERY_DATE) would be an efficient way to count order items that have reached the DELIVERED state but due to partial deliveries, it's not quite that simple. Instead, you have to test that DELIVERED QUANTITY = ORDERED QUANTITY.

State counts record if an event has completed a milestone. They are useful because repeated milestones mean you cannot use milestone dates alone to evaluate progress

Event status business rules can become complex. They should be evaluated once during ETL processing and the results stored as additive state counts to provide simple, consistent answers for all BI queries.

Durations

Milestone timestamps can be used in pairs to create duration facts. These should be named by modeling them with stakeholders

The multiple *when* details of an evolving event can be used dimensionally like any other details (for grouping and filtering), but they can also be used in pairs to calculate the elapsed time between milestones. Some of these *durations* will be key measures of process performance. It's not always obvious which ones are significant or what they should be called by looking at the raw *when* details. You find out by using timelines to modelstorm the durations with stakeholders. You should also discover the appropriate unit of time measurement (day, hour, or minute), and the acceptable minimum and maximum intervals between events that can be used as alert thresholds to drive conditional reporting applications.

Identifying and naming the right duration measures enables stakeholders to efficiently analyze process bottlenecks.

Additional Process Performance Measures

Quantities from different milestones can be combined to create process performance measures

Just as the multiple *when* details of a newly modeled evolving event can be used to create interesting durations, other quantity details from the separate discrete events can be combined to create additional process performance measures. For example, you could use ORDER REVENUE, COST AT SHIPPING, and DELIVERY COST to calculate MARGIN. You should model these additional derived measures with stakeholders to capture their formulas and business names, and add them to the event table with examples.

Event Timelines

Use event timelines to visually model milestones and durations

The best way to discover the important milestone *when* details and duration measures of an evolving event is to use an *event timeline*—like Figure 8-6. You should draw a timeline showing each of the milestone dates of an evolving event in chronological order, so that you can examine each milestone pairing visually, and ask stakeholders for business names for the intervals between them. The most important intervals are likely to have pre-existing names—a sure sign that they have business value and should be modeled as facts—but new and *significant* intervals can quickly be discovered and named in this way too.

You should try to get a name for each significant duration but when you have several milestone dates, you can end up with a lot of potential durations—too many to name in some cases. The number of durations is equal to: (Number of timestamps x (Number of timestamps − 1) / 2). So if an evolving event has six milestones, you have 6 x 5 / 2 = 15 possible durations.

Start by modeling the fixed points on the timeline: the initial *when* detail and any target dates

Typically, the most interesting durations will be those measured from the initial event date (Order Date) or from a target date (Delivery Due Date). Start by adding these fixed points on the timeline. These are the fixed value (**FV**) dimensions of the evolving event. With these in place use the white space on the timeline to prompt stakeholders for the other milestones events and their chronology.

Once you have all the events on the timeline (you may have copied the event sequence from your event matrix), you can then start discovering durations by pointing at the milestone pairs and asking stakeholders to name the gaps between them. Any meaningful duration you discover should be added to the timeline, as in Figure 8-6, which shows three important durations for an evolving order.

Model durations by naming the gaps between milestone events

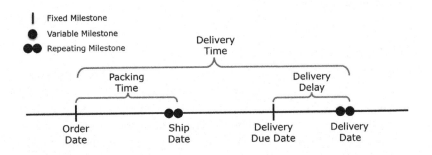

Figure 8-6
CUSTOMER
ORDERS
event timeline
showing repeating
milestones

After naming the durations on the timeline, add them to the evolving event table with example values. As mentioned in Chapter 2, you may question the wisdom of adding so many derived facts (**DF**) to the event table, but the event table is still a BI requirements model, not yet a physical accumulating snapshot design. Its purpose is to document the measures stakeholders will need, not dictate a physical structure. By adding a duration to the event table you are documenting its name, unit of measurement (UoM), and value range. You are *not* making a decision about how, if at all, it will be physically stored. Duration definitions can be implemented as database views or report items in BI tool metadata layers.

Add durations to the evolving event table as derived facts, to document their UoM and range of values

Figure 8-7 shows three durations—PACKING TIME, DELIVERY TIME, and DELIVERY DELAY—added to the event as derived facts. Their definitions can be recorded using simple spreadsheet-like formula by numbering the event milestones **DT1** to **DT4**. For example, PACKING TIME is defined as **DT2 – DT1**: the interval between ORDER DATE [DT1] and SHIP DATE [DT2]. The DTn numbering can also be used to record the chronological order of the milestones.

Number milestone dates **DT1-DTn** to reference them in duration definitions

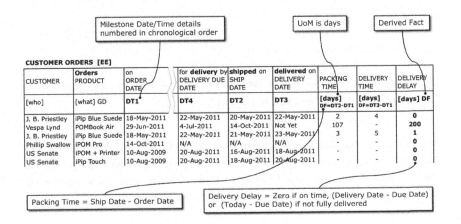

Figure 8-7
Duration measures

DF   : Derived Fact, calculated from other columns in the same table.
DTn : Date/Time, numbered in chronological order for use in duration formulas.

All the durations within an event should be defined using the same unit of measure; for example, all [days] or all [hours]. This avoids errors when durations are compared or used in calculations.

Using Timelines for Documentation

Timelines should be used to permanently document duration definitions within the model

Although the **DF** formulas in the column types of Figure 8-7 are useful for ETL and BI developers, the best way to document the meaning of each duration for the wider audience is to use an event timeline. The timelines you create in a model-storming workshop should *also* become a permanent part of the model documentation, along with the other BEAM✳ artifacts: event tables, dimension tables, hierarchy charts, and the event matrix.

Timelines are part of the definition of an accumulating snapshot. They also make great training material for BI users

Timelines are to evolving events as hierarchy charts are to dimensions. Dimension tables need hierarchy charts to document the levels of their conformed hierarchies. Accumulating snapshots need timelines to document their event sequences and durations. Just as you can use relative spacing on a hierarchy chart to show relative aggregation, spacing on a timeline can show the relative durations of stages within a process, and highlight the most time-consuming events that must be carefully monitored. Timelines are an essential part of the training material for stakeholders who need to work with complex evolving events.

Timelines can be added to the footers or summaries of reports, as simple static graphics, to explain the meaning of the duration figures they contain.

Using Timelines for Business Intelligence

Use dynamic timelines for data visualization on reports and dashboards

Timelines are not only useful for modeling and documenting event sequences, they make great tools for visualizing process flow in BI applications too. Dynamic or animated versions of the timelines you model can be used on reports and dashboards to display live status counts and durations. In Figure 8-8, an example dashboard for monitoring CUSTOMER ORDERS shows the average durations between milestone events and the number of order items at each stage.

BI developers can create dynamic timelines within reports by displaying duration measures as horizontal stacked bar charts.

The Back of the Napkin, Dan Roam (Portfolio, 2008) Chapter 12, "When can we fix things" contains some great ideas on drawing timelines to solve *when* problems. Other chapters describe how to draw pictures to solve other *7Ws* (*who, what, where, how many, why* and *how*) related business problems.

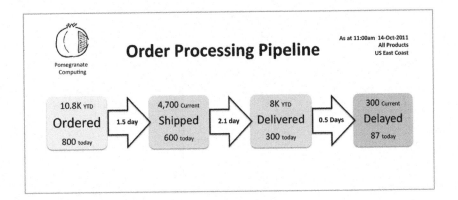

Figure 8-8
Timeline dashboard

Developing Accumulating Snapshots

When you have added all the useful evolving measures to an evolving event, it is time to profile its data sources and, all being well, design an accumulating snapshot fact table such as ORDER FACT [AS], shown in Figure 8-9. This is an accumulating snapshot version of the original transactional ORDER FACT [TF] from Chapter 5. How you go about developing this or any accumulating snapshot depends on the data profiling results. If profiling confirms that all the milestones have a 1:1 relationship *and* can be obtained from the same source system then you can build the accumulating snapshot directly. This would be the approach for the LENDING FACT [AS] snapshot in Figure 8-3. Because there is a 1:1 relationship between book loans and book returns, no detail is lost, and most importantly for ETL, because these different transactions are handled by a *single* operational system (for each library) there will be no conformance issues in merging them.

When milestone events have a 1:1 relationship *and* are handled by the same operational system, accumulating snapshots can be developed directly

ORDER FACT [AS] has a more complex 1:M or M:M relationship between its milestones which are handled by multiple sales and logistics systems managed by Pomegranate, its distributors and carriers. Attempting to populate this fact table directly is a high risk, "big *development* up front" strategy. (Another form of BDUF that you should avoid). It is unlikely that an accumulating snapshot with such complex sourcing issues could be successfully delivered in one or two normal length development sprints. So, while it's being developed what would be demonstrated, or validated by stakeholder prototyping? Nothing? That's not particularly agile. Instead each of the accumulating snapshot's milestones can initially be developed and delivered, on a more agile basis, as separate transaction fact tables.

If milestone events have more complex relationships *or* are handled by different operation systems, accumulating snapshots should be developed incrementally

If an evolving event is modeled retrospectively, you will already have all (or most) of the discrete event definitions for its milestones (you may have discovered additional milestones while modeling the evolving event). These are the blueprints for transaction fact tables that can stage the milestone events prior to merging them in the ultimate accumulating snapshot. If you don't yet have these, you can model them using the techniques described in Chapters 2-4 by pulling out their verbs from the milestone prepositions and asking: "who does each of these?"

Transaction fact tables are used to stage accumulating snapshot data, validate the design and deliver early BI value

Figure 8-9
ORDER FACT
Accumulating
Snapshot

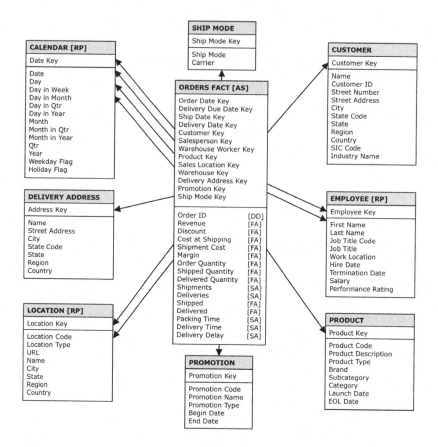

Staged
accumulating
snapshot ETL
processing will need
to be streamlined if
real-time DW/BI
requirements exist

For real-time DW/BI, the latency introduced by staging each milestone in its own fact table first may prevent an accumulating snapshot being updated urgently enough for current day reporting requirements. If streamlining the ETL process becomes paramount *and* the milestone fact tables are not needed for queries, they can become un-indexed staging tables that are truncated at the end of every load cycle or be replaced by ETL processes that act as virtual tables, piping their inserts or updates directly to the inputs of the accumulating snapshot process. If a real-time snapshot *and* queryable detailed fact tables are required, the staging tables can be implemented as un-indexed real-time partitions (covered shortly) that are fully indexed and merged with their fact tables by conventional overnight ETL.

Fact Types

Additivity describes
how easy or difficult
it is to sum up a fact
and get meaningful
results

If the most important property of a fact table is its granularity, the most important property of a fact is its *additivity*—which tells you whether or not its values can be summed to produce meaningful answers. This is important because stakeholders almost never want to see individual fact values. Instead they want to summarize them, and the easiest way to do that is to sum them. Facts are divided in three types based on their additivity: *Fully additive, non-additive and semi-additive.*

Fully Additive Facts

(Fully) additive (**FA**) facts produce meaningful results when summed using any combination of the available dimensions. For example, REVENUE in Figure 8-1 can be summed across customers, products, time, and locations—and will always produce a correct total revenue. Additive facts are the easiest to use because there are no special rules about which dimensions they work with, so default measures can be quickly defined in BI tools using SQL sum( ) function. For this reason it is always best to record fact information in its most additive form.

(Fully) additive facts can be summed using any combination of their available dimensions

The first rule for defining an additive fact is to use a single unit of measure. For example, while modeling an event you may identify a quantity that is recorded in multiple currencies that are documented as [£, $, ¥]. The corresponding fact needs to be converted into a *standard* currency, otherwise the fact will not be additive across currency.

Additive facts must use a single standard unit of measure

Store facts in a single unit of measure to make them additive and avoid aggregation errors. If BI applications need to view facts in different units of measure—e.g., report sales in local and standard currency, or product movements in shipping crates rather than retail units—provide *conversion factors*. These should be stored centrally in the data warehouse (as facts) rather than in the BI applications—because they can change.

Non-Additive Facts

Non-additive (**NA**) facts cannot be summed, even if they are in the same unit of measure. For example, UNIT PRICE cannot be summed to produce a meaningful total—even if all unit prices are recorded in dollars. Instead UNIT PRICE can be averaged, or used to create an additive SALE VALUE (UNIT PRICE × SALE QUANTITY) fact. BI users will likely want to use this additive measure more often than UNIT PRICE, so it should be stored in the fact table, and if storage is an overriding concern, the non-additive fact should derived, at query time, by just the reports that need it.

Non-additive facts can never be summed to produce meaningful answers

Percentages are non-additive; two product purchases with a discount of 50% do not equate to a 100% discount. Because of this, percentages make terrible facts, but they do make great measures and KPIs that BI users will want to see on reports and dashboards. Facts like DISCOUNT should be stored as an additive monetary amount (as in Figure 8-1), allowing BI tools to calculate the correct percentages within the context of a report.

Percentages are non-additive. Only their additive components should be stored as facts

Timestamps are non-additive facts, but pairs of timestamps can be subtracted to produce duration facts that can be treated as additive or semi-additive.

Non-additive facts
can be aggregated
using other functions
such as min, max or
average

Percentages and unit prices can easily be converted into additive facts, but other quantities cannot. These facts have to be clearly documented as non-additive along with their compatible alternative methods of aggregation for creating useful measures. For example, TEMPERATURE NA is a non-additive fact that can be aggregated using functions such as min, max, and average.

Semi-Additive Facts

Semi-additive facts
are harder to work
with than additive or
non-additive facts

Additive facts are easy to work with—they can be summed with impunity. Non-additive facts require a little more creativity to aggregate, but after an appropriate measure formula has been found they too are relatively straightforward to deal with: you simply never sum them up. *Semi-additive* facts are more problematic.

Semi-additive facts
can be summed but
not across their *non-additive dimension(s)*

A semi-additive (**SA**) fact can be summed up some of the time but you can't sum it up all of the time. To be more precise: a semi-additive fact cannot be summed across at least one dimension: its *non-additive dimension*. For example, yesterday's STOCK LEVEL cannot be added to today's STOCK LEVEL. It is non-additive across the time dimension. But STOCK LEVEL *is* additive across other dimensions. It can be summed for all stores and/or all products (apples and pomegranates?) to give a correct total stock level, as long as the query is constrained to a single day—a single value of the non-additive dimension.

To fully document a
semi-additive fact
the SA fact code is
used in conjunction
with at least one NA
dimension code

Semi-additive facts are fully documented by marking them as **SA** *and* their non-additive dimension(s) as **NA**. If there is a single semi-additive fact in a fact table or if all semi-additive facts have the same non-additive dimension(s) this is sufficient. However, if there are multiple semi-additive facts with differing non-additive dimensions, the **SA** and **NA** codes are linked by numbering, to pair each **SA** fact to its **NA** dimension(s). For example, Figures 8-2 and 8-10 show the BEAM✲ table and matching enhanced star schema for STOCK FACT, a daily periodic snapshot of in-store inventory. Both show STOCK LEVEL SA1 is non-additive across STOCK DATE KEY NA1, whereas ORDER COUNT SA2 is non-additive across PRODUCT KEY NA2. This semi-additive fact documentation can be used to correctly define measures in BI tools and some multidimensional databases. SQL doesn't natively understand that some numbers are semi-additive, this can cause averaging and counting issues for the unwary BI developer.

Averaging Issues

Semi-additive facts
can be averaged but
not by using AVG( )

Although semi-additive facts cannot be summed over their non-additive dimensions, they can often be averaged (carefully) over them. Unfortunately the SQL AVG( ) function may not be up to the job; for example, if stakeholders ask:

**What was the average stock of Advanced Laptops
in the SW region last week?**

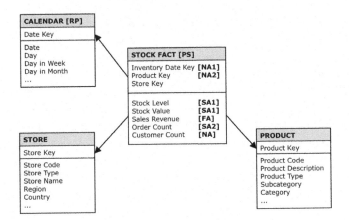

Figure 8-10
Periodic snapshot
containing
semi-additive facts

and the stock data is as follows: the product category "Advanced Laptop" contains two products: POMBook Air and POMBook Pro; The SW region contains 10 stores; Each day last week, every SW store stocked 20 POMBook Airs and 60 POMBook Pros (let's keep it simple); Last week had 7 days (like every other week).

AVG(`Stock_Level`) will return 40, which is the wrong answer to the stake-holders question. 40 is the average of 60 and 20 which is what you get when half the data has a value of 60 and the other half has a value of 20. The AVG() function—the equivalent of SUM(`Stock_Level`)/COUNT(`*`)—sums up 70 store/day records with 20 laptops and 70 with 60 (5,600) and divides by the number of records (140). To get the correct average for a category in a region, you must not divide by the number products (in the category) or the number of stores (in the region). Instead you must only divide by the number of non-additive dimensional values (7 days). The correct SQL for this is: SUM(`Stock_Level`)/ COUNT(DISTINCT `Stock_date`). The correct answer is: 800.

Periodic semi-additive facts, such as balances, must use a time average which divides the total by the number of non-additive time periods in the query

Averaging a semi-additive balance correctly, requires you to understand the time granularity of its fact table. For a daily snapshot, an average is calculated by dividing by the number of distinct days: the number of non-additive time periods.

Counting Issues

ORDER COUNT in Figures 8-2 and 8-10 is yet another example of a semi-additive fact that you must handle carefully. As long as queries are constrained to a *single* product, ORDER COUNT can be summed across days and locations to give a total number of unique orders. But if a query needs the total number of orders for the "Advanced Laptop" category it's in trouble because it will over-count any orders that contain both POMBook Airs and POMBooks. Unfortunately, there is no way to get the correct answer from STOCK FACT.

Unique counts are semi-additive or non-additive facts

Storing counts, such as ORDER COUNT or CUSTOMER COUNT, in a periodic snapshot can seem like a great idea for query efficiency (to save re-counting millions of records), but once they have been calculated to match the granularity of a

Atomic-level fact tables are required to provide fully additive unique counts

snapshot they may not be as additive as you hope, often turning out to be semi-additive or non-additive when you try to sum them further. If so, the only way to calculate a correct unique count is to go back to the transactions and count them distinctly within the context of the query. The status counts SHIPPED and DELIVERED, in Figures 8-5 and 8-9, do not suffer from this problem because they count order item states uniquely at their atomic-level of detail, whereas the event counts SHIPMENTS and DELIVERIES do, because they count shipments and deliveries aggregated to the order item level. If stakeholders want the total number of deliveries this month vs. last month they cannot get the answer from ORDER FACT [AS] using `sum(Deliveries)`. Instead they need to use DELIVERY FACT [TF] to `count(distinct Delivery_Numbers)`.

Think of degenerate dimensions as non-additive facts. They cannot be summed but can be counted distinctly to produce useful additive measures. For example, `count(distinct Receipt_Number)` provides an additive count of unique sales transactions/shopping baskets.

Heterogeneous Facts Pattern

Heterogeneous products, that are described differently, are often measured in the same way

In Chapter 6, we discussed product dimension design for handling heterogeneous products, which involved moving large sets of exclusive (**X***n*) attributes into their own more efficient swappable subset dimensions. Thankfully, heterogeneously described products are often measured homogenously; for example, a large retailer might sell everything from milk to DVD players, but it doesn't matter if items are best described by fat content ("2% semi-skimmed") or technical features ("Blu-ray recording"), they are all measured the same way: by quantity sold, revenue, cost, and margin, using the same sales fact table.

Heterogeneous products that have heterogeneous facts can give rise to inefficient "one size fits all" fact table designs

Problem/Requirement

However, in certain businesses—such as banking—heterogeneous products will have *heterogeneous facts*: very different ways of being measured. This can make fact table designs that attempt to provide an integrated view of the business, very inefficient. For example, Figure 8-11 shows a small portion of a monthly account snapshot that will allow all major product types (checking, saving, mortgages, loans, and credit cards accounts) to be analyzed. Unfortunately this "one size fits all" fact table will be very wide and sparsely populated. The dimensional keys and a small set of core facts that measure all account types (ACCOUNT BALANCE and TRANSACTION COUNT) would always be present, but the majority of the facts are marked as exclusive (**X***n*) with their validity based upon the defining characteristic PRODUCT CATEGORY [DC]. These will be null most of the time, making the table "fact rich but data poor". Depending on the database technology used, the null facts may take up far less storage space than valid facts, but if there are hundreds of facts in total across all lines of business this design will still be extremely difficult to manage and likely to perform poorly.

Figure 8-11
Exclusive facts

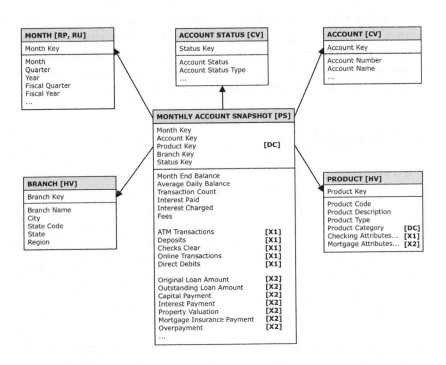

Solution

Limit MONTHLY ACCOUNT SNAPSHOT to the common facts (and possibly a few frequently used specialist facts like INTEREST CHARGED and CHARGES) and create a small set of *custom fact tables,* one for each major product family based on the exclusive fact sets as in Figure 8-11. The *core fact table* will contain a row for every account each month, and the custom fact tables—such as MONTHLY CHECKING FACT and MONTHLY MORTGAGE FACT shown in Figure 8-12—would contain rows for their account types only. The custom fact tables will contain the common facts, too—so that BI users don't have to query multiple fact tables.

Create a *core fact table* for cross-product analysis and *custom fact tables* for each exclusive fact set

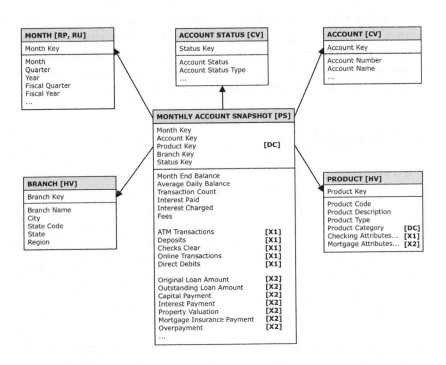

Figure 8-12
Core and custom fact tables for exclusive facts

When heterogeneous products have many heterogeneous facts, even if they share a common granularity, a monolithic fact table design may not be ideal. If the facts come from different operational systems with different access methods and maintenance cycles, separate core and custom fact tables will be easier to build and maintain, and can be a better fit with BI user groups.

Factless fact tables record events where there is nothing to measure except the event occurring

Factless Fact Pattern

While some fact tables can have too many facts, others can contain none. *Factless fact tables* are used to track events where there is nothing to measure except the event occurrence itself. For example, SEMINAR ATTENDANCE FACT in Figure 8-13 contains one row for every prospect (and existing customer) who attends a sales seminar to hear about Pomegranate products. Prospects do not pay for the privilege, nor are the seminar costs notionally allocated to them, so there are no monetary facts. The only thing to measure is the number of people who attend, which can be obtained by simply counting the rows in the fact table.

Figure 8-13
Factless fact table

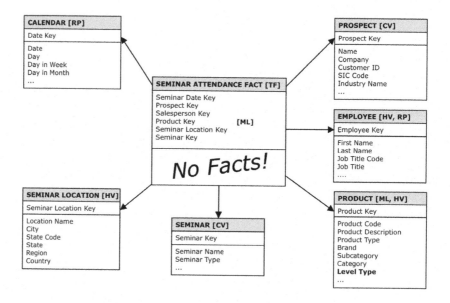

Factless fact tables can be used as coverage tables *to record dimensional relationships in the absence of other events*

Factless fact tables are also used as *coverage tables* to track dimensional relationships in the absence of other events; for example, a promotion coverage table that records products on promotion—regardless of sales, or a monthly healthcare eligibility snapshot that records *the fact* that a person is covered by a medical plan that month. Coverage fact tables are often used in combination with transaction fact tables to answer questions about what didn't happen (but should have); e.g., "Which products were promoted but didn't sell?" or "How many people were covered but didn't claim?"

To answer the "Who didn't attend but should have?" question about seminars, there is a case for making SEMINAR ATTENDANCE FACT a normal fact table by adding an ATTENDANCE fact. This would be 1 if an invited prospect attends and 0 for a "no show". Normally fact tables don't record events that didn't happen, because there are just too many of them. Airlines don't record all the flights you *didn't* take today—even if you are their best frequent flyer. But in the case of sales seminars Pomegranate didn't invite the whole world, so the number of extra records for invitees that did not attend would be manageable.

If the number of non-events is not too high, a 0/1 fact can be added to count "what didn't happen"

A dummy fact (always equal to 1) can be added to factless fact tables to provide an additive fact that can be summed. This makes it easier to build aggregates of large factless fact tables that can be used "invisibly" by aggregate navigation (see **Aggregation** later in this chapter). The aggregate will have the same fact but it will hold values other than 1. Also, some BI tools only recognize a table as a fact table if it has at least one fact.

A dummy additive fact (equal to 1) can be added to support aggregate navigation

In Figure 8-13, the PRODUCT dimension is defined as a multi-level (ML) dimension and the PRODUCT KEY in SEMINAR ATTENDANCE FACT is marked as ML too, documenting that it *makes use of* the multi-level feature of the dimension. This design allows the star schema to record attendance for seminars that are single product launches and seminars that promote entire product categories.

Fact Table Optimization

Because fact tables are so large—accounting for the vast majority of the storage and I/O activity of a dimensional data warehouse—it is essential to design them for high performance. The techniques for optimizing fact table performance are *downsizing, indexing, partitioning,* and *aggregation.*

Downsizing

The first way to improve performance is to design fact tables that are as compact as possible without compromising their usability. The following checklist gathers together techniques for reducing fact table row width:

Improve fact table performance by reducing row width

- Use integer surrogate keys as dimensional foreign keys. Keep business keys in dimensions.

- Use date keys instead of datetime data types—especially if time is unused.

- Reduce the number of dimension keys—combine small *why* and *how* dimensions (see Chapter 9).

- Move free text comments and lengthy sets of degenerate flags into their own physical dimensions and replace them with short foreign keys (See Chapter 9).

- Don't store a large number of facts that can easily be calculated intra-record; e.g., don't store all the durations that can be calculated from a smaller number of milestone timestamps.

Limit fact history to only the data that is useful for BI

The next thing to consider is the length of each fact table. You should try to limit history to what the BI users really need. Don't use fact tables as an expensive archival strategy. If the auditors need more history than the BI users, they should get that from the operational system of record, *not* the data warehouse. Regulatory requirements are not analytical requirements, so don't automatically load 20 years of transactional history just because it exists. If the business has changed substantially in that time how far can queries go back and make valid comparisons? Also, the further back you go the harder it becomes to load the data because data quality challenges tend to increase.

When modeling business events with stakeholders, ask for event stories describing the earliest *when* details that BI users will need to work with.

The most interesting data is the most recent. If you have years of history to load, start with the current year and work backwards—partitioning can help to do this efficiently. Don't bother loading the oldest data until stakeholders ask for it.

Indexing

Create query indexes on foreign keys to support "star join optimization"

After you have done all that you can to control the size of a fact table the next issue to consider is how to index it for query performance. Here you should seek your DBMS vendor's advice on defining some form of "star join index." This generally involves creating a bitmap index on each dimensional foreign key—but techniques vary by DBMS and by version, with new data warehousing index strategies being added all the time (we hope).

More query indexes can improve BI performance but slowdown ETL

Whatever indexing techniques you use, there is inevitably a trade-off between query performance and ETL processing time. Your priorities should be heavily biased towards query performance—but BI users can only query what you can manage to load in the available time—so index thoughtfully!

Accumulating and period-to-date snapshots also need an ETL update index

In addition to query indexes, accumulating snapshots and period-to-date (PTD) periodic snapshots need an ETL index to support efficient updates. This will be an OLTP-style unique index using **GD** columns such as the ORDER ID degenerate dimension in CUSTOMER ORDERS. Transaction fact tables and most periodic snapshots are insert-only so they do not require a unique index, as long as ETL processes can guarantee fact uniqueness.

If a fact is frequently used for ranking or range banding you should consider indexing it to speed up sorting, and joining to a *Range Band* dimension (described in Chapter 9).

Partitioning

Partitioning allows large tables to be stored as a number of smaller physical datasets based on value ranges. If your DBMS supports table partitioning you should consider partition large fact tables on the surrogate key of their primary date dimension. Partitioning on date can be made simpler by carefully designing your calendar dimension surrogate keys (see Chapter 7, **Date Keys** for details). Partitioning has a number of benefits for ETL, query performance and administration:

Large fact tables can be partitioned on date key ranges

- **ETL performance:** Partitions with local indexes that can be dropped and rebuilt independently allow ETL process to use bulk/fast mode loads into an empty partition while they are un-indexed. If only the most recent partitions of accumulating and PTD snapshots are being updated, unique update indexes (that are used for ETL, not queries) can be dropped on historic partitions. Partition swapping allows ETL to update the data warehouse while queries continue to run.

Loading into empty partitions speeds up ETL processing. Partition swapping enables 24/7 BI access

- **Fact table pruning:** Many fact tables need a fixed amount of history (24 months, 36 months). Monthly partitions allow older data to be efficiently removed by truncating a partition rather than row-by-row deletion of millions of records.

Partitions can be truncated to rapidly delete unneeded history

- **Real-time support:** Fact tables that need to be refreshed frequently throughout the day can be implemented using real-time "hot partitions". These are special un-indexed in-memory partitions that are trickle-fed from the operational source. During the day queries use these like any normal partition, and at night their data is merged with the fully indexed historical partitions.

Un-indexed "hot partitions" can support real-time ETL inserts

- **Query performance:** DBMS optimizers will ignore partitions that are outside of a query's date range, and some can read multiple partitions in parallel. But splitting a table into too many small partitions can also hurt performance, especially for broad queries that must "stitch" many partitions together. This can be avoided by creating aggregates to answer the broad queries.

Query optimizers can use partition pruning and parallel access to speed up certain queries

For more information on real-time partitions and ETL processing see:
The Data Warehouse Toolkit, Second Edition, **Ralph Kimball, Margy Ross (Wiley, 2002), pages 135–139.**
The Data Warehouse ETL Toolkit, **Ralph Kimball and Joe Caserta (Wiley, 2004), Chapter 11, "Real-Time ETL Systems."**

Some DBMSs allow you to partition on more than one dimension. This can be useful when a particular dimension is frequently used to constrain queries or represents the way source data extracts are organized for ETL processing; for example, by organization, geography, or data provider.

Aggregation

Aggregates act as *group by indexes* for existing fact tables

An aggregate (**AG**) (fact table) is a stored summary of a base fact table. It acts like a *group by index* on the base facts—speeding up queries that do not need to return detailed figures. They are an essential complement to traditional *where clause indexes*. A star-join index optimizes highly constrained queries that need to summarize *smaller* quantities of data, whereas aggregates optimize broad, loosely constrained queries that need to summarize *large* quantities of data. Aggregates are *derived fact tables* that are very similar to periodic snapshots, dimensionally and in terms of granularity. They differ from periodic snapshots in that they do not provide any new facts. Instead, they simply contain summarized versions of the additive facts from base fact tables.

DBMS aggregate navigation automates aggregate usage

Historically, data warehouse queries were written to use specific aggregates in the form of summary data marts. Today, many DBMSs provide aggregate navigation that automatically redirects queries to the best (smallest) aggregate. When this happens, the aggregates are *invisible* to the BI users and query tools.

Small high performance aggregates can be designed using the *lost, shrunken* and *collapsed* patterns

Aggregates must be designed so that they match the GROUP BY *and* WHERE clauses of the most popular queries, or they will be not be used. They also must be designed so that they are many times smaller than existing fact tables—to provide performance improvements that justify the cost of maintaining them. Twenty times smaller is a useful guideline—which can lead to a corresponding query performance boost. The three types of aggregate design in a dimensional data warehouse are *lost, shrunken, and collapsed.*

Lost Dimension Aggregate Pattern

Lost dimension aggregates are created by summarizing a fact table using a subset of its dimensions. Figure 8-14 shows a lost dimension aggregate formed by dropping the customer and store dimensions.

Figure 8-14
Lost dimension aggregate

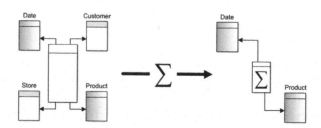

Lost dimension aggregates are the easiest aggregate type to build, because no dimensional joins are needed; for example, a *lost* aggregate can be built by:

```
CREATE MATERIALIZED VIEW Daily_Product_Sales AS
SELECT Date_Key, Product_Key, SUM(Revenue)
FROM Sales_Fact
GROUP BY Date_Key, Product_Key
```

At least one of the lost dimensions must be a granularity dimension (GD)—part of the fact table granularity—for the aggregate table to be smaller than its base fact table. Choose which dimensions to drop wisely, so that the aggregate is sufficiently smaller but can still be used to answer a broad range of queries.

Shrunken Dimension Aggregate Pattern

Shrunken dimension aggregates are created by summarizing a fact table using one or more shrunken or rollup (**RU**) dimensions instead of the base dimensions. Figure 8-15 shows a shrunken dimension aggregate that was formed by rolling up Dates into Months, and Stores into Regions.

Shrunken aggregates use rollup dimensions

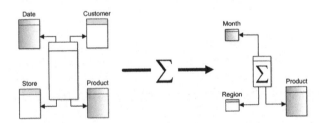

Figure 8-15
Shrunken dimension aggregate

Notice that the Customer dimension has been dropped. This is not uncommon for shrunken dimension aggregates—because dropping the most granular dimension is often needed to significantly reduce the aggregate's size. Sales by Month, Region, Product, *and Customer* would contain nearly as many rows as the base fact table— thereby negating its performance benefits.

Aggregates can shrink and lose dimensions

Shrunken dimension aggregates are more complex to build, requiring additional rollup dimensions and dimensional joins, and more difficult to maintain using incremental refresh. But they can be designed to satisfy a broad range of queries.

Materialized views can be used to build aggregates and their matching rollup dimensions. When building rollup dimensions, you can reuse their base dimension key to create rollup keys if you carefully select the first or last key value that matches the rollup dimension granularity. For example, you can use the DATE KEY of the last day of each month as the MONTH Dimension's MONTH KEY, or use the STORE KEY of the first store in a region as the REGION Dimension's REGION KEY. The actual surrogate key value selected does not matter, as long as it is used *consistently* in the rollup dimension.

Materialized views can be used to build shrunken aggregates and their matching rollup dimensions

Collapsed Dimension Aggregate Pattern

Collapsed dimension aggregates are created by summarizing a fact table using selected dimensional attributes, and storing the facts and the dimensional attribututes in a single, denormalized summary table. Figure 8-16 shows a collapsed dimension aggregate for Sales by Quarter and Product Type.

Collapsed
aggregates are
pre-joined
aggregates

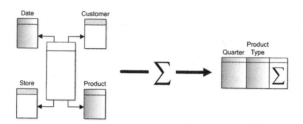

Figure 8-16
Collapsed
dimension
aggregate

Collapsed dimension aggregates can offer additional query acceleration because the dimensions and facts are pre-joined. However if many attributes are included the increased record length will make the table too large. An aggregate might have 20 times fewer records than its base fact table but if it is three times wider it will not deliver sufficient performance improvements to justify itself.

Aggregation Guidelines

The following guidelines will help you get a good set of aggregates in place:

- Budget up to a 100% overhead for aggregate storage and ETL processing.

- Create aggregates that are approximately 20 times smaller than their base fact tables. Spread aggregates, by designing aggregates of aggregates (400 times smaller than the base fact tables).

- Use (fast refreshable) materialized views whenever possible to build aggregates, and enable DBMS aggregate navigation and query rewrite features.

- Design *invisible aggregates* that the DBMS will automatically redirect queries to. Don't allow BI users, reports, or dashboards to become directly dependent on an aggregate. Hide them from query and reporting tools.

- Trust base star schemas to handle highly constrained queries using star join indexes—and focus aggregates on addressing broad summary queries.

- Monitor aggregate utilization, drop those that are seldom used, and add new aggregates as query patterns change.

- Make sure that you initially build aggregates that will speed up comparisons against budgets, targets, and forecasts. These are the most obvious quick-win aggregates.

Mastering Data Warehouse Aggregates by Christopher Adamson (Wiley, 2006) provides definitive advice on designing, building, and using invisible aggregates within a dimensional data warehouse.

Drill-Across Query Pattern

Problem/Requirement

As new star schemas and business processes are added to the data warehouse, BI users' questions will inevitably become more sophisticated because they will want to perform *cross-process analysis*. When they do, it's important to understand how their queries should access multiple fact tables to compare and combine measures. For example, Figure 8-17 shows two HR processes: salary payments and absence/leave tracking that need to be compared to answer the question: "Which employees were highly paid but were frequently absent in 2011?"

Cross-process analysis requires queries to access multiple fact tables

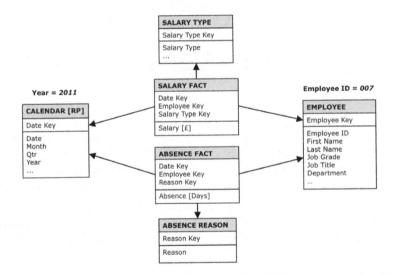

Figure 8-17
Querying multiple fact tables

Because the two fact tables SALARY FACT and ABSENCES FACT share conformed EMPLOYEE and CALENDAR dimensions it appears straightforward to join them using their common surrogate keys, as in the following query:

Joining two fact tables – don't try this at home!

```
SELECT Employee_ID, Employee, SUM(Salary), Sum(Absence)
FROM   Salary_Fact s, Absences_Fact a, Calendar c, Employee e
WHERE  s.Employee_Key = e.Employee_Key
AND    a.Employee_Key = e.Employee_Key
AND    s.Date_Key     = c.Date_Key
AND    a.Date_Key     = c.Date_Key
AND    c.Year         = 2011
AND    e.Employee_ID  = "007"
GROUP BY Employee_ID, Employee SORT BY 3
```

While the above SQL appears perfectly valid, it will not produce the correct totals for James Bond or any other employees—if the "007" constraint was removed.

Queries that attempt to directly join fact tables using single SQL select clauses can overstate the facts!

Report 3: 2011 Employee Analysis, in Figure 8-18, shows the results of the previous query—but first take a look at the two smaller reports that preceeded it. Report 1 shows that employee James Bond has received three salary payments totalling £160,000. Report 2 shows that he has been absent 6 days. Now look at Report 3. It shows that James earned £320,000 and was absent 18 days. Something is clearly not right here: his salary has doubled and his absences have tripled!

Figure 8-18

Overstating the facts

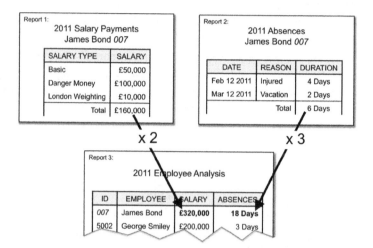

Joining across a M:M relationship causes over-counting because SQL joins first, then aggregates the "too many rows" created by the join

This over-counting is known as the "many to one to many problem", "fan trap" or "chasm trap". It occurs when the tables being joined have a M:M relationship. SQL has to evaluate the WHERE clause, which performs the joins ahead of the GROUP BY clause, so in the example the many Bond salaries (3) are joined to the many bond absences (2) creating too many rows, which are then summed up. Even if the fact tables have a 1:M relationship, any facts from the 1 side of the relationship will be overcounted. This is an insidious problem because the aggregation that's inherent in most BI queries will hide the "too many rows". The only totally safe join between fact tables is when there is a 1:1 relationship. This is very rare and hard to guarantee. Even then performance can be poor when millions of facts are joined.

Multiple fact tables should be accessed using *drill-across* queries that issue *multi-pass SQL*

Solution

BI applications can avoid the M:M problem by performing *drill-across* queries. Drilling across means lining up measures from different business processes using conformed row headers. A drill-across query does this by issuing *multi-pass* SQL: sending separate SELECT statements to each star schema. These separate queries aggregate the facts to the same conformed row-header level before they are merged to produce a single answer set. Drilling across would provide the correct answer to Report 3 by running a query to summarize salaries by Employee ID and another to summarize absences by Employee ID and then merging (full outer join) the two correctly aggregated answer sets.

Drill-across or multi-pass query support is a key feature of BI tools. It helps to manage query performance by keeping individual queries simple. By accessing fact tables one at a time the queries can be optimized as star joins and take advantage of aggregate navigation. They may also be run in parallel by the DBMS.

Choose BI tools that have drill-across/multi-pass functionality. As an alternative to multi-pass, some tools will generate multiple inline views within a single query.

Drill-across also supports distributed data warehousing. You can scale a dimensional data warehouse by placing star schemas and OLAP cubes on multiple database platforms in multiple locations. Multi-pass queries allow these to be accessed as a single data warehouse. Distributed data warehouses can use different hardware, operating systems, and DBMSs for each database server—as long as they contain stars or cubes with conformed dimensions that can be queried by a common BI toolset using drill-across techniques.

As a general rule, fact tables shouldn't be directly joined. Most fact tables have a 1:M or M:M relationship, which results in the facts being overstated when measures are calculated. Instead they should be queried by *drilling across*.

Drill-across works very well when queries need to combine summarized facts; for example, when business processes are compared at a monthly or quarterly level, individual multi-pass queries will access millions of facts but the answer sets will be aggregated to a conformed row-header levels *before* they are returned, and BI tools will only have to merge reports' worth of data—a few hundred rows.

Consequences

However, drill across doesn't work for every type of cross-process or multi-event analysis. For example, Figure 8-19 shows the sad state of a BI user who is trying to compare orders and shipments. He is trying to ask questions such as "What was the average delay on shipping an order item over the last six months?" and "How many unshipped items are there YTD this year vs. last year?" but his queries never seem to finish, or perhaps even start. The problem is these questions require individual line items from each transaction fact table to be compared before they are aggregated. This can result in multi-pass SQL that returns millions of rows that the BI tools must attempt to merge. Even when smart BI tools can construct the correct in-database joins, performance can still be poor.

Multi-pass SQL summarizes fact tables one at a time, then joins the results

Drill-across enables distributed data warehousing. Stars can be placed on different DBMSs

Drill-across queries work well for summary-level process comparisons

Drill-across queries become inefficient when cross-process analysis involves atomic-level comparisons

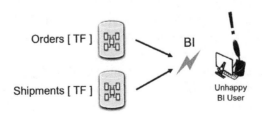

Figure 8-19
Unhappy BI user: difficult drill-across analysis

Missing evolving
events cause BI
pain and suffering

Derived Fact Table Patterns

Problem/Requirement

The unhappy user's comparison problems, in Figure 8-19, are not so much drill-across limitations, as poor or missing design. Orders and shipments are not discrete events that can be fully analyzed in isolation using transaction fact tables. They are evolving event milestones that constantly need to be compared to each other *and* to deliveries, returns and payments to provide key measures of process performance. Ad-hoc queries shouldn't have to try to join these events together every time, especially if there are complex M:M relationships between them.

Solution

Figure 8-20 shows what the user really needs: an orders accumulating snapshot that can be queried using simple single-pass SQL. Following the agile approach to Developing Accumulating Snapshots, outlined earlier in this chapter, this snapshot is delivered as a *derived fact table* (**DF**), by merging the two existing order and shipments transaction fact tables.

Figure 8-20
Happy BI user:
derived fact table
to the rescue

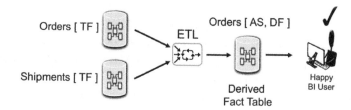

*Derived fact tables
solve difficult BI with
simple ETL rather
than complex SQL*

Derived fact tables are built from existing fact tables to simplify queries. They use additional ETL processing and DBMS storage, rather than more complex BI and SQL, to answer difficult analytical questions. In addition to aggregates, there are three other types of derived fact table: *sliced, pivoted,* and *merged.*

A sliced fact table
contains a subset of
a base fact table

- **Sliced fact tables** contain subsets of base fact tables; for example, UK sales derived from a global sales fact table. Sliced fact tables can support restricted row-level access and data distribution needs as well as enhanced performance for users who only need a subset of the data. They are often used in conjunction with swappable dimensions (**SD**) that contain matching subsets of dimensional values.

A pivoted fact table
transposes base fact
table rows into fact
columns

- **Pivoted fact tables** transpose row values in a base fact table into columns; for example, a fact table with nine facts derived from a base transaction fact table with a single fact that records nine transaction types. Pivoted fact tables make fact comparisons and calculations simpler. The same rows-to-columns approach can also be used to create *bitmap dimensions* (see Chapter 9) that support combination constraint queries.

- **Merged fact tables** combine facts and dimensions from two or more base fact tables, summarized to a common granularity; for example, a fact table that combines targets with summarized actual sales, or an accumulating snapshot derived from milestone transaction fact tables. Merged fact tables simplify cross-process analysis by replacing complex drill-across queries and expensive joins with single star queries.

A merged fact table combines multiple base fact tables, summarized to a common granularity

DF: used as a table code to identify a derived fact table constructed from one or more existing fact tables. Used as a column code to identify derived facts that can be calculated (possibly in a view) from other facts.

Data warehouse designs routinely fail to take full advantage of derived fact tables. Often there is a false impression that once the fact tables on the matrix have been loaded: "That's the data stored now, the major ETL development is done, and everything from here on out is BI". This can leave BI users and developers struggling to answer increasingly complex business questions. In all forms of agile development, project teams hold end of sprint meetings, known as *retrospectives,* to discuss what was successful and what could be improved. For DW/BI, retrospectives should include BI developers sharing their most common reporting complexities with the team to see whether these queries can be simplified by derived fact tables and other ETL enhancements.

DW/BI retrospectives should re-examine the design periodically, to see if additional ETL or derived fact tables can simplify difficult queries

Merged fact tables are often referred to as *consolidated data marts* when they are used to combine and summarize facts from several different business processes on a periodic basis. These "one-stop shop" data marts are incredibly popular with stakeholders because they provide high performance fact access in a format suitable for simpler BI tools. Common consolidated data marts include:

Consolidated data marts are the periodic equivalent of accumulating snapshots

- **Customer relationship management data marts** that provide a so-called "360° customer view" by summarizing measures from all the individual fact tables that relate to "customer touch points".

- **Profitability data marts** that combine revenue with all the elements of cost, to support product or service profitability analysis.

Consequences

There is often pressure from business stakeholders to dispense with the details and build highly summarized consolidated data marts directly from operational sources to provide "quick win" key performance indicator (KPI) dashboards. Unfortunately, data marts that summarize many different business processes and consolidate multiple operational sources are literally the last thing you should build. Apart from the ETL risks, the lack of detail rapidly undermines confidence in the KPIs when users cannot drill-down deep enough to explain the figures and view actionable information. Instead, consolidated data marts should be developed incrementally as derived fact tables: *derived from* atomic-level fact tables.

Don't attempt to build consolidated data marts before you have loaded atomic detailed star schemas

Summary

- *Transaction fact* (**TF**) tables record the atomic-level, point-in-time facts associated with discrete events.

- *Periodic snapshots* (**PS**) provide additional atomic-level facts by sampling continuous business processes and new aggregated facts by summarizing atomic transactional facts at regular intervals.

- *Accumulating snapshots* (**AS**) bring together the milestone events of a business process and combine their transactional facts to provide additional performance measures

- Both periodic and accumulating snapshots provide high performance access to measures that would be impossible or impractical to calculate at query time, from atomic transaction fact tables alone.

- Apart from its type, the most important definition of a fact table is its *granularity*, which must precisely state, in business terms or dimensionally (**GD**), the meaning and uniqueness of each fact table row.

- *Event timelines* are used to visually model the milestone events and duration measures of evolving events that can be implemented as accumulating snapshots.

- Accumulating snapshots that need to be sourced from multiple operational systems or contain *repeating milestones* (with 1:M or M:M relationships) should be developed *incrementally*—by first implementing transaction fact tables for their individual milestone events.

- Fact *additivity* describes any restrictions on how a fact can be summed to produce a meaningful value. *Fully additive* (**FA**) facts can be summed with no restrictions, using any combination of available dimensions. *Semi-additive* (**SA**) facts must not be summed across their *non-additive* (**NA**) *dimension(s)*. *Non-additive* (**NA**) facts must not be summed.

- Fact tables can be optimized by appropriate *downsizing, indexing, partitioning* and *aggregation*.

- Cross-process analysis should be handled by *drilling-across* multiple fact tables one at a time using *multi-pass SQL* or by building *derived fact* (**DF**) tables that merge commonly compared fact tables.

WHY AND HOW

Dimensional Design Patterns for Cause and Effect

There is occasions and causes why and wherefore in all things.
— *William Shakespeare (1564–1616), "King Henry V", Act 5, scene 1*

How am I doing?
— *Ed Koch, Mayor of New York 1978–1989*

Some of the most valuable dimensions in a data warehouse attempt to explain why and how events occur. *Why* dimensions are used to describe direct and indirect causal factors. They are often closely linked to the *how* dimensions that provide all the remaining event descriptions that are not related to the major *who, what, when* and *where* dimension types. Together *why* and *how* represent *cause* and *effect* and complete the *7W* dimensional description of a business event.

Why and *how* dimensions are closely linked: they describe *cause* and *effect*

In our final chapter we cover dimensional design patterns for describing *how* events occur and *why* facts vary. We focus particularly on bridge table patterns for representing multiple causal factors and multi-valued dimensions in general. We describe how bridge table weighting factors are used to preserve atomic fact granularity and avoid ETL time fact allocations. We also describe how bridge tables can be augmented with multi-level dimensions and pivoted dimensions to efficiently handle *barely* multi-valued reporting and complex combination constraints. We conclude with step, range band and audit dimension techniques for analyzing sequential events, grouping by facts and handling ETL metadata.

This chapter describes *why* and *how* dimension design patterns

- Direct and indirect causal factors
- Attributing multiple causes to a fact
- Dealing with *barely* multi-valued dimensions efficiently
- Handling complex combination constraints
- Understanding sequential behavior
- Range band reporting
- Tracking data quality and lineage

Chapter 9 Design
Challenges
At a Glance

261

Why Dimensions

Why details become causal dimensions that help to explain why facts occur in the way they do

The *why* details of an event become *causal dimensions,* such as promotion, weather, or just reason. Causal dimensions explain why business events occur when they do, in the way that they do. They describe what stakeholders believe are the influential factors for a business event; for example, price discounts driving up sales transactions, or storms triggering home insurance claims. Causal factors fall into two categories: *direct* and *indirect.*

Direct causal factors have a recorded influence on the facts

Promotional discounts are examples of causal factors that are *directly* related to the facts. You know with *absolute* certainty when they are or are not related to a sale because the promotional code (or discounted product code) and the discounted price are recorded or not recorded as part of the sale transaction.

Indirect causal factors may or may not have influenced the facts

Other causal factors—such as weather conditions, sporting events, or advertisement campaigns—are only *indirectly* related to facts. Stakeholders may know that these took place at the same time, in the same location as the facts they want to measure, but they can only *speculate* that they had an effect on them.

Causal factors can be *internal*: under the control of the organization, or *external*: beyond its control

Causal factors can also be described as *external or internal*. Weather and sporting events are examples of external causes that an organization has no control over (unless it is sponsoring the sporting event). Whereas, price discounts and advertising are examples of internal causal factors which the organization does control. Some internal causes—like seminars, sales calls and advertising—can be significant business events in their own right, and warrant dedicated fact tables to analyze their associated costs and activities by *who, what, where,* and *when.* In these cases causal dimensions may be conformed across multiple *cause and effect* star schemas that typically represent process sequences.

Internal *Why* Dimensions

PROMOTION is an internal *why* dimension that can contain a mixture of direct and indirect causal attributes

Figure 9-1 shows a simple PROMOTION dimension. This is an internal *why* dimension that would typically contains a combination of discount, display and advertising descriptions. These are a mixture of direct and indirect causal factors. DISCOUNT TYPE is a direct causal factor captured on every transaction along with a DISCOUNT amount fact ($0.00 when there is no discount). Advertising attributes such as CHANNEL are indirect causal factors if there is no way to know for sure that customers saw the adverts. However, if the DISCOUNT TYPE is "Coupon" or "Discount Code" and an advert contains the information that the customer must supply at the point of sale, then it becomes a direct causal factor.

The special "No Promotion" record (PROMOTION KEY zero) will be the most used record in the PROMOTION dimension, if most products are not on promotion every day.

Figure 9-1
PROMOTION
dimension

PROMOTION

PROMOTION KEY	PROMOTION NAME	PROMOTION CODE	DISCOUNT TYPE	START DATE	END DATE	DAYS	CHANNEL
SK	C	C	C	D	D	N	C
0	No Promotion	None	None	-	-	1	N/A
1	Spring Fling	FLING	Percentage	1-Mar-2011	1-Jun-2011	93	Web
2	Dog Days	DOGS	2 for 1	2-Jun-2011	1-Sep-2011	92	TV
3	Back to School	RODNEY	Coupon	2-Sep-2011	1-Nov-2011	61	Magazine
4	Holiday	HOLIDAY	percentage	1-Dec-2011	31-Dec-2011	31	Newspaper

While a PROMOTION dimension may be a small dimension, with only of few hundred promotional condition combinations, it can be challenging to build and assign to the facts because of its mix of direct and indirect causal factors. Direct causal factors are usually straightforward to assign because they are captured by the operational system but many of the interesting indirect causes may *not* be. For example, a sales system will not (reliably) record whether discounts are also promoted by TV ads or special (in-store or on-website) product displays because this information is not needed to complete each sale transaction and print a valid invoice/receipt (which must show any direct discount details). A richly descriptive promotion dimension will require this information to be sourced from elsewhere—typically from less formal data sources, like spreadsheets and word processing documents, and its ETL processing will need to be sophisticated enough to assign the full combination of promotional conditions correctly.

The DW/BI team may have to build small data entry applications to capture causal descriptions and timetables when this information is "known to business but not known to any system."

If BI users need to analyze promotion return on investment (ROI), the data warehouse will need an additional *Promotion Spend* Fact table—using the same conformed PROMOTION dimension. BI users can then run drill-across queries against both PROMOTION SPEND FACT and SALES FACT to compare promotion costs to sales revenue uplift.

Unstructured *Why* Dimensions

In some cases valuable direct causal details are attached to transactions as unstructured comments. These potentially large textual columns should be removed from fact tables and placed in separate dimensions, to maximize fact table performance for the majority of queries that just want to rapidly aggregate the additive facts. The resulting text dimensions are *why* dimensions. Figure 9-2 shows an example COMMENT dimension that contains reasons that salespeople have given for varying the price for specific customers. This could be turned into a better *why* dimension by adding additional attributes that codify the free-format text reasons based on interesting keywords. Embellishing the table with low cardinality sets of descriptive tags would provide better report row headers and more consistent filters.

Indirect causal values are often more difficult to source than direct causal values

PROMOTION may be conformed across sales and promotion cost star schemas

Direct causal factors are often captured as free-format text reasons. These *non-additive text facts* should be removed from fact tables and placed in *text dimensions*

Figure 9-2
COMMENT
Dimension

COMMENT

COMMENT KEY	COMMENT
SK	T
-1	No Comment
0	
1	Loyal customer. Gave her a discount on large...
2	Free accessory as previous product was faulty.

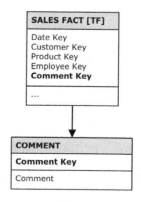

SALES FACT [TF]

Date Key
Customer Key
Product Key
Employee Key
Comment Key

...

COMMENT

Comment Key

Comment

In the absence of structured *why* details, a simple COMMENT dimension will still allow BI users to search events using causal keywords and display comments on reports when they find exceptional transactions. COMMENT dimensions can be improved in future iterations by adding additional attributes and using "text-mining" ETL routines to tag comments.

External *Why* Dimensions

WEATHER is an external *why* dimension. It could be added to any fact table with a time and location granularity that matches the weather feed

Figure 9-3 shows an example WEATHER dimension. This is an external *why* dimension. It does not attempt to document *every* distinct temperature and weather condition—it contains general weather descriptions that are useful for reporting and analyzing non-weather events, *not* weather facts. Because weather is dependent on time and location, any event with a *where* detail can potentially include weather as a dimension; for example, events that might be usefully analyzed by weather include product sales, travel reservations, seminar attendance, insurance claims, and television viewing. Adding a weather dimension requires an external feed that matches the event's time and location granularity.

Figure 9-3
WEATHER
Dimension

WEATHER

WEATHER KEY	WEATHER DESCRIPTION	PRECIPITATION	TEMPERATURE DESCRIPTION	1 WEEK PRE-STORM	1 WEEK POST-STORM
SK	C	C	C	[Y/N]	[Y/N]
0	Normal	None	Normal	N	N
1	Calm Before Storm	None	Normal	Y	N
2	Post-Storm	None	Normal	N	Y
3	Heat Wave	None	Unseasonably Hot	Y	N
4	Rainy Day	Rain	Normal	N	N
5	Cold and Rainy	Rain	Unseasonably Cold	N	N
6	Snowy Day	Snow	Normal	N	N

Causal dimensions—such as weather—that do not alter the granularity of fact tables can be added *later* when a reliable external data source has been found.

Multi-Valued Dimensions

One of the challenges of causal dimensions—especially with external indirect causes—is that there may be *more than one* cause for any given fact. For example, Figure 9-4 shows an EVENT CALENDAR table that documents several sporting events that may have influenced product sales in July 2010. This table makes it easy for BI users to answer the question: "How much did we make during the World Cup?", because they don't have to remember the dates, just pick the *single* event from a drop-down list. As such this table is *WHERE clause friendly* and could be used to store other event types with dynamic date ranges for which consistent date range filters would be useful; for example, "Business" events like "Last 60 days, Current year", "Last 90 days, Current Year" and the same ranges from the previous year.

Causal factors are *multi-valued dimensional attributes* where there is more than one cause of the same type for a fact

Weighting Factor Pattern

Problem/Requirement

If BI users want to group (rather than filter) a report by the *multiple* sporting events they can get into trouble because many of these sporting events overlap. They must be careful how they interpret a report that shows $30M sales during the World Cup and $10M sales during Wimbledon. They must not add totals that overstate the sales. The business has not made $40M because Wimbledon took place during the World Cup. This problem arises because EVENT is a *multi-valued dimensional attribute*—it can have more than one value for a single atomic-level fact like a customer product purchase.

Grouping by a multi-valued attribute can cause over-counting

Figure 9-4
Event Calendar

EVENT CALENDAR

EVENT	START DATE KEY	END DATE KEY	DAYS	EVENT TYPE
PK	PK, SK	SK	N	C
World Cup	11-Jun-2010	11-Jul-2010	31	Sport
Wimbledon	21-Jun-2010	04-Jul-2010	14	Sport
Tour De France	03-Jul-2010	25-Jul-2010	23	Sport
British Grand Prix	11-Jul-2010	11-Jul-2010	1	Sport
British Open Golf	15-Jul-2010	18-Jul-2010	4	Sport

Solution

For BI users who need to group by multiple events, Figure 9-5 shows an alternative version of the sporting schedule that is more GROUP BY friendly. EVENT DAY CALENDAR stores each (sporting) event and date combination—a 14 day event like Wimbledon will be stored as 14 rows. This may appear a little wasteful but it has two benefits:

Over-counting can be avoided by providing a weighting factor

- Each date/event combination can be given a weighting factor to allow facts to be allocated amongst the multiple events that occur on the same day.

- It simplifies the fact table join—this is now a simple inner join on the single EVENT DATE KEY just like a standard CALENDAR dimension instead of a BETWEEN join on START DATE KEY and END DATE KEY.

Figure 9-5
Event Day Calendar

EVENT DAY CALENDAR

EVENT DATE KEY	EVENT	EVENT TYPE	WEIGHTING FACTOR
PK, SK	PK	C	[%]
21-Jun-2010	World Cup	Sport	50%
21-Jun-2010	Wimbledon	Sport	50%
...	...	...	...
11-Jul-2010	World Cup	Sport	**33%**
11-Jul-2010	Tour De France	Sport	**33%**
11-Jul-2010	British Grand Prix	Sport	**34%**
...	...	...	...
14-Jul-2010	Tour De France	Sport	100%
15-Jul-2010	Tour De France	Sport	50%
15-Jul-2010	British Open Golf	Sport	50%

> Must add up to 100% for each day

Weighting factors for each *multi-valued group* (e.g., all the events on a day) must total to 1

If you take a look at the example data in Figure 9-5 you will see that the weighting factors for any one date add up to 1 (100%). For example, on June 21 2010 both the World Cup and Wimbledon are taking place so they both receive 50% of the sales activity by giving them a weighting factor of 0.5 (50%). Whereas, on July 14 2010 the Tour De France is the only significant sporting event taking place (perhaps this is the only event that Pomegranate has sponsored that day) so it gets a weighting factor of 1 (100%). Now when sales are grouped by EVENT, sales revenue can be "correctly weighted" by multiplying each atomic revenue fact by the sporting event weighting factor for the day it was recorded, as shown in the SQL below:

```
SELECT  Event, SUM(Revenue * Weighting_Factor) as Weighted_Revenue
FROM    Sales_Fact s, Event_Day_Calendar d
WHERE   s.Sale_Date_Key = d.Event_Date_Key
GROUP BY Event
```

Consequences

Of course these may not be the "correctly weighted" figures at all—if a business sells more tennis rackets than soccer balls, the Wimbledon/World Cup split should be quite different. Allocation is usually problematic because different stakeholder groups have different ideas about how the atomic facts should be split. However, the one thing no one can argue about is the weighted total. If the weighting factors always adds up to 1 for any day, the grand total for all the days covered by a report will be correct—so long as no events are filtered out.

The "correct" weighting factor split can depend on the facts being queried and who is doing the querying

Useful *impact* reports can be constructed by querying both the weighted facts and unweighted versions of the facts. The unweighted facts can be displayed in the body of the report for each row header; for example, World Cup $30M and Wimbledon $10M. The weighted facts can be aggregated within the BI tool to produce a correct grand total for the report; for example, $30M for the two events (because they completely overlap).

Modeling Multi-Valued Groups

Sporting events in the previous example are multi-valued *indirect* causal factors. Because they are not fundamental details of product sales events—they are only related to time—the multi-valued modeling challenge they represent can be addressed after the sales star is implemented or (better still) ignored altogether. This is not the case when a *direct* causal factor is a significant *multi-valued detail* of an event. For example, imagine you are modelstorming Pomegranate's medical insurance claims. When you ask the stakeholders "Who does what?" they reply:

Multi-valued (**MV**) event details are discovered by telling *group themed* stories

> Doctor claims amount.

By working through the *7Ws* you discover that a DOCTOR (*who*) claims an amount for a TREATMENT (*what*) given to a PATIENT [Employee] (*who*) on a specific TREATMENT DATE (*when*), as shown in the BEAM✳ event table, Figure 9-6. These are all single-valued details that convert readily to dimensions. But a problem arises when you come to the *why* question:

> Why does a doctor treat a patient?

When you ask for examples for the resulting DIAGNOSIS *why* detail, you discover that a claim contains *multiple* diagnosis—there is typically *more than one* thing wrong with a patient—and the diagnosis codes (ICD10 codes) submitted as part of every claim are not linked to the specific treatments.

> **MV**: multi-valued *why* detail. Group example data shows multiple diagnosis for a single treatment.

Figure 9-6
MEDICAL
TREATMENTS
event table
containing
group themed
examples

MEDICAL TREATMENTS [DE]

DOCTOR	claims CLAIM AMOUNT	on TREATMENT DATE	for TREATMENT	to PATIENT	with DIAGNOSIS	with CLAIM ID
[who]	[$] FA	[when]	[what] GD	[Employee]	[why] **MV**	[how] GD
Goldfinger	$500	9-Mar-2011	Plaster Cast	Bond	Broken Arm, Stress, Myopia	G-2011-4
Goldfinger	$5,000	9-Mar-2011	Laser Correction	Bond	Broken Arm, Stress, Myopia	G-2011-4
Dr. No	$100	2-Jun-2011	Pain Killers	Bond	Headaches, Jellyfish Stings	N-2011-7

You capture this business knowledge about multiple diagnoses by marking DIAGNOSIS as **MV** to denote a *multi-valued detail*. Generally you discover MV details by getting stakeholders to tell *group themed* stories. You do this after they have told all their other *themed* stories (*typical, different, missing, repeat*) by pointing at each detail and asking stakeholders if they can give you an example of the *same* type of event that would contain groups of that detail; e.g. a group of customers or a group of products. For most events and most details they won't be able to because multi-valued details (and multi-level (**ML**) details, which you also find this way) are the exception rather than the rule—thankfully.

Multi-valued (**MV**) and multi-level (**ML**) event details are discovered by telling *group themed* stories

Changing the granularity of a fact table to remove a M:M relationship "hard-codes" fact allocations

Multi-Valued Bridge Pattern

Problem/Requirement

The multi-valued group of diagnosis for each treatment creates a M:M relationship between the event and a diagnosis dimension. This could be addressed in the star schema design by changing the physical fact table granularity from one row per claim line item to one row per claim line item *per diagnosis* (CLAIM ID GD, TREATMENT_KEY GD, DIAGNOSIS_KEY GD). However, this causes a significant allocation problem. If 10M claims have an average of 5 itemized treatments for an average of 3 diagnosis codes each this would immediately triple a 50M row fact table to 150M rows. While the extra 100M rows will adversely affect query performance, the real issue is what facts do you put on these extra rows? Doctors submit 50M "atomic" claim amounts, how do you go about splitting these amongst their multiple diagnoses to create 150M additive CLAIM AMOUNT facts? Looking at the example events you may have some ideas on how Bond's treatment costs should be allocated to his symptoms but with hundreds of millions of claim facts to process, automating this would be difficult and few stakeholders will agree on how you should "hard-code" these fact allocations.

Use a *multi-valued bridge table* (**MV**) to resolve a M:M relationship between a fact table and a dimension

Solution

Fact allocation problems can be avoided by leaving the fact table granularity unaltered, and using a *multi-valued bridge table* (**MV**) instead, to resolve the M:M relationship. For example, DIAGNOSIS GROUP [MV], shown in Figure 9-7, can be used to join unaltered claim facts to a DIAGNOSIS dimension. It does this by storing the multiple DIAGNOSIS KEYs of a claim as separate rows of a *diagnosis group*, each with a now familiar WEIGHTING FACTOR. Diagnosis groups are created and assigned a surrogate key (DIAGNOSIS GROUP KEY) as unique claim diagnosis combinations are observed during ETL. These bridge table keys are added to the facts as they are loaded so that tables can be joined as in Figure 9-8.

Figure 9-7
DIAGNOSIS
GROUP
multi-valued
bridge table

DIAGNOSIS GROUP [MV]

DIAGNOSIS GROUP KEY	Contains DIAGNOSIS KEY	on WEIGHTING FACTOR
SK, PK	SK, PK	
1	Broken Arm	0.33
1	Stress	0.33
1	Myopia	0.34
2	Headaches	0.50
2	Jellyfish Stings	0.50

Total weighting factor for a diagnosis group must be 1

Bridge tables avoid the political issues of hard-coding fact allocations

Not only does the bridge table resolve the technical problem of the M:M relationship, it sidesteps the political issues of how to split the atomic facts and provide greater reporting performance and flexibility. By not increasing the number of facts and altering their values, queries that stick to the normal single-value dimensions to analyze busiest doctors, sickest patients or most expensive treatments run as fast as possible and produce "unarguable" answers. Even queries that filter on one specific ICD10 code produce similar fast "unarguable" answers. Only when BI users want to analyze by *multiple* diagnoses do they have to consider the weighting factors and argue about allocations. When they do, they can choose to ignore weighting factors and look at the unweighted treatment costs, use the default (crude) weighting factors in DIAGNOSIS GROUP (which add up to 100% for each diagnosis group) or model their own weighting factors in swappable versions of DIAGNOSIS GROUP and use those instead.

Bridge tables provide flexible multi-valued reporting. Users can choose how they weight the facts at query time

When a multi-valued dimension, such as DIAGNOSIS, is constrained to a single value the multi-valued allocation problem goes away for that query and any additive facts, such as Claim Amount, can be summed without over-counting.

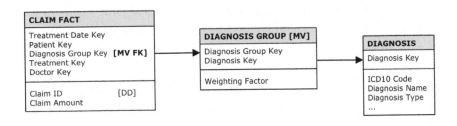

Figure 9-8
Using a
multi-valued
bridge table

If diagnosis combinations seldom repeat, a simple ETL process could create a new diagnosis group for *every* claim using the CLAIM ID as a DIAGNOSIS GROUP KEY. This would avoid having to add a new foreign key to the claim facts as the degenerative CLAIM ID would already be present. However, if combinations frequently reoccur a more sophisticated ETL process can reuse common diagnosis groups (to reduce bridge table growth) by using a dedicated surrogate key for the bridge table. This approach would be likely to have greater BI value because frequently occurring groups could be more easily found (by ranking on DIAGNOSIS GROUP KEY—breaking our rule on hiding surrogate keys) and their weighting factors adjusted by hand if necessary.

Consequences

When you discover a potential multi-valued dimension you should first check that the granularity of the facts is correct before complicating the design with a bridge table. If this is an aggregation of the available operational details you may be able to turn the multi-valued dimension into a normal dimension by going down to the atomic level of detail. For example, if you modeled an invoice fact table with a granularity of one row per invoice then PRODUCT would be a MV dimension. Modeling the atomic invoice line items easily solves this. However, if you are already at the atomic-level you can avoid "splitting the atom" and creating meaningless (unstable subatomic) measures by using a bridge table.

Check that fact granularity is correct (atomic) before using a bridge table design

A bridge table over-complicates queries that rollup a *barely* multi-valued dimension to a single-valued level

Use a multi-level (**ML**) dimension to avoid joining through a bridge table

Optional Bridge Pattern

Problem/Requirement

Causal (*why*) dimensions are not the only multi-valued dimensions. Frequently the *who* dimension for a single fact can be multi-valued. For example, multiple doctors can perform a surgical procedure and multiple customers can purchase a joint policy. Multi-valued uses of *who* dimensions can be implemented by building bridge tables as in the previous pattern. However, using bridge tables in every query can be excessive when a multi-valued *who* dimension is only *barely* multi-valued and the majority of queries want to rollup the facts past the multiple *individuals* to a single-valued *who* hierarchy level. For example, most product sales are made by a single employee but a small percentage are made by teams of two employees working together. Employee level sales reports need to split any team sales facts between employees based on their seniority or role within their teams, but most reports only need to total sales to the branch level or above—ignoring the members of a team by using the branch where the team is based.

Solution

When a dimension is *barely* multi-valued, a bridge table can be avoided by making the dimension multi-leveled (**ML**) so that it contains additional records for the small number of multi-valued groups needed. For example, the multi-level EMPLOYEE [HV, ML] dimension, in Figure 9-9, holds normal employee records for sales consultants and additional records for sales teams made up of two or more consultants. It contains example dimension members for two employees Holmes and Watson, and handles facts where they have worked together (when the game is afoot) by treating their team "Holmes & Watson" as a pseudo-employee. This allows EMPLOYEE to join directly to the sales fact table (as in Figure 9-10) and rollup all their individual and joint sales to the appropriate branch at the time of sale. For example, Watson's individual sales will be rolled up to Afghanistan or London depending on when they occurred. His joint sales with Sherlock Holmes will always be rolled up to London.

Figure 9-9

Multi-level EMPLOYEE dimension containing additional team rows

EMPLOYEE [HV, ML]

EMPLOYEE KEY	EMPLOYEE NAME	BRANCH	Start Date	End Date	CURRENT	LEVEL TYPE
SK	C, MD, CV	C, MD, HV			[Y/N]	C, MD, NC
Holmes	Sherlock Holmes	London	14/01/2008	01/01/3000	Y	Employee
Watson	John Watson	Afghanistan	14/01/2008	19/09/2010	N	Employee
H & W	Holmes & Watson	London	14/01/2008	19/09/2010	N	Team
Watson (2)	John Watson	London	20/09/2010	01/01/3000	Y	Employee
H & W (2)	Holmes & Watson	London	20/09/2010	01/01/3000	Y	Team

All SK column examples values will be replaced by integer surrogate keys in the physical model. The (2) records show the effect of an HV attribute change for employee John Watson (moving back to London).

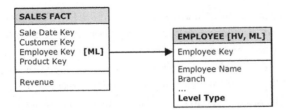

Figure 9-10
Joining the multi-level dimension directly to the facts

For most queries that need to total sales the efficient direct join will be ideal, but those queries that calculate team sales splits will still need to treat EMPLOYEE as multi-valued. They can do so by joining through an *optional bridge table*, such as TEAM shown in Figure 9-11, that provides the team split percentage (the equivalent of a weighting factor) for each team member. The presence of the optional bridge effectively makes the direct join a shortcut that can be used whenever PERCENTAGE is not needed.

A bridge table will still be needed for queries that must use a multi-valued weighting factor

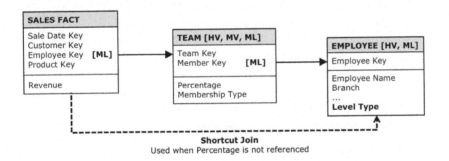

Figure 9-11
Joining through the TEAM optional bridge table

To be able to optionally join through a bridge, or directly to the facts, both the optional bridge table and the ML dimension must use the same surrogate keys, effectively making them swappable dimensions. For example, the Figure 9-12 BEAM✳ diagram for TEAM shows that the bridge table key TEAM KEY is actually a foreign key role of EMPLOYEE KEY. TEAM uses the special pseudo-employee key values, shown in Figure 9-9, to record the members and percentage splits for each team. It also uses normal employee key values on the records where TEAM KEY and MEMBER KEY are the same and PERCENTAGE is 100. These act like teams of one, allowing the bridge table to join employees to 100% of their individual sales facts—the equivalent of a direct join.

An *optional bridge table* must use the same surrogate key values as its multi-level dimension

TEAM [HV, MV, ML]

TEAM KEY	contains MEMBER KEY	with PERCENTAGE	with MEMBERSHIP TYPE
SK [Employee]	SK [Employee]	[%]	C
H & W	Holmes	80	Team Split
H & W	Watson	20	Team Split
Homes	Homes	100	Employee
Watson	Watson	100	Employee
Watson (2)	Watson (2)	100	Employee
H & W (2)	Holmes	50	Team Split
H & W (2)	Watson	50	Team Split
H & W	**H & W**	**100**	**Team**
H & W (2)	**H & W (2)**	**100**	**Team**

Figure 9-12
Multi-valued *and* Multi-leveled bridge table

Adding multiple levels to the bridge table increases reporting flexibility

TEAM contains an additional attribute MEMBERSHIP TYPE to describe these "Team Split" and "Employee" records. It also records a third membership type of "Team" for some of the 100% records (highlighted in bold in Figure 9-12). These records allow the bridge to join facts to the team level records (e.g. "Holmes & Watson") in EMPLOYEE as well as normal employee records. This makes TEAM [HV, MV, ML] a multi-level (**ML**) as well as multi-valued bridge table, enabling it to be used to flexibly query both team sales and employee sales in a single pass. For example, consider the following query:

```
Select Employee_Name, Sum(Revenue)
From Employee E, Team T, Sale_Fact S
where E.Employee_Key = T.Member_Key and
      T.Team_key = S.Employee_Key
Group by Employee_Name
```

Bridge table levels must be carefully filtered to avoid double-counting

This returns both team sales and employee total sales (including their team sales) — a very useful report — but care must be taken not to add a grand total because it would double-count team sales. Filtering on MEMBERSHIP TYPE removes this limitation and makes the following additive reports available:

- employee individual sales (excluding their team sales):
    ```
    Where Membership_Type = "Employee"
    ```

- employee team sales (excluding their individual sales)
    ```
    Where Membership_Type = "Team Split"
    ```

- employee total sales
    ```
    Where Membership_Type in ("Employee", "Team Split")
    ```

- team sales:
    ```
    Where Membership_Type = "Team"
    ```

- teams sales and employees individual sales (excluding their team sales):
    ```
    Where Membership_Type <> "Team Split"
    ```

This last filter is the equivalent of the shortcut join that avoids the bridge table.

Multi-level bridge tables are complex to build and complex to use correctly

Consequences

Multi-level bridge tables are complex. Including the multiple levels provides complete reporting flexibility, but at a price. Queries must filter the bridge table correctly to avoid double-counting or misinterpreting the results. Keeping the multiple levels in the dimension and bridge synchronized also requires significant additional ETL processing. For example, one change to Watson's location requires 2 new rows in EMPLOYEE and 4 new rows in TEAM to keep Watson and the Holmes & Watson team in sync. All these new rows have been marked (2) in Figures 9-9 and 9-12 to highlight the second versions of Watson, his team, and his team splits in the two tables created by his return from Afghanistan to London.

Pivoted Dimension Pattern

Problem/Requirement

A number of Pomegranate products are highly configurable (e.g. the POMCar). For marketing and manufacturing purposes, BI users would like to analyze customer option choices, particularly which options are frequently chosen together, and which options are added to base products that already had certain other "options as standard". The options themselves are also products and services stored in the PRODUCT dimension—some can be sold standalone, others cannot. Figure 9-13 shows a proposed enhancement to the order processing star schema to handle the option analysis requirements. It includes an OPTION PACK [MV] bridge table that allows the PRODUCT dimension to play the additional roles of custom ordered option (by adding OPTION PACK KEY to ORDERS FACTS) and standard option (by adding a STANDARD PACK KEY foreign key to PRODUCT).

BI users want to analyze event combinations

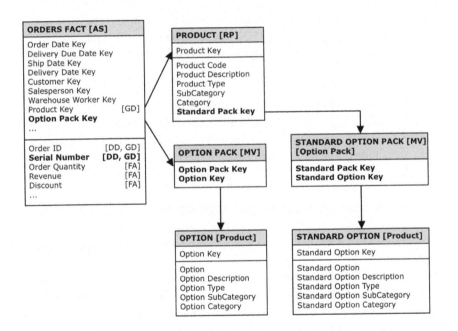

Figure 9-13
OPTION PACK
bridge table added
to ORDER FACTS

By creating two role-playing views (OPTION and STANDARD OPTION) it is easy to construct a query for the users' first question type:

> **How many products with option 4 as standard were customized by adding option 5?**

Their second question type:

> **What were the most popular customized products ordered with option 2 *or* option 3?**

is also straightforward because the unique SERIAL NUMBER of each customized product has also been added to ORDERS FACT. This enables customized products to be counted distinctly so as not to double-count orders where the customer has chosen both option 2 *and* option 3 for the same product.

Counting unique events that are filtered on *multiple multi-values* requires an appropriate unique degenerate ID in the fact table to be counted *uniquely*.

Unfortunately, even with the role-playing bridge table and a unique degenerate ID the proposed design does not *easily* answer their third question type:

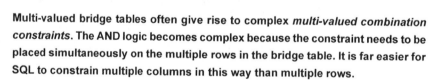

How many products were purchased with options 2, *and* 3 *and* 14, but without options 4, *and* 5 *and* 190?

Combination analysis can involve complex set logic SQL

The AND logic of the option combinations complicates matters. The users cannot answer this question with simple SQL that might contain: "WHERE Option=2 and Option=3…" because OPTION can be equal to both 2 *and* 3 at the same time! Instead they must:

1. Run 3 queries to find products with one of the 3 required options.
2. INTERSECT the results to find only the products with all 3 options.
3. Run 3 more queries to find products that have the 3 unwanted options.
4. INTERSECT the results to find the products with all 3 unwanted options.
5. Use SQL MINUS to take the second set of products away from the first.

These 9 subqueries can be executed as a single SQL SELECT but users would not be able to construct them (or other combination questions) using simple ad-hoc query tools. Even if they could, the queries would not necessarily perform well.

Multi-valued bridge tables often give rise to complex *multi-valued combination constraints*. The AND logic becomes complex because the constraint needs to be placed simultaneously on the multiple rows in the bridge table. It is far easier for SQL to constrain multiple columns in this way than multiple rows.

Use a *pivoted dimension* to turn complex row constraints into simple column constraints

Solution

If the number of options available across all customizable products is limited (e.g. 200 in total) and relatively static (e.g. new options are only added once a year) this *row problem* can be turned into a *column solution* with a bit of lateral thinking. Figure 9-14 shows an OPTION PACK FLAG dimension. This is a *pivoted dimension* (denoted by the code **PD**) that stores the same option combinations as the bridge table, but as columns rather than rows. It requires 200 columns to do so but these columns are just bit (or single byte) flags and they make combination constraints very easy to build in SQL. For example, the filter for the previous user question becomes:

```
WHERE Option2 = "Y" and Option3 = "Y" and Option14  = "Y" and
      Option4 = "N" and Option5 = "N" and Option190 = "N"
```

The example data in Figure 9-14 shows that option pack the users are looking for is OPTION PACK KEY 1. This is the same value as the more complex set based queries would eventually find in the bridge table because the pivoted dimension and the bridge table use the same surrogate key—they are swappable versions of each other. This means that the fact table does not need to be altered to add the pivoted dimension if the bridge table key is already present. There is value in having both tables because the bridge table and OPTION dimension combination is *GROUP BY friendly* and *single value WHERE clause friendly* while the pivoted dimension is *combination WHERE clause friendly*. To make the pivoted dimension *user-friendly* as well it should be built with meaningful names for each option column; for example, MEMORY UPGRADE, CPU UPGRADE, RAID CONFIGURATION etc.

A bridge table and pivoted dimension are swappable dimensions that can be used together

OPTION PACK FLAG [PD]

PACKAGE KEY	OPTION 1	OPTION 2	OPTION 3	OPTION 14	OPTION 200	OPTION PACK
SK	C1, ND1	C1, ND1	C1, ND1	C1, ND1	C1, ND1	T, ND1
0	N	N	N	N	N	No options
1	N	Y	Y	Y	N	2, 3, 14
2	N	N	N	Y	Y	14, 200
3	Y	Y	Y	N	N	1, 2, 3
4	Y	N	N	Y	N	1, 14

Figure 9-14
OPTION PACK
pivoted dimension

In Figure 9-14, the pivoted dimension has an additional OPTION PACK attribute containing comma separated lists of option codes. This can be used in a query GROUP BY clause or displayed in a report header/footer to describe the filters that have been applied. In the user-friendly version of the pivoted dimension this would be a long text column containing a list of descriptive option names (sorted in alphabetic order). It can be useful to provide both versions; e.g., an OPTION PACK NUMBER list of codes and an OPTION PACK list of descriptions.

Add comma separated list attributes to flag dimensions to make them more report display-friendly

If you need to build a column flag dimension, create the multi-valued bridge table version first. Maintaining this type of table is easier with standard ETL routines and simple SQL. After the bridge table is in place you can then create more elaborate ETL routines that pivot its rows to create and maintain the column-orientated version with meaningful column names generated for the descriptive row values using *SQL generated SQL*.

While bridge tables and pivoted dimensions often go together, the need for a pivoted table is not limited to multi-valued dimensions. For example, if the granularity of ORDERS FACT was one record per product option order line item (the product plus each of its custom options as fact rows), this would avoid the multi-valued bridge but the pivoted dimension would still be needed to easily answer the combination questions. It would just be more work to build the pivoted dimension

Even without a bridge table, a pivoted dimension is needed to cope with complex ad-hoc combination queries

from scratch without the bridge and the fact table would still need to be altered to add the OPTION PACK KEY.

Column flag dimensions should only be populated with observed combinations, otherwise they can easily grow to be bigger than fact tables. A bit flag dimension with only 20 columns has over a million possible combinations.

If bridge table rows contain quantities, a pivoted dimension can contain count columns

If the business problem was more complex and varying quantities of each option could be chosen to configure a product, the OPTION PACK bridge table would need to contain an OPTION QUANTITY attribute and the OPTION PACK [PD] pivoted dimension would contain option count columns rather than [Y/N] flags. Similarly, if small numbers of options and options quantities were handled as separate fact rows (to avoid a bridge table) and comparisons or combinations were constantly used then a *pivoted fact table* might be created with option count facts.

Pivoted dimensions are limited to relatively small and stable value populations

Consequences

Pivoted dimensions are limited by the maximum number of columns available in a database table (usually between 256 and 1024) and the ETL involved in automating the maintenance of volatile combination values is complex. A pivoted dimensions works well for Pomegranate because there are only a few hundred relatively stable options (with several new ones being add manually each year) but it could not cope with a possible 155,000 ICD10 diagnosis codes.

How Dimensions

How dimensions are often degenerate (**DD**) IDs that provide useful links to operational source records and unique count measures

How dimensions document any additional information about facts that are not captured by other dimensions. The most common *how* dimensions are degenerate (**DD**) transaction identifiers stored in fact tables. These dimensions describe how facts come to exist by tying them back to the original source system transactions. They can also be invaluable for providing unique transaction counts. For example, an ORDER ID in an ORDERS FACT table can be used to count how many orders contained at least one laptop product line item. Using `COUNT(DISTINCT Order_ID)` ensures that individual orders with several line items for different laptops will not be over-counted. As mentioned earlier, a degenerate ID that can be uniquely counted is essential if a star schema has one or more multi-valued dimensions.

Look out for conformed degenerate dimensions and add them to the event matrix to help you discover event sequences and milestone dependencies that can be modeled as evolving events.

Too Many Degenerate Dimensions?

Most transaction fact tables will contain at least one degenerate transaction ID that cannot be stored more efficiently in a separate dimension table because its cardinality approaches that of the fact table itself and it has no additional descriptive attributes. However if a fact table contains many additional degenerates you should try to prune these to keep the fact table record length under control using the following guidelines:

- If degenerates will be used to group or filter or will be browsed in combination, they should be remodeled as attributes in a separate dimension.

- Any degenerates that contain large unstructured comments should be replaced by a surrogate key to a COMMENT dimension (as in Figure 9-2).

- If a degenerate [Y/N] flag will be frequently counted it can be remodeled as a low cardinality additive fact with the values 0, 1 that can be summed. This is especially useful as aggregates can be built that use this fact.

- If the degenerate is high cardinality and will be counted distinctly it should remain in the fact table where it will act as a non-additive fact.

- If a degenerate flag describes the type of value in an adjacent fact it may represent data that would be better modeled as separate additive fact columns without the flag. For example, a REVENUE fact and a flag REVENUE TYPE with the values: 'E' for estimate and 'A' for actual, should instead be modeled as two facts: ESTIMATED REVENUE and ACTUAL REVENUE.

- Sometimes a degenerate meets more than one of these criteria. For example, a flag may be frequently counted, and used for grouping and constraining. In which case, you can model it as both a fact and a dimensional attribute.

Large sets of degenerate dimensions within a fact table should be remodeled as separate dimensions

Some degenerates can be remodeled as useful additive and non-additive facts

Creating *How* Dimensions

If you identify degenerates that should be remodeled as dimensions, check to see if any belong in existing dimensions. For any that do not, define a new dimension with its own surrogate key and relocate the degenerates to it, replacing them in the fact table with the new surrogate key. This new dimension is often called a "junk" dimension, because of its tough-to-classify mix of attributes. But it really is not junk at all. Instead, it is a non-conformed *how* dimension, specific to just this set of facts, that can often be usefully named after its matching fact table. For example, a CALL DETAILS FACT table may need a CALL DETAIL *how* dimension, and a SALES FACT table may need a SALE TYPE dimension. If a fact table has multiple small non-conformed dimensions—typically *whys* and *hows*— they can often be merged to reduce the number of keys in the fact table.

Move degenerates to a physical *how* dimension named after the fact table and replace them in the fact table with a surrogate key

Don't tell stakeholders that any of their data is "junk", especially when you are modelstorming with them. If you are looking for a less pejorative term for your non-conformed *how* dimensions, call them *miscellaneous dimensions*.

Range Band Dimension Pattern

Problem/Requirement

BI users want to group by the facts but need to rollup the answers

BI users want to group by facts, such as REVENUE and ORDER QUANTITY, and count the unique occurrences of customers, products or transactions. They need to use a fact like a dimension and treat a dimensional attribute like a measure. Converting a dimensional attribute like CUSTOMER ID into a measure can be straightforward using COUNT(DISTINCT …) but it requires more work to turn raw facts into good GROUP BY items. Because facts are mostly high cardinality, continuously valued numbers, grouping by them rolls up very little data and produces too many report rows: more data dump than readable report.

Solution

Provide a *range band* dimension to "turn facts into dimensions"

Numeric range band dimensions such as RANGE BAND, shown in Figure 9-15, are another type of *how* dimension. They are *how many* dimensions or *"How do you turn a fact into a dimension?"* dimensions that convert continuously valued high cardinality facts into better discrete row headers. Chapter 6 described how high cardinality dimensional attributes should be stored as range band labels that are more useful for grouping by. Range band dimensions allow this to be done dynamically at query time to facts and other numeric dimensional attributes.

Figure 9-15
RANGE BAND
dimension

RANGE BAND

RANGE BAND GROUP	LOW BOUND	HIGH BOUND	RANGE BAND
PK, C, ND1	PK, N	PK, N	C, ND1
5 Money Bands	0	99.99	$0 to $99
5 Money Bands	100	499.99	$100 to $499
5 Money Bands	500	999.99	$500 to $999
5 Money Bands	1000	1999.99	$1,000 to $1,999
5 Money Bands	2000	Max Value	$2,000 and above
4 Age Bands	0	10	Age 0 to 10 Years
4 Age Bands	11	29	Age 11 to 29 Years
4 Age Bands	30	59	Age 30 to 59 Years
4 Age Bands	60	Max Value	Age 60 or More

Range band dimensions convert high cardinality facts into useful low cardinality report row headers

Figure 9-15 is an example of a general-purpose range band dimension that can store any number of *range band groups*. The example data shows two groups: "5 Money Bands" that would be used to group REVENUE into 5 bands and "4 Age Bands" that can be joined to a customer or employee age to group a population into 4 bands. Figure 9-16 shows how the RANGE BAND dimension is joined to SALES FACT to count the number of products sold in each of the 5 revenue ranges—effectively converting the REVENUE fact into a dimension on-the-fly. The SQL for the query would be:

```
SELECT   range_band, SUM(quantity_sold)
FROM     sales_fact, range_band
WHERE    range_band_group = "5 Money Bands"
AND      revenue BETWEEN low_bound AND high_bound
GROUP BY range_band
```

Range band dimensions allow BI users to define new bandings at any time—by simply adding or changing dimension rows. The price for this flexibility will be slower query performance because SQL between joins are difficult to optimize. If certain facts are frequently used for range banding they can be indexed to improve join and sort processing. Normally only the dimensional foreign keys are indexed. Facts are usually not indexed because indexes do not speed up their aggregation. But for range banding queries, the facts are acting like dimensional foreign keys.

Index facts that are frequently used for range banding

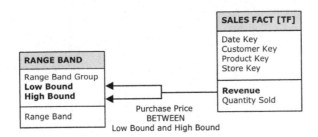

Figure 9-16
Range banding
a fact

Consequences

RANGE BAND GROUP, LOW BOUND, and HIGH BOUND form the primary key (**PK**) of the RANGE BAND dimension, and must therefore be unique. You should set up the LOW BOUND and HIGH BOUND values for each range band with care: they should not overlap, and no gaps should exist. In addition, the RANGE BAND names must be unique within each RANGE BAND GROUP. The short code **ND1** (No Duplicates) in Figure 9-15 has been added to these columns to indicate that they form a no duplicates group (number 1)—the combination of column values within the group must be unique.

Range bands must be carefully defined. They must be unique with no gaps and no overlaps

Step Dimension Pattern

Problem/Requirement

Chapter 7 covered techniques for overloading sequential events, such as flights or web page visits, with first and last locations. These powerful dimensions not only provide extra *where* information, they typically describe *why* a sequence of events started and *how* it finished. For example, the first URL in a web visit can be converted into a REFERRAL *why* dimension that describes the banner ad or search string that triggered each click, and the last URL can become a *how* dimension that describes each click by its outcome; for example, "Just browsing" or "Big shopping trip". Armed with this additional *why* and *how* information, BI users will often want to analyze the position of all the intervening events relative to these pivotal cause and effect events.

BI users want to understand sequential behavior by analyzing events relative to the cause and effect events within a sequence

A step dimension
numbers each event
in a sequence

Figure 9-17
STEP dimension

Solution

The humble looking STEP dimension, in Figure 9-17, helps BI users understand sequential behavior. It allows ETL processes to explicitly label events with their position in a sequence (from its beginning and from its end), along with the length of the sequence. For example, a web browsing session of four page views by the same visitor (IP address) within an agreed timeframe would be represented as four rows in a PAGE VIEWS FACT table. The first page view event would be labeled as step 1 of 4 by assigning it a STEP KEY of 7 (see Figure 9-17). The next page view would be labeled as step 2 of 4 using STEP KEY 8, and so on.

STEP

STEP KEY	STEP NUMBER	TOTAL STEPS	STEPS UNTIL LAST	LAST STEP
SK	N	N	N	[Y/N]
0	0	0	0	-
1	1	1	0	Y
2	1	2	1	N
3	2	2	0	Y
4	1	3	2	N
5	2	3	1	N
6	3	3	0	Y
7	1	4	3	N
8	2	4	2	N
9	3	4	1	N
10	4	4	0	Y

A STEP dimension
enables positional
analysis (better
story telling) using
simple single-pass
queries

BI users can use the STEP dimension to easily identify page views belonging to sessions of any length, rank pages by position within sessions, and answer questions about the beginning, midpoint and ending of sessions for any interesting subset of customers, time, and products. They can quickly find the good and bad ("session killer") last page visits of a session (LAST STEP = "Y"), or those that precede session killers (STEPS UNTIL LAST = 1) using simple, single-pass SQL. Answering questions like these without a STEP dimension would be too difficult for all but the most SQL-savvy BI users.

Step dimensions
can play multiple
roles to describe
sequences within
sequences

A STEP dimension can also play multiple roles for an event; for example, Figure 9-18 shows a PAGE VIEWS FACT table with two STEP dimension roles: STEP IN SESSION which describes page position within the overall session, and STEP IN PURCHASE which describes how close each page is to a purchase decision. Each time a visitor clicks on a link to place a product in a shopping cart, STEP IN PURCHASE would be reset and the next mini-sequence length calculated.

Figure 9-18
Using the STEP
dimension to
describe web page
visits

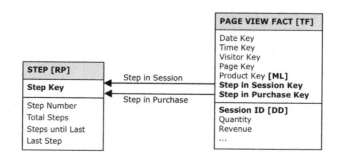

The STEP IN PURCHASE dimension role lets BI users analyze page visit sequences that lead to product purchases *and* ones that don't: page views that don't lead to a purchase would have a STEP IN PURCHASE KEY that points to the "Not Applicable" row 0 in STEP.

Events that are not part of a sequence use STEP row 0

Consequences

STEP dimensions are relatively simple to populate from spreadsheets, but they grow surprisingly quickly as the maximum number of steps increases. The formula for calculating the number of rows needed for n total steps is: $n \times (n+1)/2$. Therefore, 200 steps = 20,100 rows, and 1,000 steps would be more than half a million rows! If 200 steps are more than adequate for 99% of all sequences, pre-populate your STEP dimension accordingly, and create special step number records greater than 200 if/when they are needed. These records would use special STEP KEY values (e.g. the negative step number) and would contain the STEP NUMBER but have missing values for the other attributes to denote that they are steps in "exceptionally long" sequences. Often exceptionally long sequences are the result of ETL processing errors or poorly defined business rules that fail to spot the end of a normal sequence.

STEP dimensions grow in size quickly. You should set a maximum number of steps for the majority of sequences

Although designing and creating a STEP dimension is straightforward, attaching it to the facts can require significant additional ETL processing. The events that belong to the same sequence have to be identified by an appropriate business rule (for example, all the page visits from the same IP address that are no more than 10 minutes apart) and counted in a first pass of the data; only then can the correct STEP KEYs be assigned to each fact row in a second pass.

STEP dimensions require additional ETL processing to make two passes of the data

Overloading facts with STEP information and other richly descriptive *why* and *how* dimensions takes significant additional effort from the ETL team. You should make sure you take them to lunch—on a regular basis.

Audit Dimension Pattern

Problem/Requirement

No treatment of *how* and *why* would be complete without covering the perplexed stakeholder's questions:

> **How did this data get into our data warehouse?**
>
> **Why are the figures so high/low?**

Too often the answers to these questions are locked away in *an ETL tool metadata repository*—inaccessible to BI users who need this information the most.

Stakeholders want to query data lineage

An audit dimension
provides summary
ETL metadata in a
dimensional format

Solution

Figure 9-19 shows an AUDIT dimension that presents ETL statistics and data quality descriptions in a dimensional form—tied directly to the facts—where they can be queried by BI users, and used to provide additional context within the body of reports or as header or footer information. The AUDIT dimension surrogate key—AUDIT KEY—represents each execution of an ETL process. For example, if there are five different ETL modules that support the nightly refresh of the data warehouse, there would be at least five new rows added to the AUDIT Dimension each night. Each of these rows would have a unique AUDIT KEY, which would appear in the fact table (and dimension) rows that were created or updated by the given ETL execution—providing basic data lineage information on each fact (and dimension): where it came from, and how it was extracted and loaded or last updated.

Figure 9-19
AUDIT dimension

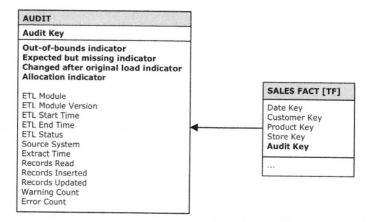

Audit dimensions
can be expanded to
provide basic data
quality indicators

Figure 9-19 also shows additional indicator attributes (in bold) that describe data quality and completeness. The Audit dimension would contain additional rows for each ETL module so that unusual facts records can be explicitly flagged if they contain out of bounds (defined by example data, data profiling, or historical norms), missing, adjusted or allocated values.

Audit dimensions
turns metadata into
normal data that can
be used to query the
facts

Audit dimensions leverage the value of ETL metadata. By making it available within each star schema they elevate metadata to the position of "real" data— another *how* or *why* dimension that BI users can use to group or filter their reports to help explain the figures they see.

You can find additional information on creating and populating Audit dimensions in *The Data Warehouse ETL Toolkit,* by Ralph Kimball and Joe Caserta (Wiley, 2004) pages 128–131

Summary

- *Why* dimensions are used to store direct and indirect causal reasons. Direct causal factors such as price discounts are typically easier to implement and attribute to facts than indirect factors because they are captured as part of a business event and do not need to be inferred from additional internal or external sources.

- Unstructured *why* details are often captured as free text comments. These should be stored in a COMMENT *why* dimension rather than as degenerate dimensions within fact tables.

- *Multi-valued* (**MV**) *bridge* tables are used to resolve multiple causal factors and other multi-valued dimension relationships. Bridge tables avoid having to change the natural atomic granularity of a fact table and hard-coding fact allocations at ETL time. Using a bridge table allows BI users to choose how to weight the facts at query time. They also avoid multi-valued issues altogether when queries do not use the multi-value dimension.

- *Optional bridge* tables and multi-level dimensions that share common surrogate keys can be used to efficiently handle *barely* multi-valued dimensions. Queries that do not need to deal with a multi-valued dimension level and its weighting factor can attach the multi-level dimension directly to the facts to rollup to single-valued hierarchy levels.

- *Pivoted dimensions* (**PD**) are built by transposing row values into column flags or column counts. They are used to simplify combination constraints that would otherwise be difficult to place across multiple-rows. Pivoted dimensions are often implemented as swappable versions of multi-valued bridge tables. For query flexibility it is useful to have both the row-oriented bridge table for grouping and the column-oriented pivoted dimension for combination filtering. It is also easier to build a pivoted dimension once the bridge table is in place.

- Degenerate *how* dimension (**DD**) transaction IDs ensure that facts are traceable back to source systems. They also provide unique event counts for use in multi-valued queries.

- *Physical how* dimensions are typically non-conformed dimensions that are specific to a single fact table. These *miscellaneous dimensions* provide a home for the unique combinations of degenerate dimensions that are too numerous to leave in the fact table. They reduce the size of fact tables and make it easier for users to browse the dimensional values combinations.

- *Range Band* dimensions support the ad-hoc conversion of continuously variable facts and dimensional attributes into report-friendly discrete bands for grouping and filtering.

- *Step* dimensions allow facts to be analyzed using their relative position within event sequences. They enable BI users to discover events that closely follow or precede other significant cause and effect events. The help the data warehouse to tell better stories.

- *Audit* dimensions make ETL data lineage and data quality metadata available within star schemas so that it can easily be used with BI reports.

I keep six honest serving-men
(They taught me all I knew);
Their names are **What** and **Why** and **When**
And **How** and **Where** and **Who**.
I send them over land and sea,
I send them east and west;
But after they have worked for me,
I give them all a rest.

...

—*Rudyard Kipling, The Elephant's Child*

Time for a DW/BI Retrospective

Appendix A: The Agile Manifesto

Manifesto for Agile Software Development

We are uncovering better ways of developing software by doing it and helping others do it. Through this work we have come to value:

Individuals and interactions over processes and tools

Working software over comprehensive documentation

Customer collaboration over contract negotiation

Responding to change over following a plan

That is, while there is value in the items on the right, we value the items on the left more.

The Twelve Principles of Agile Software

We follow these principles:

- Our highest priority is to satisfy the customer through early and continuous delivery of valuable software.
- Welcome changing requirements, even late in development. Agile processes harness change for the customer's competitive advantage.
- Deliver working software frequently, from a couple of weeks to a couple of months, with a preference to the shorter timescale.
- Business people and developers must work together daily throughout the project.
- Build projects around motivated individuals. Give them the environment and support they need, and trust them to get the job done.
- The most efficient and effective method of conveying information to and within a development team is face-to-face conversation.
- Working software is the primary measure of progress.
- Agile processes promote sustainable development. The sponsors, developers, and users should be able to maintain a constant pace indefinitely.
- Continuous attention to technical excellence and good design enhances agility.
- Simplicity—the art of maximizing the amount of work not done—is essential.
- The best architectures, requirements, and designs emerge from self-organizing teams.
- At regular intervals, the team reflects on how to become more effective, then tunes and adjusts its behavior accordingly.

APPENDIX B: BEAM✳ NOTATION AND SHORT CODES

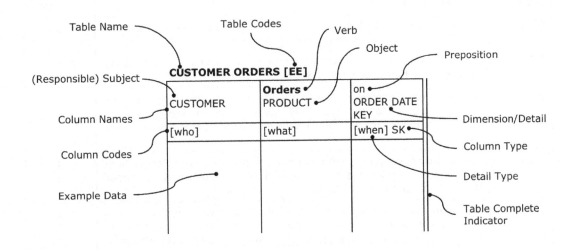

Table Codes

Event Story and Fact Table Types

CODE	MEANING/USAGE	CHAPTERS
[DE]	**Discrete Event.** Event represents a point in time or short duration transaction that has completed. Implemented as a transaction fact table.	2, 8
[RE]	**Recurring Event.** Event represents measurements taken at predictable regular intervals. Implemented as a periodic snapshot fact table.	2, 8
[EE]	**Evolving Event.** Event represents a process that takes time to complete. Implemented as an accumulating snapshot fact table.	2, 4, 8
[TF]	**Transaction Fact table.** Physical equivalent of a discrete event [DE]. Typically maintained by insert only.	5, 8
[AS]	**Accumulating Snapshot.** Physical fact table equivalent of an evolving event [EE]. Maintained by insert and update. Typically contains multiple milestone date/time dimensions with matching duration and state count facts.	8
[PS]	**Periodic Snapshot.** Physical fact table equivalent of a recurring event [RE]. Typically contains semi-additive facts.	8
[AG]	**Aggregate.** Fact table that summarizes an existing fact table.	8
[DF]	**Derived Fact table.** Fact table that is constructed by merging, slicing, or pivoting existing fact tables.	8
{Source}	**Data source.** Default source system table or filename.	5

Dimension Table Types

Code	Meaning/Usage	Chapters
[CV]	**Current Value**. Table contains only current value dimensional attributes. Also known as a *type 1 slowly changing dimension*.	4, 5, 6
[HV]	**Historic Value**. Table contains at least one historical value dimensional attribute. Also known as a *type 2 slowly changing dimension*.	4, 5, 6
[RP]	**Role-Playing**. Dimension is used to play multiple roles; for example, `Salesperson` and `Manager` are both roles of the `Employee [RP]dimension`. `Calendar[RP]` is the most common role-playing dimension.	4
[RU]	**Rollup**. Dimension is derived from a more granular dimension. For example, `Month[RU]` is a rollup of the `Calendar` dimension containing conformed dimensional attributes `Month`, `Quarter`, and `Year`.	4
[SD]	**Swappable Dimension**. Part of a set of dimensions with a common surrogate key that can be used in place of each other. Swappable dimensions are often used to provide subsets of a large dimension population for efficiency; for example, `Business Customer` is a swappable subset of `Customer`. Swappable dimensions can also be used to provide alternative historical views and national language support.	6
[ML]	**Multi-Level**. A dimension containing additional members representing higher levels in the dimension's hierarchy. Used when a fact table can be attached to a dimension at different levels. For example, sales transactions can be assigned to an individual Employee or a Team/Branch, and web advertisements can be for a specific product or a product category.	6
[HM]	**Hierarchy Map**. A table used to resolve a recursive relationship. Represents a variable-depth hierarchy. For example, `Company Structure[CV,HM]` is a current value hierarchy map (does not track hierarchy history).	6
[MV]	**Multi-Valued**. A bridge table used to resolve a many-to-many relationship between a fact table and a multi-valued dimension. Or A hierarchy map [HM] that contains child members with multiple direct parents. For example, `Reporting Structure [MV,HM]` is a hierarchy map that connects employees to more than one direct manager. MV tables often contain a weighting factor that allows facts to be allocated across the multiple values at query time.	6, 9
[PD]	**Pivoted Dimension**. A dimension that represents multiple row values as a set of column (bit) flags—used to simplify combination selection. Often built by pivoting a multi-valued bridge table or a fact table.	9
{Source}	**Data source**. Default source system table or filename.	5

Column Codes

General Column Codes

CODE	MEANING/USAGE	CHAPTERS
MD	**Mandatory**. Column value should be present under normal conditions. Column is defined as nullable so it can handle errors.	2
NN	**Not Null**. Column does not allow nulls. All SK and FK columns are not null by default.	5
ND NDn	**No Duplicates**. Column must not contain duplicate values. The numbered version is used to define a combination of columns that must be unique.	9
X*n*	**Exclusive**. A dimensional attribute that is not valid for all members of a dimension. Used in conjunction with a DC defining characteristic. Number coded to identify mutually exclusive attributes or attribute groups and identify the defining characteristics it is paired with. Also used to denote exclusive facts that are only valid for certain dimensional values.	3, 8
DC DC*n,n*	**Defining Characteristic**. Column value dictates which exclusive attributes or facts are valid. For example, `Product Type` DC defines which `Product` attributes are valid. Number coded when multiple defining characteristics exist in the same table.	3, 8
[*W-type*] [dimension]	**Dimension type or name**. The *W (who, what, when, where, why, how)* type of an event detail or the dimension name when a detail is a role; for example, `Salesperson [Employee]` where `Salesperson` is a role of the `Employee` dimension. Also used to show a recursive relationship within a detail table.	4, 6
{Source}	**Data source**. The name of a column or field in a source system. Can be qualified with a table or filename if necessary (when different from the table default).	5
~~Unavailable~~ ~~MD~~	**Unavailable or incorrect**. Column name or column code annotation denoting that source data is unavailable or does not comply with the current column type definition. For example, ~~MD~~ denotes that the source system does not treat the data as mandatory as it contains null or missing values. ~~Gender~~ denotes that `Gender` is not available.	5

Data Types

CODE	MEANING/USAGE	CHAPTERS
C Cn	**Character data type**. The numbered version is used to define the maximum length. Overrides the default length.	5
N Nn.n	**Numeric data type**. The numbered version is used to define precision. Overrides the default precision.	5
DT DTn	**Date/Time data type**. The numbered version is used in duration formulas for derived facts; for example, `Delivery Delay DF=DT2-DT1`. Numbering can also denote default chronological order of milestones within an evolving event.	4, 5, 8

D Dn	**Date data type**. The numbered version is used in duration formulas for derived facts; for example, `Project Duration DF=D2-D1`. Numbering can also denote chronological order of milestones within an evolving event.	5, 8
T Tn	**Text**. Long character data used to hold free format text. The numbered version is used to define the maximum length. Overrides the default length.	5
B	**Blob.** Binary long object used to hold documents, images, sound, objects, and so on.	5

Key Types

CODE	MEANING/USAGE	CHAPTERS
PK	**Primary Key**. Column or group of columns that uniquely identify each row in a table.	5
SK	**Surrogate Key**. integer assigned by the data warehouse as the primary key for a dimension table. Used as a foreign key in fact tables. Used to denote that example data in a BEAM✲ table column will be replaced by an integer foreign key in the physical model.	5
BK	**Business Key**. A source system key.	3, 5
NK	**Natural Key**. A (source system) key used in the real world	5
FK	**Foreign Key**. A column that references the primary key of another table.	5
RK	**Recursive Key.** A foreign key that references the primary key of its own table. Often used to represent variable-depth hierarchies. Stores information needed to build hierarchy maps; for example, `Parent Company Key` in `Company`.	6

Dimensional Attribute Types

CODE	MEANING/USAGE	CHAPTERS
CV CVn	**Current Value attribute**. A dimensional attribute that holds the current value only. Source system updates overwrite the previous value. Supports current value (as is) reporting. Also known as a *type 1 slowly changing dimensional* attribute. The numbered version relates a CV attribute to a previous value (PV) version of itself; for example, `Territory CV1` and `Previous Territory PV1`.	3, 6
HV HVn	**Historic Value attribute**. A dimensional attribute that tracks historical values. Source system updates cause a new version of the dimensional record to be created, preserving the historically correct values. Supports historical value (as was) reporting. Also known as a *type 2 slowly changing dimensional* attribute. The numbered version is used in combination with CV to define *conditional* HV attributes. These are CV attributes that act as HV attributes only when another HV attribute with the same number changes; for example, `Street CV, HV1` will only track changes when `Zip Code HV1` changes at the same time.	3, 6

FV	**Fixed Value attribute.** A dimensional attribute that should not change; for example `Date of Birth`. FV attributes however can be corrected. When FV attributes are corrected they behave like CV attributes: the previous incorrect value is not preserved.	3
PVn	**Previous Value attribute.** A dimensional attribute that records the previous value of another current value attribute. Also known as a *type 3 slowly changing dimensional* attribute. PVn is always used in conjunction with a matching CVn to relate the previous value to the current value; for example, `Previous Territory PV1` and `Territory CV1`. PV attributes can also be used to hold initial or "as at specific date" values; for example, `Initial Territory PV1` or `YE2010 Territory PV1`.	6

Event Detail and Fact Column Types

CODE	MEANING/USAGE	CHAPTERS
MV	**Multi-Value.** Event detail contains multiple values that must be resolved using a bridge table when converted to a dimensional model. Fact table FK that points to a multi-value bridge table.	6, 9
ML	**Multi-Level.** Event detail represents various levels in a hierarchy such as individual employee or teams/branches that must be handled by a multi-level dimension that contains additional members representing the required levels. Fact table FK that points to a multi-level dimension *and* makes use of the additional levels.	6
DD	**Degenerate Dimension.** Dimensional attribute stored in a fact table. Has no additional descriptive attributes; therefore, does not join to a physical dimension table. Typically used for transaction IDs (*how* details); for example, `Order ID DD`.	2, 3, 4, 5
GD GDn	**Granular Dimension.** A dimension or combination of dimensions that defines the granularity of a fact table. The numbered version is used when alternative dimension combinations can define the granularity. For example, `Call Reference Number GD1` or `Customer GD2`, `Call Time GD2` define the granularity of a call detail fact table.	2, 8
FA	**(Fully) Additive fact.** A fact that produces a correct total when summed across any combination of its dimensions. For a fact to be additive it must be expressed in a single unit of measure. Percentages and unit prices are not additive.	5, 8
SA SAn	**Semi-Additive fact.** A fact that can be correctly totaled by some dimensions but not others. Semi-additive facts have at least one non-additive (NA) dimension. For example, an account balance cannot be summed over time: its non-additive (NA) dimension. Semi-additive facts are often averaged over their non-additive dimension. SA is always used in conjunction with at least one NA dimension foreign key to relate the semi-additive fact to its non-additive dimensions. The numbered version is used to relate multiple semi-additive facts in the same table to their appropriate NA dimensions. For example, `Stock Level SA1` is non-additive across `Stock Date Key NA1` whereas `Order Count SA2` is non-additive across `Product Key NA2`.	8

NA NAn	**Non-Additive fact**. A fact that cannot be aggregated using sum; for example, `Temperature NA`. Non-additive facts can be aggregated using other functions such as min, max, and average. A non-additive dimension of a semi-additive fact. The numbered version is used to relate non-additive dimensions to specific semi-additive facts when multiple SAs exist in the same table.	8
DF DF= formulae	**Derived Fact**. A fact that can be derived from other columns within the same table. May be followed by a simple formula referencing other facts or date/time details by number; for example, `Unit Price DF=Revenue /Quantity`.	8
[UoM] [UoM1, UoM2,...]	**Unit of measure**. Unit of measure symbol or description; for example, `Order Revenue [$]` or `Delivery Delay [days]`. Lists multiple units of measure required for reporting, with the default standard unit (**UoM1**) first. All quantities are stored in the standard UoM to produce an additive fact.	2, 4

APPENDIX C: RESOURCES FOR AGILE DIMENSIONAL MODELERS

Here is our list of recommended resources to help you implement the ideas contained in the book.

Tools: Hardware and Software

Use Inclusive Tools. Take Pictures

We're very interested in the use of tablet devices for collaborative data modeling, but until they support seamless shared drawing and become ubiquitous, to the point where *everyone* is comfortable using them to scribble all over your nascent designs, we recommend that you use low-tech whiteboards, flipcharts, large Post-It notes, or whiteboard-on-a-roll for your modelstorming sessions.

The Wi-Fi–enabled cameras in smartphones and tablets can be tremendously useful for capturing modelstorming results and quickly transferring them to a laptop for further review (stick to black ink on your whiteboards and flipcharts to help with that). There are many apps that can automate the workflow of cleaning up whiteboard images and moving them to shared folders for group viewing.

Go Large

Digital projectors are our number one high-tech collaborative modeling tools. It's amazing how quickly everyone can spot opportunities to improve a data model when it's blown up large on the wall. Invite your colleagues to the screening of your latest data model. Perhaps they can stay for a movie afterwards!

Avoid Database Modeling Tools When You're Not Talking To Databases

We recommend that you use spreadsheets and presentation software for communicating with business stakeholders, and ERD data modeling tools for communicating with databases and DBAs. ERD modeling software is invaluable for forward and reverse-engineering physical database tables and drawing detailed star schema diagrams for a technical audience, but can get in the way when working with business people.

Try Our Template

We suggest that you try the BEAM✷*Modelstormer* spreadsheet template (see **Websites** shortly). It supports the transition between BEAM✷ models and physical database models by generating SQL DDL that can be imported by many commercial database modeling tools.

Playing Planning Poker

There are a number of iOS and Android apps that simulate a deck of planning poker cards.

Books

Agile Software Development
Scrum and XP from the Trenches, Henrik Kniberg (InfoQ.com, 2007)

Not why do agile (like so many books) but how Henrik did agile.

Agile Analytics, Ken Collier (Addison-Wesley, 2011)

While our book concentrates on agile DW/BI data modeling, Ken's book is a guide to *being agile* in many of the other aspects of DW/BI projects.

Visual Thinking, Collaboration and Facilitation, Business Modeling
The Back of the Napkin: Solving Problems and Selling Ideas With Pictures, Dan Roam (Portfolio, 2008)
Blah Blah Blah: What To Do When Words Don't Work, Dan Roam (Portfolio, 2011)

Dan's books contain great ideas that will inspire you to draw simple pictures of the *7Ws* to help you discover, understand and present your dimension data stories and BI designs.

Gamestorming: A Playbook for Innovators, Rulebreakers, and Changemakers, Dave Gray, Sunni Brown, James Macanufo (O'Reilly Media, 2010)
Visual Meetings: How Graphics, Sticky Notes and Idea Mapping Can Transform Group Productivity, David Sibbet (Wiley, 2010)

Books to help you facilitate modelstorming sessions and improve upon the collaborative techniques we have introduced.

Business Model Generation: A Handbook for Visionaries, Game Changers, and Challengers, Alexander Osterwalder, Yves Pigneur et al. (Wiley, 2010)

Check out the *Business Model Canvas* for more high-level collaborative modeling ideas.

Dimensional Modeling
Star Schema The Complete Reference, Christopher Adamson (McGraw-Hill, 2010)

Dimensional Modeling Case Studies
Data Warehouse Design Solutions, Christopher Adamson, Michael Venerable (Wiley, 1998)
The Data Warehouse Toolkit, Second Edition, Ralph Kimball, Margy Ross (Wiley, 2002)

ETL
The Data Warehouse ETL Toolkit, Ralph Kimball, Joe Caserta (Wiley, 2004)
Mastering Data Warehouse Aggregates, Christopher Adamson (Wiley, 2006) Chapters 5 and 6 also provides excellent coverage of dimensional ETL.

Database–Specific DW/BI Advice
The Microsoft Data Warehouse Toolkit, Joy Mundy, Warren Thornthwaite (Wiley, 2011)

Websites

decisionone.co.uk : DecisionOne Consulting, Lawrence Corr's training and consulting firm.

llumino.com : Llumino, Jim Stagnitto's consulting firm.

modelstorming.com : The companion website to this book where you can download the BEAM✳ *Modelstormer* spreadsheet, the *BI Model Canvas* (inspired by the *Business Model Canvas*) plus other useful BEAM✳ tools and example models from the book and beyond. It also contains links to our recommended books, articles, websites, and training courses. Don't forget to register your copy on the site to receive discounts on training and the eBook version.

READER	*can upgrade* BOOK	*on* DATE	*to* BOOKS	*at* BOOK WEBSITE	*for* DISCOUNT
[who]	[what]	[when]	[what]	[where]	[why]
You	This Paperback	Today	Paperback + eBook	modelstorming.com	50% of eBook price

INDEX

E

F

G

H

Made in the USA
Monee, IL
17 August 2021